China Academic Library

This book series collects, organizes and presents the master pieces in contemporary China studies. Titles in this series include those by Chinese authors who studied and worked abroad during early times whose works were originally in English and had already made great impacts in the Western world, such as Hu Shih, Fei Xiaotong and others; as well as works by more recent authors, Chinese and non-Chinese, that are of critical intellectual importance in introducing and understanding the transformation of the modern Chinese society. A wide variety of topics are covered by the series, from philosophy, economics, and history to law, cultural geography and regional politics. This series is a key English language resource for researchers and students in China studies and related subjects, as well as for general interest readers. The book series is a cooperation project between Springer and Foreign Language Teaching and Research Publishing Co., Ltd.

Yining Li

China's Economy Since 1978

Forty Years of Reform and Opening-Up

外语教学与研究出版社
FOREIGN LANGUAGE TEACHING AND RESEARCH PRESS

Springer

Yining Li
Peking University
Beijing, China

Translated by
Kangyu Ren
Beijing Foreign Studies University
Beijing, China

ISSN 2195-1853 ISSN 2195-1861 (electronic)
China Academic Library
ISBN 978-981-95-5732-5 ISBN 978-981-95-5733-2 (eBook)
https://doi.org/10.1007/978-981-95-5733-2

Jointly published with Foreign Language Teaching and Research Publishing Co., Ltd
The print edition is not for sale in the mainland of China. Customers from the mainland of China please order the print book from: Foreign Language Teaching and Research Publishing Co., Ltd.

Sponsored by Chinese Fund for the Humanities and Social Sciences (本书获中华社会科学基金资助).

Translation from the Chinese Simplified language edition: "改革开放以来的中国经济" by Yining Li, © Encyclopedia of China Publishing House 2018. Published by Encyclopedia of China Publishing House.

This Springer imprint is published by the registered company Springer Nature Singapore Pte Ltd.
The registered company address is: 152 Beach Road, #21-01/04 Gateway East, Singapore 189721, Singapore

Competing Interests The author has no competing interests to declare that are relevant to the content of this manuscript.

Contents

Chapter 1
Introduction: Breaking Away from Path Dependence and Moving Forward under the Guidance of a New Development Ideology

1.1 Why Do we Stick to the Old Development Mode?

After World War II, several newly independent countries in Asia and Africa longed to shake off poverty as soon as possible, and they followed the advice of some economists and committed themselves to attracting foreign capital. Nevertheless, they remained trapped in poverty in spite of increased economic growth rate and per capita GDP, because there were only limited changes to their original systems.

The difficulties of these developing countries have been critically examined by some economists from a new perspective who argue that it is harmful for these countries to focus only on development and introduction of foreign capital through blind liberalization of investment and excessive export of national resources without changing their systems. They will eventually fall into the low-income trap. While some, at best, may reach a middle-income status, they will then be trapped in middle-income category eventually. Hence there is a new term called path dependence. What does path dependence mean? It suggests that following the old pattern is the safest way to develop. By stepping in previous footprints, one need not take responsibility, and at the same time could avoid the risk of taking on a new road. Many countries realized the problems in the old way and contradictions between the old and the new ways, but are still sticking to the path-dependent approach.

Clinging to the old patterns has gradually become a convention. Even if some developing countries can elevate themselves out of the low-income status and reach the middle-income level, they will often fall into the middle-income trap again given that they still follow the old way. We can see this in the case of Greece. From the late twentieth century to the early twenty-first century, Greece's per capita income, or GDP per capita, had exceeded that of the past, reaching more than $12,000, which is usually considered as a benchmark. After exceeding this benchmark, the United Nations and the World Bank would congratulate this country for surpassing the middle-income level. However, Greece had not changed its system. When the financial crisis hit, the country suffered a lot and immediately dropped back below the

Y. Li, *China's Economy Since 1978*, China Academic Library,
https://doi.org/10.1007/978-981-95-5733-2_1

middle-income mark. Therefore, it suggests that sticking to the old path is not necessarily risk-free, and could be even much riskier than changing to a new development mode.

1.2 Why Is it Revolutionary to Replace the Old Development Mode with a New One?

This is an issue that many economists around the world are discussing. For China, the impact of the old development mode was well entrenched because this development mode had lasted and been believed in for many years. Strictly speaking, in China, it was only after the 18th National People's Congress (NPC) that the central leadership regarded the replacement of old modes by new modes as a revolution—a revolution in development mode. While replacing the old development mode with a new one has been repeatedly stressed along with an emphasis on supply-side structural reform, the impact of path dependence could not be underestimated. It is widely believed that the pace of reform and the implementation of a new development mode should not be in haste based on China's national conditions. Therefore, in China's economic transition, path dependence becomes an ideological obstacle. It lies in a lack of a sense of urgency, since it not only represents a transition of development pattern, but also entails a concurrent change in the allocation of resources. Then a big problem occurs: The traditional development mode would not automatically step down. Therefore, the old mode has to be ousted in an effort to establish new ways of development.

Consequently, we can conclude that it is necessary to distinguish the new development mode from the old one. The old development mode is to follow the old path; thus, the responsibility remains that of the predecessors. As there is nothing new, the risk of innovation can be avoided. Meanwhile, a new development mode must be realized through revolutionary reforms. One of the most important policies, for example, is to allow enterprises to be the leading players in the market, making their own management decisions and taking full responsibilities for their profits and losses. Technological innovation is another critical issue for a new development mode, which is crucial for the creation of new products, new capacity, new features, etc. Without various innovation, the old development mode cannot be replaced and driven out of history.

Based on the above discussions, it is apparent that in China, the market, which is key to resource allocation, must be put at the forefront. Meanwhile there are some other sectors of the economy that are also important, such as the public welfare, national security, and research & development in new technologies. In this case, along with market regulation, the government should also play a planning, leading, and supporting role. How to transform the economy, then? In brief, under normal circumstances, market mechanism must play a dominant role. Otherwise, we will be at a disadvantage. But the government should still lead and support non-profit, public welfare, and other special industries.

1.3 The Reform cannot be Delayed

Why is this issue so urgent now? Because the reform cannot be delayed, and time should not be wasted on the debate over which is better: the old production mode or the new production mode. With the economy moving forward, enterprises have competitors both at home and abroad. If we do not reform, we will lose our competitiveness and could even go out of business.

Following the old path, i.e., path dependence, will only end up delaying the economic transition. What is this economic transition? Simply put, the old economic mode will turn into the new one. The old economic mode values quantity and speed, while the new mode emphasizes quality and efficiency. Enterprises compete with each other. If they do not feel pressure, they do not tend to change their status quo; once they face the pressure to be surpassed, they will make a change. The idea of die or live should be brought forward at present. However, that is not what we are doing.

What are we doing now? We acknowledge that transition is feasible, but we tend to take it slow and not rush. Why? How to solve unemployment problem once the pace of transition is quickened? Once the pace of transition is accelerated, and goods become in short supply, will it cause prices to rise? If we do so, where is the market for the new products; will our innovation bring a more significant risk before we have a little faith in success? There are all sorts of problems, and the solution to these firstly relies on an in-depth study of the theories put forward by the 19th NPC. The theories have clarified that the transformation of our development ideology should be emphasized. We can only move forward through fundamental rather than patchy reforms. We might blindly think that access to all development paths is available, and that we no longer need to work so hard and so fast. However, this is not enough for the long-term economic transformation. Therefore, the issue should be put forward here.

The rapid development experienced by many countries worldwide is temporary and unsustainable; therefore, economists believe that rapid development is not the norm. And for some countries, medium-to-high growth is also not the norm, and their speed of development is not stable and may slow down again. With the economy growing, China should not get obsessed on high-speed development but maintain medium-to-high growth based on its current situation. What about after medium-to-high growth? It depends. We have to take medium-to-high growth for the sake of sustainable development. As to reducing excess inventory, strengthening areas of weakness and lowering costs, etc., all of these still need to be done. Because if we do not take advantage of the opportunities to address inadequacies and move forward, other enterprises will do. It is not a matter of whether one enterprise undertakes the corresponding reform or not. It is a matter of whether its staff can continue to be employed here, and whether it can continue to dominate its market and fend it against competitors. For China, medium-to-high growth is a necessity to maintain economic normality.

What can be done to ensure continuous development in the future for China? The top priority is to pay close attention to our corporate rivals—other enterprises both at home and abroad. When other enterprises experiment successfully with new products and new capacity, we will be forced to reform, otherwise we may lose competitiveness and even collapse. This is not a bad thing; however, the real transformation of economic development mode emerges from competition. Only by making various trade-offs and choices can enterprises survive in the long run. Thus, enterprises should realize that the transformation phase is also the stage to prepare the human capital for the future, and once the transformation begins, it is going to be fast. It will be helpful if this is acknowledged.

There is no end to reform. If we follow the old way, sooner or later we will fail. Then why don't we get started and seek reform? Thus, the so-called "second undertaking" is particularly important for private enterprises. Meanwhile, enterprises are exactly at the stage of second undertaking. Without this, enterprises would not survive the next competitive stage. The talents should also be cultivated along this direction. There is a huge shortage of talents. More people can improve their skills and enhance their knowledge for the new jobs through training. All in all, we cannot depend on the past path. Only by competition, transformation, and innovation will Chinese enterprises have a better and brighter future.

— *China Economic & Trade Herald*, issue No. 4, 2018

Chapter 2
1978: Technical Education and Capitalist Industrialization: Research on the Formation of Technical Forces in Western Europe and the United States

In order to achieve industrialization, a nation must have corresponding technical forces, including a certain number of qualified scientific researchers, engineering technicians, and skilled workers. However, when industrialization is initiated, the existing technical forces are always insufficient. There is a wide gap between the need for industrialization and a lack of existing technical forces. What measures had some Western capitalist countries taken to promote the formation of technical forces in the process of industrialization? What can we learn from their experiences? This is the main topic of this article.

2.1 I

Capitalist industrialization began in the United Kingdom (UK) around the late eighteenth or early nineteenth century. The first stage of this process is usually called the industrial revolution, that is, the process from handicraft workshops to modern industry. "The starting point of modern industry is the revolution of instruments of production, and the transformed instruments of production have obtained the most advanced form in the organized machine system of factories (Marx 1975)." How were the new means of production used in modernized large industry manufactured? How were the "transformed means of production" combined with the work force? For the first nation to carry out the industrial revolution, these issues deserve special attention, because at the beginning of this process, there were not enough technicians and skilled workers with advanced technology in the society.

The traditional handicraft production in Medieval Western Europe provided the necessary material and human resources for the industrial revolution in Britain in the eighteenth century. A clock workshop, for example, was the best place to train excellent mechanical artisans for the future, because the watchmakers had superb manual skills and could skillfully operate advanced machineries available at that time, leading

Y. Li, *China's Economy Since 1978*, China Academic Library,
https://doi.org/10.1007/978-981-95-5733-2_2

to high precision products. British millers were also outstanding. According to the records, even ordinary millers had certain knowledge of mathematics, understood leveling surveyance and measurement, and were able to calculate speed and strength as well as draw plans. These watchmakers and millers were an essential part of the first generation of British technical force during the industrial revolution. Such forces became designers and manufacturers; furthermore, some even grew to be operators of new products and equipment.

However, the number of watchmakers, millers and other artisans with high manual skills (such as pump makers, carriage makers, assemblers, blacksmiths, etc.) was limited and couldn't meet the demand of the British capitalist industry. In particular, the manufacturing of various machines had different technical requirements for people: Manufacturing spinning machines, looms, and some tool machines were relatively simple, while machines such as steam engines required higher-level technologies. When James Watt received the charter to make his own designed steam engine, John Smeaton, a famous British engineer, predicted that Watt could not make it because it required high accuracy. In order to make a steam engine for commercial application, Watt looked for skilled workers everywhere, but it was challenging. The cylinder was not well cast and the piston leaked and could not be operated. Watt spent a total of twenty years applying his design in production. This was not only the case with steam engine manufacturing, but also with the development of ironmaking industry during the British industrial revolution. Some iron mill owners in Britain often spent a lot of money to recruit skilled workers all over the country, even going to Belgium to hire.

Since Britain was the first country to experience industrial revolution, the formation of its technical force obviously had historical characteristics. This was a relatively slow process: It took about two generations from handicraft skills to mastering advanced machinery production and technology, from relying on watchmakers and millers to cultivating mechanical craftsmen and "engineers" for special machinery production.

Another historical feature of the formation of British technical forces was that school education played a relatively limited role in this process. The growth of technicians mainly depended on personal exploration and the accumulation of their own experience, and the training of skilled workers mainly depended on the transfer of skills and knowledge among individuals. This feature also attributed to the special economic status of Britain at that time.

According to Marx, "In the previous production stage, the limited knowledge and experiences were directly related to labor itself and did not develop into an independent and separate force. Therefore, the whole had never exceeded the scope of the accumulation of means of production. This accumulation had been enriched from generation to generation and expanded slowly and gradually. (Master the know-how of every craft with experiences) (Marx 1978)." Britain, the first to carry out the industrial revolution, could not get rid of the significant influence of the medieval handicraft way in the formation of technological power. People ignored the practice of cultivating such power through school education, especially higher education. In the 1860s when Britain urgently needed colleges and universities to train technicians, there were none available. It was not until nearly one hundred years later, in the mid-nineteenth century, that the municipal universities in Birmingham, Manchester, London, Liverpool and other cities undertook the task of training technicians. In 1851 and 1860, two professional colleges of higher technology, The Royal School of Mines and The Royal Institute of Naval Architects, were established.

During the industrial revolution when skilled workers were urgently needed, the training of skilled workers was also ignored in Britain. At the beginning of the industrial revolution, only some private remedial schools in certain rural areas of Manchester taught mathematics and business knowledge, and institutions such as secondary vocational schools were neglected. The capitalists generally felt that it was better for workers to remain ignorant so as not to be rebellious, therefore they were skeptical and resistant to any plan for workers to receive school education (Fairchild 1923). As a result, industry was developing, machines were being popularized and used, but the number of skilled workers was insufficient. Factory owners regarded apprentices as cheaper labor, so they would rather recruit more apprentices than students who were trained in vocational schools. It was not until 1823, sixty years after the beginning of the industrial revolution, were formal vocational schools established in big industrial cities such as London and Glasgow, which was followed by other cities. It was not until 1851 that the British government allowed the establishment of industrial night schools. Nevertheless, it had been ninety years since the beginning of the industrial revolution.

Why did Britain adopt a path of inheriting handicraft skills from masters to apprentices in cultivating its own skilled labor for a long time? Britain was the first country to carry out the industrial revolution. It was understandable that it could not learn from the experiences of other countries in developing modern capitalist industries. At that time, there was no technical personnel familiar with machinery production, so Britain had to inevitably rely on the traditional technology and ways of learning of the medieval handicraft industry. However, it should be emphasized that Britain's capitalist industrialization began in a context where it was unrivaled among its peers. Britain had never had the pressure of *speed problem*, nor had it been aware of the importance and urgency of *growth rate*. Competitors had not appeared yet. Therefore, why was it needed to accelerate the cultivation of technical forces? Since the cheap apprenticeship system can still ensure high profitability for the British capitalists, why should they spend money to set up vocational schools to cultivate a group of people who might be well educated, having more knowledge and learning rapidly but be not so *obedient*? This was what the British capitalists had in mind at that time.

2.2 II

The capitalist industrialization of continental Western European countries and the US occurred thirty or forty years, or even longer, after that of Britain. When they upgraded from handicraft workshops to large-scale machinery production, Britain had successively established advanced textile, machinery manufacturing, transportation, and other departments. Facing the industrial advantages of Britain, these Western latecomers almost invariably adopted the following two methods: One was to employ Britain's technical forces, the other was to attach importance to school education and cultivate their own technical forces.

Before Britain lifted the ban on the emigration of technicians in 1825, other countries repeatedly used high wages to lure British technicians and encouraged them to sneak across the border. According to statistics, there were at least 2000 British technicians on the Western European continent in 1825. After abolishment of the ban, continental countries recruited even more British technicians. The first wave was before the 1840s. At that time, they mainly worked in the textile and machine manufacturing industries. The second wave was after the 1840s. They mainly worked on railway, canal, and bridge construction sites. Some British workers with special skills were particularly popular with foreign employers. For example, in the US, John Fitch tried to hire British technicians who had worked for Watt to make steam engines. For another example, after Samuel Slater came to the US from Britain, he used to have a great vogue because he could build an advanced British Arkwright spinning machine according to his memory, and even made some improvements. When it comes to France in the first half of the nineteenth century, British technicians were employed in ironworks, machine factories, and cotton textile mills. Some factories employed hundreds of Britons, including managers, technical experts, supervisors, and ordinary workers. The Netherlands, Belgium, and Germany also employed a large number of British technical experts and technicians. A railway initially built on the Western European continent relied on British technical force from designing to track laying. Even after the completion of the railway, these countries still engaged British experts and technicians for operation management and locomotive maintenance. The role of British technicians in the early stage of capitalist industrialization in Western Europe cannot be underestimated. Their greatest role lies not in their own technical work, but in the promotion and impartment of advanced technology.

In the process of American capitalist industrialization, relying on foreign technical personnel was also important. According to statistics, from 1820 to 1859, 1.05 million skilled workers and 11,200 professionals moved to the US (Nourse 1971). Without such a large number of technical professional immigrations, it would have been difficult to gain efficiency even if the US imported advanced machinery and equipment from abroad or manufactured by themselves.

In the process of industrialization in Western capitalist countries that carried out the industrial revolution later, although these countries had relied on British technology to a large extent, they generally realized that this reliance could not be a long-term arrangement. For the US, the situation was particularly special because the skilled workers and professionals entering the country were immediately integrated into the domestic technical force. For the countries of Western Europe, the recruited British technicians and skilled workers were foreigners after all. They were well paid but less obedient, uneasy to work with, and homesick. At the same time, with the development of the capitalist economy in these countries, there was an increasing demand for technicians and skilled workers. Foreign technical forces alone could not meet this demand. Of course, the apprenticeship system also existed in these countries. However, these countries did not emphasize relying on that system, instead mainly opted for school education, which had become an important way to form their technical power in the process of capitalist industrialization.

Germany and the US are the two most prominent examples. Germans were aware that they were fifty years later than Britain in industrial development. If they repeated the old path of the British, they would never catch up with Britain. Therefore, Germany needed to take the road of developing technical education and establishing higher vocational colleges (Wilbur 1972). Germany had implemented a compulsory primary educational system since the early nineteenth century. The enrollment rate of school-age children had been increasing. In Prussia, the enrollment rate of school-age children was 43 percent in 1816, 68 percent in 1846, and 97.5 percent in the 1960s. Germany's secondary education and vocational education were well-known all over Europe. German schools emphasized not only applied science teaching but also basic theory training. Many technical and vocational schools had been set up throughout Germany. In particular, Germany attached great importance to the technical education of young workers and apprentices in factories. Amateur technical night schools and Sunday schools were quite common. Germany stipulated that the factory owner should be responsible for the amateur technical education of the factory's young workers and apprentices. More often than not, it was compulsory to enter night schools and Sunday schools. In the contract signed between the manufacturers and the apprentices, there were provisions for apprentices to receive part-time education, which both sides should observe. German universities also attached great importance to the training of researchers in natural science theory and applied science. According to the survey and comparative study at that time, Germany ranked first in European countries in national reading, writing and math ability, workers' skills, the combination of engineers' scientific principles and application training, and high-level scientific research, while Britain was far behind in all four aspects, except the second (workers' skills) perhaps. In terms of education funds, Germany ranked first in Europe. According to statistics, the cost of education in 1880 was $69 million, accounting for 1.6 percent of the GDP. In 1900, the cost of education was $150 million, accounting for 1.9 percent of the GDP (Fishlow 1971). Only the US was comparable in such growth rate and share in GDP.

The US also began to focus on cultivating technical forces through school education very early. As early as 1773, there were some private vocational schools in Salem, Massachusetts, to train seamen who were in urgent need at the time. Consequently, the number of this type of school continued to increase. By 1890, there had been 808 night schools in 165 cities and towns, with 150, 770 students. In 1825, the

US established the first higher technical college, the Rensselaer Institute of Technology in Troy, New York. Higher technical colleges had developed rapidly since the 1860s. By 1904, there were already 147 higher technical colleges. Among them, 36 were supported or partially supported by the Federal and State governments, and 102 were related to universities. This situation happened to be a sharp contrast with that in Britain.

Germany and the US, which carried out the industrial revolution later, did not repeat the old path taken by Britain in developing their own technical forces, that is, rely mainly on schooling and on foreign technical forces to teach advanced technology in the early stages of industrialization, which was one of the reasons why they caught up and surpassed Britain economically.

2.3 III

As the technical forces of the US and Germany grew, Britain, which insisted on the traditional approach to training its own technicians and skilled workers, increasingly appeared to lag behind. This was fully demonstrated in the late nineteenth and early twentieth centuries.

Taking the shipbuilding industry for an example, Britain maintained its position as the dominant maritime power for two hundred years, and its shipbuilding technology was unparalleled. Since the late nineteenth century, although Britain was caught up by the US and Germany in important industrial sectors such as metallurgy, mechanical engineering, chemistry, and electricity, Britain remained far ahead in the shipbuilding industry. For example, after 1900, when the German company Krupp tried to get orders from Japan, it emphasized that its ability to build warships was the same as that of the best British-designed warships. During the same period, the US government intended to invite Vickers or Armstrong, the largest company in the British shipbuilding industry, to build modern dockyards and naval arsenals in the US to help develop American warship building. But how long could Britain maintain this advantage? At the end of the nineteenth century, when the British shipbuilding industry still dominated in the world, people with access to insider stories noticed that the British shipbuilding industry did seem to be declining because of a lack of technical forces. It is important to understand that until then, the British shipbuilding industry continued to train its technical workforces in a traditional way, neglecting both formal and amateur vocational education. The British capitalists continued to favor apprentices as the cheapest form of labor and apprentices were widely used in shipyards. In the factories of the Ministry of Navy, qualified mechanic involved a seven-year apprenticeship. In private shipyards in general, apprentices were also required five years to graduate. During the five-year period, the first year was spent in the sand tilling yard doing odd jobs such as fire making and mopping, followed by two years of irregular training in carpentry, one or two years of metalwork in the assembly yard, and if lucky, one might thus enter the drawing room, where he would learn from scratch again. At the end of the apprenticeship, he had little theoretical knowledge and forgot everything he had learned before the apprenticeship. Most of the apprentices were contracted not to leave the factory. However, during this period, shipbuilding technology was developing rapidly, and shipbuilders who were apprentices could not adapt to technical development. Some factories also held technical night schools to improve the skills of the apprentice and young workers. Due to the long working hours (6 am to 5 pm) and frequent overtime work in shipyards, the effect of afterwork vocational schools was limited. Formal vocational education in the shipbuilding industry was as little appreciated as the afterwork ones. Although the Royal Institute of Naval Architects was founded in 1860 (incorporated into the Royal Naval College in 1873), only 166 shipbuilders graduated from the Institute and the College between 1865 and 1904. Another formal school that trained advanced shipbuilding technicians was the University of Glasgow. Its shipbuilding class had about forty enrollments each year at the beginning of the twentieth century. However, it was stipulated that students required five years of apprenticeship at the time, and they could not prepare properly during their apprenticeships. As a result, only two students completed their degree requirements on average each year. By contrast, full-time shipbuilding classes in Germany at Charlottenburg and Danzig had 280 students at that time, and full-time shipbuilding classes in the US at Cornell University, MIT, the University of Michigan, and Weber College had more than 100 students, with a combined total surpassing that in Britain. It should be particularly noted that at that time, Germany required students who enrolled in higher technical institutions to have only one year of practical experience before enrolling, while the US did not have such requirements. In this way, the excessively long apprenticeship system and the requirement of five-year apprenticeship experience before enrollment in Britain not only limited the enrollment number and unnecessarily increased the age of students in school, but also interrupted the continuity of learning and gave students a poorer foundation for higher technical education because what they had learned in the past were forgotten.

Why did Britain attach little importance to technical education until then, and persist in training technicians through the apprenticeship system? Apart from the fact that the British capitalists regarded apprentices as cheap labor, another important reason was that the British capitalists always regarded school education as something that did more harm than good to itself. In the case of shipbuilding, the British shipbuilding capitalists believed that the opening of vocational schools would train competent technical personnel who would not necessarily benefit Britain (because they might serve its foreign countries) or their own company (because they could be employed by other companies). They believed that the apprenticeship system was good enough to train its workforce in operating all kinds of machinery and equipment, building all kinds of ships, and still enjoying reputation among foreign countries. Therefore, the innovations and changes in scientific research, design, and production in the shipbuilding industry, as well as their relationship with vocational education, were rarely considered seriously.

The severe consequence of downplaying the role of technical education in the development of British industry may not be visible in the short term, but in the long term, the damage caused was difficult to estimate. This is one of the differences between education and the material production. If industrial and agricultural production is disrupted, the consequences would be significant and quickly recognized. In contrast, if education is neglected and its serious effects are not perceived for a while, it often has already brought about greater harm by the time it is identified. Moreover, it is much more difficult to make up for this damage because the cycle of education is longer. In the case of the British shipbuilding industry, in the early twentieth century, apprentices aged 18 or 19 became the major players in the shipyards during World War II. The limited skills they had accumulated through personal experiences were increasingly lagging behind to the new level of science and technology, and they had no contact with the latest achievements of other sectors related to shipbuilding and lacked the necessary theoretical basis for understanding them. Their personal experience seemed unilateral and narrow, and some of their skills were obsolete. Although by this time, the British shipbuilding capitalists had changed their attitude toward technical education and had become more attentive to it, the serious consequences of the previous negligence had taken its toll. In the 1920s and 1930s, the industry remained at the same level at the beginning of the twentieth century.

The decline of British Shipbuilding Industry since the late nineteenth century is a typical case. Shipbuilding was once one of the pillars of Britain's establishment of maritime supremacy and a symbol of its high technology, because building a battleship integrates advanced technologies such as metallurgy, machinery manufacturing, communication, artillery and so on. Yet this sector had been irrevocably declining in Britain. The British economy was overtaken by the US and Germany, which was the result of the uneven development of the political economy of capitalism. Since latecomers were not bound by a large amount of old fixed capital and could make extensive use of new science and technology, they could leap forward in a relatively short period and quickly catch up with and overtake the existing champions while the latter were bound by the old industrial sectors and old machinery and equipment, thus developing more slowly. However, the history of economic development of Western capitalist countries clearly demonstrates that the growth of technical forces is always one of the primary conditions for ensuring economic development, and the formation and growth of a technical force that ensures and promotes economic development depends on the development of education and its level. Therefore, the lack of attention to technical education would inevitably contribute to the backwardness of the British economy, which cannot be ignored. The neglect of technical education in Britain in the nineteenth century had far-reaching effects. To some extent, the stagnation of the British economy during the World War II resulted from the neglect of technical education in Britain in the previous century.

2.4 IV

In the late nineteenth century, the change in the mode of scientific activities was far less significant than the change in the form of production organization. Science remained a field of solitary research or simple cooperation involving one or a few people, and scientific research had not yet been organized into large industries or developed into an enterprise of collective activity. This situation began to change significantly at the turn of the new century. After the industry had developed to a certain extent, scientific research became more expanded, instruments and equipment more complex, and cooperation and collaboration more needed. The same was true for investment. Thus, research institutions supported by large enterprises replaced individual inventors in many fields. After the 1930s, due to the further development of production and scientific research, especially due to the need for certain highly integrated scientific research projects, joint research institutions organized and directed by the capitalist countries took on an increasingly important role.

The new active mode of scientific research accelerated the progress of research work. While the existence of monopolies certainly prevented the application of certain science and technology that could be unfavorable to the monopolies themselves, the arms race and competitive pressure between monopolies managed to shorten the time gap between discovery, invention, and application in actual production, making the pace of technological development in Western capitalist production much faster in recent years.

New active mode of scientific research and accelerated technological upgrades in production generated more urgent demands on the growth of technical forces than any previous time. Even Britain, which downplayed the role of technical education at the beginning of capitalist industrialization, changed its view based on its own historical experience and admitted that it was lagging behind the US and Germany in the training and development of human resources. Today, all Western capitalist countries, including Britain, treat both formal and afterwork vocational education as important ways to develop their technical forces. Although the apprenticeship system still exists, it obviously no longer plays an important role. Under the conditions of modern science and technology, the developed capitalist countries have not advocated prolonged apprenticeship years nor made it a necessary condition to have long service years before entering higher vocational schools and colleges.

All countries are increasingly recognizing the important role of technical education for economic growth. This role is manifested in several ways.

First, it helps maintain a scientific research and design team for the nation, which can make discoveries and inventions in science, and make innovations and transformations in production technology. Without such a team, the best a country could do in science and technology is to simply follow other countries' footsteps. It is almost impossible to have significant breakthroughs.

Second, it builds a skilled workforce capable of mastering and applying advanced production methods. Without such a team, even advanced production tools and production methods are unlikely to function fully.

Third, it produces a team of production and technical managers adapted to the level of industrialization. Without such a team, a lot of manpower, material, and financial resources in the production process will be wasted, and the superiority of advanced production technology will not be brought into play.

Fourth, it raises the scientific and cultural level of the whole society, provides the conditions for the promotion and use of new products, as well as the spread and improvement of advanced technologies and knowledge. It also expands the basis for the growth of technical forces in the future, and ensures a continuous supply of high-quality researchers, engineering technicians, managers, and skilled workers.

Fifth, it enables the preservation and dissemination of accumulated scientific knowledge and productive experiences. This kind of dissemination can break the restriction of national borders and time. The accumulated scientific knowledge and productive experience, as the common wealth of mankind, will be transmitted from one nation to another and from one generation to the next through education.

In recent years, with the increasingly closer connection between production and science, the acceleration of technological transformation, the higher precision in production technology and the more complex technical requirements, the role of the whole education, including technical education, has inevitably become more and more significant in promoting economic growth.

The American economist Kuznets conducted a comparative study of economic growth across countries. His observations remain valuable to this day. For example, he argued that in modern economic growth, the "stock of knowledge" has a transnational nature and that all countries depend on the transnational "stock of knowledge" in their economic growth. He explained that manual craftsmanship used to be integrated and embodied in an individual, while the useful knowledge needed for modern economic growth is embodied in mathematical formulas, which are open, easily communicated, and utilized worldwide. Therefore, we must rely on education to impart knowledge, and can no longer rely on handicrafts and apprenticeship to transmit personal knowledge any more.

The American economist Denison analyzed the sources of economic growth. On the basis of estimation, he classified the factors contributing to a country's economic growth into three major categories: the increase in the amount of labor input (including the increase in the number of employees and the total number of working hours, as well as the improvement in the quality of labor, etc.); the increase in the amount of capital input; and the increase in the amount of output per unit of input. From 1929 to 1957, the average annual growth rate of real national income in the US was 2.93 percent, of which 2 percent was due to the increase in the amount of labor input and the amount of capital input, and the rest due to the increase in the amount of output per unit of input.

According to Denison's analysis, 23 percent of the growth in US national income during this period was attributable to the improvements in the quality of labor, and 32 percent due to increases in the quantity of output per unit of input. At the same time, the contribution of increased employment and working hours in economic growth has declined relatively. Modern economic growth does not depend primarily on the increase of employees and their working hours. Therefore, the increasing role of education here is self-evident. The improvement of labor quality is related to education, as well as to the increase of output per unit of input (including the improvement of resource utilization efficiency, the increase of rationality of business scale, scientific progress and the shortening of their application cycle).

Denison, in his book *Why growth rates differ? The Postwar Experience of Nine Western Countries* (published in 1967) illustrated the role of education in the improvement of labor quality that has contributed to economic growth in major Western European capitalist countries. In the case of Britain, the average annual total growth rate between 1950 and 1962 was 2.29 percent; and the average annual growth rate of labor quality was 0.37 percent, which shows that 12 percent of the total growth could be attributed to the improvement of labor quality. The improvement of labor quality played a more significant role in the British economy than in France, Italy, West Germany, the Netherlands, Denmark, Norway, and other countries. Following the *policy failures* of the nineteenth and early twentieth centuries, during which the role of education in the shaping technical forces was underestimated, Britain ultimately recognized and prioritized education as a critical driver of economic growth. Since World War II, only in some developing countries have the quality of labor improved slowly, either because of historical reasons or because the authorities underestimated the role of education in shaping technical forces. For example, in Mexico, from 1940 to 1964, the average annual growth rate was 6.34 percent and that for labor quality was 0.39 percent, which shows that only 3 percent of the total growth was attributed to the improvement of labor quality. In India, the average annual growth rate was 3.74 percent and that for labor quality was 0.03 percent from 1950 to 1960, meaning only 1 percent of the total growth was attributed to the improvement of labor quality (Engerman 1971). Here, let's not comment on whether Dennison's economic growth factor method has a sound economic theoretical basis, nor discuss whether the actual role of education in economic growth can be accurately calculated according to Dennison's method. At least his following conclusions still have a certain reference for understanding the relationship between education and economic growth: The more developed a country's economy is, the more urgent the demand for technical power, and the more important the role of education in both developing technical power and driving economic growth.

Hence, the US, despite leading the capitalist world in terms of technical forces, still makes it one of the country's priority tasks to accelerate the training of high-level technical personnel. According to the Department of Labor, in 1968, 8.5 million domestic adult workers (over 25 years of age) had completed at least four years of college education, 37 million had graduated from high school, and around seven million had received schooling less than eight years. By 1980, 13 million adult workers had completed at least four years of college education, 52 million had graduated from high school, and about five million had eight years of schooling. It was estimated that from 1968 to 1980, the US would need approximately 10.4 million new college graduates, 4.3 million of whom would replace workers who had deceased, retired, or otherwise left the workforce, and the rest 6.1 million would be appointed as they adapt to economic and technological developments. During this period, higher education in the US had been developed rapidly, with two-thirds more people receiving bachelor's degrees and twice as many receiving Master's and doctoral degrees by 1980 compared to 1968. Nevertheless, according to the Department's projections, there would still be an overdemand of engineers by 1980. Within the field of science, chemists, geologists, and geophysicists would also be in a shortage of supply. In addition, the US would need more personnel in planning and management.

2.5 V

From the historical perspective above, we examined the general situation of formation and development of technical forces in Western capitalist countries since the industrial revolution. In this section, we will focus on an analysis of the limitations of the formation of technical forces in the process of capitalist economic development. With the development of the capitalist economy, the basic contradiction of capitalism has become increasingly pronounced. In terms of the formation of technical forces, it shows the contradiction between the organization of capitalist units using technical forces and the disorder of the whole society in the formation and development of technical forces. This contradiction is inherent to the capitalist economy.

The formation and development of technical forces are fundamentally driven by the needs of capitalist production. The need for technical forces, the training and deployment of these technical forces, and the organization of labor and production in terms of technology, all depend on the capitalist enterprises' imperative goals for surplus maximization. From this point of view, the individual units for training and employment could subject to certain degree of planning and organization. But as far as the whole society is concerned, enterprises are in a state of intense competition. The units that train technical forces (schools) are largely isolated from the units that employ them (enterprises), and the entire labor market, including researchers, technicians and skilled workers, remains subject to the law of supply and demand. Moreover, the capitalist economic crisis and its periodicity also inevitably affect the cultivation and use of technical forces. Therefore, no matter how the capitalist governments formulate the so-called "human resource policies" and "human resource programs," it is difficult to realize the planned formation and development of the technical forces for the whole society.

The coexistence of unemployment and job vacancies is an inherent feature of the capitalist system. In *Das Kapital,* Marx quoted a paragraph from *the Report of the Factory Inspectors* on October 31, 1866, explaining that in Britain at that time, on the one hand, a large number of workers were unemployed, and on the other hand, "many machines had to be shut down for a lack of labor (Marx 1975)." Among scientific researchers and technicians, unemployment and job vacancies also coexisted. For example, in the US in 1972, despite the Department of Labor complaining about the shortages of engineers or chemists, and despite large enterprises actively recruiting senior technical personnel, approximately 100,000 industrial scientists, engineers and technicians were still unemployed (Happiness 1972), and one in four chemistry graduates could not find a job (Business Week 1972).

Under the conditions of the capitalist wage-labor system, competition in the labor market is fierce, and it is no exception for scientific researchers and technicians. Especially in recent years, due to the great progress of scientific research and the accelerated pace of technological upgrades, certain professionals, even if they were once adapted to the needs of then advanced technology in their fields, might imme diately lag behind the times and became redundant to employers, unless they could have the opportunity to continue their research and study in the relevant disciplines, or they could still attach to the latest productive or scientific reality. In 1971, a survey entitled *Engineers are redesigning their line of work* was published in the American magazine *Happiness*, with a thought-provoking subheading: no longer a hero. It was written within the text that the development of technology was relentlessly turning the knowledge of engineers into something obsolete very quickly, and people who had just graduated from college for only a few years were also frustrated because they were under threat from and could be replaced by younger graduates with more cutting-edge knowledge. According to the survey, 40 percent of engineers claimed that "if they had the opportunity to choose a career once again, they would choose another line of work (Happiness 1971)."

The existence of unemployment means a huge waste of human resources, while job vacancies signify a waste of material resources (in the form of idle technical equipment and inefficient use of raw materials). The coexistence of unemployment and job vacancies is inevitable in the formation of technical forces under the capitalist system.

The study on the formation of technical forces in the economic development of Western capitalism is of great practical importance. What we need to find out is: What are the experiences and lessons for us to learn from the Western capitalist countries in terms of developing their own technical forces?

First, there are several effective measures that the Western capitalist countries, which started industrialization later but developed faster, implemented to promote technical education that we can learn from. Some examples are giving importance to primary and secondary education in the process of industrialization, emphasizing education in basic mathematics and science in secondary schools, and organizing many forms of formal and afterwork technical education actively.

Second, with the progress of industrialization, Western capitalist countries have increased their spending on education both in absolute terms and in the share of GDP.

Third, although the apprenticeship system has played a role in the training of skilled workers, with the progress of industrialization, and the increasingly close connection between science and production, countries had to shift their focus to the development of school education. For the apprentices, vocational education should be strengthened and strict examination should be ensured. The lack of emphasis on schooling, as was in Britain in the nineteenth century, and the reliance on traditional methods of craft skills training, have been historically proven to be a failure.

Fourth, practical work experiences are important for students entering higher vocational colleges and universities, but the emphasis on practical work experiences should not be one-sided at the expense of ignoring coherent study, the age of the student, and guiding effect of theories for practice. As was the case in nineteenth-century Britain, the requirement of five-years industry experiences for entering ship-building engineering colleges and university courses had not been conducive to accelerating the development of technical skills. Universities may admit and accommodate workers in long service, but this should not have been made an eligibility requirement for admission.

Fifth, while introducing advanced foreign technology, we should also pay attention to the formation and growth of indigenous technical teams so that we can master advanced technologies and be able to innovate. If China's technical force is temporarily insufficient (in terms of quantity and quality), then foreign experts and skilled workers could be used in a certain period. Countries in Western Europe had done so in the early stages of industrialization, and the results were relatively remarkable. The foreign experts and skilled workers should be allowed to play a role in the transfer of technology and experience so that we can quickly establish our own technical force.

We have a superior socialist system which could avoid the negative experience in Western capitalist countries that ran on profit maximization and a huge waste of human and material resources. Historically, it took more than two hundred years for Britain to build up the technical forces that could adapt to modern production conditions, and roughly one hundred and fifty years for both the US and Germany to achieve this. This is a long process. We firmly believe that our country will build a great and excellent technical team in a relatively short period.

—*Advances in Social Sciences,* issue 4, 1978.

References

Fairchild EC (1923) *Labor and the Industrial Revolution,* Allen & Unwin, London, p. 131.

Nourse (1971) "Capital Formation in Early Industrial America: a Re-examination of the Issues." In: Fogel and Engerman (ed.) *The Re-interpretation of American Economic History*, Palgrave, London, p. 279; U.S. Census Bureau (1949) *Historical Statistics of the United States: 1789-1945*, Govt. Print. Off. Washington, p. 34.

Wilbur (1972) "The Industrial Expansion of England." *Lloyds Bank Review*, October, p. 44.

Fishlow A (1971) "Levels of Nineteenth-Century American Investment in Education." In Fogel and Engerman (ed.) *The Re-interpretation of American Economic History*, Palgrave, London, p. 271.
Engerman SL (1971) "Human Capital, Education, and Economic Growth." In: Fogel RW, Engerman SL (ed) *The Re-interpretation of American Economic History*, Palgrave, London, p. 253.
"Happiness" Magazine, April 1972, p. 69.
"Business Week" Magazine, September 23, 1972, p. 54.
"Happiness" Magazine, June 1971, p. 72.

Chapter 3
1979: Discussion on the Role of Capital-Intensive and Labor-Intensive Economies for Developing Countries' Modernization

The actual costs of production are based on labor consumption. The means of production consumed in the production process is materialized labor, while actual labor would also be consumed. Therefore, the real costs of production include two parts: materialized labor consumption and actual labor consumption. Due to different production technologies and the features of products, the proportion of these two parts in the costs of production vary from product to product. Hence, there are labor-intensive and capital-intensive economies. The former refers to the economy in which actual labor consumption accounts for the more significant proportion, while the latter is the opposite. This division is related to the type of technological innovation. If "labor-saving" technical measures (that is, the proportion of labor consumption in product costs can be reduced) are adopted, the proportion of the capital-intensive economy will increase. If "capital-saving" technical measures (that is, the ratio of materialized labor consumption in product costs can be reduced) are

"Capital-intensive economy" and "Labor-intensive economy" were originally concepts in Western economics. Some foreign economists classify economic types based on the proportion of materialized labor and living labor in product costs, referring to those with a large proportion of materialized labor as capital-intensive economies and those with a large proportion of living labor as labor-intensive economies.

These two concepts only refer to materialized labor as capital and exclude living labor from the category of capital, which is unscientific. The bourgeoisie has always confused capital with means of production, that is, viewing capital as a thing rather than as a production relationship. We know that any industrial capitalist must divide his capital into two parts, one to purchase means of production and the other to purchase labor power. According to Marxist concepts, the former is called constant capital and the latter is called variable capital. Marx's division of capital into constant and variable capital is a great achievement, which is of great significance in revealing the true source of surplus value.

Y. Li, *China's Economy Since 1978*, China Academic Library,
https://doi.org/10.1007/978-981-95-5733-2_3

adopted, the ratio of the labor-intensive economy will increase.[1] This paper examines the evolution of developing countries' economic structures in the modernization process, based on the above classification of economies, and then tries to theoretically explore a technological innovation approach that is beneficial for developing countries in both short and longer term.

3.1 The Traditional Way of Capitalist Industrialization Is to Develop a Labor-Intensive Economy First

According to economic history, among the new technologies adopted by the earliest capitalist industrializers, there were both "labor-saving" technologies (such as the use of flying shuttles and Spinning Jenny, which greatly increased labor productivity in weaving and spinning) and "capital-saving" technologies (such as replacing water turbines with steam engines, thereby increasing the proportion of labor consumption and reducing the proportion of capital factors) (Temin 1971). However, labor-intensive economies were dominating in the national economy. Britain, France, the

---

The proportion of means of production and labor force belongs to the category of capital composition. From the perspective of Marxist theory, the composition of capital, in terms of physical form, is always composed of a certain amount of means of production and labor force. There is a certain proportion between the two, which generally depends on the level of development of production technology. The higher the level of production technology, the more means of production each labor force drives, and the more materialized labor consumed in product costs: The lower the level of production technology, the opposite is true. It is precisely because the proportion between means of production and labor force reflects the level of development of production technology that it is called the technical composition of capital. The composition of capital is not only manifested in physical terms but also in value terms. In terms of value form, capital is composed of the value of means of production and the value of labor power, that is, constant capital and variable capital. The proportion between these two parts of capital value is called the value composition of capital by Marx.

There is a close connection between the technical composition and value composition of capital. Changes in the technical composition usually lead to a corresponding change in the value composition. Similarly, changes in the value composition usually reflect changes in the technical composition. To show the organic connection between the two, Marx called the value composition of capital determined by and reflecting the changes in the technical composition the organic composition of capital (i.e., C:V). The organic composition of capital is an important concept in Marxist political economy, which is significant for studying and explaining many major issues in the capitalist economic process, such as relative overpopulation, average profit, and the problem of production prices.

It can be seen that "capital-intensive economy" and "labor-intensive economy" actually refer to two different types of economies with high and low organic compositions of capital. However, since these two concepts can still reflect the factor composition in the economy from some aspects, they can be used.

[1] A technological reform may reduce both the consumption of materialized labor and the consumption of living labor in product costs. In this case, it will be classified according to which part of the product cost decreases more. If the consumption of materialized labor and living labor decreases proportionally, then this technological reform is called "neutral."

US, and Germany developed the cotton textile industry first. Under the technical conditions at that time, compared with products from other sectors, wage accounted for a more significant proportion in the total costs for the cotton textile industry. In contrast, capital investment required by the industry was less. In these countries, capital-intensive sectors, such as steel and machine manufacture, gradually developed only after the cotton textile industry had expanded to a certain level. The economists have already concluded this.

The progress of a labor-intensive economy has three main impacts on a country's economic development. First, it requires less investment and has quick result, bringing profits in a shorter period of time and increasing accumulation. Second, at any given level of investment, more labor force would be in need. Third, under the condition of lower wages, it has greater international competitiveness and can win the international market promptly. However, in the early stage of capitalist industrialization, capitalist countries mainly focused on the first aspect mentioned above in the process of developing labor-intensive sectors.

In the earliest capitalist industrialized countries, the capital available for industrial investment was inadequate. There was still a lack of financial institutions, securities markets, and credit instruments to mobilize domestic funds for the industries. Or, these institutions and agencies may have emerged, but they were not in full function. Too much capital was concentrated in commercial or non-industrial capitalists. At the beginning of industrialization in Britain (the end of the eighteenth century to the beginning of the nineteenth century), France, and Germany (the first half of the nineteenth century), the economic power of industrial capitalists were relatively small. The establishment of industrial enterprises mainly relied on domestic financial accumulation, and the new enterprises were small and medium-sized. Although the US could use the foreign capital that flowed from Western Europe in the first half of the nineteenth century, most of the capital was used in transportation and public utilities with only a small amount invested in the industries (Berrill 1963). In the US, capital was still scarce, resulting in high interest rates. Therefore, the common urgent problem that Britain, France, Germany, the US, and other countries encountered first at the beginning of industrialization was insufficient capital. They could not develop a capital-intensive economy at that time and could only develop a labor-intensive economy first.

How to increase employment was not a major problem in the early stage of capitalist industrialization. At that time, the urban population was small, and the labor productivity in agriculture had always been low. Those unemployed or rolling stones had more opportunities to emigrate abroad. So, the governments of those capitalist countries did not regard employment level as a policy goal, neither did the capitalists care. Nevertheless, the development of a labor-intensive economy in the early stage of industrialization did absorb a large number of urban and rural unemployed, although it was not the primary purpose.

The focus of developing a labor-intensive economy in the early stage of capitalist industrialization was to enable products with greater international competitiveness to capture foreign markets. The commodities produced with advanced technologies at the time, whether in the capital-intensive sector or the labor-intensive sector, gained advantages in the international market. Although products from France, the US, and Germany were less competitive, they still had a large domestic market. They also had the opportunity to enter markets in adjacent regions. The competition in the international market was far less intensified than later. Products in labor-intensive sectors with relatively higher wages could still be sold. At that time, the specific historical environment made it possible for the earliest industrializers with relatively higher wages to develop labor-intensive economies first.

3.2 It Is Difficult for Developing Countries to Develop Capital-Intensive Economies First

The industrialization in developing countries was many years later than that in advanced industrial economies. During this period, the world's political, economic, and technological conditions had undergone dramatic changes. Due to various historical reasons, the developing countries themselves also have some characteristics different from those of advanced industrial countries at the beginning of their industrialization. Generally speaking, these changes and features can be summarized in five aspects.

First, due to continuous advancement of science and technology, superior technologies could be introduced and adopted in both capital-intensive and labor-intensive sectors.

Second, the capital outflow has already been a feature of monopoly capitalism, and international financial institutions and credit instruments had been fully developed. This made it possible to use a large amount of foreign capital in economic development, making up for the lack of domestic financial accumulation.

Third, the government's role in economic development has generally been emphasized. The practice of relying mainly on private capitalists to establish new industrial sectors, as in Britain, the US, and France in the early industrialization period, was considered inefficient. In establishing a new industrial sector, the demand for government support and direct participation is increasing, and the government also believes that it has the responsibility to do so.

Fourth, due to the increase in productivity, the volume of commodities in the world market has increased, and the competition among countries has dramatically intensified. As a result, products with high costs, high prices, old styles, and poor quality would be quickly abandoned by the world market.

Fifth, the long period of colonial exploitation and domination entrenched the vassal status of developing countries in exporting raw materials and importing industrial products. The unequal exchange of processed and primary products led to a tremendous financial loss for developing countries. The developing world demanded an urgent change. As a result, industrialization and modernization have become the priorities for these countries. Any ruling party must put this at the forefront of its governance goals, which did not occur in the capitalist countries that started industrialization more than a hundred years ago.

Based on these changes and characteristics, developing countries naturally prioritized the development of capital-intensive sectors of the economy when preparing for modernization, because these sectors were equipped with advanced technology, having high productivity and a relatively small proportion of living labor. Developing countries find that in the current international market competition, the developed industrial countries rely on their capital intensity and high productivity to make their products internationally competitive. In developing countries, it is widely believed that if they do not introduce "labor-saving" advanced technologies, establish their capital-intensive sectors, and increase their capital-intensive levels, they will not be able to catch up with developed economies.

Objectively, developing countries also have the possibility of developing capital-intensive economies. With current production technology, there are ready-made "labor-saving" advanced technologies and complete sets of equipment that can be imported. If the country's capital is insufficient, foreign investment can generally be available as long as certain conditions or obligations are in place. If private capitalists have inadequate funds or are unwilling to take risks, the government could directly invest in the projects. In short, if developing countries intend to create capital-intensive economies first, the process will be much easier than that over a hundred years ago.

In the 1940s and 1950s, some Western economists had explored the approaches of industrialization and modernization in developing countries. One argument was that developing countries must promote domestic processing industries with advanced technologies and equipment as soon as possible to replace the import of industrial products and traditional exported commodities—primary products. According to this proposition, developing countries should first introduce "labor-saving" technologies and develop capital-intensive sectors in the economy. Then, they could establish sectors such as smelting, machine manufacturing, and transportation equipment that were highly productive and could compete with the products of the capital-intensive sectors of advanced industrial countries. Because only in this way could the government reduce the import of industrial products from developed industrial countries (products mainly from capital-intensive sectors). This proposition precisely conforms to the idea that developing countries are eager to realize industrialization and modernization, increase productivity, and upgrade from the domestic technological and economic backwardness. Certain countries in Asia and Latin America, which embarked on industrialization in the 1940s and 1950s, actually regarded this proposition as a guide for formulating economic development policies.

However, practice has shown that this approach of prioritizing capital-intensive economies did not work, i.e., it did not lead to increased economic growth rates in these developing countries. In addition, this approach had also brought a series of new difficulties and obstacles to economic development.

Although developing countries could use foreign capital in economic development to introduce labor-saving advanced technologies, the products of these newly established enterprises generally still could not compete in the international market. The reasons are as follows.

First, there are "economies of scale" problems in development process of enterprises. Capital-intensive enterprises can only fully play their technical and economic advantages under a certain scale (McQueen 1973). If capital-intensive enterprises established in developing countries could not have the appropriate scale as their counterparts in the advanced economies, their products would still lack international competitiveness. Moreover, if these enterprises want to reach the same scale, there were considerable difficulties in access to financial resources and management skills.

Second, a capital-intensive enterprise with advanced technologies and high productivity can fully take its technical and economic advantages only when it cooperates with other relevant enterprises and departments. It often does not exist in isolation, but is often embedded in a financial system that serves developed production technology. Unlike advanced industrial countries, however, developing countries lacked such an economic system of advanced technologies. Therefore, even if a few highly capital-intensive enterprises or sectors were established, it was still difficult to fully function and make their products internationally competitive (Singer 1963).

Third, with the continuous development of science and technology, even if capital-intensive enterprises or sectors were established at the advanced level at that time, they still needed to innovate and adopt more advanced scientific and technologies. To this end, there must be corresponding scientific and technological research capacity. In these respects, conditions in developing countries were far inferior to similar sectors and enterprises in advanced industrial countries. Therefore, after some time, capital-intensive enterprises established at the advanced level in developing countries would still lag behind the technological level of similar enterprises or sectors in the world, and their products would still lack international competitiveness.

Suppose developing countries first develop capital-intensive enterprises or sectors. In this case, they may not achieve the expected goal of replacing capital-intensive enterprises or sectors' products imported from advanced industrial countries or replacing their traditional export commodities—primary products. On the contrary, capital-intensive enterprises and sectors require a lot of investment and a long construction period. They cannot rely on their products that lack international competitiveness to obtain sufficient income denominated in foreign exchange. As a result, it is difficult to repay foreign debts and interest expenses would increase, hindering the country's industrialization and modernization process.

In addition, developing countries often have relatively rich resources in labor. However, the long-term economic stagnation in the past had resulted in large unemployment in the society. The redundancy in labor is common, especially in agriculture. In the process of industrialization and modernization, with the development of the economy, those unemployed and the laborers who are freed from agriculture could obtain job opportunities. Otherwise, the potential of social instability would increase. However, suppose that we focus on introducing and adopting "labor-saving," in this case, capital-intensive new technologies, and first develop a capital-intensive economy, then only a small part of labor could be absorbed in the new industries, and excessive work would still exist. In this way, when developing countries begin to industrialize, they will encounter the unemployment problem later than in advanced industrial countries. Correspondingly, out of political considerations, developing countries have to take "full employment" and "zero poverty" as their primary policy goals at the beginning of industrialization, as the advanced industrial countries do now (Adelman 1975). However, once "unemployment benefits" and other expenses are included in fiscal expenditures, it will worsen the current financial difficulties.

3.3 If Developing Countries Only Focus on the Development of Labor-Intensive Industries, they cannot Become Free from their State of Economic Dependence

In the 1960s, the Western economists formed another view on the technological innovation approach in the process of industrialization and modernization in developing countries, which suggested that developing countries should focus on the development of a labor-intensive economy, but not adopt "labor-saving" technological innovation and make efforts on developing the capital-intensive economy. In the 1960s and 1970s, the economic growth in some previously underdeveloped countries and regions in Asia maintained at a relatively high level and attracted more attention of advanced industrial countries in the international market. This made some Western economists who held the ideas mentioned above even more eloquent. It seemed that their point of view was entirely tenable.

This view is one-sided and ultimately not beneficial for developing countries to get rid of their economic dependency.

It is undeniable that when developing countries focus on labor-intensive economies at the beginning of industrialization, the following effects could take place as it did in the early capitalist industrialized countries. First, it requires less investment and can deliver immediate effects, gaining profits in a short period of time and then increasing the accumulation. If foreign capital is still in need, the amount could be decreased and then the interest expenses would be less, followed by a faster process of settlement. Second, under a certain amount of investment, more labor force would be needed, which would help alleviate employment pressure. Third, it is conducive to products' entrance into the international market. Notably, developing countries generally have abundant labor resources and relatively low wages. Therefore, if they grow a labor-intensive economy and adopt current global technologies for production, their products will be internationally competitive. In this way, more foreign exchange income can be obtained.

It is also undeniable that when all other conditions are equal, the development of a labor-intensive economy in developing countries has two other favorable conditions, compared to that of a capital-intensive economy. On the one hand, compared with a capital-intensive economy, a labor-intensive economy has lower requirements for the technical proficiency of the labor force. Developing countries generally lack a large technical sector, which would become an obstacle to developing a capital-intensive economy. However, if the focus is on developing a labor-intensive economy, this obstacle will be relatively small. On the other hand, "capital-saving" or new labor-intensive technologies are more accessible than "labor-saving" or capital-intensive new technologies. If developing countries want to create new labor-intensive technologies, they generally do not need to change the current production system. They often need to only select some existing production technology projects, adopt and promote them, or only need to reorganize production activities. The labor-intensive technological innovation is mainly about a reform of the process, which is easy to be imitated. The first company to adopt this new technology can certainly get high profits. Other companies can also adopt the same new technology, and the technological gap between them will not last for long, so the technological innovation is usually fast.

The situation above shows the advantage of developing countries to focus on creating a labor-intensive economy. But this is only one side of the issue. While emphasizing this aspect, it is easy to overlook the other element of long-term strategic significance.

Firstly, in Western economics papers that emphasize the development of labor-intensive economy in developing countries, the economy is treated as a purely open system, which means that it is entirely based on the world market. As a result, large-scale imports and exports have become the conditions for its survival. Of course, a completely closed economy is detrimental to a country's economic development. That will be the other extreme, in which a country relies on foreign trade and takes the world market as its primary destination for its industrial products, or relies mainly on imports for raw materials and capital equipment. Such an economy will be fragile and cannot withstand disruptions. In the long run, this is by no means a wise way.

Secondly, if a developing country's economy is based on the international market in industrialization and modernization, then even if there is no severe global economic crisis, large-scale war, or other huge turbulence, continued inflation in the capitalist world will still adversely affect the domestic economy. As mentioned above, if a developing country first develops a capital-intensive economy, then fiscal deficits, foreign debt and interest burdens, and balance of payments deficit will lead to domestic inflation. Conversely, if these countries focus solely on developing labor-intensive economies that heavily depend on the world market, they will inevitably suffer from rising domestic prices as a result of the global price increases.

Thirdly, the unequal exchange pattern between developed capitalist countries and developing countries remained largely unchanged through developing countries' emphasis on labor-intensive economies. If developing countries export primary products from labor-intensive sectors, the nature of their exchanges with developed capitalist countries' exports remains the same as before industrialization. When developing countries are exporting processed labor-intensive products in exchange for processed capital-intensive products from developed capitalist countries, such exchanges remain unequal because those processed capital-intensive products are exclusive for developing countries themselves. However, processed labor-intensive products exported by developing countries are non-exclusive, which can also be made by developed capitalist countries. The wages in developing countries are relatively low. Therefore, the price of processed labor-intensive products is relatively favorable. Such products can be sold on the international market meaning that the producers can manipulate prices of capital-intensive products in developed capitalist countries. In contrast, the prices of labor-intensive products in developing countries will depend on market competition. As a result, developing countries are still at a disadvantage in trade and are often subject to exploitation and extortion by developed capitalist countries.

Finally, the economists who advocate a priority on developing a labor-intensive economy in developing countries entirely neglected the issue of establishing their advanced defense industry system. However, installing of an advanced defense industry system must create a highly capital-intensive economy.

Therefore, we can conclude that if developing countries only focus on developing labor-intensive economies, they cannot grow out of economic dependency. However, this disadvantage can easily be concealed under aggregate indicators such as the increase of GDP, national income and economic growth rate. The advantages of developing a labor-intensive economy may be overstated. GNP does not reflect the composition of products or the degree of dependency a country's economy on the world market. And the growth of national income does not reflect the change in the domestic income distribution structure or the difference in the ratio between a country's export and import price indexes. A high economic growth rate might mean an increase in the unitary degree of a country's exports, a sharp decline of a country's domestic sectors critical to the national economy, or a deformed expansion of industries that are less important to the national economy. Without sectoral and structural analysis of the national economy, it is impossible to understand the actual effects on intensifying the development of labor-intensive economies in developing countries.

3.4 Developing Countries Should Choose the Type of Technological Innovation Based on their Specific Conditions

In the 1940s to the 1950s, some Western economists advocated that developing countries should adopt new "labor-saving" technologies and develop capital-intensive economies first, but this approach proved to be ineffective in practice. Since the 1960s, the proposal that developing countries adopt new "capital-saving" technologies and emphasize labor-intensive economies has also turned out to be one-sided. The result would still be detrimental to developing countries. So, what new technology should the developing countries choose and which kind of economy should they establish? This issue still needs further study. But at least it must be affirmed that each decision should be based on the country's actual situation, and there is no fixed and ironclad development model in reality.

Some developing countries are rich in both natural resources and human resources. The others may only have abundant natural resources with a small population or may own great human resources without sufficient natural resources. Due to different historical conditions and current levels of economic development, some developing countries are still lagging far behind in both industry and agriculture. In contrast, the modern sectors in some developing countries have merely reached an elementary level. What is closely related to this is that the level of science and culture, as well as the technical proficiency of workers vary from country to country. In this way, for developing countries with abundant natural endowment and relatively sparse population, but with a good balance of payments, it is possible to introduce and promote "labor-saving" new technologies and establish capital-intensive enterprises. As long as other social and economic conditions can be coordinated well, the difficulties and resistance encountered in developing a capital-intensive economy can be reduced and even avoided. On the other hand, for some regions and countries with relatively high population density and insufficient natural resources, they could only survive by bulk import and export trade temporarily. If their existing balance of payments situation deteriorated, it would be simply impossible or unfavorable to introduce and adopt new "labor-saving" technologies and establish capital-intensive enterprises and departments. The only viable option is to first develop a labor-intensive economy to alleviate the acute problems of employment and balance of payments. However, the two extremes mentioned above are exceptions rather than the norm.

Developing countries with rich natural resources, large populations, and an elementary level of industrial development are more common. Generally speaking, they would have a debt in the balance of payments, but the deficit would not be too large. In such countries, a more reasonable way is to adopt and promote "labor-saving" new technologies, "capital-saving" new technologies, and new "neutral" technologies simultaneously (new technologies with neither emphasis on "labor-saving" nor "capital-saving" technologies, that is, new technologies that can reduce the consumption of materialized labor and actual labor in the actual production cost in the same proportion[2]). A more reasonable economic structure is capital-intensive and labor-intensive economies with equal attention and an appropriate proportion. Why is this development method more reasonable? It is apparent from the political and national defense perspective that a country's advanced defense industry has to be built on a highly capital-intensive economy. From an economic point of view, this can simultaneously lead to the development of both labor- and capital-intensive economies.

In the process of industrialization and modernization, developing countries must address the following five economic issues simultaneously.

---

[2] Conceptually, "neutral" technology should not be confused with "intermediate technology." The former is determined by the proportion of each part of product costs, while the latter is divided according to the scale and level of technological advancement. "Neutral" technology may be "large-scale technology" (often also the most advanced technology) or "intermediate technology" (often relatively advanced technology). And "intermediate technology" may be "labor-saving," or "capital-saving," or "neutral."

First, to increase accumulation and the rate of investment. Second, to resettle a large number of unemployed people in society. Third, to increase foreign exchange income. Fourth, to develop a national economy in balance, and to improve the coordination of economic activities and the fragmented sectoral structure left over from the past. Fifth, to increase the level of real wages on the basis of the growth of productivity. These five issues are interrelated and mutually in check. If they are not handled properly, the vicious circle of economic stagnation, rising unemployment, balance of payments deficit, imbalanced national economic structure, and falling real wages are inevitable. Since the 1950s, there have been many lessons among developing countries. Paying equal attention to the development of labor-intensive and capital-intensive economies helps to balance these issues.

The adoption of new "labor-saving" technologies and the establishment of advanced capital-intensive enterprises and sectors will rapidly increase labor productivity and provide conditions for the technological transformation of the entire national economy. At the same time, it can fill the greenfield in the structure and products of the national economic system, gradually improving economic coordination out of fragmentation left over from the past.

However, establishing capital-intensive enterprises and developing capital-intensive sector means that labor-intensive enterprises and sectors must also be developed accordingly. On the one hand, unemployment can be alleviated. The existing unemployed in the society and the labor force made redundant by the enterprises and sectors with increased productivity can be resettled. On the other hand, the profitability, accumulation, and investment rate can be increased or improved. At the same time, the export of labor-intensive industrial products and foreign exchange income can be increased, which is necessary for the further introduction of advanced technologies from abroad.

In terms of the types of technological innovation, no sector in a developing economy should simply focus on substituting machines for the workforce to achieve high productivity. Instead, it should also emphasize the adoption and promotion of new "labor-saving" technologies. In this case, even if there is sufficient capital, the problem of labor placement will be difficult to address because the share of the capital-intensive economy in the national economy has increased too fast. Therefore, "capital-saving" and "neutral" technological innovation should never be ignored. Here, let's take the three sectors of the steel industry, television industry, and agriculture as examples.

Adopting "labor-saving" new technologies in the steel industry can have the same steel output with less workers. Still, it is also possible to adopt "capital-saving" new technologies to reduce the iron-to-cook ratio or the power consumption per unit of output. The former technological innovation will increase the number of unemployed steelworkers in the society with the same steel output while the latter will maintain the original size of the workforce. Both technological innovations can reduce the cost of production, but in detail, the ratio of materialized labor consumption to living labor consumption changes in different directions. It is the same in the television industry. The establishment of a new automated TV factory or transforming an original non-automated TV factory into an automated one is manifested in a significant increase in each worker's annual TV production capacity. If the output remains the same, the number of workers in need will be reduced. Even if the production increases, the demand for new workers will be relatively reduced. These will increase the employment tension in the society. However, if technical measures are taken to reduce the quota of raw material consumption and the rate of defective products based on the existing production equipment and workforce, it can still increase the international competitiveness without laying off workers. In agriculture, one can not only focus on the use of "labor-saving" new technologies (replacing workforce with machines), but also emphasize the use of "capital-saving" new technologies (i.e., obtaining the same output with less fertilizer, seeds, oil, and electricity per acre of arable land). Therefore, it can prevent the capital intensity from increasing too rapidly during technological change, making it easier to resettle a large number of agricultural labor forces.

In short, as far as the entire national economy is concerned, the agriculture and television industries are labor-intensive economies relative to the steel industry. However, as for any sector in these industries, it includes both capital-intensive and labor-intensive parts. In the process of industrialization and modernization, developing countries should consider the following five economic goals: to increase accumulation, to expand employment, to increase foreign exchange income, to fill gaps in sectors and products in the national economy, and to increase real wages on the basis of productivity growth. To achieve these goals, both labor-intensive and capital-intensive sectors in the entire national economy and labor-intensive and capital-intensive parts in each industry should develop proportionally and in balance. Therefore, it is necessary to pinpoint the type of technological innovation in the process of industrialization and modernization according to the actual situation of the country and the specific conditions of each economic sector. By doing so, the "labor-saving," "capital-saving," and "neutral" technologies can be equally valued and adopted, and various technological innovations can maintain an appropriate proportion.[3]

3.5 Is it Feasible to Pay Equal Attention to Labor-Intensive and Capital-Intensive Economy?

Theoretically, the simultaneous development of labor-intensive and capital-intensive economies in developing countries is beneficial because this can reap their benefits and avoid shortcomings. But in practice, a series of new problems will emerge. Can inflation be controlled? Is the transfer of labor between sectors and regions easy to

[3] This article discusses technological innovation classified by "capital-saving" and "labor-saving." It does not address the issue of the level of advancement of introduced technology. Whether it is "capital-saving" technology or "labor-saving" technology, there are the most advanced and relatively advanced. According to the experience of developing countries in the 1950s, introducing the most advanced technology is not necessarily the most beneficial. In some aspects, it is more advantageous and faster to introduce technology that is not the most advanced for developed capitalist countries but is still relatively advanced for developing countries. See Bauer's cited book, page 273.

implement? Can companies with lower productivity in similar products survive in the competition?

The issues involved here are obviously beyond the economics scope of technological innovation. We know that the developing countries mentioned here are developing productivity. From the perspective of the relations of production, developing countries as a category include those that are based on different systems of ownership and means of production, and on different ways of organization and management. Technological innovations can help solve some of the problems developing countries encounter in modernization, but it cannot solve all problems. Moreover, even for those problems that can be solved, the solutions differ depending on the relationship of production.

The issue of inflation in technological innovation in developing countries is challenging under capitalist relations of production. When capital-intensive and labor-intensive economies are adopted simultaneously, the fiscal and international balance of payments may not deteriorate as they first did. However, since the domestic economy is closely related to the capitalist world market, price increases caused by external inflation will affect the domestic economy. The resultant domestic anti-inflation measures will either affect the economic growth and technological advancement (e.g., through contractionary fiscal and credit policies) or impact the balance of payments (e.g., through income indexation policies). Given the existing capitalist world trading system and financial system, developing countries based on capitalist relations of production cannot entirely separate their domestic economic part from the foreign-related part (or genuine economic part). Therefore, this problem may exist for a long time.

Suppose developing countries want to establish capital-intensive and labor-intensive economies and to maintain coordination simultaneously, they must try to allocate labor reasonably so that work can be adapted to national economic development needs and deployed in various sectors and regions. Under a capitalist system, the principle of supply and demand in the labor market comes into play. When factors such as the lifestyle, habits, and residence of workers do not play a role, and workers can move freely, then the main factor affecting labor allocation would be the wage rate. But employers decide wage rates based on expected profitability and labor supply and demand. When productivity and normal profitability are too low, employers may either stop operating or significantly reduce the wage level. With the simultaneous development of capital-intensive and labor-intensive economies, and the coexistence of capital-intensive and labor-intensive enterprises in the same sector, there must be some sectors, enterprises, and regions that are short in labor, because employers are unwilling to increase wages and workers are reluctant to move to those places where they think the wages are too low. The only way is that the country provides long-term profit subsidies to employers or wage subsidies to workers, increasing fiscal expenditures. However, it still cannot solve the issue of rational allocation of labor. The production technology and equipment, capital intensity, and the technical requirements for work are all different. Technical conditions may also restrict the transfer between sectors and regions.

Similarly, under capitalist conditions, there is fierce competition among employers. When developing countries develop capital-intensive and labor-intensive economies simultaneously, or when capital-intensive and labor-intensive enterprises coexist in the same sector or sectors with substitutable products, employers will inevitably strive to adopt advanced technologies to maintain their survival and expand their production. Companies with poor technical equipment will be eliminated and crushed. Capital will shift to more profitable sectors. Accelerated depreciation and early asset renewal, which have become common in developed capitalist countries, will also appear in such developing countries. The capital intensity of the entire economy will continue to increase amid fierce competition. Therefore, proportional and coordinated development of capital-intensive and labor-intensive economies will become empty talk. Competition and dispersed production make it impossible to maintain an appropriate ratio between "labor-saving" and "capital-saving" technological innovation. To prevent private enterprises with poor technical equipment from being crowded out and to support the survival of small and medium-sized private enterprises with low productivity, the state must provide large subsidies for a long period of time, which is another substantial financial expenditure.

From this point of view, if the private market economy is allowed to play its role, and the principle of profit maximization remains the fundamental principle for all economic activities, it is difficult for developing countries to place equal emphasis on capital-intensive and labor-intensive economies. What is good for the society is not necessarily good for private capitalists. Private capital will be used in the areas that are best for itself. As a result, specific sectors of the national economy will decline, while other sectors will grow abnormally and excessively.

Therefore, based on a capitalist system of private ownership and the means of production, the simultaneous development of capital-intensive and labor-intensive economies is likely to face significant resistance in developing countries. This is fundamentally determined by the nature of capitalist industrialization and modernization. With capitalist "planning" as a supplement to the private market economy, state regulation, nationalization of certain industrial sectors, floating exchange rates, and import quota system, etc., can help ease the contradictions between the capital-intensive part and labor-intensive part of the economy. However, these are not the fundamental ways to solve the problem.

All these tell us that the socialist economic system has significant advantages in realizing modernization. Therefore, we should pay equal attention to the capital-intensive and labor-intensive economy, develop both parts of the economy in a proportionate and coordinated manner, select the types of technological innovation suitable for the country's specific conditions in a planned way, develop the agriculture, light industry, and heavy industry in different capital-intensive degree by local conditions, and make full use of the country's rich labor resources and rationally distribute them in various sectors and regions. These are genuinely feasible only under a socialist economic system. At the same time, in developing capital-intensive economy and labor-intensive economy, these countries use foreign capital and advanced technologies, and rely on a country's favorable conditions to improve the international competitiveness of products and expand exports. Thus, the relationship between the domestic economy and the world market will become closer. Then will it be strongly affected by capitalist world inflation? The superiority of the socialist economic system can be fully demonstrated here. It is possible to prevent or significantly reduce the impact of capitalist inflation on the domestic economy by implementing foreign trade and foreign exchange policies and ensuring the smooth progress of socialist economic construction. It is also all the more challenging amidst a process of capitalist industrialization and modernization.

— *The Journal of World Economy,* issue No. 6, 1979.

References

Temin P (1971) "Steam and Waterpower in the Early Nineteenth Century." In: Fogel and Engerman (ed.) *The Re-interpretation of American Economic History*, Palgrave, London, pp. 229-230, 234.

Berrill K (1963) "Foreign Investment and Take-off." In: Rostow WW (ed) *The Economics of Take-off into Sustained Growth*, Palgrave Macmillan London, p. 291, 293, 297.

McQueen M (1973) *Development Economics: Problems and Policies*. Weidenfeld & Nicolson Ltd. London, pp. 107-108.

Singer HW (1963) "Report on the Proceedings Summary Record: Statement at the Conference on Rostow's 'Leading Sectors and Takeoff'." In: Rostow WW (ed) *The Economics of Take-off into Sustained Growth*, Palgrave Macmillan London. p. 303.

Adelman I (1975) *Development Economics: A Reappraisal of Goals*. The American Economic Review, Vol.65(2):306-307.

Chapter 4
1980: The Role of Education in Economic Growth

In my speech "Technology Education and Capitalist Industrialization: A Study of the Rise of Technological Power in Western Europe and America (delivered at Peking University's 1978 *May Fourth Science Forum*, and carried in *Social Science Front*, issue No. 4, 1978)," I dwelled on the relationship between education and economic growth in light of economic history. What I was driving at was that education is a major recourse for nations to groom technological personnel, and that only by putting a premium on education and the cultivation of talents can less developed nations boost their economic growth rates and catch up with and surpass the developed countries. As I put it in that speech, the role of education in economic growth has five aspects.

First, education provides society with a supply of researchers and designers who can venture into the unknown, innovating in science, renovating and transforming productive technology. Without such contingents, the best a nation can do is to tag along after other nations, but in that way, you cannot score major breakthroughs in science and technology.

Second, education provides society with engineers and technicians who can master and apply advanced means of production. Without such technocrats, even if a nation has acquired sophisticated tools of production, it cannot put them to best use.

Third, education brings forth production and technology managers well adapted to society's level of industrialization. Without teams of such managers, the production process can be prone to colossal waste in human, material, and financial resources, making it impossible to benefit from the superiority of advanced productive technology.

Fourth, education enhances society's scientific and cultural attainment, and sets the stage for promoting new products and disseminating and upgrading knowledge in science and technology. At the same time, education also lays the groundwork for the future growth of a nation's technological prowess, and guarantees the supply of a constant stream of high-caliber researchers, engineers and managers, and skilled workers.

Y. Li, *China's Economy Since 1978*, China Academic Library,
https://doi.org/10.1007/978-981-95-5733-2_4

Fifth, education enables society to preserve and disseminate its accumulation of scientific knowledge and productive experience free from barriers of time and space and national boundaries. It is through education that such accumulated knowledge and experience are spread from one nation to another and from one generation to another as humanity's shared assets.

I would like to go on with my observation of the relationship between education and economic growth on the basis of the speech I made and published two years ago. However, this paper has a different focus. While in my previous speech I looked into the major role education plays in expanding the economy and raising its growth rate, this paper underlines education's important role in ensuring economic stability and sustained growth, and in providing effective solutions to problems that have occurred or may occur in the process of economic growth. In other words, my previous speech was about economic growth per se, whereas this paper is a study of employment, balance of international payments, income distribution, financial balance, and other issues occurring in the process of stabilizing and sustaining economic growth. Furthermore, while my previous speech proceeded from the perspective of the economic history of Western Europe and America, this paper takes China's socialist economy as its focus and background.

This paper is delivered in four chapters dealing respectively with education's relationship with employment, balance of international payments, income distribution, and fiscal balance, so as to illustrate education's role in guaranteeing economic stability and sustained growth.

4.1 The "Structural" Nature of the Employment Problem Can be Solved by Developing and Restructuring Education

Theoretically speaking, any nation can grow its economy either by expanding its workforce or by investing more in machines and equipment and improving workers' technical know-how and skills. The adoption of labor-saving technology and equipment may help cut down the material production sector's demand for workers in the course of economic growth. Consequently, given a constant population growth rate, economic growth itself cannot ensure full employment. The number of jobs to be created through output increase is determined not only by the rate of production expansion, but also by which approaches are adopted for such expansion. If a country develops its economy not by hiring more workers but by adopting new technology and equipment and improving workers' cultural and technical proficiency, then the ability of its material production sector to absorb the workforce will be limited.

On the other hand, economic growth also entails a process of change in a nation's economic structure. The inexorable law of material production is that some old manufacturing industries decline or are phased out while new ones rise and grow. The ratio between material and non-material production in the national economy is changing as well. It is an irrevocable trend in economic growth for some non-material production industries to grow in strength along with their shares in the national economy. With the national economic structure changing constantly, those working in languishing or failed industries need to find new jobs elsewhere. The rising industries in material production, and particularly the burgeoning industries in non-material production, often run short of workforce. Thus, the emergence and growth of new industries in both material and non-material production are major reasons why a nation can increase employment amidst economic growth.

The changing economic structure of a nation implies changes in both industrial and geo-economic structures. In China, underdeveloped regions may achieve a relatively higher economic growth rate, whereas developed regions may slow down, or grow at a relatively lower pace. Regions that either suffer a low growth rate or maintain a high growth rate mainly by spending more on technology and equipment will produce a glut of factory layoffs that will have to seek employment elsewhere, whereas regions with a high growth rate, those with a labor shortage in particular, are likely to accept the job hunters.

These situations prove clearly that the employment problem confronting a country in the process of economic growth is mainly "structural." That is to say, the success or failure in tackling this problem hinges on whether the workforce structure—the makeup of workers of different trades, industries and locations in a region's total number of workers—is commensurate with local economic growth rates and economic structural changes, and whether the workforce itself can meet the technical needs of local economic growth. When the structure of a workforce does not match the local economic growth rate and the changing local economic structure, and when workers' technical proficiency level falls short of the needs of economic growth, unemployment will unavoidably exist alongside a surplus of unfilled job vacancies.

This paradoxical coexistence of unemployment and superfluous vacancies means that while people are looking frantically for jobs, many jobs are left unfilled. How is it that people lose jobs while the economy keeps growing? The answer is that if economic growth is achieved for the most part by raising labor productivity while the population growth rate remains high, those coming of employment age are likely to fail to land suitable jobs. Even if these people are a non-factor, industries and regions with slow or stagnant growth lay off workers. This is particularly true of developing countries, where agriculture—known for its low labor productivity—often dominates the national economy. In the industrialization process, large numbers of villagers who have just quit farming may find it hard to land jobs. Unemployment—concealed unemployment[1] included—thus becomes unavoidable.

Why, then, are there vacancies that remain unoccupied? This is because, when the workforce structure does not tally with the prevailing economic growth rate and economic structure, the rising industries in both material and non-material production cannot find what they want badly: skilled workers and competent engineers, technicians, researchers, and managers. The same labor shortage can also occur in

[1] Referring to individuals who know that no suitable jobs are available but choose not to register as being employed, even though they would prefer to have a job—*Translator*.

established industries in material production that maintain growth by relying heavily on new technology and equipment, so much so that even workers on their payrolls cannot measure up to what such new technology and equipment require of them. Seemingly unwanted jobs may also occur in newly developed places where required workers are in short supply. This is an outstanding problem with developing countries, where, for historical reasons, skilled workers that can keep pace with industrialization are scarce.

Generally speaking, the number of the jobless can never match the number of jobs awaiting them in a national economy. The ratio between the two numbers differs with the changes and readjustments in a nation's economic growth rate and economic and workforce structure. However, even if the two numbers match each other, they cannot offset each other, because workers of different proficiency levels and fields of work are not interchangeable under modern production and technological conditions. In the long run, the coexistence of unemployment and unfilled job vacancies in a nation's economic growth is not temporary, but, most probably, perpetual. That is to say, job vacancies may disappear when long-time job seekers have found their jobs, but will occur again when new layoffs arrive on the scene. Unemployment, concealed unemployment included, is a waste of human resources, while job vacancies left unfilled are a waste of material resources—for them to exist at the same time is not only detrimental to economic growth, but also holds back the adoption and popularization of new technology and economic restructuring. The result is that the economy remains mired in low efficiency. Chronic joblessness can also be a major destabilizing factor for society.

In a nutshell, employment problems in a growing economy are attributable to the failure in reconciling the conflict between unemployment and unfilled job vacancies. Such is the "structural" nature of employment.

The employment problems confronting China are complicated. Some are universal to all economies, some are common to developing nations in economic development, but others are peculiarly China's own. These three categories of employment problems are intertwined. The universal one stems from the fact that the increasing use of sophisticated machines and technological equipment has whittled down producers' need for workers, unskilled workers in particular. Those common to developing nations arise from the new job needs of large numbers of unskilled laborers that have just quit farming at the time of an agrarian society's transition to industrialization. The employment problems peculiarly of China's own are partly to be blamed on incompetent labor administration, but most of them are attributed to the lopsided economic development resulting from the ten-year chaos of the Cultural Revolution that considerably narrowed down people's job options. These problems were aggravated by the excessive population growth in the late 1950s and the early 1960s. Today, those born in those years are coming of age or will soon become eligible for jobs. If the employment problems for these people cannot be properly handled, both society and the economy will be in jeopardy. The situation is also complicated by a dire shortage of skilled workers and the low labor productivity of those in their jobs. The dilemma facing China today is that while many job-seeking youths are having trouble finding jobs, factories, too, find it hard to fill jobs with qualified workers.

A country's aggregate volume of labor resources is derived by multiplying the total number of workers with their average level of technical competency—the chief indicator of labor quality. In that sense, China's aggregate volume of labor resources is by no means abundant because its workers' average skill proficiency is low despite their sheer numbers.

The solution to our nation's employment problems, in the final analysis, is to create a constant supply of new jobs to keep pace with economic growth. If we cannot create new jobs, the need for labor will shrink with the adoption of new technology, even if population growth is kept at a low level.

How to create new jobs? This involves the diverse economic sectors and forms of public ownership under the socialist system, as well as such factors as economic administration, various types of technical innovation, and the ratios between sectors and economic growth rate. These issues, however, are beyond the scope of this study. The topic at hand is this: Supposing substantial numbers of new jobs are created by readjusting and revamping the ownership structure, the economic system and the ratios between economic sectors, and by riding the nation's robust economic growth, can the nation come to grips with its employment problems? Given the "structural" nature of employment in our country, we can assert categorically that the disparity between the structure of the workforce and that of the national economy will never be eradicated without corresponding development in education and without restructuring the education system. The dilemma between "people hunting for jobs" and "jobs seeking takers," too, will remain for a long time to come. The important role of education in tackling employment problems rests precisely on its ability to deliver the nation from that dilemma.

Developing education and spending more on it can help dovetail the workforce structure with a growing economy's need for workers at different technical levels and in different fields of work. To achieve that end, we have got to adapt our educational structure to the changing economic growth rate and structure, and act on the long-term need of economic growth to readjust the categories of schools and the setup of academic programs, and to variegate the schooling terms. Long years of observation reveal two options in this regard. In the first option, when existing and prospective job seekers are not outnumbered by anticipated unfilled job vacancies, the main thrust of our effort can be directed at further improving education and raising workforce quality, so that every worker that has been educated or trained can qualify for more demanding jobs, thereby enhancing labor productivity and further promoting the adoption of new technology. In this way, not only can the needs of economic growth be met, but the number of unfilled job vacancies can be curtailed as well. In the other option, when the total number of existing and prospective job hunters outgrows the anticipated number of unfilled job vacancies, we can lay equal stress on improving and universalizing education, so that more high-caliber professionals can be cultivated for the national economy while legions of job-waiters are tooled with one kind of skill or another to qualify for suitable jobs. To achieve this end, apart from further restructuring the economy to increase job vacancies, attention should also be paid to developing secondary technical and vocational education so as to put more job seekers through training. The school term for students can be lengthened so as to curtail the number of prospective job hunters and better prepare students culturally and technically for future economic growth needs. In other words, we would rather let our youngsters learn more knowledge and skill than keep them waiting for jobs when they are ill-prepared in both skill and knowledge.

As things stand today, it is believed the second option is more workable for China for a long time to come. Thus, in education development and reform, we cannot go single-mindedly after improvement to the neglect of the role of education in tackling the "structural" employment problem.

We should also remember that education reform cannot be accomplished overnight. For one thing, economic growth itself demands that our schools supply large numbers of well-educated and skilled workers who measure up to its needs. Failing this, stable and sustainable economic growth will be out of the question. For another, the economy's ever-changing sectoral, regional, and technological structures call for the adaptation of the education system. A certain level of national economic development is always consistent with a certain structure of education, with the latter changing in sync with the former. This fact should be considered when mapping out long-term national human resource plans.

So much for my analysis of the "structural" employment issue. The employment problems facing China today are "structural" in the main, but they do not stop merely at being "structural." "Individual occupation selectivity" is another social employment issue for present-day China. When job openings are available, people can still choose to stay jobless. They do not lack the needed education and skill, but they make this choice out of occupational considerations. The causes of this employment problem are manifold, but education can still play a role in tackling it. This is because the mission of educators is not limited to teaching cultural knowledge and technical expertise. Character building and education in revolutionary values are essential to students in this country.

4.2 Investment in Education as a Prerequisite for Developing a Knowledge-Intensive Economy; the Gradual Increase of Knowledge-Intensive Exports as a Strategic Measure to Improve China's Balance of International Payments Amidst Economic Growth

As to the patterns of technological innovation for developing nations in the modernization process, I have voiced my opinions in my article "On the roles of capital-intensive and labor-intensive economies in the modernization process of developing nations" (*World Economy*, issue No. 6, 1979). Because what I wanted to drive at in that article was that developing countries are not going anywhere if they choose to develop a capital-intensive economy more than anything else, I made no mention of the differences between skilled and unskilled labor and of the developmental trends of a labor-intensive economy. In this study, however, to explain why investment in education is a boon to stable and sustained economic growth, I find it necessary to look further into the patterns of technological innovation, or, to be specific, the role a knowledge-intensive economy can play in economic growth.

Theoretically speaking, a nation out to seek economic growth must boost its financial savings and raise funds for investment purposes. If the supply of funds is in shortage at home, something can be done to procure foreign funds under appropriate credit conditions and in light of the situation of the world capital market. The plus side of the use of foreign capital is that it helps overcome immediate foreign exchange and capital shortfalls and brings in advanced technology from other lands. However, in the long run, the commitment to repaying both principal and interest will eventually become a problem for the borrower. If the nation cannot increase its foreign exchange revenue from exports or other sources, balance of payments deficit may become a major hindrance to sustaining its economic growth.

Let us imagine a nation that is before or at the beginning of industrialization that has an abundant workforce, whose wages are low, and whose traditional exports of labor-intensive products have a competitive edge on the world market. Such a nation can use its foreign exchange earnings from exports to meet its domestic demand for technology and commodity imports and improve its balance of international payments. However, when industrialization reaches a certain stage, labor-intensive exports will gradually lose their edge and put the nation at a disadvantage for the following reasons.

First, a growing economy inevitably boosts national income gradually. While per capita national income rises on a yearly basis, worker wages go up as well. As a result, the gap in average wage between the nation and the developed industrial nations is likely to narrow down, thus diminishing the benefits of the "entry ticket" the nation can get from its low wages on to the world market. What merits particular attention here is that industrialization is a common trend for all nations. When industrialization arrives at a certain stage in the said nation, other less developed nations will follow suit and strive to expand exports and absorb advanced foreign technology. These "latecomers" are most probably in the possession of abundant workforce and even lower wages, and their exports of labor-intensive products are more competitive on the world market because they are made by workers with even lower pay. If the said nation goes on to depend on labor-intensive products for exports after it has increased workers' wages on the basis of economic growth and increased national income, it is bound to come across newer and tougher competitors on the world market, a situation that is obviously not in its favor.

Second, a considerable part of the products of a labor-intensive economy are primary ones. Economic growth is likely to boost the demand for primary products in nations pursuing industrialization. For instance, the demand for mineral products or farm and sideline produce tends to swell with the rise of new industries, urban development, development in communications and transport, and improvement in people's material and cultural lives. Yet the effort to sustain massive exports of primary products can be inhibited by economic growth and growing domestic demand for such products. If that happens, the nation's balance of international payments will be adversely affected.

Third, even though the output of labor-intensive products can grow in pace with a nation's economy, such a growth rate is generally low. Moreover, their supply is restrained by natural resources and productive technology. This is because living labor accounts for the lion's share of production costs, whereas materialized labor makes up a smaller portion of it. As a result, the growth of labor productivity is relatively slow. Supposing a nation in economic growth needs to import advanced technology constantly and repay the principal with interest on procured foreign capital, it must expand exports to meet that need. If that nation counts mainly on labor-intensive exports in return for foreign exchange earnings, it may not maintain its balance of international payments by expanding such exports because of their low growth rate and serious supply restraint. If the nation wants to expand its exports and maintain its balance of international payments, it can only have one of the three options. Option One: to export more non-labor-intensive products to pick up the slack in the slow growing supply of labor-intensive products. Option Two: to slash domestic demand for labor-intensive products and curtail its growth rate to guarantee exports. Option Three: to transform production technology for labor-intensive products and increase their labor productivity, so as to increase output and expand supply. Option One calls for changing the nation's traditional dependence on labor-intensive products for export revenue. Option Two is predicated on cutting home demand and restraining domestic growth rate, that is, to expand exports at the expense of domestic demand and economic growth. Option Three will bring down labor intensity in the nation's labor-intensive economy and gradually deprive it of its competitive edge. No matter what option is chosen, it is not only difficult but also against the law of economic growth for a nation to keep counting on labor-intensive products for export revenue when industrialization reaches a certain stage of development.

It should also be noted that even if a nation can still benefit from labor-intensive exports at a certain stage of industrialization (when, for example, its wages are low enough, there are still no tough competitors on the international market scene, domestic demand for primary products has not grown strong enough to affect exports, or its labor-intensive economy is still robust enough to stabilize such exports), it gets a raw deal if it goes on selling labor-intensive products in return for non-labor-intensive imports. This is because the history and system of the world economy have determined that trade between non-labor-intensive and labor-intensive products on the international market is an unequal exchange of value, a situation that is not going to change anytime soon. This being the case, why should nations stick to labor-intensive products as the major source of export revenue after they have gone through a certain stage of industrialization? Why can't they replace labor-intensive products with non-labor-intensive ones that can definitely stand them in good stead in world trade?

As shown previously, observed from whatever perspectives, heavy dependence on labor-intensive exports should definitely be relinquished when industrialization reaches a certain stage even though it is a necessity at the beginning. On no account should the practice of letting labor-intensive products take up the lion's share of exports become a long-term state policy.

This poses a problem: Since it is both difficult and inappropriate for a nation to allow labor-intensive products to go on dominating its exports at a certain stage of industrialization, what is to be done with its balance of payments deficit in the course of economic growth? Supposing that nation's international revenue from non-trade items is fixed, what should it do to increase exports so that it can boost imports and repay the principal and interest of foreign debts?

The way-out rests in developing a capital-intensive economy, exporting capital-intensive products, or replacing home-made capital-intensive products with similar imports. Feasible though these options are, they are by no means simple. Some developed industrial nations in the world economy today have turned international trade to their advantage through long years of painstaking maneuvering. This, plus the abundant capital in their hands, is of good service to them in exporting capital-intensive products. It is no mean task to compete with the capital-intensive products from these countries, let alone gain the upper hand in such a competition.

For this reason, developing nations that are latecomers to industrialization should spare no effort to develop and export something else after they arrive at a certain stage of industrialization, and that is the products of a knowledge-intensive economy.

The knowledge-intensive economy, observed from the perspective of labor quality and technological innovation, is actually a way of categorizing innovations, industries, and products. As illustrated in the foregoing, the strength of a country's labor resources manifests itself in both the number and quality of laborers. Labor quality is not factored in when categorizing national economies into capital-intensive and labor-intensive types. Rather, economies are differentiated in this regard merely in terms of the ratio between labor and capital goods inputs in production by natural physical units. By contrast, in calculating the labor input by natural physical units, every person (or work hour) represents an equal amount of labor input; in calculating the input of capital goods, only their values are considered—the degree of sophistication of technology embodied in the capital goods and the technical proficiency of the workers using such goods are not factored in. However, an analysis in light of labor quality shows, firstly, labor input is naturally divided into skilled and unskilled labor input, and secondly, the input of capital goods is also naturally divided into those that, on one hand, embody technological sophistication and are applied by skilled labor, and on the other, do not embody the sophistication of technology used and are operated by unskilled labor. Thus, national economies can also be categorized into skilled-labor-intensive ones and unskilled-labor-intensive ones. In a skilled-labor-intensive economy, labor is skilled, and the input of capital goods embodies mature technology in the hands of skilled labor. By the same token, products can also be classified as either skilled-labor-intensive or unskilled-labor-intensive. Knowledge-intensive products are exactly skilled-labor-intensive products.

If a nation rich in workforce can not only keep upgrading workers' scientific and technical proficiency, imbue them with high labor productivity, and enable them to innovate production technology, but can also employ skilled workers and use capital goods that embody the sophistication of technology in production, then its products will not customarily be labor-intensive but skilled-labor-intensive or knowledge-intensive. Such products are a crystallization of the latest science-and-technology achievements mastered by that nation's labor—workers, technicians, scientists, and researchers included—and the advanced technical levels they have attained. They also epitomize the latest progress in production technology and the high labor productivity the nation has achieved. If that nation can export this kind of product in return for unskilled-labor-intensive imports, rather than sell labor-intensive products in exchange for capital-intensive products, it can still be competitive on the world market even though its wages are rising with economic growth, and it can also open up one market after another to promote sales. Furthermore, because the nation has stopped exporting labor-intensive products, it can steer clear of the extant terms of exchange in international trade that are detrimental to labor-intensive products, thereby forestalling economic losses that might be incurred by the system of unequal exchange.

Technological innovation knows no bounds; nor will improvement of labor productivity stop at a certain level. A developing nation striving for modernization enjoys broad prospects in both economic growth and balance of international payments so long as it sets its skilled-labor-intensive economy on a track of ceaseless development.

Thus, the important role of educational investment becomes apparent in coordinating economic growth and the balance of international payments. Without steady follow-up investment in education, we can never achieve universal and remarkable development in the workforce's technical and work proficiency, bring forth high-caliber scientists and researchers, and revamp productive technology without letup. For this reason, investment in education is the prerequisite for developing a skilled-labor-intensive or knowledge-intensive economy.

To sum up, increasing investment in education is a strategic measure for improving the balance of international payments in the course of economic growth. Ours is a socialist nation. Where is our comparative strength in international trade? It lies in none other than the export of certain labor-intensive products. We have got to make the most of this strength, and develop it unremittingly. However, we should never make it a long-term state policy for foreign trade, to say nothing of the inevitability that this strength of ours will dwindle gradually with national economic growth. From a strategic point of view, we must heighten the skilled-labor intensity of every export commodity and the skilled-labor intensity of every exporting company. Our nation will stay competitive on the world market for a long time to come if our exports of farm products are no longer customarily labor-intensive, but improved strains and quality products that epitomize advanced science and technology and the latest research and development achievements; if our exports of industrial goods are no longer run-of-the-mill products of the labor-intensive processing industry, but quality goods that reflect the distinctively innovated Chinese technology and nascent research results; and if what we sell to the world market are no longer ores, coal, crude oil or other mineral products but a good variety of quality products that are fashioned out of mineral raw materials and that mirror China's new achievements in science and technology. Then the more productive our industrial and agricultural departments are, the more competitive our country will be on the world market. All these things, when done in due course, will put our nation's workforce at an advantage not only quantitatively but also qualitatively. With our "knowledge" crystallized in produce and labor service, we will remain invincible in the world market.

4.3 To Increase Wages and Improve Economic Efficiency Is the Nation's Cardinal Mission that Can be Attained—To a Certain Extent—Through Investing in Education

The topic of this chapter is the relationship between income distribution and economic efficiency. In a capitalist economy, the trade-off between "equality" and efficiency has special connotations. Under capitalist ownership of capital goods, "equality" is based on recognizing the capitalist hired-labor system, whereas efficiency is an outcome of capitalist competition. Fundamentally speaking, there will never be true equality so long as the capitalist hired-labor system remains, but this is irrelevant to the theme of this study. Nevertheless, the relationship between income distribution and economic efficiency is a major issue that merits attention.

To care for people and cultivate them is the purpose of socialist production. To develop production is to improve people's material and cultural well-being, and bring forth workers' talent. However, to develop production, we have got to be particular about efficiency and motivate our workers. Theoretically speaking, the principle of distributing to each according to one's work, if carried out to the letter along with sound social welfare measures, is conducive to the development of production and enhancement of efficiency, as well as a guarantee for workers' pay raise provided development in production is ensured. However, workers' average income in this nation is low, and the influence of egalitarianism on income distribution very much alive. Both facts hamper economic growth, sap people's enthusiasm, and render workers' pay rise all the more difficult. The egalitarian pattern of income distribution that has kept wages at a low level for a long time cannot be eradicated without painstaking efforts.

To illustrate this issue, and to explain the role education can play in readjusting the relationship between income distribution and economic efficiency, it is necessary to begin this study with the income distribution theory.

Generally speaking, in economic growth there may be two income distribution patterns. One is to pay workers entirely according to the quantity and quality of work done. Under the other pattern, the state takes steps to regulate people's income by making allowances for low-income earners and limiting or deducting from the income of those highly paid. Proponents of the first pattern argue that paying people entirely according to the quantity and quality of work done represents a fair and square evaluation of the labor or service provided by every member of society, and that this is the only way to duly reward those who work hard and sanction those who malinger or dillydally, and to motivate people to work to the best of their ability and talent. Supporters of the second pattern hold that to reward people entirely according to the quantity and quality of work done is unfair because such quantity and quality are not entirely determined by whether people work hard or not. They argue that people differ in the ability to earn a living because there are broad differences in talent, intellectual attainment, physical strength, family background, and education, and especially because people cannot choose the social and work environment and the capital goods they are supposed to use in production. For example, because some happen to be using highly productive machines while the others are not, someone may have worked hard, but the quantity and quality of work he does compare unfavorably with what is done by someone else who does not exert himself but has better talent and family background and works in a better environment. These factors embody the limits of the practice of rewarding people entirely according to the quantity and quality of work done, and are responsible for the fact that some people work harder than others but make less money while others do not work as hard but earn more. It thus stands to reason for the state to adopt regulating measures to give allowance to low-income people and limit the incomes of highly paid people.

Supporters of either income distribution pattern try to make their cases also by citing income distribution's beneficial effect on economic growth. Supporters of the first pattern believe that paying people entirely according to the quantity and quality of work done can inspire every worker to take the initiative into his hands and improve his expertise and skill, thereby promoting national economic growth. According to them, people's enthusiasm will be dampened, and their work efficiency reduced, if they are not paid according to the quantity and quality of work done, or if their incomes are evened up arbitrarily. Supporters of the second pattern believe that the first pattern tends to widen the income gap between members of society, thereby adversely affecting the mindset of some people, so that low-income people may become so frustrated and disappointed as to hurt the national economy.

The controversy surrounding these two income distribution patterns, however, makes little sense for capitalist economies. A capitalist society cannot possibly pay workers according to the quantity and quality of work done, and its class nature determines that it cannot regulate the income of members of various classes in reasonable ways. The superior socialist system makes fair income distribution possible, as it can maximizes economic growth by dispensing income on a rational footing. The superiority of socialism, however, is yet to be brought to full fruition in China. Egalitarianism in income distribution and low average worker income are established facts in this country for a variety of reasons. Ambiguity in production goals compels people to produce for production's sake year in, year out. The belief that the more egalitarian it is, the better income distribution becomes makes it impossible to distribute income reasonably and motivate workers with it. As a result, the economy grows at a snail's pace, labor productivity remains penuriously low, and workers' disposable incomes cannot be increased, so much so that social stability and unity are affected. The situation has reached a point where something has got to be done about it. But what exactly is to be done? In my opinion, when we discuss how to regulate the relationship between income distribution and economic efficiency, we must proceed from our nation's established income distribution pattern, from the egalitarianism that has been prevalent across the land for years, and from the current average income of workers. History cannot be reversed. It won't do to conjure up an income distribution pattern based on the assumption of "what we would have done if we were living in the pre-liberation year of 1949." Important though it is for us to explore such a pattern, it cannot solve real-world problems because the established wage standards make it easy to raise wages and hard to reduce them, and because the established welfare benchmarks make it easy to raise welfare and hard to reduce it.

Given the *status quo* in our nation, we are not getting anywhere if we stop paying people according to the quantity and quality of work done and increasing people's average income, and allow egalitarianism to go unchecked. It will not work, either, if our government acts impetuously, turns a blind eye to the real practices of income distribution and the welfare steps that have been taken, and carries to extremes the practice of paying people strictly according to the quantity and quality of work done. Considering the historical circumstances under which the current income distribution practice has come about, I believe the order of the day should be to gradually increase workers' pay in the process of developing production. Egalitarianism and low average worker income are the main causes behind low work efficiency; and low work efficiency is a major hindrance to economic growth. Our mission at hand is to root out egalitarianism and carry out the principle of distributing to each according to his work. That is to say, under the precondition of raising workers' actual income, we must do what we can to pay them in light of the quantity and quality of work done. If we keep doing this, workers' income is bound to grow considerably within a few years. However, a universal rise of average worker's pay may also result in the income of some people rising more quickly than others, thereby widening the income gap. If the growing income gap disgruntles some people, it will not be too late for the government to remedy the situation with regulatory steps, such as increasing the private income tax rate and levying an inheritance tax within the framework of a progressive tax system. In my opinion, we have got to foresee this potential trend and refrain from taking premature countermeasures. The problem will be taken care of sooner or later.

Coordination between income distribution and economic efficiency amidst economic growth involves not only the longstanding distribution pattern and the past and present wage and welfare systems, but also a number of ideological issues. For instance, such important ideological issues as workers' political awareness, social mores and values, and people's understanding of what "equality" and "happiness" really mean can affect, one way or another, people's enthusiasm, initiative, and efficiency at work, and the balance between income distribution and economic efficiency. We must be careful about the countermeasures we are going to take against these ideological issues if we are to increase workers' pay without crippling their enthusiasm for work or hurting economic efficiency.

What, then, is the role of education in coordinating the relationship between income distribution and economic efficiency? Can education investment speed up the accomplishment of the above-mentioned tasks? There is no doubt that education has a certain ideological impact on those being educated, thereby helping them foster a sound outlook on life, a sense of social responsibility and other values that should not be overlooked. It is also indisputable that this impact is not an issue. What is at issue is the content of such education and the approaches to it. In this study, however, I want to draw attention to the following four pertinent economic issues.

First, as education can improve people's money-making ability by raising their cultural and technical levels, an effective way to help low-income workers make more money is to put them through certain professional education or training. If the principle of distributing to each according to his work is followed in real earnest, a worker schooled in professional knowledge and technical expertise can earn more than those who lack such knowledge and expertise. Thus, he is a beneficiary of the education he has received. Regular and spare-time education can both help individuals increase their private income. Therefore, those who have passed a certain level of academic or technical examinations should be issued a diploma or certificate and paid accordingly in the workplace. Developing education can upgrade the quality of the entire nation's workforce and boost the work efficiency of those who have been educated. This is particularly the case in this age of modern science and technology, where a growing economy badly needs quality workers who can never be replaced no matter how many low-quality workers there are. Low-income people will be stuck in the low-income brackets, and their work quality will remain low if they do not receive professional training. It is thus clear that developing education helps bridge income disparity, increases efficiency, boosts the economy and increases workers' average income.

Second, the lack of labor mobility is detrimental to the effort to enhance economic efficiency and increase income. However, labor mobility is a complex issue that is beyond this study. What I want to say right now is this: Supposing the workforce in our nation has become somewhat more mobile through institutional and other reforms and readjustments, this leaves another important problem to be addressed, that is, there are people who, for lack of professional knowledge and skills, are not able to adapt themselves to the changing economic structure and ever-improving technology by changing their jobs. In the course of economic growth, large numbers of villagers quit farming as a result of raised productivity in agriculture, but their poor adaptability to new careers makes it hard for them to be absorbed by other sectors in need of workforce. Thus, large numbers of them have stuck in agriculture, where their labor cannot be fully utilized. Social efficiency suffers as a result. What merits particular attention is that, under these circumstances, low efficiency, lack of vocational adaptability, and low income are interrelated, and can also be addressed by relying on education development. Only through education can low-income people change their jobs when and where necessary, and get higher pay; only when their abilities and talents are brought into play in their new jobs can society reduce its loss in efficiency.

Third, low income not only affects its earners but also carries over to their younger generation. This is true everywhere, and socialist China is no exception. A socialist society is theoretically free from hereditary tenures, workplace discrimination and cliquishness, but children from low-income families have few schooling opportunities and even fewer opportunities to go to college. When they start work, they have fewer chances to get new jobs, let alone jobs with high pay. I think we should admit that their problem is caused by economic factors. A comparison of low-income families with high-income families shows that if income disparity has become a reality in the first generation, by the time of the second generation, a few low-income families may quit poverty, but most of them will remain poor or even become poorer. This is because, judging from the Chinese reality, among the generation of people in their forties and fifties, families with poor education generally have more children than others. In these families, few housewives hold jobs; it is a factor which kept per-family income at a low level. Low income leads to low level of education, and low level of education leads to low income, and the vicious cycle goes on and on. It goes without saying that the government may take steps to provide children of low-income families with more educational opportunities. But this way of doing things can backfire, because in an environment where higher education is underdeveloped while the remnant influence of feudalism still lingers, government steps can degenerate into some people's tools for selfish gains. When that happens, there will be serious consequences: The efficiency of the national economy will be eroded, and a drain of precious human resources will occur. To break the vicious cycle suffered by low-income families without affecting economic efficiency and dashing talented people's hope for education, we must develop education. We must expand higher education and vocational education dramatically to increase the rate of school enrollment of low-income families' children and prepare them for high-income jobs in the future. At the same time, we should never do anything that might either erode society's economic efficiency or deprive gifted people of the opportunity to continue their education and bring their talent into full play.

Fourth, with the whole picture of the national economy in mind, low-income people and their families cannot be asked to improve their income level on their own. If our economy today were still under the kind of turmoil and sabotage that we saw during the decade-long Cultural Revolution, or if our economic growth was very slow, little could be done to address the low-income levels as a social problem, no matter how hard these people worked to raise their incomes or improve their and their children's future money-making ability. The effective solution to income distribution problems in the course of economic growth comes down to national economic development, GDP growth, consistent technological innovation, and ever-increasing labor productivity. This is precisely where the role of education comes into play in regulating the relationship between income distribution and economic efficiency amidst economic growth. As I have said in the previous chapter, improving labor quality is a major guarantee for economic growth, while any achievements in innovating technology and raising labor productivity can be regarded as the accumulated results of investment in education.

Incidentally, I use the term "high-income" in this study as a reference to a certain group of individuals or families in the context of China's income distribution situation. It is relevant only to what happens in China, where the income levels of both workers and government functionaries are on the low side. This renders any comparison of China with the absolute statistics on average international income meaningless. Instead, it makes a lot more sense to compare the consumer-goods structure (the percentage of food expenses in a family's income in particular) and the hourly wage's purchasing power (the exchange ratio between hourly wage and durable consumption goods in particular). For this reason, while riding economic growth to raise the income level of low-income families, we should also work to improve the income of all workers and government employees, so that every family can see changes in their consumption composition and the exchange ratio between hourly income and durables. Of course, this arduous task cannot be accomplished without a whole package of government steps. To develop education and increase funding for it is one such significant step. This is because only with a quality workforce and robustly growing labor productivity is it possible for everyone to make enough money and for production costs to drop enough to bring down the prices of consumer goods, change every family's consumption structure, and raise everyone's hourly income higher enough to afford more consumer goods. These changes are interconnected and mutually promoting. Universal changes in family consumption structure and universal increases in worker wages can yield more jobs and make it easier to solve employment problems.

4.4 Despite the Conflict of Rising Educational Funding with Fiscal Balance at the Present Stage of Economic Development, Investing in Education Helps Boost Fiscal Revenue Amidst Economic Growth

Developing education calls for more funding. Where shall the money come from? The mere mention of this question arouses concern about an added burden on state treasury. That is why people are saying the need to develop education and increase the funding for it is in conflict with the effort to maintain fiscal balance.

At the present stage of China's economic development, government funding is crucial to education development. But is government the only source of funding for education? Of course not. To solve employment problems and create more jobs, we cannot count on direct government investment alone and turn a blind eye to nongovernmental fund-raising efforts. By the same token, we cannot set our eyes only on state coffers and relinquish social fund-raising efforts if we are to develop education and put more people through school. In this study, however, let us forget about raising funds for education from nongovernmental channels and suppose that government funding is the only financial resource for education in this country.

In that case, there is no lack of theoretical support for the concern that increasing educational funding will result in fiscal deficits. Supposing the financial revenue is fixed or its growth rate is rather low while the growth rate of educational investment and spending on teachers' salaries are high, then financial deficits become unavoidable. Deficits increase money supply, which in turn causes prices to rise. Furthermore, if fiscal revenue is fixed while expenditure for national defense, administration and other purposes is curtailed to a maximum, increasing educational funding is likely to cut directly into investment in material production. This may reduce the economic returns from material production (or its profit growth rate), and inflate production costs (or bring down the cost reduction rate). In both scenarios, fiscal revenue and balance will be adversely affected, which may eventually trigger price increases.

However, we may see another possibility if we look a bit farther. Increasing educational investment is beneficial to both economic growth and the effort to maintain fiscal balance in the course of economic growth. Other things being equal, the source of increasing net revenues for an enterprise lies in its success in managing labor productivity to outgrow wage costs, expanding commodity production and reducing consumption of raw materials induced by improved labor productivity. As far as the entire national economy is concerned, increasing labor productivity to boost enterprise revenues is a reliable way to raise fiscal revenues and stabilize prices. In this light, the role of boosting educational investment speaks for itself. This is because, as I have said previously, increases in labor productivity can be regarded as an outcome of educational development.

This point of view can be further elaborated in three ways.

Firstly, insofar as its nature is concerned, education investment should be seen as a productive investment. Like investment in material production (such as building a factory or adding machinery and equipment), educational investment can also help increase the GDP. The difference between the two kinds of investment is that while investment in material production embodies itself in increasing the quantity and quality of material products, investment in education is reflected in workers' improved cultural and technical proficiency or in increasing the number of laborers who measure up to certain industrial or job requirements. The results of the former investment are plain for all to see, whereas the outcome of the latter can be easily overlooked, so much so that educational expenditure has for a long time been regarded as non-productive. If the role of education in promoting national economic development is still perceived in that old light, the inevitable conclusion is that adding educational funding can only upset fiscal balance. If, on the contrary, spending on education—an investment in human capital—is deemed conducive to heightening the cultural and technical proficiency of the workforce, thereby raising labor productivity and speeding up economic growth, then it is ultimately beneficial to fiscal balance.

Secondly, spending on education as a productive investment is characterized by a cycle that is longer than the construction cycle of the infrastructure, such as transportation and power supply. Of course, there is no lack of cases in which educational spending brings quick economic returns, such as certain short-term training programs for technical workers. Generally speaking, however, it takes time to groom workers to a certain proficiency level in culture and technology, and it takes a much longer time to bring forth professionals of a certain caliber. Such facts give rise to the misunderstanding that education is like "distant water that cannot slake immediate thirst." As a matter of fact, that misunderstanding can be averted if people take a strategic point of view and regard education as a productive investment capable of yielding lasting economic returns, and if they can see the continuous role education can play in economic growth. To put it another way, if you are frustrated to see money being spent on education year in, year out, then you must be patient enough to wait until the number of laborers of a high cultural and technical caliber starts growing with each passing year. Just as education spending has about the same long harvesting cycle as infrastructure investment, so it can bring the same significant benefits to the national economy.

Thirdly, as a productive investment, education benefits society with its salubrious effect on the national economy as a whole. That effect can be easily neglected if we lose sight of the whole picture of society and the national economy, or if our vision is limited to a certain region, industry, or firm. Of course, the direct effect of education investment can be felt in an individual region, industry, or firm, especially in the case of certain types of local school or a factory's training school for technicians. This, however, is less important. Social gains from educational investment are a lot greater. Such gains are reflected, for one thing, in the fact that, by changing jobs or locations, educated workers will spread to all economic sectors and regions, and for another, in the improved scientific and cultural attainments of the entire population and the emergence of a rich crop of new inventions and innovations. Every invention or innovation is the fruit of long-accumulated investment in education, and, therefore, belongs to the entire society. With these inventions and creations, society is able to raise labor productivity, promote economic growth, improve workers' living standards and work conditions, create more jobs, and increase per capita national income. All these are the benefits society can reap from education. In all, if we shift our point of departure from a single region, industry or firm to take in the panorama of society, our judgment of the actual economic returns of education will not be limited to what a region, industry or firm has spent on education, nor shall our evaluation of the beneficial effect of education investment be restrained by the size of a partial investment. Clearly, even though increasing education spending in the course of economic growth may temporarily expand fiscal expenditure or curtail the income of some localities, from a long-term point of view and by taking the overall situation into account, such spending is paramount to raising labor productivity, and effective in sustaining growth in national income and fiscal revenue.

Now that the benefits of developing education to the maintenance of fiscal balance in the long run are established, how should we look at the conflict between short-run increases in education spending and the need for fiscal balance? Let us return to the two hypotheses I have set at the beginning of this chapter.

Hypothesis One: Fiscal appropriation is, at present, the only source of funding for education. As a matter of fact, it is unnecessary to regard fiscal appropriation as the only source of funding for education, because nongovernmental fund-raising efforts hold great potential in this regard. How such potential should be tapped depends on the making and enforcement of government policy. We can save a huge amount of government spending on education as long as our policy allows nongovernment entities or individuals to run schools. Schools can be run effectively by involving nongovernment entities or collectives, and there is no lack of success in this field. I see nothing wrong with individuals running schools. Accomplished doctors, artists, accountants, translators and so on, are doing our nation and our youngsters a service by taking apprentices and teaching them knowledge or skills individually or by teamwork. These individuals are doing a lot of good to both the country and people when they run private vocational, technical or continuous education schools by tuition and cultivate talents for society without asking the government for a single penny. We would rather see young people in school than have them stay idle. As well as schools, abundant work-study programs are available for these people. To insist on running schools according to certain "rules" or "stereotypes" can do nothing but hold back development in education and put unwarranted burdens on the state treasury.

Hypothesis Two: Supposing fiscal revenue is fixed and defense and administrative expenditures have been pared down to a minimum, more spending on education can mean less investment in material production and result in fewer economic returns, to the jeopardy of fiscal revenue. Reality, however, has never been that simple. As we all know, investment in material production is just one condition for boosting aggregate production. There is at least another condition, and that is the economic returns from investment. If we can increase economic returns from investment in material production, speed up funds' turnover rate, and maximize the economic returns for every dollar spent, then we will see no reason why such investment cannot be downscaled. The former condition has been overestimated for a long time while the latter condition is overlooked, as if the more the investment is made, the higher the accumulation rate will become, with no consideration given to the economic returns of such investment. Astonishing waste is the inevitable result, and there is no lack of bitter lessons in this regard. Given a fixed fiscal revenue, why can't we do more to raise the turnover rate of funds and improve the efficiency of investment in material production? To speed up the training of technicians and managers is an effective way to enhance the economic returns of investment in material production. As long as we can find ways to raise the economic returns of such investment, it will not hurt the aggregate output, companies' economic returns, or government revenue to develop education with money saved from it under a fixed fiscal revenue.

4.5 Conclusion

In this study I have looked into the positive role education investment can play in tackling problems in employment, international payments, income distribution, and long-term fiscal balance in the course of China's economic growth. We have no alternative but to speed up educational development by spending more money on it, if we are to ensure stable and sustained economic growth, tackle the nation's "structural" employment issue and weaknesses in international trade, and coordinate the relationship between income distribution and economic efficiency. The economic history of other nations indicates that it is easy to achieve temporary economic growth, but difficult to gain stable and sustained economic growth on the basis of coordinated development in all fields of socio-economic development.

In the West, class antagonism and other fundamental conflicts inherent in capitalism are worsening; and unemployment, inflation, international payment deficits, and unequal income distribution are entangled with the need for economic growth in an insoluble mess. Even if these capitalist nations can increase investment in education, the best they can accomplish is to ease the situation temporarily—there is no way they can find real solutions to their problems. Despite that fact, since the 1960s Western economists have been emphasizing the role of education in economic growth and urging their governments to take human capital investment policy and human resource planning as important measures to ensure long-term economic growth.

Socialism is a superior system. Problems of one kind or another do occur in our economy, but these problems are not inherent in the socialist system. On the basis of eliminating private ownership of capital goods under capitalism and carrying out the distribution policy of "from each according to his ability, to each according to his work," it should be a great deal easier for our nation to coordinate diverse social and economic interests in the course of economic growth. Education definitely has a bigger role to play in this regard than under the capitalist system. How is it, then, that education has not played such a role in the past? This question merits careful thinking. In my opinion, apart from long years of interference from ultra-leftist ideology and the sabotage of the Lin Biao Clique and the "Gang of Four," it also has a lot to do with our short-sightedness, our failure to consider socialist economic development from the viewpoint of national development strategy, and our lack of understanding of the role of education in long-term economic growth. To those who cannot see the nature and role of education in perspective, education is a "soft" task that can be laid aside or delayed at will. Something is amiss, however, with that line of thinking. Therefore, I wrote this article with the same intention as when I wrote my thesis "Technical education and capitalist industrialization: A study of the rise of technological power in Western Europe and America" two years ago. That is, to send this message to our government policymakers: You have got to put a premium on education! When you mobilize society to raise money and open up schooling opportunities for our workforce, please make sure you will increase fiscal spending on education by a wide margin and thereby accelerate the development of education in our nation.

— *Journal of Peking University (Philosophy and Social Sciences)*, issue No. 6, 1980.

Chapter 5
1981: Import Substitution or Export Substitution: An Exploration of China's Current Import and Export Strategies

5.1 What is Import Substitution and Export Substitution?

A closed economy is mostly internally oriented, whereas the open economies of developing countries can be divided into two types: One is basically internally oriented, and the other is externally oriented. Therefore, there are two types of import and export strategies for developing countries: import substitution for the former and export substitution for the latter.

What is import substitution? It refers to a strategy in which developing countries, which mainly depended on imported manufactured goods, now replace them with domestic products. In this regard, these countries need to establish domestic processing industry for their markets, reducing their reliance on foreign supply of manufactured goods and preserving domestic markets for indigenous enterprises. However, in developing import substitution, some equipment and certain raw materials for manufacturing substitutions of imported goods still need to be imported due to a domestic shortage in supply. As a result, besides earning foreign exchange through non-tradable items, exporting primary products for a certain period is also necessary in order to pay for the imported goods and maintaining the balance of payments. Therefore, import substitution usually relies on the export of primary products as a prerequisite.

What is export substitution? It refers to a strategy in which developing countries, which mainly export primary products, are transformed to export manufactured goods. For this purpose, these countries need to establish domestic processing industry sectors that aim for foreign markets, and make the products (including semi-finished ones) internationally competitive. Besides, export substitution also aims to earn foreign exchange and further strengthen the balance of payments mainly by exporting competitive industrial products. Again, there is often no adequate domestic supply in equipment and raw materials in developing export substitution. Certain manufactured goods still need to be imported, so the total import expenditure increases substantially along with economic growth. Nevertheless, the balance

Y. Li, *China's Economy Since 1978*, China Academic Library,
https://doi.org/10.1007/978-981-95-5733-2_5

of payments position may remain unchanged or even be improved, just because the total revenue of export is also increasing.

The focus of the two strategies in an open economy is different. Import substitution focuses on the domestic market, while export substitution eyes for the international market. Import substitution is an "export-for-import" strategy, while export substitution is the opposite. In modern Western theories of development economics, many economists believe that export substitution is a more advanced and mature strategy than import substitution. To them, the latter will sooner or later be switched to the former, serving as a symbol of economic maturity of developing countries. How to account for this argument? It should be admitted that although it makes sense to some extent, it is still a view derived from one-sided analysis and based on specific conditions, and some economists in developing countries have already proved the latter's unavailability. From our perspective, the discussion on export and import strategies must be combined with the real-time conditions of a given country, and there is no one-size-fits-all economic model that applies across regions and historical periods.

5.2 Two Kinds of Developing Countries: Large and Small

The first issue here is the distinction between large and small developing countries. Let us leave aside the differences in social systems but consider the size and population. Large developing countries have vast land and large population, while small countries have small size and population. Large countries tend to be more affluent in natural resources than small countries and have a higher self-sufficiency rate. Sometimes the distribution of resources is highly uneven among small countries, some of which are scarce while others are adequate. Due to such differences in resource endowment, even if they are open, the degree of openness is different between large and small countries. In terms of long-term development prospects, large countries with relatively abundant resources are not as highly dependent on the international market for import and export as small countries with a lower self-sufficiency rate of resources.

In addition to resource conditions, the domestic market capacity of large and small developing countries should also be considered. Large countries have larger populations and domestic market capacities than small countries. There is a direct relationship between domestic market capacity and economies of scale in the industry. Industrial enterprises must reach a particular scale to reduce the production costs of industrial goods. Otherwise, they may lose competitiveness in the international market with higher costs, and their survival in doubt due to inefficiencies and losses.

From the perspective of economies of scale, we can recognize the difference in market location of industrial goods between large and small developing countries. Small countries have small population and domestic market capacities. If the industrial products are sold mainly in the domestic market, it is difficult for many industrial enterprises to reach a moderate scale, which is detrimental to the economy. On the contrary, large countries have sizeable domestic market capacities. If the industrial products are sold mainly to the domestic market, many industrial enterprises can reach a moderate scale and thus make profits. Therefore, the study of economies of scale shows that, if a small country wants to develop profitable industry sectors, it is necessary to explore the international market. This entails that a minor part of the products is sold in the domestic market with a smaller capacity, and a larger part of the products is sold abroad. It is a practice conducive to reducing costs and increasing profits. The greater capacity a country's domestic market has, the less necessary it is to adopt this approach.

5.3 About Structural Imbalance

A structural imbalance may occur in economic development, which is caused by issues of economic structure. In a capitalist economy, structural imbalance leads to a structural economic crisis. Structural imbalance and cyclical imbalance are not directly related. They may coexist or exist alternately. Structural imbalance is prevalent among non-capitalist economies, which is manifested in the following ways. The first is the incoordination between industrial sectors, which results in insufficient supplies of power, raw materials, or food. The second one is the incoordination between the production and transportation sectors. Backward conditions of transports and blocked circulation of goods may force specific sectors operate under capacity. Then the economy stagnates, productivity decreases, fiscal revenue declines, prices rise, and so on. Besides, the structural imbalance is usually chronic. Moreover, it could intensify under certain conditions, thus leading to an overall decline in production, a sharp increase in fiscal deficits, an increase in unemployment, and a relatively significant and sustained increase in prices.

Since economic structure issues cause structural imbalance, they cannot be eliminated within a short period of time once it is formed. Therefore, it should not be handled hastily. Otherwise, side effects may occur and the imbalance may worsen. Structural imbalance should be eliminated by gradual adjustments on the structure. Therefore, gradual adjustments and reform measures are necessary.

Research on structural imbalance in development economics is of great significance to formulating a country's import and export strategies. Western researchers gradually accept that the practice of "reducing overproduction and unemployment through export" is not mainly aimed at the structural imbalance. Instead, it is about the fact that when domestic demand is insufficient, the issue of excess products can be more or less solved by expanding sales in foreign markets.[1] With the expansion

[1] This is a simplified way of argumentation, as it does not consider international trade wars or other countries' measures to boycott imports or retaliate, nor does it consider the issue of global imbalance synchronization.

of export and increase in revenue, the demand for domestic products can be further expanded,[2] leading to a resurgent domestic market.

However, in dealing with structural imbalance, "reducing overproduction and unemployment through export" is not always effective and easy to be achieved. In general, expanding foreign markets does not always help to eliminate structural imbalance. It may alleviate some of its symptoms, but it is also likely to aggravate previous issues. This depends on the extent of the initial structural imbalance, the composition of the exports and their share in the GDP. If the supply of raw materials and fuels for manufacturing exports is already strained, or the transportation of exports under pressure, expanding the export may increase foreign exchange earnings or internal revenue,[3] but the supply and transport pressures may aggravate structural imbalance. The benefits gained from the increased exports may not be able to compensate for the losses caused by the further aggravation of structural imbalance to the national economy. Therefore, such export growth may not be worthwhile from the macroeconomic perspective. Moreover, the export growth is difficult to sustain because the increasingly intense structural imbalance will prevent export expansion, and even lead to its contraction.

It is clear that any general discussion on export strategies, or the superiority of export substitution compared over import substitution, fails to address the essence of the issue.

Of course, under structural imbalance, export expansion can be exchanged for specific imported equipment to ease the domestic imbalance, but it usually involves a formation of production capacity. Before this, it is important to note the tension in supply of certain raw materials and fuels that may be exacerbated by export expansion.

5.4 It is Necessary to Face up to the Disadvantages of Export Substitution Strategy

Experts who study economic development often mention the advantages and disadvantages of the import substitution strategy. The advantage of import substitution is that it makes developing economies more stable and less subject to the interference of international political and economic factors. At the same time, the disadvantages of import substitution are usually considered as follows. Firstly, it protects relatively backward domestic industry sectors and keeps the production technologies far behind foreign ones. Secondly, it may ignore the economic effects of foreign trade. Since the strategy here is "export for import," it is easy to take only the acquisition of foreign exchange as the goal rather than profitability. In addition, within a certain period of time, primary products have to be exported in exchange for imported equipment,

[2] The premise here is: Assuming that a certain share of export income is used to purchase domestic products, rather than using all export income to purchase imported goods or for savings.

[3] The conditions mentioned in the previous two notes are also applicable here.

obviously leading to a disadvantageous position in international trade. In this regard, it is not as favorable as the export substitution strategy.

Meanwhile, the superiority of export substitution strategy is also mentioned frequently by experts. For example, it enables developing countries to promote the production of competitive industrial goods, expand foreign markets, and even introduce these goods to developed countries, thus generating higher foreign exchange earnings. Moreover, the industries of these developing countries participate in international market competition to narrow the gap with the advanced international technological level. On the other hand, if the strategy is "import for export," the goal of export is not simply to obtain foreign exchange but also to make profits, and the economic effects of foreign trade tend to be considered. All of these are based on practical experiences from several countries. However, as previously noted, an export strategy that works for one region or country may not be effective for another, and the advantages of the export substitution strategy are not always achievable under all conditions. As for the disadvantages of the export substitution strategy, they are often ignored. However, for socialist developing countries like China, these disadvantages should be paid enough attention to.

The first disadvantage of export substitution strategy is that it makes a country's economy overly reliant on demand from other countries. Thus, if a depression or crisis occurs in its importing countries, the exporter's economy will experience a substantial shock, such as a sharp drop in exports, factory closures, and unemployment.

The second disadvantage of such a strategy is that it makes the economy overly subject to the price level in the international market. In this way, once the external prices experience sharp fluctuations, including those exported by the country and the raw materials and fuels imported for their manufacture, the exporter's economy is also likely to suffer from major shocks.

The third disadvantage of the strategy is that it makes a country overly subject to other countries' economic policies. If other countries or national alliances take aggressive economic measures like tariff barriers, import restrictions, export subsidies, currency devaluation, and embargoes on raw materials, the exporter's economy is likely to be significantly affected. The related economic policies may even be implemented as a countermeasure. Under this circumstance, the exporting country is often involved involuntarily in an intense international war of currency, trade, and investment.

These three disadvantages exist in the export substitution strategy itself, relating to the size of the country, and the nature and extent of imbalance in the economy. The smaller the country is, the more apparent these disadvantages may be. Compared to a cyclical imbalance, a country with structural imbalance will be more likely to be exposed to the disadvantages after adopting an export substitution strategy. At the same time, the more severe the structural imbalance is, the more significant the disadvantages of the strategy will be.

Since import substitution involves the export of primary products in exchange for the import of equipment during a specific period, the disadvantages of export substitution such as being more likely subject to external economic depression or crises, price fluctuation, and economic policy in other countries may also exist when the import substitution strategy is adopted. However, as mentioned earlier, a significant difference between import substitution and export substitution is that the former focuses on the domestic market, i.e., "export for import," and the latter concentrates on the international market, i.e., "import for exports." In this way, import substitution is less intervened by international political and economic factors. This is what we should not forget.

5.5 It is Inadvisable for China to Adopt Export Substitution Strategy at the Current Stage

The discussions above are about the general comparison between import substitution and export substitution from a theoretical perspective. Now let us turn to the issues related to the actual economic situation in China. Our general view is that the export substitution strategy advocated by Western theorists of development economics is not currently applicable to China.

How do we make such an argument? It is mainly based on the three reasons discussed earlier.

First, China is a large country with abundant resources and a large population of over 1 billion. The capacity of our domestic market becomes larger as per capita income grows. From the perspective of economies of scale, our industry sectors and enterprises can meet the demand of moderate scale under the condition that the domestic market is the central merchandising location. At the same time, some small developing countries that lack such a broad domestic market must sell products mainly to foreign countries. Moreover, from the perspective of self-sufficiency rate, China is rich in resources as a whole, unlike some small developing countries that lack resources and rely deeply on the international market. Therefore, China does not necessarily have to take export substitution strategy as a large country with a broad domestic market and relatively abundant resources.

Since it is unnecessary to adopt an export substitution strategy, which has some disadvantages previously mentioned, why do we still take an export substitution strategy?

Second, a structural imbalance remains to be a severe problem in our economy. The reason for the existence of the structural imbalance certainly includes historical factors (for example, the economic structure in our semi-colonial and semi-feudal economy was extremely irrational before the founding of the People's Republic of China, or PRC). However, we must conduct more in-depth analyses of how structural imbalance is formed in the long period after the PRC was established. If structural imbalance still exists in a socialist country thirty years after the revolution, it cannot be simply blamed on the unreasonable economic structure before the founding of the PRC. It should be admitted that we have not paid much attention to structural issues in economic development since the establishment of the PRC. On the contrary, the adventurous ideology of speedy success for a long period, the bias toward output value in the area of production, the neglect of infrastructure construction, and especially the failure to carry out the socialist goals of production, have all led to a continued existence of structural imbalance. Current and future adjustments should aim precisely to eliminate this structural imbalance.

As pointed out before, under the condition of structural imbalance, expanding foreign markets does not necessarily help to eliminate the structural imbalance in general and sometimes even aggravates it. The reasons are as follows. Assuming that there is a shortage of exported products, the domestic supply will become even tighter. Even if products exported are not in short supply, the supply of certain raw materials and fuels will become tighter for production. Even if the supply of these raw materials and fuels is not too tight to cause a further structural imbalance in the domestic economy, there is still a need to consider the pressure on transportation. Thus, in the case of structural imbalance, if export substitution strategy is adopted, the benefits gained from increased export do not necessarily compensate for the losses to the national economy caused by a further aggravation in structural imbalance. Therefore, the judgment from the overhead view is not suitable for China to adopt an export substitution strategy.

Third, the price and wage system that can be adapted to export substitution strategy in China has not been perfect at the current stage. Export substitution strategy is related to a country's domestic market capacity, economic structure, and price and wage system. Therefore, a developing country needs to develop a system adapted to export substitution strategy so that this strategy can be truly realized. In addition, there are many issues involved in the price and wage system, such as labor management, tax, exchange rate, and corporate leadership. Since the success of export substitution depends on some conditions, such as the competitiveness of industrial products for the international market and the adaptability of relevant enterprises to the changing situations in the international market, the benefits of export substitution cannot be realized without the adaptation of the price and wage system to an export substitution strategy.

As for China, we have not been able to adapt to the requirements of the export substitution strategy in terms of the price and wage system. If an export substitution strategy is to be adopted, a complete reform must be undertaken. However, it is never easy, and it must be considered in relation to a series of essential economic and social issues. Of course, it does not mean that our current price and wage system is reasonable and permanent. On the contrary, reform of the system is inevitable. Even if it is to be implemented in the future, the focus will be on the interest of the economy and society as a whole, not just for the strategy of export substitution.

5.6 Combined Strategy of Both Import and Export Substitution

If the disadvantages of import substitution cannot be ignored, and export substitution strategy is not applicable at the current stage, what kind of an import and export strategy should be taken? A closed economy of self-sufficiency is certainly not the direction of our economic development because it is harmful to our socialist economy and even challenging to be achieved. Both import and export trade need to grow alongside our economic growth. An open economy is an inevitable trend of our economic development, which is entirely consistent with our interests. Regarding foreign trade, the issue does not lie in a choice between a closed economy or an open economy, but what kind of an import and export strategy to adopt under an open economy.

China has a vast domestic market and a higher self-sufficiency rate of resources. However, a structural imbalance has been in place till now. In addition, we still lack a price and wage system that is compatible with the export substitution strategy. Therefore, the current focus of trade should be on the domestic market. However, without ignoring the disadvantages of import substitution and some advantages of export substitution, it is possible we can find an alternative strategy that combines both import and export strategy, which possesses their advantages and avoids their disadvantages? Based on the experience and lessons of our foreign trade in the past thirty years, and those of other countries in the world (including developing and developed countries), we can envisage a new strategy, i.e., a selective strategy of combined import and export substitution under the superior condition of our socialist system.

"Selective" here means that under the premise of the country's overall arrangement, differentiated approaches can be implemented based on the specific situation of the products. Export substitution can be applied to the selected products of specific regions or industry sectors, while import substitution for some other products of specific regions or industry sectors.

In order to avoid the aggravation of domestic structural imbalance, those industry sectors or enterprises that implement the export substitution strategy should sell their products on the international market under the condition that domestic supply of raw materials and fuels will not be affected. The superiority of China's human resources in the international economy should be fully utilized here to increase the competitiveness of these products on the international market and generate more foreign exchange income. At current stage, when the price and wage systems have no space for significant changes, localized and flexible measures can be taken to ensure the development of these sectors and enterprises. However, when they have not opened up the channel for export and temporarily lack competitiveness on the international market, measures like export subsidies are still essential.

In order to protect the domestic market for industrial goods and reserve it for domestic enterprises, import substitution should be carried out in combination with import restriction measures. In order to avoid protecting backward industry sectors and enterprises without allowing foreign firms to crowd out their domestic counterparts, import substitution should be implemented in conjunction with the encouragement of technological cooperation, exchange, and competition among similar domestic enterprises. In the domestic market, advanced domestic products should be allowed to win over the backward ones and the same for enterprises. Those running with high costs and significant losses without realistic prospect to improve should be converted or transformed in order to truly protect the domestic market and obtain the benefits of import substitution.

As long as China's structural imbalance has not been eliminated, an emphasis on the domestic market is still necessary even if both import and export substitution strategies are adopted. However, for certain regions, such as coastal provinces or sectors, the externally oriented economy might be more suitable. Such import and export strategy is good for China's national conditions.

—Speech at a Symposium on Import and Export Trade Development Strategy Held by the Institute of World Economics, Chinese Academy of Social Sciences on December 1981

Chapter 6
1982: Effective and Rational Investment Under Socialism

What is effective investment? To put it simply, it is the kind of investment that works promptly in putting together production capacity, boosts the supply of aggregate social product, and stimulates economic growth. What is rational investment? In short, it is the kind of investment that maintains basic price stability, creates many job opportunities, and raises labor force income while spurring economic growth. Whether investment is effective or not is determined by whether it has increased aggregate social product; and the effectiveness of investment is measured by the growth rate of aggregate social product. In contrast, whether investment is rational or not is determined by whether it has met the following goals: (1) boosting the economy; (2) maintaining basic price stability; (3) creating more jobs; and (4) raising labor force income. And the rationality of investment is measured by its actual results in meeting these goals. Effective investment may or may not be rational investment. Under socialism, it is not enough for investment to be merely effective. No effort should be spared to turn effective investment into rational investment, and with the largest possible degree of rationality at that.

6.1 Investment—Primary Dynamo Behind Economic Growth

Economic activity is a dynamic process in which one period of production, distribution, exchange and consumption circumscribes the next period. To allow production, distribution, exchange, and consumption to take place on a larger scale in the next period, a certain amount of national income from the previous period must be spent in investment. The amount of investment determines the degree of changes in economic scale. Therefore, for a given return on investment, economic growth rate is always predicated on a given rate of investment, i.e., the percentage of national income spent on investment.

Y. Li, *China's Economy Since 1978*, China Academic Library,
https://doi.org/10.1007/978-981-95-5733-2_6

Investment always manifests itself as the primary driving force behind economic growth. The term "primary driving force" refers to the initial impetus that can set a stagnant economy on the track of growth. Without this initial impetus, no economy can be delivered from stagnation.

The relationship between supply and demand or between production and consumption may be thrown off balance in economic activity. The same can happen between economic sectors and between economic regions. If this lack of coordination is allowed to deteriorate further, it can bring down the economic growth rate or, worse, lead to zero or negative growth. Investment is indispensable if this situation is to be remedied and sustained economic growth ensured. Here, investment is still the primary driving force in adjusting economic structures, coordinating supply and demand, and maintaining economic relations in equilibrium.

Stagnant development of productive technology, worn-out equipment and outdated technological processes, misuse of equipment and raw materials, or failure to eliminate weak production links in good time in the course of economic activity can erode workforce productivity or inflict financial losses. If these conditions are allowed to continue, they will not only hold back economic growth but also adversely affect government revenue for the obvious reason that financial losses in enterprises invariably diminish government revenue. To reverse shrinking workforce productivity and compensate for enterprise losses, it is necessary to increase investment while adopting necessary management countermeasures. This is precisely where investment can be used as the primary driving force to renovate production technology, raise workforce productivity, and boost corporate profits and government revenue.

The reason why investment becomes the primary driving force on these occasions is that the significance of investment does not lie in the demand for it, but in the chain reactions it causes in economic activity. The demand arising from investment is, after all, limited, but the chain reactions it causes in economic activity can play a much larger role in national economy.

More investment means higher income, and higher income can stimulate investment. If this virtuous cycle can be made to last, a cumulative process will result in which investment brings along more investment, and income brings about still more income. This is how economic growth happens, how technology is upgraded and labor productivity grows, and how growth in corporate profit and government revenue are realized. By the same token, without the initial investment, there will be no subsequent investment; and without the income yielded by the initial investment, a constant flow of income will be out of the question.

This being the case, it is clearly unwise to underestimate or overlook the tremendous role investment can play as the primary dynamo behind economic growth.

My above analysis is, of course, built upon a given condition of management. It is not uncommon that mismanagement results in low labor productivity, sluggish economic growth, and financial losses. For this reason, this situation can be changed to a certain extent simply by improving management, without increasing investment.

My analysis is also based upon the initiative and motivation of the workforce. It is not uncommon that the lack of initiative or motivation, or the failure to motivate the workers and give full scope to their initiative limits workforce productivity to such a low level as to reduce the economic growth rate and incur corporate losses. In that scenario, we can also change the situation not by investing more but by taking proper steps to motivate workers and put the initiative into their hands.

6.2 Effective and Ineffective Investment

The effectiveness of investment rests with its ability to fuel economic growth, but not all kinds of investment have such ability. Investment may also be ineffective. Ineffective investment refers to the kind of investment that yields zero or negative growth.

Investment effectiveness or ineffectiveness has dual implications: microeconomic and macroeconomic. In microeconomic terms, investment becomes effective if it can boost the investor's output (that is, increase the investor's net output value). Otherwise, it is ineffective. In macroeconomic terms, investment becomes effective if it causes the national economy to grow (that is, increases national income); failing this, it is ineffective. Because all investment must go through certain processes from the start of the action to the yield of increases in production and national income, the time factor must be considered, that is, the length of interval from the beginning of investment to the date when output begins to grow and national income begins to rise. That duration varies in length with the situation in different sectors. However, no matter how long it takes, the effectiveness or ineffectiveness of investment hinges on whether the economic growth it has brought about is positive, zero, or negative.

If the time factor is not considered, investment is ruled ineffective only if it cannot enhance production capacity or contribute to aggregate social product. Any investment can be ruled effective if it enhances production capacity or increases aggregate social product. Thus, the number of ineffective investments should be kept low, because most investment can yield production capacity and add to aggregate social product after a certain period of time, thereby contributing to economic growth one way or another.

However, it is far from enough to judge the effectiveness of investment or the lack of it this way. The time factor must be cared, that is, the length of time it takes from the onset of an investment action to the realization of output and national income increases. I have defined effective investment at the beginning of this article as something that is prompt in bringing about production capacity. In other words, no investment can be effective if it is overly time-consuming.

You may wonder why my definition of effective investment should contain the word *prompt*. In what light should we understand that word? How can we tell whether investment is effective or ineffective based on our understanding of that word? As we all know, investment refers to the occupation of a certain amount of available capital for a certain period of time, whereas the available capital occupied by investment is part of the newly created value in the national economy that may be put to other uses in material production. Used properly, it can raise aggregate social product and elevate economic growth. Therefore, investment entails a certain degree of "probable" or "potential" increase in aggregate social product and economic growth rate. If this amount of money used as investment is prompt in bringing about production capacity, this "probable" or "potential" increase can be converted into an actual increase in aggregate social product. If this amount of money is left idle, it will never yield actual increase in aggregate social product. If an amount of money that can be invested to yield production capacity promptly is left idle, it obviously means losses in aggregate social product and national economic growth rate.

Supposing this amount of money is used as investment but takes a longer time than usual to enhance production capacity, it does absolutely nothing to boost aggregate social product or economic growth during that extra inactive period of time. Because, in this regard, inactivity is synonymous with losses in both aggregate social product and economic growth. During that extra time this amount of money should be regarded as ineffective investment. Moreover, even after it has yielded production capacity and begun to contribute to aggregate social product, it must make up for the losses it has caused previously to the national economy. Only after that can it qualify as effective investment.

This is why, when assessing investment effectiveness, we should consider the time required to build production capacity.

How, then, should the word "prompt" in the wording "being prompt in yielding production capacity" be understood? Because of the differences in industries and investment projects, it is necessary to use the average time it takes for a specific industry or investment project to build production capacity as the benchmark. Investment that takes less than the average time to achieve the anticipated result can be regarded as being "prompt." The less time it takes to be effective, the "prompter" it becomes. Investment projects that take more than the average time to foster production capacity should be deemed "tardy in bringing about production capacity." The more time it takes in this process, the "tardier" it becomes.

With this benchmark, the effectiveness or ineffectiveness of investment can be defined as follows:

1. Investment that cannot yield production capacity or contribute to aggregate social product is ineffective investment;
2. Investment that takes less than the average time to yield production capacity is effective investment;
3. Investment that takes more than the average time to yield production capacity can be deemed effective only after it has reaped production capacity, contributed to aggregate social product, and made up for the losses it incurred during the extra time it took to yield such a production capacity. Before it has met these goals, it should be regarded as ineffective investment.

6.3 Rational and Irrational Investment

No study of investment is complete if it focuses only on whether it has furthered economic growth or not. As the primary driving force behind economic growth, the positive role of investment lies not just in boosting aggregate social product and economic growth rate, but also in coordinating economic relations and goals of development. In that sense, investment is actually a balancing force in an economy, and hence investment is deemed rational only if it acts as such a balancing force.

Investment, however, may play an opposite role, that is, to disrupt the balances of economic relations and goals of economic development. Instead of keeping the economy on an even keel, it can throw the economy off balance or aggravate economic disequilibrium. Such is one of the attributes of irrational investment.

If investment is irrational, it may still help increase aggregate social product in the short run when it is effective. But in the long run, what appears briefly as effective investment can disturb economic relations, cause or aggravate economic disequilibrium, and result in a stagnation or downturn in aggregate social product.

Thus, it is more important to see whether investment is rational or not than to judge if it is effective or ineffective. The concept of rational and irrational investment belongs in macroeconomic investment theory. When we talk about rationality or irrationality of investment, we do it in the context of macroeconomics.

Whether investment is rational or not depends on what role it plays in (1) economic growth, (2) price stability, (3) job creation, and (4) increase in labor income. Investment is considered irrational if it performs badly in one of these four fields, but it can be regarded as rational if it contributes to one field while the other three fields remain roughly constant. Investment becomes more rational if more such fields have improved while fewer of them remain constant.

Therefore, the definition of rational investment can be put more specifically:

As far as the role of investment in the aforementioned four fields is concerned, investment is rational if it has improved one of these fields while the others show no sign of decline.

If economic growth has picked up after investment is made, and the other three fields remain intact, that is, they have neither improved nor deteriorated, this is a typical case of effective investment also being rational, or to put it differently, effective investment and rational investment becoming the same thing. The minimum requirement for investment to be at once effective and rational is that it can at least promote economic growth while maintaining the status quo of the other three fields.

To combine effective investment with rational investment under that minimum requirement is just the starting point of arranging investment. We should try to improve all the four fields after investment is made. The more rational investment is, the more effective it becomes and the longer it can stay effective. The reason for this is clear: Without increasing aggregate social product, basic prices stability cannot be maintained, new job positions cannot be created in the national economy, and labor income will decline, and as a result, the national economy as a whole will deteriorate, and sustained economic growth becomes out of the question.

As much as the time factor should be considered when investment effectiveness or ineffectiveness is studied, the same should be done when investment rationality or irrationality is observed. This is because only by generating production capacity can investment play its role in coordinating economic relations, but it takes a period of time for that to happen. The length of this period is determined by the characteristics of the economic sector and the investment project in question.

What merits attention in this regard is that investment impacts price stability, the creation of jobs, and labor income in different ways. Before production capacity is generated, because there is only financial input and no output in aggregate social product, *the amount of currency in circulation grows,* which will have a negative impact on price stability. If, after production capacity is yielded, the growth rate of aggregate social product resulting from the investment is still lower than the growth rate of the amount of currency in circulation, it may still have a negative impact on price stability, a possibility that should not be overlooked. The situation, however, is different with the creation of new jobs. Investment may begin creating jobs immediately after it is made, because the investment action itself can absorb some workers. However, after investment has brought about production capacity, it may either increase employment (including the jobs created by this investment itself and the jobs created by other industries or firms under its impact), or reduce employment (including fewer job opportunities in other industries or firms under the impact of this investment and fewer job opportunities directly caused by the termination of the investment project). With regard to real labor income, apart from the investment-induced changes in price level and employment that are likely to affect labor income, the investment-induced changes in labor productivity are a more important factor that inevitably affects changes in labor income. Before production capacity is realized, few significant changes will happen to labor productivity. Therefore, during the interval from the start of investment to the materialization of production capacity, changes in labor income are mainly related to changes in price level and employment, whereas after production capacity is created, changes in labor productivity will have an increasing impact on labor income.

Thus, to judge if investment is rational or not, not only its impact on price stability, job creation, and real labor income after it has brought about production capacity, but also its impact on these fields during the interval from the outset of the investment to the yield of production capacity should be observed. If the former impact is considered but the latter neglected, it is likely that the investment in question may have already had a negative impact, and a seriously negative impact at that, on the balance of national economy before it reaps production capacity. In that scenario, even if investment has generated new production capacity, its earlier negative impact on national economy may be so grave as to hold back the effectiveness of production capacity or offset its positive impact on balancing the national economy.

6.4 Discrepancy Between Effective and Rational Investment

As I have pointed out in the foregoing, the criteria for judging effective investment are different from those for rational investment. The roles of effective investment and rational investment in the economy are different as well. Effective investment is not necessarily rational investment. Even if effective investment is also rational, it is not necessarily the most rational investment. On the other hand, although rational investment must also be effective, it may not be the most effective investment. The discrepancy between effective investment and rational investment is apparent.

For instance, a specific investment project or investment in one certain field may be effective because it can raise aggregate social product, but it may have a negative impact on price stability by taking up so much funding for so long as to affect the amount of currency in circulation before it creates production capacity. After creating production capacity, the investment in question may also diminish the job positions it has created and cause other industries and firms to reduce their job positions. Even if it has created production capacity, the investment can still cause real labor income to dip due to price changes, job market fluctuations, and declining labor productivity. Given these possibilities, and by taking its multiple goals and the balance of national economy into consideration, effective investment is likely to be irrational or have just a small degree of rationality at best.

Observed from the perspective of multiple goals and the balance of national economy, a certain investment is rational because it has improved at least one of the four fields—economic growth, basic price stability, job creation, and labor income—while the other fields have shown no sign of deterioration. However, because rational investment has to attain multiple goals, its capacity to boost aggregate social product may be lower than maximal (for instance, if the investment is not put into a highly sophisticated automated factory), although it can still boost aggregate social product to a certain extent. In this case, it cannot be counted as the most effective investment.

How, then, should we deal with the discrepancy between effective and rational investment? We may study the question from a normative or a positive approach.

A normative approach calls for realigning the goals of investment in the order of importance, urgency, and priority of the multiple goals that the investment aims to attain. Then overall consideration should be given to the problems to be solved through this investment and the means of solving these problems, so as to find out to what extent effectiveness and rationality of this investment can be coordinated. According to the aforementioned definition, investment is rational if it has improved at least one of the four fields while the others show no sign of deterioration. The question now is which one of these four fields should be improved first. The answer must be based on a study of the actual situation to see which one of the four goals is most attainable. However, the answer also involves judgment of values, that is, which goal is more important and which goal is less important. To observe investment through normative analysis is to prioritize the four goals from judgment of values in order to make rational investment.

The positive approach follows established norms and rules, or assumes that all goals are equally important, to find ways to coordinate effective and rational investment. The solution to the discrepancy between effective and rational investment is related not only to the preconditions of a given investment but also to the methods of raising and operating the fund needed for this investment. The next chapter explores, from the viewpoint of positive study, the preconditions of investment and how to raise and operate the fund of investment.

6.5 Resource and Marketability for Effective and Rational Investment

The shared attributes of effective and rational investment are that, firstly, both can only take place where there are sufficient and usable economic resources, and secondly, there must be markets for the products of the production capacity they have created. In other words, economic resources and marketability are prerequisites for investment to be at once effective and rational.

Economic resources fall into two categories: material and human. Material resources, that is, means of production, include production equipment, raw materials, fuels and power, means of transportation, and storage facilities. Human resources encompass unskilled and skilled labor force, the latter including technical and management professionals. These resource conditions are indispensable for every investment project.

Now that effectiveness of investment hinges on its speed in putting together production capacity and boosting aggregate social product, it is difficult, or even impossible, to turn investment promptly into production capacity in the absence of means of production and human resources. Even if an investment project has been completed, it still cannot increase aggregate social product if it has no sufficient supply of means of production—such as raw materials, fuels, power, and spare parts for maintenance and repair purposes—and adequate labor force, or if transportation, storage and other factors fail to meet production needs. In this regard, investment—the primary driving force behind economic growth—is based upon the adequacy of useful economic resources. Investment can put together production capacity rapidly where idle productive resources and a variety of idle workers are available. It can also quickly bring about production capacity where productive resources and labor force are unavailable but can be obtained through minor readjustments, or where economic resources are in short supply but there is an adequate foreign exchange reserve to be used to buy those deficient resources from foreign markets. However, in the latter scenario, things tend to be complicated because it involves the balance of foreign trade and of international payments. In the absence of all the above-mentioned conditions, investment becomes ineffective because it cannot promptly create production capacity.

Given that the rationality of investment is determined by whether it can meet the four goals of economic growth, basic price stability, job creation, and real labor income, effectiveness—that is, promptness in creating production capacity—becomes the minimum requirement for rational investment. Because adequate supply of economic resources is a prerequisite for the speedy creation of production capacity, such supply must also be guaranteed for rational investment. Otherwise, it cannot meet all four goals at the same time.

The next consideration is the market conditions for investment, that is, the product salability of an investment project. Whether such a product is made for production or consumption purposes, there must be people willing to buy it at a certain price. If production is carried out only for the purpose of meeting certain output quotas and the product cannot be sold out and has to be piled up in warehouses, the investment will not be able to contribute to economic growth. This conclusion is understandable, because investment can be rational only if it contributes to aggregate social product, maintains basic price stability, creates new jobs, and increases real labor income. Those roles can never be realized if nobody wants to buy the product of an investment project. Furthermore, investment may have a negative impact on prices and labor income if its product cannot be sold out. Such investment is irrational.

Is product marketability also a prerequisite for effective investment? Because whether investment is effective or not is determined by whether it can bring about production capacity promptly and boost aggregate social product, people may argue that the effectiveness of investment is irrelevant to product marketability. They believe that investment is effective as long as it can produce a certain number of products, regardless of product salability. In their eyes, investment becomes ineffective only if it cannot create production capacity or cannot do it fast enough—investment should not be deemed ineffective if it can bring about production capacity speedily even though its products are unwanted on the market. This idea, undoubtedly, is not correct.

This idea is wrong in that it only accepts the literal meaning of production capacity, and severs production capacity from product marketability. It is, therefore, a misunderstanding of production capacity. We know that the production capacity of a factory built with an amount of investment is only nominal if it does not produce and supply products. If the factory's products cannot meet market demand and only belong in warehouses, this factory is a non-factor at best because of its failure to supply society with usable products. We would rather this kind of factory did not do anything, for the fuel, power, raw materials and so on it consumes could have been used for meaningful purposes. Therefore, production capacity created by investment should be real, rather than nominal. It should supply society with marketable products instead of things that cannot be sold out. If the effectiveness of investment and the creation of production capacity are understood in that light, product marketability must be regarded as a precondition for effective investment.

The argument that the effectiveness of investment is unrelated to the marketability of its product exactly mistakes nominal production capacity for real production capacity. The effectiveness of investment depends on the real production capacity it creates, not just the nominal capacity.

6.6 Profitability of Effective and Rational Investment

Investment profitability is an important theoretical issue. Even if the product of an investment project can be sold out, what will be the consequences if it can only be sold out at a lower price than its production and interest costs?

First of all, this kind of investment cannot be recouped in that case. Moreover, even after the investment project is completed, further expenses are needed to keep production going; otherwise even the original scale of production cannot be maintained. This kind of investment, even if it can bring about production capacity and its products are marketable, poses more losses than gains, and should never be allowed to happen.

Nevertheless, if we extend our vision from an individual investor to the entire national economy, different opinions may occur on investment profitability.

The national economy is an integrated entity, in which all sectors are organically connected. Some sectors or firms may have the needed economic resources and their products can meet market demand. But, for one reason or another, their products are priced equal to or lower than their production costs and interest expenses, and therefore, they cannot generate a profit. Should investment be made in such a sector or firm? Is profitability an overriding condition for investment? It seems that neither question can be answered with a simple yes or no, because both involve how the macroeconomic effectiveness of investment should be measured.

As illustrated in the previous chapter, effective investment has both macroeconomic and microeconomic implications, while rational investment belongs in the macroeconomic realm. Observed from a macroeconomic point of view, some kinds of investment in certain sectors or firms are unlikely to make a profit, but can contribute to faster growth in other sectors or firms and to the balance of national economy and coordination among investment goals. This kind of investment is still necessary, and can be regarded as both effective and rational.

Defenders of investment that is at once ineffective and irrational in practice may also cite the macroeconomic effectiveness of investment to back up their argument that this kind of investment should not be canceled. They may accuse those who want to do so of lacking macroeconomic far-sightedness. They can always find a "reason" to justify any investment project they like, arguing that it is so important to the national economy that it cannot be ditched even if it is not making money. Indeed, this issue can easily become controversial, and can never be settled if we accept the existence and significance of the macroeconomic results of an investment project without setting benchmarks for its effectiveness and rationality in macroeconomic terms.

This is where econometrics comes in handy. Despite its limitations, the methods of econometrics are still useful for analyzing investment effectiveness and rationality in macroeconomic terms on certain occasions and under certain premises and presumptions.

The resource and market conditions for investment should be considered in the first place. Investment, no matter what kind it is, must be guaranteed with an ample supply of means of production and human resources, both of which are prerequisites for production capacity. The products invested in should also meet market demand, otherwise they can only become part of warehouse stockpiles and their production capacity is nominal at best. Various econometric methods can be employed when we analyze the resource and market conditions for an investment scheme. Generally speaking, we can employ the input–output analysis to determine the situation regarding resource supply and market demand.

The conditions for investment profitability come next. Investment profitability in microeconomic terms can be computed with cost–benefit analysis. Relationships in this regard are relatively simple. By factoring in the given output and price conditions, as well as production costs and interest expenses, we can clarify whether an invested project is making or losing money. Then the deadline for recouping the investment —normally a major benchmark for judging the microeconomic effectiveness of an invested project—can be set with reference to the production cycle.

The situation is a lot more complex when it comes to judging if an investment project is making a profit or not from a macroeconomic perspective. Investment rationality in the field of material production and investment effectiveness in macroeconomic terms cannot be studied without comparing various relations in the national economy and dissecting the input–output relationship between sectors in the national economy. If the product of Sector A is not only supplied directly to consumers but also needed by Sectors B, C, and D for their production, while the products of Sectors B, C, and D are also both supplied directly to consumers and needed by Sectors E, F, G, and H for production purposes, and if that cycle goes on and on, then the results of follow-up investment in Sector A will be reflected not just in that sector's augmented income but also in the augmented incomes of Sectors B, C, D, E, F, G, and H. Suppose there is a certain ratio between income and employment, then the results of follow-up investment in Sector A will be reflected not just in its increased number of jobs but also in the changes that have taken place in the number of jobs in the other sectors. Using counterfactual analysis, we can compare the results of the following two approaches: First, to study total income, net income, employment, and other variables before Sector A was invested in; second, to study the changes in the variables such as total income, net income, and employment in the other sectors after Sector A was invested in. From this comparison we can get to know the degree of profitability of investment in macroeconomic terms. Suppose that a certain investment project does not make money for itself, but contributes to the growth in total income, net income and employment in other economic sectors, and the benefits to the national economy from the growth in these sectors outweigh the losses caused to the national economy by the investment project's failure in making a profit, then the investment can still be considered as a gain to the national economy. As a matter of fact, there is an investment-recouping period for the project, but such a period is reflected in the national economy. If, on the contrary, a comparison of the two approaches indicates that the investment does make a profit for itself but has inflicted losses in total income, net income, and employment on other sectors, or that the investment is losing money while these sectors' increases in gross income, net income, and employment are negligible so that the benefits the investment has yielded for the national economy are barely enough to offset the losses it has inflicted on the national economy, such an investment is deemed detrimental to the national economy. If allowed to continue under the excuse of cherishing its macroeconomic results, the said investment becomes irrational, and—in macroeconomic terms—ineffective as well.

6.7 Relationship Between Investment Fund Supply, Public Finance, and Investment

To make investment both effective and rational, due attention must be paid to the supply of funding. Suppose an investment project has favorable resource and market conditions and its product can be sold briskly enough to guarantee an after-sale profit, but it cannot continue or has to stop midway because of fund shortage, then it cannot put together production capacity in good time, and cannot become effective investment. Furthermore, this kind of investment is irrational because it is a loss to the national economy when the money spent fails to yield production capacity.

If, on the contrary, an investment scheme can yield production capacity promptly but spends too much to achieve the purpose, it may also disrupt public finance or money circulation, thereby exerting an adverse impact on price stability. Thus, it can never become rational investment.

What can be done to avoid improper supply of funding and ensure effectiveness and rationality of investment? Let us begin answering this question by studying the relationship between investment and public finance.

Under socialism, fiscal appropriations are an important source of reinvestment. They generally have a direct impact on the volume and scale of investment and its effectiveness. More importantly, the impact of such appropriations also extends to the relationship between the multiple goals of investment and to investment rationality.

When we try to coordinate the relationship between economic growth and basic price stability, we face the urgent task of preventing the demand for monetary funds from running out of control, or, to put it another way, we must prevent the amount of currency in circulation from growing too fast. Inflation is eventually attributed to the failure of the growth in aggregate social product to outpace the growth in the amount of currency in circulation. Inflation can be prevented or erased only by boosting the growth rate of aggregate social product, reducing the growth rate of the amount of currency in circulation, or both.

Fast growth in the amount of currency in circulation is mainly an outcome of fiscal deficit or bank credit expansion. Therefore, when there is a serious fiscal deficit, especially when such a deficit has lingered for several years, fiscal appropriation designed to increase investment funding must be used cautiously. Otherwise, the amount of currency in circulation may be further increased.

However, insofar as investment is the primary driving force behind economic growth, the lack of sufficient investment can neither boost aggregate social product nor change the situation where aggregate social product grows slower than the amount of currency in circulation. Tightening up investment alone can neither eliminate fiscal deficit nor effectively keep inflation away from the door. This is because economic sectors are interlinked and only by constantly restructuring these sectors and their products can the proportional relationships in the national economy be coordinated. However, restructuring sectors and products calls for follow-up investment on most occasions. If investment is tightened up merely to eliminate deficits and forestall inflation, the national economy will fall further out of proportion and coordination. Worse, it can also land some industries or firms that may expand production and make a profit in financial loss, thereby doing a disservice to the effort to turn the fiscal situation around and eradicate inflation.

From the perspective of increasing aggregate social product, technical renovation and equipment upgrading are material conditions for labor productivity increases, but both call for follow-up investment. If investment is tightened up merely to wipe out deficits and forestall inflation, it is very difficult to boost labor productivity and aggregate social product by improving their material conditions. Furthermore, if other conditions remain unchanged but equipment cannot be upgraded for lack of necessary investment, workforce productivity will decline. As a result, the industries and firms that could have been producing and making a profit will lose money, and public finance and the effort to control inflation will be jeopardized as well.

To ascribe the rise of financial deficits or inflation merely to investment growth is to oversimplify a complex matter. Effective and rational investment is actually an important means by which to eliminate deficits and inflation, rather than to aggravate them. It is ineffective or irrational investment—investment that drags on and fails to yield production capacity, investment in unmarketable products, investment that is made in marketable products but incurs heavy losses or distorts economic relations—that should be held responsible for deficits and inflation.

This being the case, what merits the attention of the fiscal department is that they should curtail or cancel all the investment projects that lack resource and market conditions or fail to yield macroeconomic returns. However, investment projects that yield production capacities promptly, produce marketable products, make profit, and are conducive to the growth of total and net income of various sectors in the national economy, should not be curtailed or axed. Effective and rational investment is a dynamo behind a robust and booming national economy, and a robust and booming national economy is the solid foundation of public finance and a guarantee for stable fiscal revenue. The financial department can avoid inappropriate supply of investment funding as long as it takes a scientific attitude toward investment, that is, to invest in what should be invested in and not to invest in what should not be invested in.

6.8 Choice of Investment Funding Raising Channels

Fiscal funding is a major financial source for investment, but certainly not the only source for it. Under socialism the money needed for investment purposes comes from at least four avenues: fiscal appropriations, nongovernmental fund-raisers, business reserve funds, and bank credits.

Short-, medium- and long-term bank credits can be used as a source of money for all purposes of investment. Their strength lies in that they can urge investors to tighten up financial auditing and pay due attention to the microeconomic results of their investment projects. The bank, by screening investment plans and monitoring the spending, plays a definite role in enhancing the macroeconomic results of investment.

Apart from money raised by way of savings and bond purchases, the funds from nongovernmental sources also include the money procured from people of all walks of life to run cooperative firms and boost domestic development.

Business reserve funds refer to the portion of profit that firms are allowed to retain on the principle of autonomy to buy equipment, upgrade technology, expand production, reduce costs, and increase output.

Of the four major sources of funding, fiscal funding is not always the principal one. People can make their choices according to investment needs and financial situation. No matter what source is chosen, however, the aforementioned investment conditions should always be kept in mind. On no account should ineffective and irrational investment be made. Whenever an investment project gets off the ground, no effort should be spared to maximize its effectiveness and rationality.

A point that can be easily forgotten is that nongovernmental fund-raisers are not only a substitute for government investment but also a method to withdraw money from circulation. The role of such fund-raisers in substituting for government investment comes through when investment projects originally to be funded with fiscal appropriation revert to social fund-raising. However, investment is not just a supply of money. Guaranteed material supply is indispensable, too. The money raised from nongovernmental channels needs to be spent on means of production. However, means of production needed for investment purposes are basically provided by the government department in charge of supplying them. If the government department does not possess sufficient means of production needed for an investment project, it means that the resource conditions for the project are not ripe. Just as I have said in my analysis of investment conditions, investment without adequate supply of means of production is ineffective and irrational and, therefore, should be abrogated. By the same token, if a nongovernment-funded investment project fails to get off the ground, it will not adversely affect the national economy. If the government department has sufficient means of production for an investment project, it means that the material conditions are ripe and that the project in question can be undertaken. In this case, the government department contributes to the national economy by supplying the needed means of production and withdrawing money from circulation. Otherwise, if nongovernmental funding is replaced with fiscal funding, it cannot withdraw money from circulation even though it could also be used for investment purposes.

From another point of view, in the absence of fund-raisers, what is the best use for money held in nongovernmental hands? This kind of money may end up in banks as saving deposits, or be spent on consumer goods. If it ends up as saving deposits, banks will have to think about how to put the money to good use. When there is investment demand, supply of money by bank credit plays the same role as nongovernmental money-raisers. However, if the money does not become saving deposits but is spent on consumer goods, especially on those in short supply, market supply will be strained. For this reason, if investment conditions are suitable and money can be raised from nongovernmental sources, such investment projects are more rational than others.

—*Finance & Trade Economics*, issue Nos. 1 & 3, 1982

Chapter 7
1983: Factor Analysis in Educational Economics

This paper attempts to discuss the appropriate size of schools, the technical composition of education, and the reasonable distribution of schools from the theoretic perspective of educational economics, in combination with the specific situation of China.[1]

7.1 Factor Input and School Size

7.1.1 I

To improve the economic performance of intellectual investment, policymakers should prioritize research on the input of educational institutions.

This input usually consists of two parts. The first part is the input that does not vary with the output, and the second part is the input that varies with the output.

The first part, called "input I," includes educational expenditures that directly or indirectly affect output, or provide a premise and guarantee for it. For example, an educational institution needs certain dormitories, teaching equipment, books, and other materials. The depreciation value and maintenance costs of these materials, as well as the payment to those who fix and manage them, belong to "input I" that has an indirect effect on output. In China, the basic salary of all formal faculty members is also classified as "input I," which has a direct effect on the output. The characteristic of "input I" is that no matter how much the educational institution produces (the increment of students' knowledge and skills) in a certain period, a certain amount

[1] The author's discussions in "Technical education and capitalist industrialization" (in "Social Science Front" 1978 No. 4), "On the role of education in economic growth" (in "Chinese Social Science" 1981 No. 2), and "On the macroeconomic effects of intellectual investment" (in "Chinese Social Science" 1981 No. 4) are the starting point for the discussion in this article.

Y. Li, *China's Economy Since 1978*, China Academic Library,
https://doi.org/10.1007/978-981-95-5733-2_7

of "input I" is indispensable, and its amount remains constant. It requires the same level of "input I" no matter how much the output is (even zero, i.e., there are no teaching activities and the increment of students' knowledge and skills is zero). Therefore, "input I" in the field of intellectual investment is similar to the concept of *fixed cost* in production economics, which does not correlate with output in the short and medium terms. However, the "input I" in the field of intellectual investment should not be simply regarded as a "fixed cost" in production economics, where only managers' wages are included in fixed costs, not workers' wages. In production economics, labor's wages, like those of raw materials and fuel, vary with output and are classified as variable costs. In the field of intellectual investment, the basic salary of all formally employed teachers is classified as "input I," because it should be paid even in the case of no output. Thus, despite of teachers' direct impact on the output, their position is similar to that of the producer in the field of production.

The second part, called "input II," varies with the amount of output. In China, the bonus or overwork compensation for administrators and formal teachers, as well as the salary of substitute teachers or part-time teachers who are not in the formal system, belong to "input II." The expenditure on teaching and management for the increment of students' knowledge and skills, such as the cost of experiments in direct teaching, student internships, and teaching materials, also belong to "input II." If there is no output in the educational institution, this "input" is unnecessary. As output increases, the amount of such input increases accordingly. Therefore, "input II" of intellectual investment is similar to the concept of variable cost in production economics but has a narrower scope, as the basic salary of full-time teachers is included in "input I," not "input II" (students' financial aid is excluded for simplification).

7.1.2 II

Although the concepts of "input I" and "input II" in the intellectual investment field are not the same as the concepts of fixed and variable costs in the economics of production, the research on the principle of fixed and variable costs' movement is still applicable for the intellectual investment field.

According to the concept of "input I," whatever the output of an educational institution is, "input I" is a constant if the output is within a certain range. Therefore, "input I" appears as a line parallel to the horizontal axis on a Cartesian plane with input as the vertical axis and output as the horizontal axis.

According to the concept of "input II," when the output of an educational institution is zero, "input II" is also zero. As output increases, "input II" increases accordingly. Therefore, on a Cartesian plane mentioned above, "input II" appears as a curve ascending from the origin to the upper right.

Since the total input is equal to the sum of "input I" and "input II," the curve of total input will be a curve ascending to the upper right from the intersection point of "input I" and the vertical axis in the above plane.

In the field of intellectual investment, the average input is the ratio of the total input to output.

The principle of the variation on average input is as follows: When the output is zero, the average input cannot be zero, but a positive value, because there is always "input I." When output increases gradually from zero, the average input will diminish accordingly. When the output reaches a certain amount, the average input will increase accordingly as the output continues to increase.

Thus, on a Cartesian plane, the average input appears as U-shaped curve, which falls first and then rises.

Since the total input is composed of "input I" and "input II," the average input can also be divided into "average input I" and "average input II." "Average input I " is the ratio of "input I" to output, and "average input II" is the ratio of "input II " to output.

"Average input I" decreases with the increase of output because "input I" is a fixed quantity that does not vary with output. When output increases, the average amount of "input I" per unit of output will diminish. The larger the output, the smaller the average "input I." On the chart above, the curve of "average input I" will take on a lower right sloping shape.

The graph of the "average input II" curve is also U-shaped like the average input curve because the "average input II" diminishes first as output increases. When the output increases to a certain level, the "average input II" will increase.

In the field of intellectual investment, the amount of new input refers to the amount of inputs required for each additional unit of output. In simple terms, the marginal input is the quotient of the increment of total input divided by the increment of output, i.e.:

the marginal input = the increment of total input / the increment of output

= (the increment of "input I" + the increment of "input II") / the increment of output.

Since "input I" is fixed, the increment of "input I" is zero within a certain amount. Thus, the new input is equal to "input II."

the marginal input = the marginal "input II"

= the increment of "input II" / the increment of output.

In this way, on a Cartesian plane with input as the vertical axis and output as the horizontal axis, the marginal input curve is U-shaped, i.e., it decreases first and then increases with the increase of output.

For an educational institution, if the amount of new input is less than the average input, then the average input will decrease with the increase of output, because the new input will drag down the average input. If the new input is larger than the average input, then the average input will increase as output increases, because the new input pulls the average input up. If the new input is equal to the average input, then the new input will neither drag the average down nor pull the average up, so the point at which the new input is equal to the average input is the lowest point of the U-shaped average input curve.

Similarly, if "marginal input II" is less than "average input II," then "average input II" decreases with the increase of output. If "new input II" is larger than "average input II," then "average input II" must increase with the increase of the output. If the "marginal input II" is equal to "average input II," then "marginal input II" should neither reduce, nor increase "average input II," so "marginal input II" is equal to the lowest point in U-shaped "average input II" curve.

Understanding the relationship between total input, average input, and marginal input in the field of intellectual investment is helpful for the research on improving the economic performance of the educational investment.

In the field of intellectual investment, "input I" constitutes a large proportion of total investment, while "input II" accounts for a much smaller share. It is different from the situation in the field of material production, where payment for labor is included in variable costs rather than fixed costs. In addition, the variable costs of raw materials and fuel, which varies with output, also accounts for a large part. The "input II" of intellectual investment is different. Thus, while the issues related to input in educational institutions are similar to those in production economics, they also have their own unique characteristics. The foundation for determining the amount of input into an educational institution can be summarized as follows.

To determine the input of an educational institution, it is necessary to know the regularity of the change of the average input and new input. It is most favorable when the new input is equal to the average input, because at this point, the average input is the lowest. Stopping the input before reaching the lowest point cannot benefit the diminishing average input, as the average input can be further reduced by increasing the input. Stopping the input after passing the lowest point of the average input curve will suffer a loss of increasing average input, as the latter increases with each additional unit of input.

As mentioned earlier, the amount of marginal input equals to the amount of "marginal input II." Therefore, the input is also relatively favorable when the marginal input (i.e., "marginal input II") is equal to "average input II." At this point, the "average input II" is the lowest. Stopping the input before this point will not benefit from diminishing "average input II," because the "average input II" will continue to decrease if the input continues to increase. Stopping the input after passing the lowest point of the "average input II" curve will suffer a loss because the "average input II" will increase.

The problem is that the input and output levels at the lowest point of the average input curve do not match those at the lowest point of the "average input II" curve. The amount of the average input consists of "average input I" and "average input II," and according to the characteristics of the intellectual investment, the "average input I" accounts for a large proportion, and the proportion of "average input II" is very small. Therefore, when the new input curve intersects the curve of "average input II," the average input curve is far from reaching the lowest point. If the input is stopped at the lowest point of the "average input II" curve, the full benefit of the minimum average input will not be obtained.

For an educational institution, input should not be stopped at the lowest point of the "average input II" curve but should continue to increase until reaching the lowest point of the average input curve. After passing the lowest point of the "average input II" curve and before reaching the lowest point of the average input curve, each additional unit of input will increase the "average input II" as output increases, but the average input will continue to decrease, which is obviously positive for the educational institution.

7.1.3 III

If we take the total input of an educational institution as an indicator of its scale, i.e., the total input of an educational institution suggests its scale, increasing the total input of an educational institution means expanding its scale.

As mentioned above, the total input can be divided into two parts: "input I" and "input II." With the increase of the total input, the amount of "input I" is fixed, and "input II" increase with the increase of the total output. Therefore, increasing the amount of "input II" will cause an increase in the total output, which means the expansion of the scale of the educational institution. But as output increases, the ratio of the total input to output (i.e., the average input) diminishes first, showing that the increase of the educational sector's scale is advantageous at first, as it can lead to the diminishing average input.

However, when the output increases to a certain amount, if the total input continues to increase to make the institutional scale increase continuously, the condition will become unfavorable. This will make the positive condition of decreasing average input gradually disappear, and make the adverse conditions, such as decreasing efficiency caused by increasing the size of educational institutions, gradually come into effect. The result is that when the size of educational institutions increases to a certain extent, the average input will have to increase.

Thus, it can be seen that the concept of an appropriate size of enterprises in production economics is also applicable in the field of intellectual investment, suggesting that the optimal size of an educational institution should be neither too small nor too large, but moderate. If it is less than the optimal size, the average input cannot reach the lowest point that is available. If it is larger than the optimal size, the average input must exceed the lowest point. Both situations need to be avoided for the educational institutions.

It can be concluded that the moderate size of an educational institution is precisely the size that can minimize its average input.

It's most favorable if each educational institution can reach its optimal size. But in reality, due to various reasons, educational institutions are not in moderate size and need to take some measures to achieve it based on their specific conditions.

Since the size of an educational institution could be represented by its total input, if its size is greater than its moderate size, it means that its total input is greater than the total input it needs at the moderate level, and vice versa.

From a theoretical point of view, the appropriate scale of the education units can be reached through adjusting the total amount of input, but the reality is more complicated. Because in the field of intellectual investment, "input I" accounts for a large proportion in the input, while "input II" accounts for a small proportion. In addition, "input I" is fixed and the way "input I" works to increase output (school buildings, teaching equipment, books and materials, administrators, formal faculty members, etc.) are often beyond the capacity of an educational institution to change.

Therefore, to achieve a moderate scale of educational institutions, feasible measures should be considered, which can be divided into the following two scenarios.

(1) Measures Needed if the Current Scale is Larger Than Optimal

If the current size of an educational institution is greater than the moderate size, it indicates that the amount of input is greater than the amount needed to achieve the moderate size. In theory, the input should be reduced.

However, the proportion of "input I" in the total input is very large. Then it's difficult to reduce this part by the educational institution itself. Even if it could, the space is often very limited. As for "input II," which accounts for only a small proportion of the total input, and is directly related to the amount of the output, a reduction in "input II" would affect the output in the same direction. In the case that "input I" is constant and accounts for a large proportion of the total input, the average input will be larger after the output starts to decrease, which is even less in line with the minimum average input required by the moderate scale.

According to the above analysis, the measure for an educational institution to realize its optimal scale should be to increase the output from the current amount of input. This can be illustrated by the formula for the average input.

the average input = ("input I" + "input II") / output = Total input / output.

Since neither "input I" nor "input II" can be significantly reduced, the average input can only be reduced by increasing the output.

Output is represented by the increment of knowledge and skills, which is equal to the number of the educated multiplied by the increment of knowledge and skills per person. If the number of the educated is constant and the increment of knowledge and skills per student increases, the output will increase. Alternatively, assuming that the increment of knowledge and skills per student remains constant while the number of the educated increases, the output will also increase.

Then we can conclude that, in a scenario in which the current size is greater than the optimal scale, an educational institution should adjust current input that could either increase the number of the educated, or to improve the average increment of students' knowledge and skills, or to adopt both.

The idea of increasing the number of the educated seems paradoxical from the outset, for if an educational institution is too large, it should enroll more students. This is in fact not contradictory, because the scale of an educational institution is measured by the amount of input, and the moderate scale is based on the amount of input when the average input is lowest, while the idea of increasing the enrollment proposed here is based on the premise of not increasing the amount of average input. If input is constant, recruiting more students can reduce the average input. This process continues until the size of the school is reduced to a moderate size, i.e., the lowest average amount of input.

Of course, from the perspective of educational decision-makers, if it is believed that the scale of an educational institution is too large to recruit more students, except for making efforts to improve the increment of knowledge and skills of each student, it can also reduce the input (mainly refers to "input I") under the condition of stable output. For example, some managers and teachers in the institutions who do not affect the output can be transferred out, thus reducing the wage costs in "input I." In addition, materials such as dormitories and teaching equipment, which do not affect output, can be transferred out of the institution as well, thus reducing the depreciation value and maintenance costs of these assets in "input I." This makes it possible to reduce the size of the educational institution to meet the requirements of achieving optimal size.

(2) Measures Needed if the Current Scale is Smaller Than the Optimal

If the current size of an educational institution is less than its moderate size, it indicates that its current amount of input is less than the amount needed to achieve the moderate size. In theory, it should increase the inputs.

However, the "input I" can't be increased by educational institution itself. Though "input II" is likely to be increased, the effect of increasing "input II" would be limited because the latter's proportion is very small.

In this situation, measures for an educational institution to achieve a moderate scale should also be to achieve more output out of the current amount of input, which can still be explained by the average input formula.

the average input = ("input I" + "input II") / output = Total input / output.

It should be known that when an educational institution is at its optimal size, its average input is the lowest. The input at the lowest point of the average input can keep the educational institution at a moderate size. According to the trajectory of the U-shaped average input curve, the average input before the lowest point of the curve is less than the moderate scale of investment required and is an uneconomical input. By the same token, the input beyond the lowest point of the average input curve is greater than the appropriate scale of the requirements of the input, which is also uneconomic.

Therefore, without increasing the input, educational institutions whose existing scale is smaller than the optimal could achieve their optimal scale by maximizing the use of existing inputs, especially the effect of "input I." As the output goes up, the average input goes down. The way to increase output is also to increase the number of the educated or to enhance the average student's knowledge and skills, or both.

This seems to be another contradictory phenomenon, because in order to achieve a moderate scale, the educational institutions on a larger scale should increase their output, and the existing educational institutions on a smaller scale should also increase their output. In fact, this is not contradictory, because the appropriate scale of an educational institution is determined by the lowest average input, so both the larger and smaller institutions should strive to reduce the average input to the lowest point. How do they reduce the average input? According to the characteristics of the intellectual investment, "input I" accounts for a large amount of the total input, and cannot be increased or decreased by education units themselves. Thus, education units should increase output at given input and reduce the average input to the lowest point, in order to comply with the requirement of the optimal scale.

Of course, from the perspective of the educational policy, if the size of an educational institution is seen as too small, in addition to increasing the output, the authority can increase the amount of input, especially "input I." If the current scale is smaller than the appropriate scale, the new amount of investment will pull down the average amount of investment after expanding the scale, ripping the benefits of economies of scale. This process of scale expansion will continue until the amount of new input equals to the amount of average input, i.e., until the amount of average input reaches the lowest point on the curve.

7.2 Factor Substitution and the Technical Composition of Education

7.2.1 I

The factors of input can be divided into material and human factors. In some cases, these factors are interchangeable, while in other cases, they are not.

In the economics of production, substitutability of factors indicates that factors are combined in variable proportions so that the curve on the Cartesian plane, with one factor's input as the vertical axis and that of the other as the horizontal axis, must be inclined to the lower right. The non-substitutability of the factors, on the other hand, indicates that the factors are combined in a fixed proportion so that the equal-yield curve takes on a shape of a straight line parallel to the vertical axis intersecting with another straight line parallel to the horizontal axis. Similarly, in the field of intellectual investment, the factors are either grouped in variable proportions or in fixed proportions. In this sense, the shape of the equal-yield curve of intellectual investment is similar to that in production economics.

But the factor substitution of an educational institution's input has its own characteristics. Let's first analyze those caused by the composition of inputs. According to what has been mentioned above, "input I," which does not change with output, accounts for a large proportion of the educational input in China. In addition, the basic salary of formal teachers is included in the "input I." Moreover, the increase or decrease of "input I" usually cannot be determined by the educational institution. As a result, it is difficult for the latter to consider teachers as the substitution factors when deciding its output, which greatly affects the solution of the whole factor substitution problem.

This situation is different from that discussed in the economics of production, which considers that labor wage is included in variable costs in relation to output. As production increases, the size of the workforce can be adjusted to realize the factor substitution by replacing workers with machines or vice versa. This kind of factor substitution will be reflected in adjusting the variable costs. However, in the area of intellectual investment, "input II" varies with output, and it only includes bonus and overwork remuneration of formal teachers, together with only a small amount of the salaries of substitute and part-time teachers. Even if teachers are replaced with material or the opposite, the amount of "input I" is fixed. Therefore, when teachers are replaced with additional material, they still have to be paid with basic salaries. In the case of replacing the material with additional teachers, educational institutions cannot increase the number of formal teachers. In other words, it is impossible to increase "input I," and we can only realize such substitution by increasing "input II." Thus, the characteristic of factor substitution for educational input is non-flexibility.

Now consider the influence of professional characteristics of teaching staff on factor substitution. In the teaching activities organized by educational institutions, teachers impart knowledge and skills to students. Sometimes such teaching activity is impossible to be replaced by additional inputs of material, and sometimes it can, but the quantity of teaching will be affected, which means that output will be adversely affected. For example, merging small classes into large ones, or switching to remote teaching to reduce the number of teaching staff actually indicate that the educational institution replaces teaching labor with additional material input. The effect on output is not the same as that of diminishing marginal substitution (DMS) rate in the economics of production. The law of DMS in the economics of production is that in the process of factor substitution, with the increase of the substitution, more factor A needs to be used to replace the same amount of factor B, or the amount of factor B that can be replaced by the same amount of factor A will decrease. Hence, the equal-yield curve on the Cartesian plane must be convex to the origin when it tilts to the lower right. In the field of intellectual investment, when factors can be interchanged, the law of the DMS also plays a role, i.e., more additional factor input is needed to replace another factor of equal amount in order to maintain the original output. But the influence of teachers' professionalism on factor substitution makes a difference here. Because teachers' work is professional in that it imparts the knowledge and skills, and there is a limit to the ratio of the number of teachers to that of students. If this limit is exceeded, the amount of knowledge and skills learned by the educated will be reduced. Suppose the educational institutions do not consider the specialty of teachers, and they arbitrarily increase the number of students for each teacher and use more additional material input to replace the same amount of teaching labor, then the output will eventually be adversely affected. Therefore, under such substitution, when the teacher-student ratio exceeds a certain level, the output generated by the combination of input factors is the equal-yield, so the output of the combination of each factor does not show an equal-yield curve slanting to the lower right and convex to the origin on the above Cartesian plane. Such characteristic of factor substitution in the educational input is its limitation. Though the factor substitution of the educational institutions is inflexible and limited, there are still two reasons for an educational institution to make the substitution.

First, factor input represents educational expenditure. In order to improve the economic efficiency of intellectual investment, an educational institution should make a best use of less educational expenditure to achieve the same output. There's a difference in various factors' monetary value. Suppose factor A needs relatively more expenditures while factor B needs less, then for an educational institution, more factor B should be used than factor A if both factors can be interchangeable, which is positive to reduce the expenditure.

Second, the scarcity differs among different factors. It's an objective fact for the intellectual investment and will exist for a long time. The scarcity of these factors could or could not be represented by the monetary value, because there is no complete factor market. In this way, every educational institution must make use of more relatively abundant factors and less relatively scarce factors according to its own material and human resources. From this point of view, there are two reasons why factor substitution is important. On the one hand, such factor substitution can reduce educational expenditure. On the other hand, such substitution should be an indispensable guarantee of a certain output. If factors are scarce and cannot be obtained from the factor market, it is impossible to produce a certain amount of output.

In particular, factor substitution is even more necessary if the aim is to increase output when different factors have different degrees of scarcity. If the relatively scarce factors cannot be replaced with those relatively abundant, the increase of output is for sure not guaranteed.

7.2.2 II

Since factor substitution is necessary, how to make a suitable factor substitution for each educational institution, given that it's inflexible and limited? This will be discussed by the following two cases.

(1) the Factor Substitution Strategy Under Inflexible Condition

As mentioned above, the inflexibility of input factor substitution in educational institutions is related to the large proportion of "input I." "Input I" includes the base salary of formal staff, and the change of "input I" is not usually determined by the educational institution. Therefore, measures must be taken to formulate countermeasures of factor substitution based on the real situation, mainly including the following ways:

First, if "input I" is constant, the existing materials should be fully used at capacity, and the input of non-teaching human resources should be reduced, making those who are capable of teaching be transferred to the work of teaching. In this way, on the one hand, it realizes the substitution of human resources by the input of material factors (i.e., to replace the non-teaching staff whose number can be reduced). On the other hand, it makes these non-teaching staff meet the needs of increasing output.

Second, if "input I" remains constant and the number of formal staff in the "input I" is relatively large, the expenditure for human resources in the "input II" should be reduced, and the expenditure for material input should be increased. The additional material input should be used to give full play to the role of formal staff: The human resource in surplus in "input I" can be fully utilized by substituting material input for human input in "input II."

Third, if "input I" is constant and the material in "input II" is relatively large, the expenditure on the material of "input II" should be reduced, and the expenditure on human resources should be increased. The additional human resources should be used to give full play to the role of the material input. Such factor substitution is to make full use of the redundant material factor in "input I" by substituting human input for material input in "input II."

(2) the Factor Substitution Strategy Under Inflexible Condition

As discussed above, the limitation of factor substitution in educational input is related to staff expertise. Therefore, an educational institution must consider the specialty of teachers first to make the countermeasures of factor substitution. The main stratcgics arc as thc following.

First, the factor substitution should be controlled within a certain level of teacher-student ratio.

The teacher-student ratio here refers to the ratio of the number of teachers directly engaged in teaching to the number of students.

In the process of replacing teachers with material input, if the latter is too much and the quality of teaching falls, then such substitution is out of the limit. As for whether or to what extent the quality of teaching declines, it can be measured by the increment of knowledge and skills.

Second, factor substitution implementation is taken it is needed to increase the number of the educated.

The output of an educational institution equals to the increment of knowledge and skills of its students, which is also equal to student number times the average increment of the students. As service providers, educational institutions have certain output objectives. Therefore, assuming that the teacher-student ratio exceeds a certain level after factor substitution and make the average increment of educated people's knowledge and skills decrease, it's still acceptable on some occasions as long as the targeted output is unchanged (which refers to the increase of the number of the educated after factor substitution to offset the decrease in the increment of knowledge and skills of each student). In other words, such factor substitution could be allowed in urgent need. But it should not be regarded as a normal countermeasure, only a special one, because the standard measurement of knowledge and skills is always the level of knowledge of the educated.

At the same time, even in special cases where excessive factor substitution is required, appropriate remedial measures should be taken to avoid the decline of knowledge and skill increment in the process of factor substitution, such as increasing the supply of teaching references, strengthening after-class and tutorial before the exam, and so on.

7.2.3 III

From the perspective of educational economics, factor substitution exists as an issue for each educational institution. Therefore, how should intellectual investment and macro-policy decision-makers deal with this issue?

On the one hand, the character of intellectual investment and the limitation of educational input should be recognized, and that the advanced and automatic teaching equipment is important but not omnipotent. Such equipment could replace teachers' work to some extent, but it couldn't replace them all. Even when it could replace teachers' work, the teaching quality could be affected if the teacher-student ratio decreased beyond a certain level because of the decline in the number of teachers. This is different from the material production. For example, the number of workers could be reduced to the lowest level in an advanced and automatic factory because multiple machines can be operated simultaneously, with the growth of the output doubled and quality not affected. But will that happen in intellectual investment? Suppose a formal school could increase the investment in equipment and replace a large number of teachers with audio and video teaching facilities, is this the realization of high-quality education? In reality, this is not the case at all. The direct contact in and out of class between teachers and students can not only transform the experience but also exchange their feelings and ideas. Besides, teachers' behaviors always have a potential impact on students, and their political attitude, moral character, and dedication to education have an important influence on students, as well as their study attitude and research methods. In addition, teachers can teach in accordance with students' specific circumstances. These are all the reasons why the audiotape and fluorescent screen cannot replace teachers. Therefore, one thing for sure is that both basic and specialized course teaching is inseparable from teachers. Especially in primary and middle school education, where teachers directly impart skills and knowledge to students, their work cannot be substituted by teaching equipment. Moreover, the quality of teaching by correspondence varies greatly according to the teachers' guidance. The object of a teacher's work is people rather than materials, which is why teachers' work is different from producer's work in producing materials.

On the other hand, to the extent that it is necessary to replace the factors without reducing the increment of the knowledge and skills of the educated, the decision-makers of intellectual investment should allow each educational institution to undertake such factor substitution. If institutions have problems in factor substitution due to their inability to determine the amount of "input I," helps should be provided to do so, such as helping them reduce redundant human resources, providing them with the teaching equipment needed to replace the factors, and so on. Therefore, even if the non-flexibility of input factor substitution of a single educational institution will not disappear completely, it can be reduced to some extent, i.e., the flexibility of factor substitution can be increased. As long as relevant officials recognize both the necessity and the non-flexibility of the factor substitution in education and take concrete measures to reduce such non-flexibility, it could be undertaken to improve the economic effect of intellectual investment.

As for the national economy, the government can either replace the input of teaching facilities with more teachers or replace teachers with more advanced teaching facilities as factor substitution. Therefore, just as the economics of production is divided into labor-intensive and capital-intensive economies according to the proportion of factor input, education investment can also be divided into two types according to the proportion of factor input, from the perspective of the technologies involved. They are the light-structured education, consisting of more input of teaching labor and less facilities, and the heavy-structured education, consisting of more teaching facilities and less labor. The sequence of education, from primary, secondary to higher education, also reflects the gradual transition from "light-structured education" to "heavy-structured education." From a macro perspective, although the factor substitution in educational economics has limitations and the input of labor is essential, such gradual transition is still the trend of educational development.

7.3 Factor Movement and School Distribution

7.3.1 I

There are many issues to discuss about school distribution. Here we only talk about several issues related to the improvement of the economic effect of intellectual investment from the theories of educational economics. For example, what is the basis for the choice on school locations? What kind of school distribution is reasonable? And how to adjust the current school distribution to improve the economic performance of intellectual investment?

Primary and secondary schools are units of basic education, which are aimed to teach school-age students in proximity. The primary school graduates would go to secondary school, and the graduates of latter would go to colleges or universities. Only some of the students have the opportunities to study in colleges and universities, the rest having to find jobs one way or another. Therefore, nearby enrollment policy must be considered in the location arrangements of primary and secondary schools, because the amount of input required for the same output could be less under a suitable policy.

For basic education, the supply of factors needed to build a school is in a relatively minor position.

The factors in the intellectual investment could be classified from different perspectives. From the perspective of the distribution of schools, the liquidity of the input factors could be a classification standard, and input factors can be divided into "illiquid," "liquid," and "incompletely liquid" in between. "Illiquid" factors include the land occupied by a school and the existing school building. The "liquid" factors include books, teaching facilities, and staff who can be transported easily. "Incompletely liquid" factors refer to those staff who are difficult in changing work locations or need care.

In basic education, "illiquid" factors account for a small proportion of the input required to establish an educational institution. The proportion of teachers who can move easily is relatively large, with the proportion of teachers who are difficult to move relatively small. Such condition brings great convenience to adjust school locations according to the population distribution, and the nearby enrollment policy is also relatively easy to implement. In basic education, the supply of factors needed to establish a school (especially a primary school) is easier to be guaranteed, whether it is the supply of "illiquid" or "liquid" factors. For example, suppose that every village or street should have a primary school, it would be easy to secure the supply of the buildings and staff. Suppose that every village or town should have a secondary school, the supply is often more complicated than that of a primary school, but generally it is not difficult.

Therefore, the *nearby enrollment policy* in elementary education stage means that schools should be arranged according to population density, or the source of students. It is the basis for the distribution of primary and secondary schools.

7.3.2 II

Colleges and universities are different from primary and secondary schools. They are specialized education units to train professional personnel for the society.

Should the distribution of colleges and universities consider the nearby enrollment policy or the density of population or students' area? In principle, this policy should still be considered, because for students, it means reducing the costs of education. For educational institutions, enrolling students in proximity means reducing the cost on student services. For the society, it means reducing the burden on transportation. Therefore, the distribution of colleges and universities should also consider that of the population. For example, if a college or university can recruit students in proximity who don't need dormitories and retain the same teaching quality, it can achieve the same output with less input.

However, demographic factors should not play as important a role in the distribution of colleges and universities as they do in that of primary and secondary schools, therefore cannot be considered as the main factor. Colleges and universities train specialized personnel for the society. Their graduates will work all over the country, not necessarily in the same location where their schools are. The nearby enrollment policy does not mean that graduates are employed nearby, especially for those who graduate from key colleges and universities, because the latter select students from the whole country, not subject to the nearby enrollment principle.

The demographic factor is relatively simple in determining the distribution of colleges and universities, but more complex issues need to be considered if we look at the factor movement in the field of intellectual investment.

The amount of "illiquid" factor of the input in colleges and universities is much more than that in primary and secondary schools. The reason why changing the location of a college or university is much more difficult than that of a primary or secondary school is related to its large proportion and amount of "illiquid" factor. But relatively speaking, such difficulties mainly come from the supply of teaching staff. Though some college teachers can change their work locations easily, there are still a large number of teachers who are difficult to move or need other care. Because of age, health, family, and all kinds of sociological reasons, it's not absolutely impossible to make the college or university teachers move with the institutions to a new place where economy is relatively backward, but the working environment and their working morale might be badly affected, followed by the decline of teaching quality. Under the system of retirement, the number of teachers retiring on schedule or in advance will increase, and it will be far more difficult to fill the vacancy of retired teachers in colleges and universities than to fill those in primary and secondary schools. The more specialized and academically accomplished teachers in colleges and universities are, the greater their immobility, and the smaller the possibility of local recruitment. These lead to some special issues in the distribution of colleges and universities. Therefore, it can be considered that the supply of factors in the distribution of colleges and universities is mainly the supply of "incompletely liquid" factors, which is actually the supply of teachers. This special issue must be considered seriously in the distribution of colleges and universities.

7.3.3 *III*

The academic environment factors that affect the distribution of higher education entities are those objective conditions, including factors of human and material resources. Colleges and universities are both educational and scientific research units. If they only pay attention to teaching and neglect scientific research, it would be hard for them to improve teaching quality, and it would be a loss for the society, suggesting that their expertise and facilities could not be fully utilized for scientific research. Besides, for colleges and universities, no matter what their teaching or scientific activities are, they need to cooperate and communicate with the outside world. With the continuous development of science and technology, it is impossible for colleges and universities to do well if they are isolated from the academic circle.

Therefore, compared with the distribution of primary and secondary schools, academic environment factors are much more important for colleges and universities. In order to improve teaching and scientific research, colleges and universities should be located in places that are convenient for academic exchanges and cooperation with academic communities and other institutions of production and scientific research. In terms of academic environment, it is more advantageous to have several colleges and universities located in the same city than to have them scattered in several cities, which is the same for the relationship between institutions of higher education and scientific research. In addition, it is more advantageous to locate specialized higher educational institutions close to, rather than far away from, large industrial enterprises. These all demonstrate the impact of an academic environment on the distribution of colleges and universities.

Moreover, the material resources needed by the establishment of colleges and universities also include the infrastructure conditions (power and transportation systems, social and living facilities, etc.). The better the infrastructure, the more beneficial it is to the teaching and research activities of colleges and universities. If colleges and universities are in areas with poor infrastructure, the improvement of these infrastructures will take a long time and require a large amount of investment. There would be an issue of who will bear the cost. If it is the colleges and universities to bear the cost, they may not be able to do so. If the cost is borne by the national or local government, they will first consider whether the investment is urgently needed, because they cannot invest a huge amount of money in infrastructure just to improve the teaching and research conditions of a particular college or university.

In general, the factors affecting the supply of teachers and the academic environment in colleges and universities are the same. Teachers are special talents and the improvement of their academic level is closely related to the academic environment. The better the academic environment of a region, the more attractive it is to the teachers of colleges and universities. The transformation of colleges and universities from a better academic environment to a worse one would increase the difficulty of teachers' mobility. Therefore, the supply of teaching staff and academic environment are two different input factors. The former is often considered from the perspective of mobility, while the latter is considered for the objective conditions that facilitate other input factors in the investment. However, if the colleges and universities could be located in the regions with a better academic environment, the teacher immobility will be relatively solved.

The academic environment also includes the regional "talent reserve" which could affect the location of colleges and universities. Regional "talent reserve" refers to the accumulative amount of talent in a region. In this regard, we may encounter some issues when investigating the academic environment. Wouldn't a region with a large "talent reserve" be even larger if colleges and universities were set up there? Compared with the regions with relatively low "talent reserve," wouldn't the gap between the abundant and rare factor regions be even larger? Can this condition be tolerated?

Teachers in colleges and universities are part of a region's "talent reserve." The "talent reserve" varies from region to region for various historical and social reasons. It would certainly be ideal to distribute talent more evenly across the country to achieve a balanced economic and cultural development among different regions. However, it should be pointed out that the distribution of talents should be subject to the needs of the economic and cultural development of the whole society, rather than just following the principle of absolute equal distribution. As the center of economic and cultural development, big cities should have a concentration of more talents. To promote collaboration and exchanges between colleges and universities and scientific research as well as improving the academic level of the whole country and regions, colleges and universities should also be relatively centralized, which not only conforms to the law of scientific and cultural development but also helps to realize the improvement of the economic efficiency of intellectual investment.

In other words, it's not necessary or possible to distribute talents geographically evenly, because the amount of a region's "talent reserve" couldn't reflect its structure. Often, one type of specialist is abundant in one region and another is abundant in another region. It's impossible to establish identical talent structure among the regions.

It can be seen that the problem is not how to make colleges and universities evenly distributed in each region, but how to transfer the graduates of these colleges and universities to areas with less "talent reserve," to gradually improve the situation of talent shortage in some regions. Unless there are special circumstances, colleges and universities should not be located in areas under the prefecture level. On the province level, it is advisable to set up colleges and universities in its capital and a few important cities. On a national scale, colleges and universities should be relatively concentrated in larger cities.

Given that a region's "talent reserve" is a component of its academic environment, the regional "talent reserve" can affect the locations of colleges and universities, meaning that a region's large "talent reserve" can be one of the reasons for setting up colleges and universities in that region. It's not a reason for regions with a small "talent reserve" to do that, but it can be a reason for allocating more graduates of colleges and universities to the regions with a small "talent reserve."

According to principle above, those comprehensive, normal, financial, medical, and art colleges and universities should be located in large and medium-sized cities, and the key comprehensive, normal, finance, economics, politics, law, medical and art universities in a small number of big cities where scientific research institutions are concentrated. From the perspective of academic environment, engineering, agricultural and forestry colleges have reasons to be located in large and medium-sized cities, and key engineering colleges and agricultural and forestry colleges and universities should be located in a few influential big cities where scientific research institutions are concentrated. As for the allocation of engineering colleges in industrial and mining areas, and agricultural and forestry colleges in rural, forest and pastoral areas, the academic environment (including the factor of a region's "talent reserve") must be considered. If a certain industrial and mining, rural, forest or pastoral areas have a suitable academic environment, with scientific research institutions and a certain number of specialized talents, to ensure the improvement of the teaching quality of these colleges and universities, it is feasible to set up relevant specialized colleges and universities there.

Finally, just as we need to consider political as well as social and economic factors in the distribution of production, it is important to consider political factors in the distribution of schools, which usually include ethnic and national defense factors. Ethnic factors mean that in order to strengthen ethnic unity and promote the economic and cultural development of ethnic minority areas, the investment in ethnic education should be increased to promote education in these areas, and more schools including colleges and universities should be set up there. National defense factor means that for the needs of national defense, some higher education institutions related to national defense scientific research should be established in safer areas, or move to safer regions, if necessary, in order to retain talents and avoid losses from war.

Ethnic and national defense factors should be regarded as the special factors in considering school locations. But they can be coordinated with the above three factors (demographic, factor supply, and academic environment) under certain conditions. That is to say when the establishment of schools in minority areas is decided on the basis of ethnic factors, or the establishment of schools in relatively safe areas is decided on the basis of national defense factors, an analysis should still be made based on the factors of demographic, teacher supply, and academic environment. This means that the most favorable location among several alternative sites should be selected to obtain an equal output with minimal input, or obtain as much output as possible with the same input.

7.3.4 IV

If the ethnic and national defense factors are regarded as given, then the distribution of demographic, factor supply, and academic environment will be the three factors affecting the locations of colleges and universities. Population distribution cannot be changed in a short period, nor is the academic environment. Moreover, the change of population distribution and academic environment of a region cannot be realized with the efforts of the education unit itself.

In general, it is easier to change the supply of production factors than to alter population distribution or educational conditions. Although some of these conditions cannot be changed by the efforts of the education unit itself, the latter can still contribute to the change of factor supply to some extent.

In terms of the supply of "illiquid" factors, they are always illiquid, and couldn't be transformed into "liquid" factors by the education sector. But the latter can expand the scale of schools and increase school buildings by reallocating the total social input of intellectual investment. It can also allocate between the existing school buildings and the land occupied by the school, or achieve the rational use of these through school merger and reorganization. Thus, in the process of adjusting the school distributions, the supply of "illiquid" factors can be improved. In general, the improvement of the primary and secondary schools' "illiquid" factors supply is easy, while for colleges and universities it is more difficult. But as long as the education authority is determined to do so with effective measures, it is still possible to improve the supply of "illiquid" factors in the distribution of colleges and universities.

The issues regarding the supply of "liquid" factors could be easily addressed by the education authority itself. Assuming that the total social input of intellectual investment remains constant, the authority can address liquidity issue through the reallocation of books, materials, and facilities of existing schools and workplace transfer of teachers who are easy to change work locations. Assuming that the total social input of intellectual investment is increasing, the authority can use additional input to make schools in some areas increase the "liquid" factors they need without reducing the existing "liquid" factors in other areas. For example, assigning newly graduated students to schools that lack teachers is a measure to increase the "liquid" factors in supply. This is usually relatively easy to achieve.

However, the issue of the "incompletely liquid" supply is more difficult to address regardless of an increased or constant intellectual investment, because it involves the job transfer of those teachers who are difficult to move, and these problems often cannot be addressed by the educational authority itself. Nevertheless, it can still increase the mobility of "incompletely liquid" factors within their capacity, so as to improve the distribution of schools, especially the supply of teachers in colleges and universities.

What can education authorities do to increase the "liquidity" of teachers? In addition to political and ideological measures, it mainly relies on improving the working and living conditions of teachers, helping them solve the problems encountered in curriculum preparation, professional training, teaching, and specific family issues. It should be recognized that the reasons why some teachers have difficulty in mobility lie in the issues in their lives. If the authorities do not take effective measures to help them solve these issues (such as difficulties in schooling and employment for their children, reuniting with the spouse, housing, family income, etc.), the mobility of teachers cannot be increased. Even if they are transferred to the workplace, teachers' work morale will be affected.

We should know that if the working and living conditions from the macro perspective of a region (which refer to the conditions of a region) where a school is located are relatively ideal, even if the micro conditions within the school (which refer to the conditions of the school) are relatively poor, the influence on teacher mobility will not be obvious. If the conditions of a region are poor in both aspects, it is not easy to make teachers focus on their work, nor is it easy to transfer teachers to these regions. Therefore, in areas where macro-working and living conditions are poor, it is necessary for the authority and school to improve the micro conditions as much as possible. It can be summarized that if the macro condition is poor and difficult to be improved, it can be compensated by improving the micro condition. If this can be done, the problem of teacher supply will be improved.

7.3.5 V

Although the supply of teachers can be improved with better working and living conditions, the authority and school are still unable to improve overall conditions. Therefore, they have responsibilities to report the situation to the central and local authorities for effective measures to improve the academic environment of the region (including infrastructure conditions). Besides, they can also organize teachers' regular directional communications to ease shortage in qualified teachers in a region.

Under the condition that teachers are "incompletely liquid" factors, although in some regions there are surplus talent or the waste of talents' potential, there's lack of teachers of this specialty in other regions. The reality is that teachers of the former regions are difficult to move to the latter regions. The reasons behind this pertain to both the personnel management system and teachers themselves. Personnel management system will not be analyzed here. Assuming that the above measures to improve the micro conditions of teachers still couldn't solve the mobility issue, then it may be feasible to adjust teachers regular targeted exchange program organized by the education authority.

The term "regular" in the targeted exchange refers to a program in which a school with talent potential sends teachers to a school with insufficient teaching staff for a certain period (minimum one or two months, maximum one or two years), without transferring teacher's household registration and the job, as well as the position and teaching subjects in the original institution.

The term "targeted" refers to the establishment of a formal connection between a school with strong teaching staff and one or several schools with insufficient teaching staff. The former sends teachers to the latter, with the former making plans for sending teachers, and the latter making plans for hosting the dispatched teachers.

Under this program, the dispatched teachers should mainly offer courses that the destination schools do not have the capacity to offer. The courses that both schools can offer are not appropriate to be offered by dispatched teachers. To carry out regular targeted communication among teachers, the courses assigned to the dispatched teachers can be taught in a more intensive way (single subject or double subjects), so that the courses of a school year can be taught in three or four months or the courses of a semester can be taught in one or two months. This is more convenient for the dispatched and both schools under the program.

Since the dispatched teachers adopt a more intensive teaching mode, additional teaching remuneration should be given by regulations without affecting their workload in the original school. Even if dispatched teachers reduce their workload in their original school due to relocation, they should also be appropriately remunerated for the extra workload at the remote school and that the change of living conditions could also increase their living expenses.

Here we have a question: Does this program improve the economic effect of intellectual investment? If it is improved, how?

If the economic effect of investment is represented by the output of the average input, i.e.,

Output of the average input = output/input.

The amount of input is increased after the implementation of the program because the dispatched teachers have to be paid additional travel expenses (even if the lecture remuneration is not calculated). If teachers are sent to another school to teach as many students as before, and teach the exact same subject, then the output is equal after the implementation of the exchange (except that the output is counted separately in both schools). Since the amount of input increases, but the amount of output is the same, from the macroeconomic perspective, the economic effect of intellectual investment decreases after teachers' participation in this program because the output of average input decreases.

Can we simply look at the economic effects of the program in this way? The problem is what kind of courses the dispatched teachers teach. Assuming that the courses offered by them could also be taught with similar teaching quality, then the output of the average input of teachers under the program will decrease, which is not in line with the economic principle. If the courses offered are those necessary to cultivate certain kind of graduates that couldn't be offered by the hosting school, it involves the quality of the graduates of the hosting school. It can be considered that any student who does not reach a certain standard of knowledge cannot be regarded as a qualified graduate. Thus, it is indispensable for a hosting school to invite teachers from other schools to teach these courses. Therefore, after implementing the exchange program, the number of graduates with a certain kind of knowledge and output could increase although the amount of input also increases. From this point of view, the exchange program is undoubtedly a measure to improve the economic effect of intellectual investment.

—*Advances in Social Sciences*, issue No. 1, 1983

Chapter 8
1984: Issues on the Unified Regulatory Mechanism of Macro- and Micro-Economies

This paper aims to raise a theoretical issue for academic discussion: Can there be a unified internal regulatory mechanism of macro- and micro-economies in a socialist economy? And how can such a mechanism be formed?

8.1 The Regulatory Mechanism in a Capitalist Economy

For some Western economists, there exists a mechanism that could adjust the macro-economy automatically in a capitalist economy. This mechanism is called "internal stabilizer." For example, the levying of individual and corporate income tax could play this role. In boom times, when both individual income and corporate profits rise, the taxation on these incomes would increase accordingly, which can restrain the expansion of aggregate demand. Conversely, during economic recessions, the decreased individual income and corporate profits lead to fewer tax levies, which in turn helps hinder the decline in aggregate demand. As another example, unemployment benefits and various welfare expenditures automatically decrease during a boom and increase under a bust, adjusting the macro-economy toward stability and avoiding dramatic inflation and demand decline. In addition, people's adherence to consumption habits is believed to help prevent excessive decreases in consumption during recessions. Since people always maintain their consumption habits and levels which they are used to in the past, they would rather save less or use their savings to maintain consumption level for a period of time despite decreased income. In this way, the decline in consumption expenditure would be less than that in income, thus being conducive to macroeconomic stability to certain extent. On the contrary, when people earn more or receive a large windfall (a grant, an inheritance, etc.), they would consider more for saving. Alternatively, when people enter their prime of life with increasing income, they would also take childcare and pension into consideration. Then they may save a portion of their income, which thereby releases the pressure on

Y. Li, *China's Economy Since 1978*, China Academic Library,
https://doi.org/10.1007/978-981-95-5733-2_8

the market brought by expanded demand. According to these Western economists, although such an internal economic regulatory mechanism might seem insufficient to fully guarantee macroeconomic stability in capitalist countries, there is no doubt that it can moderate the degree of economic decline in times of depression, and the degree of inflation during economic prosperity.

In terms of the micro-economy, it is believed that market competition improves capitalist efficiency. Competition pushes enterprises to improve their management, adopt or develop new technologies, reduce costs and increase profits. They may transform production and create a new development path, like investing in other areas of production and marketing. This is the internal regulatory mechanism in a capitalist micro-economy.

In the early 1970s, Mann, a professor at the University of Rochester and a consultant to General Motors, pointed out that if an enterprise did not maximize its profits, it might eventually be "taken over." In a modern capitalist society, investors have their eyes on enterprises, which also pay close attention to their peers. Investors are constantly trying to find out which one has a higher profit margin and a better chance to earn more. At the same time, enterprises are also analyzing their competitors' production capacity, current profitability, and future potential. If an enterprise is likely to make a higher profit based on its production capacity and potential, but is currently unable to do so due to mismanagement, then investors and competitors may acquire its stocks in various ways. They could buy the stocks at a slightly higher price in the market and then accumulate them to a certain percentage, so that they could eventually take over the targeted enterprise. Then they may reorganize the board of directors, reappoint senior management, and run the enterprise in another way for higher profits. It can be seen that each capitalist enterprise faces two possibilities. One is to adapt to the new situation, adopt new technologies and operating methods, indicating that they must gain a foothold and achieve expansion in the competition. The other is to lag behind and lose business, followed by either being "taken over" or even going bankrupt. It is precisely such a mechanism that forces capitalist enterprises to improve their economic efficiency initiatively.

In general, a capitalist economy is characterized by the fact that the internal regulatory mechanism of the micro-economy usually functions well and promotes efficiency, while the macro-economy regulatory mechanism falls short of maintaining macroeconomic stability. The above two are disconnected from each other, and the foundation of capitalist private ownership is a serious obstacle to form the internal regulatory mechanism of both macro- and micro-economies. The role of such a mechanism is specifically manifested in the simultaneous realization of two major goals: Macroeconomic stability and the improvement of corporate efficiency, both of which must complement each other.

The objectives of the macro- and micro-economies are usually inseparable. The economic realities in capitalist countries show that, on the one hand, if more enterprises suffer losses and go bankrupt because of inefficiency, there would be decreased fiscal revenues and increased unemployment, followed by a more difficult situation for macroeconomic stability. On the other hand, if the macro-economy is out of control, the micro-economy would be less dynamic and the improvement of corporate efficiency would also be impacted. For example, with high inflation or high unemployment, it is impossible for the market to allocate various economic resources to the most appropriate sectors or areas. In addition, it is not easy for enterprises to consider technological innovation in accordance with principles that are truly conducive to improving their long-term economic efficiency. If the prices of capital goods rise quickly and seem difficult to be restrained, enterprises would try to maintain stocks beyond the normal level of inventories. In this way, the speed of capital turnover would be affected, thus leading to lower efficiency of capital use. Even if such prices cannot rise freely due to some constraint, enterprises would likewise increase inventories as long as capital goods are in short supply. As another example, in the context of an instable macro-economy, the directions of corporate investment and the balanced development among sectors and areas would also be influenced, which are detrimental to the rational allocation of economic resources and the improvement of efficiency.

Thus, in the absence of a unified internal regulatory mechanism of the macro- and micro-economies, it would be difficult to coordinate the objectives of macroeconomic stability and microeconomic efficiency.

However, within capitalist private ownership, the regulatory mechanism of the macro-economy mostly relies on progressive taxation and social welfare systems implemented by the government, apart from being self-initiated by consumers' insistence on consumption habits. These two mechanisms are difficult to be integrated. In general, the mechanism of market competition tends to affect macroeconomic stability in the process of increasing corporate efficiency. While progressive taxation and social welfare systems tend to moderate macroeconomic instability but also restrict the realization of the microeconomic objective. Social welfare expenditures are often associated with deficit financing, particularly in capitalist countries. The beneficiaries of welfare policies become victims of decreased real income in an inflationary environment. A vicious circle is thus formed: More welfare expenditure adds fiscal burden on the state, which leads to credit expansion and an increase in money supply. Then there would be inflation, which reduces household real income and allowances. In this way, increasing demands for more benefits induce more fiscal burden. As long as this vicious circle is not broken, the fiscal deficits in Western countries would not be reduced.

What's more, the increase in welfare is directly related to inefficiency. In Western countries, benefits for the unemployed reduce their motivation to seek jobs and make them pickier about careers. This can be regarded as a loss in national efficiency. Moreover, while receiving certain benefits, employed workers still identify some facts of social inequality. Not only do they take the received benefits for granted, but they also think that others are paying less and getting more. All of these do not help create a real incentive for people to work and promote efficiency.

The above discussions reflect the contradictions in the regulatory mechanism of macro- and micro- economy within the capitalist system.

8.2 The Regulatory Mechanism in a Socialist Economy

Based on socialist public ownership of capital goods, it is reasonable to assume the existence of a unified internal regulatory mechanism of the macro- and micro-economies. Under a socialist system, the interests of the state, enterprises, and individuals are consistent, so the macro- and micro-economy objectives could be unified. However, some facts indicate that this may not become a reality. Moreover, even from a theoretical perspective, some issues are still to be studied. The core of this is how to establish a system of economic regulation that can make macroeconomic and microeconomic regulation interlink with each other. It should be noted that even in a socialist economy, the effects of various regulation measures are quite different. Some are severe, and some are moderate. Some can react faster and some react with a time lag. They work on different parts of the economy as well. In particular, some are beneficial to macroeconomic stability but may be negative to the mobilization of enterprises, while others have absolutely opposite effects. What needs to be studied is that, based on public ownership of capital goods, how the various regulatory measures can be integrated into a unified system so that they can be complementary and do not weaken or cancel each other out for the national economy.

Some foreign economists have discussed methods of coordinating macro- and micro-economies in a socialist society. For example, Virlyn W. Bruse proposed the doctrine of three levels of decision-making: central, corporate and individual. He believed that central decision-making should mainly solve fundamental and policy issues, corporate decision-making mostly should care about profitability, and individual decision-making should consider choices over consumer goods and jobs. When there are conflicts, coordination based on social interests should come into play. Bruse also considers that there should be a division between macro- and micro-decision-making. Economic planning is a kind of macroeconomic decision-making, the goal of which is to balance the economy, while microeconomic decision-making considers the role of market mechanisms, which aims to achieve economic benefits. Any excessive expectations are not necessary and appropriate. This is one of Bruse's theoretical visions for coordinating macro- and micro-economies in a socialist society. He considered both the balance of the macro-economy and the principle of corporate profitability, but several issues remained unsolved. For example, when there is a contradiction between central government, enterprises and individuals, how to coordinate the conflict and ensure the effectiveness of such coordination are all yet to be studied.

Ota Sik argued that in socialist countries, macro- and micro-economies could be coordinated through decentralized ownership, with the market meeting the needs of consumers and the government regulating the direction of investment, the proportion of savings, and public service programs. This is an attempt to deal with the above issue in another way. But it remains unclear how to exactly realize the division between government planning and market initiatives, and how to connect changes in the price level in the macro-economy with the determination of individual prices in the micro-economy.

Moreover, in related research abroad on coordination of macro- and micro-economy, some issues have hardly been considered. These include the unbalanced development of a country's domestic economy, the impact of structural factors and the technological revolution on the macro-economy, and the coordination of macro- and micro-economies in the transition from a less open to a more open country, etc.

Thus, even from a purely theoretical point of view, the issues on the unified regulatory mechanism of macro- and micro-economies still need to be further explored.

8.3 Theoretical Assumptions on the Unified Regulatory Mechanism of Macro- and Micro-Economies Under a Socialist System

My assumption is still premature and is presented solely for the reader's assessment.

In order to simplify this issue, assume that the enterprises mentioned here are state-owned ones that have been assigned the production tasks by the government. It is also assumed that:

First, these enterprises should use funds remuneratively. In terms of production, they receive the tasks assigned by the government, obey the country's laws, pay taxes in accordance with regulations, and have the right to sell additional products after completing the tasks of a national plan.

Second, two types of prices are set for the products of these enterprises, planned and non-planned. Products produced within the tasks of the government are sold at the planned price, and excessive products are sold at a non-planned price (i.e., often higher than the planned). It is assumed that the planned price level should be slightly above or equal to the average cost, then most enterprises would not suffer a loss. Therefore, the realized profitability is actually determined by the non-planned price level and relevant sales volume.

Third, enterprises have the right to recruit employees independently and dismiss those whom they consider incompetent. Enterprises can increase their employees' wages and bonuses after paying taxes according to regulations.

Fourth, after completing production tasks assigned by the government and paying taxes as prescribed by the regulations, the enterprises have the right to use the retained profits as a fund for the development of production, employees' welfare and incentive, etc.

Based on the above assumptions, the internal regulatory mechanism of macro- and micro-economies under socialist conditions is most likely a mechanism that combines credit, price, and taxation.

The internal regulatory mechanism of credit here refers to enterprises' remunerative use of funds. Due to this, enterprises must consider the opportunity cost of using these funds. They need to economize funds and strive for greater economic efficiency, while the government can control the macro-economy through credit management. The remunerative use of funds would exert both pressure and vitality on enterprises to achieve their microeconomic goals. At the same time, credit management would allow the growth of enterprise's efficiency to be coordinated with the growth of domestic credit in the national economy. That is to say, if the economic efficiency of enterprises increases and the retained profits boost, the absolute amount of domestic credit in the national economy would also increase, otherwise its growth rate would decrease. Instead, if the opposite circumstance occurs, the growth rate of domestic credit would then rise in response to the need for enterprises to change the current situation and improve economic performance. This contributes to revitalizing the micro-economy and preventing two phenomena: Credit contraction and credit expansion, which are detrimental to the national economy.

The internal regulatory mechanism of price refers to setting planned and non-planned prices for products, and the former are often lower than the latter. In this way, the enterprises would be motivated in production and sales. They may seek methods to save raw materials and fuel, rationalize the use of manpower and production equipment, and try to raise their revenue by selling additional products after completing the tasks of the national plan. Setting a non-planned price can motivate enterprises to achieve the goal of improving efficiency. Furthermore, it is assumed that products produced by enterprises based on national planned tasks are sold at a planned price, which also helps the government control the macro- economy through the planned price. These two price systems not only reflect the characteristics of the planned economy, but also introduce the mechanism of market competition into a socialist economy. The non-planned price level is the result of both supply and demand forces in the market, and is determined through competition among enterprises. As to the ratio of planned and non-planned prices for each product, and the proportion of sales at planned or non-planned prices in total production and sales, these are determined by the importance and scarcity of each product in the national economy. Some products may have a larger share to be sold at a non-planned price, a smaller share to be sold at a planned price, or even a completely non-planned price, and vice versa.

The internal regulatory mechanism of taxation refers to the fact that enterprises should pay taxes in accordance with various relevant regulations set by the government, and only after that can they increase wages and bonuses for employees, and use the retained profits to expand production and improve employees' welfare. Under this circumstance, the improvement of enterprises' efficiency, the expansion of their production scale and the increase in their employees' income can be directly linked to the state's macroeconomic control. The regulation of taxation should encourage enterprises that only by improving efficiency can they meet requirements for expanding production scale and raising employees' income after paying taxes. This mechanism thus contributes to the realization of microeconomic goals. In addition, tax regulations also enable the government to raise revenues and adjust the expansion of investment and the growth of consumption on a national scale. A progressive tax system with appropriate tax rates would better help achieve the goal of managing the macro-economy. In this way, the internal regulatory effect of taxation would be manifested as follows: Higher efficiency of enterprises leads to more revenues for the government, which results in a stronger capacity of the management on the expansion of investment and the growth of consumption through the progressive tax system. Thus, the improvement of efficiency would be further motivated on a new basis.

The combination of credit, price, and taxation here refers to their coordination and complementarity to each other. These three regulatory measures can exert pressure and vitality on enterprises and make it possible for the government to manage the macro-economy. Among them, the remunerative use of funds and non-planned prices play a more prominent role in facilitating the realization of micro-efficiency goals, while the planned price and the regulation of progressive taxation function more in achieving macroeconomic goals.

Based on the above assumptions, within a socialist system, the combination of credit, price, and taxation can lead to the formation of the unified internal regulatory mechanism of the macro- and micro-economies.

Assuming that the enterprises are in a state of high production costs, weak competitiveness, poor economic performance, unprofitability, or even loss, the strong pressure would force them to take measures to upgrade technologies, reduce costs, improve economic performance, expand sales market, and finally turn losses into profits.

Assuming that the enterprises are already in a profitable state, they may not be complacent, but also face further challenges. The existence of non-planned prices and the role of taxation would make them recognize the following things. On the one hand, there is peer competition, and they may lose their original markets. On the other hand, the enterprises are expected to keep improving to a higher level. At the current level of efficiency, enterprises should make full use of all conditions (including retained profits) to pursue more profits.

Assuming that the efficiency of domestic enterprises is generally low, followed by tight fiscal revenues, the government would then ease credit to enterprises. As a result, they can make use of funds remuneratively to upgrade technologies and increase efficiency, based on which, the macroeconomic instability would also be eliminated.

Assuming that there is a general increase in domestic efficiency, and each enterprise can utilize its retained profits to expand production and increase employees' income after tax. Then on the one hand, the non-planned price would fall due to an increase in the supply of products. On the other hand, the progressive tax system would function. These are beneficial to maintaining macroeconomic stability. In addition, the growth rate of domestic credit in the national economy would decline due to increased enterprises' retained profits, which would also contribute to macroeconomic stability.

In short, the unified regulatory mechanism of the macro- and micro-economies can be formed in the socialist economy, and socialist public ownership prepares for it. However, the above assumptions are based on given preconditions, which omit some important issues, such as unbalanced regional development, production and marketing of agricultural products, self-employment, social financing of collective enterprises, and changes in the market with the promotion of new technologies and openness. In addition, this paper also does not mention the role of consumer behavior as a constraint on macro- and micro-economies. Therefore, it can only be deemed as a preliminary exploration, far from being a comprehensive and systematic study. Nevertheless, I hope that the academic community can discuss these issues and jointly explore and develop theories that can contribute to the socialist economic management.

—*Foreign Economic Administration*, issue No. 4, 1984.

Chapter 9
1985: Discussions on the Regulatory Effects of Financial Measures on China's Macro-Economy at the Current Stage

The main argument of this paper is that the interest rate has little effect on the regulatory process for China's macro-economy at the current stage. This is not only due to system features but also closely related to the characteristics of the interest rate's connection with investment, savings, and consumption under current conditions. This paper won't discuss the systemic reasons, but specifically analyze the above relations.

I

In the macroeconomic regulation theories proposed by some modern Keynesian representatives, it is assumed that investment has higher interest elasticity, while consumption (along with savings) lacks or only has low interest elasticity. These assumptions more or less conform to modern capitalist countries' conditions. Modern capitalist countries often use these assumptions as the starting point for formulating specific measures to regulate the economy through the adjustment of interest rates by central banks. However, in China's socialist economy, the situation is likely to be the opposite, that is, investment lacks or only has low interest elasticity, while consumption (along with savings) has higher interest elasticity. If this is the case, it is unlikely that banks could squeeze investment so as to reduce aggregate demand by increasing the interest rate on loans to productive factories; or if the government wants to influence the investment amount by adjusting the interest rate, it should increase or decrease the interest rate by a wider margin. Therefore, the change of interest rate is not commensurate with that of the investment. If consumption (along with savings) has higher interest elasticity, then banks can stimulate or reduce aggregate demand by raising or lowering the interest rate of savings deposits. Therefore, it's necessary to discuss the main reasons why China's investment lacks or only has low interest elasticity while consumption (along with savings) has higher interest elasticity.

Undoubtedly, one of the reasons why the investment lacks interest elasticity lies in the economic system. Given that enterprises are yet to become independent economic

Y. Li, *China's Economy Since 1978*, China Academic Library,
https://doi.org/10.1007/978-981-95-5733-2_9

entities, i.e., those socialist commodity producers and operators cannot manage independently and take full responsibilities for their own profits and losses, the adjustment of interest rates and the changes in interest costs of enterprises cannot become important factors in investment regulation. But what I want to explore is the reasons beyond the system. For example, if the enterprises owned by the whole people become independent commodity producers and operators after institutional reforms, will investment no longer be inelastic or will the interest elasticity of investment immediately become higher? It doesn't seem so. This is because, in an environment where the total amount of funds available for credit is limited while enterprises are almost universally in urgent need of increased investment to upgrade or acquire technology and equipment, the primary concern for enterprises is whether they can obtain bank loans. Then it comes to the consideration of how much interest would have to be paid, and whether the resulting interest costs would become an excessive burden for the enterprises, etc. If enterprises recognize that the increased costs because of higher interest rates might affect the sales of their products, they would rather take alternative approaches, such as accelerating the turnover of their funds, reducing the consumption of production resources, improving the quality of products, increasing the variety of commodities, etc. However, enterprises are unwilling to reduce investment. They do not want to give up credit opportunities. It is more obvious for independent units, such as collective enterprises, individual businesses, and rural specialized households, in their attitude toward bank loans and interest rates. Therefore, at the present stage in China, even if the State-Owned Enterprises (SOEs) have become independent commodity producers and operators by institutional reforms, their investment may still lack or only have low interest elasticity. It is still not time for a significant change in this elasticity. Of course, this is only a general observation. It is still possible for some SOEs to consider interest rates as the primary factor in their investment decisions, i.e., to place more emphasis on their interest costs.

Based on the above analysis, the following views can be put forward.

First, if enterprises urgently need to increase investment with the background of limited supply of investment funds, then it is more important for them to raise funds rather than to consider the cost. As a result, investment will lack or only have low interest elasticity.

Second, if enterprises have great potential in reducing production costs and improving efficiency, which can be realized with the increased investment, then their net return is guaranteed even with the high cost of obtaining funds. So, in this situation, the investment will also lack or only have low interest elasticity.

The above situations do exist in China at this stage, and won't disappear in the near future. Therefore, if we want to adjust the total amount of social investment by interest rate, the effect might not be as significant as initially expected. After the economic structural reform, the situation may be a little better, but it is not appropriate to hope more.

Does this mean that we don't have to pay attention to the effect of interest rates in regulating investment? Not so. It is necessary to implement differential interest rates for different types of industrial and commercial loans. Charging interest on overdue loans and imposing penalties on the misappropriation of bank loans will also play a role. But their main functions are to force enterprises to strengthen corporate accounting and improve efficiency, rather than regulating the total amount of social investment. In other words, the main role of interest rate adjustment for production units at the present stage of China is manifested in the microeconomic sphere. It affects the macro-economy indirectly through the improvement of efficiency of production units, but not in the regulation of the total amount of investment directly. In my view, this is a feature of the relationship between interest rate and investment in China, which cannot be ignored. The recognition of this feature has policy implications.

So, what methods should China's central bank mainly adopt to influence total investment? My argument is that, when investment lacks or only has low interest elasticity, the central bank should consider direct control over investment credit and its growth rate as the main financial measures for regulating the total amount of investment. In the next stage, with the development of the economy and the formation of the above conditions favorable to the role of interest rate in influencing the changes in total investment, that is, with the gradual increase of interest elasticity of investment, the central bank can attach importance to both direct control of investment credit and the adjustment of interest rate, making them effective measures for controlling total investment. After that, when the interest elasticity of investment becomes higher, we can use interest rate adjustment as the main measure to control aggregate investment. We should take the progressive stages into account when discussing the impact of the central bank on the aggregate investment and its measures. This is precisely from the perspective of China's actual economic situation.

It is important to clarify why it is a better alternative for the central bank to control the investment credit and its growth rate directly to affect the changes in total investment at this stage. This is because, in the situation that investment lacks or only has low interest elasticity, direct control of the investment credits' growth rate has its advantages compared with the interest rate adjustment method, in influencing total investment. In addition, its allocation among sectors, regions, and enterprises, and the direct regulation of the allocation ratio of investment credits and the proportion of their growth will also be better than a differential interest rate policy. Compared with the investment credit's growth rate, that of money supply might be a broader indicator of the national economy, which involves an analysis of financial flow. However, the investment credit's growth rate, involving an analysis of financial stocks, obviously has two advantages as follows.

First, the amount of investment credit and its growth are more clearly defined and easier to calculate, while the definitions of money supply and its growth are not very specific (in definition). For example, the different money aggregates under socialist conditions (M1, M2, M3 …) still need to be clarified; therefore, the calculation of money supply is also complicated. It's inappropriate to simply apply the explanation and calculation methods of M1, M2, M3 … given by Western economics.

Second, what is emphasized here is the aggregate investment channel for the adjustment of aggregate demand, so the control of investment credit's growth rate would be more effective than that of money supply's growth rate. Of course, it's not necessarily true in all cases. This could be explained when we analyze the adjustment channel of total households' disposable income in the following section.

II

Let's then discuss the relationship between interest rates and consumption at this stage in China.

The reason why consumption (along with savings) has a higher interest elasticity is related to the characteristics of consumption and savings at the current stage in China. We may analyze savings first. The share of savings intended for pension, livelihood security, and children's future education, is not sensitive to interest rate, because its purpose will not change immediately with the increase or decrease of interest rates. On the other hand, in the case that consumption habits have been formed, the consumption structure has been set, or the certain consumer durables markets are close to saturation, household cash will be deposited in the bank as the real balance after consumption. Therefore, this share would be quite stable, which is also inelastic or only has low interest elasticity. In addition, we should consider another situation. Under extreme conditions when people lose confidence in the economy or no longer have trust in the banks, the changes in the interest rate won't change their decision of keeping money out of banks. Although these are purely theoretical analyses, they are still useful for the understanding of the relationship among interest rates, savings, and consumption in contemporary China. At present, a part of the savings, whether from labor income, inherited income, or other income (interest, dividends, rental income, etc.), is indeed intended for retirement, life security, future education of children, etc. We should understand that the effect of interest rate changes on this part of the savings deposit adjustment won't be significant. But the main problem does not lie here. It lies in the intended use of the savings deposits beyond this part, and in the current consumption situation of the residents. As already pointed out above, money deposited as the real post-consumption balance may be unaffected by changes in interest rates or have only a low interest elasticity. How will savings deposits, which are not the real post-consumption balance but merely a temporary substitute for consumption, react to changes in interest rates? This part of savings deposits will obviously have a higher interest elasticity. This is especially true in China's current situation. With the growth of the economy and the rise in the average income of residents in recent years, and with the development of the commodity economy and the increase in economic openness, the consumption structure of residents is in a dynamic process, and the old consumption habits of residents are gradually giving way to new ones. However, the durable consumer goods that residents prefer and are willing to purchase are still in short supply, and these products are far from saturation. Therefore, a significant portion of money held as savings deposit is not the real balance after consumption, but a temporary substitute for consumption. For the households, such savings deposits are temporarily deferred consumption expenditure. Similarly, savings intended for pensions, living security, or children's education costs can be considered as deferred consumption, but they are quite long-term in the time horizon, while the temporary substitute for consumption will change immediately whenever the interest rate changes.

Temporarily deferred consumption can be converted into savings deposits, turned into current consumption, or kept as cash by residents. Which form they actually take depends on three factors.

The first factor is residents' confidence in the economy and the degree of trust in the banks that take savings deposits. The degree of confidence or trust will make residents decide whether to convert their cash in hand into deposits or into commodities, and whether to turn saving into commodities or cash. The confidence in the economy actually includes expectations about prices, the quantity of goods supplied in the market, individuals' permanent income, etc. The degree of trust in banks includes not only expectations about prices, but also expectations about bank savings and interest rate policies, etc. If people lack confidence or trust, then they are bound to reduce their savings or even cash in hand and increase their purchases of goods including temporarily unnecessary or undesirable goods).

The second factor is the growth rate of consumer-goods supply (especially durable goods, including commercial housing) that is popular in the market and commensurate with consumers' ability to pay. If the supply of these goods grows rapidly, residents will have to prepare larger amounts of cash for purchase; if the opposite happens, residents will tend to deposit their cash into banks, which means turning current consumption into temporarily deferred consumption. Therefore, as long as residents believe that the supply will continue to grow without a significant increase in prices, the conversion between cash holdings and savings will depend mainly on the supply growth.

The third factor is the interest rate of deposits. Whether the deposits interest rate can adjust social consumption is closely related to the two factors mentioned above. If residents lose confidence in the economy, lack trust in banks, or the supply of popular consumer goods is growing rapidly, deposits rate will tend to play a minor role in the transformation between cash holdings and saving deposits. Conversely, if residents have confidence in the economy and banks, and market supply is growing continuously but at a low rate, then residents will still convert their cash into deposits, so the interest rate on deposits can play a more significant role in this conversion. Moreover, under the current realities in China, where it costs for cash holders to save or depositors to withdrawal, the deposit rate must be maintained above a certain level. If it is lower than this level, it will have no effect in this regard.

From the above analysis, we can see that the adjustment of interest rates on savings can play a role in the regulation of total consumption in the society. This role can be further strengthened if a differential interest rate policy is implemented for saving deposits. Even if there is no such policy, as long as the amount of cash held by residents is large, higher interest rate on deposits can still induce residents to convert their cash into deposits, that is, to delay current consumption into temporarily deferred consumption. The main reason is that consumption (along with savings) has a high interest elasticity.

III

Further analysis of the relationship between interest rates and consumption is necessary. According to what has been discussed above, the rise or fall of the interest rates on savings can adjust social consumption expenditure in the current period. However, there is still an unanswered question: The regulation of expenditure through the adjustment of the interest rates on savings isn't equal to the regulation of total household disposable income. The excessive growth of the total disposable income would be a significant sign of macroeconomic incoherence. To change this situation, how significant an impact can adjusting the interest rate have?

The total disposable income of residents can be divided into three major components: consumption, savings, and cash holdings. The adjustment mentioned above, through the rise or fall of the interest rate on savings, refers to the regulation of the proportional relationship among the three components within the total disposable income of the residents (i.e., consumption, savings, and cash holdings). Although this adjustment is one aspect of macroeconomic regulation, it is not equal to the regulation of the sum of these three components (the total disposable income of the residents), which should be considered more important. The out-of-control of the consumption fund in the macro-economy usually first refers to the out-of-control of residents' total disposable income. If the latter is fixed, we will have to adjust the proportional relationship among its components. So, the question is: Can interest rates regulate the total disposable income of the residents? If so, to what extent could it work?

I argue that, at the current stage, interest rate adjustment can only affect the total disposable income of residents to some limited extend. We know that a part of the disposable income does come from the interest income from their savings. Interest rates on savings can increase or decrease the interest income of residents, and thus can affect their total disposable income. However, the proportion of interest income in the total disposable income of residents is very small. Another part of the disposable income comes from their business income, such as that of self-employed entrepreneurs and professionals. For some business operators who borrow from banks, interest rate adjustment can affect their business income and thus the total disposable income. However, the impact in this respect is also limited. As for wages and bonuses, pensions and other social welfare income, which account for a significant share of the disposable income, it is difficult to consider a direct or apparent connection with interest rate adjustment. Therefore, it is different to regulate by adjusting the interest rate.

Just as the regulation of total investment in society can be achieved through both fiscal and financial measures, so can the regulation of the total disposable income of residents be managed using fiscal and financial means. For financial measures, as mentioned earlier in the analysis of the regulation of aggregate investment, direct control of investment credit and its growth rate should be the main measure at this stage, and the adjustment of interest rates is secondary. Only with the gradual increase of the interest elasticity of investment, the adjustment of the interest rate could become more important. For the regulation of total disposable income, the effective financial instrument at this stage, besides the fiscal measure, is to control the growth rate of money supply. Although the latter can also affect the total amount of investment, what is worthy to note here is its impact on the total amount of disposable income of the residents.

The control of the growth rate of money supply should be based on the net growth rate of national products, which is a reliable material basis. In real life, however, the growth of these two is not always consistent. There is also a problem of time lag in the adjustment of money supply. All these need to be considered beforehand. The growth of money supply should not necessarily be determined according to a fixed ratio based on gross national products, but according to a ratio decided by different compositions of national income, the control of the growth rate of money supply is still well-founded and not arbitrary.

In order to prevent the growth of wages and bonuses from being excessive, the growth rate of money supply should be controlled from a macroeconomic perspective. This means that the growth of wages and bonuses must be conditional on, if not strictly limited to, the net growth of national products. If the growth of labor wages and bonuses exceeds this predetermined range, it means that the limits of the permissible growth of money supply are exceeded, thus a shortage of money supply in the national economy will occur. Even if a shortage of money supply in the national economy does not directly affect the decision to increase wages and bonuses in the production units, the tightening of the economy as a whole due to the restriction of the growth of money supply may prevent a sustained growth of consumer funds and continue to put pressure on the market. Oppositely, if the growth rate of money supply is not controlled in relation to the net growth of the national products, then once the growth of wages and bonuses exceeds the limit of the net growth of national product, the uncontrolled growth of the consumption fund will intensify, and the resulting demand expansion will for sure cause inflation. This is the advantage of controlling the growth rate of money supply.

The function of controlling the growth rate of money supply in the operation of national economy does not stop here. Since the control of the growth rate of money supply is based on the net growth rate of the national products, the shortage of money supply will be inevitable after the growth of wages and bonus income of employees exceeds the limits of the possible net growth of national product. The shortage of money supply in the national economy not only increases the difficulties of product realization, but also affects the amount of investment credit and its growth, which may prompt the production units to adjust by rearranging production, sales, and costing, at least to prevent the continuation of the situation in which the wages and bonuses of employees exceed the limits of the net growth of national products. In other words, as long as enterprises truly become independent socialist commodity producers or operators, and competition among enterprises truly puts pressure on them, every enterprise that contributes to an excessive growth in the wages and bonuses of its own employees will be relatively disadvantaged under conditions of insufficient money supply in the national economy. In an environment of increased demand and inflation, enterprises are not easily aware of this. If they can, they are likely to take advantage of the objective situation of these to overcome the difficulties such as higher costs caused by excessive growth of wage and bonus.

If the growth rate of money supply is determined in relation to the pace of national products, the excessive growth of wage and bonus might be more or less restrained by a shortage in money supply in the national economy, with other components of the total disposable income unchanged. After this excessive growth of income gradually disappears, it will be appropriate for the growth of money supply to be linked to the net growth of national product, provided that other conditions remain the same. However, changes in interest rates do not have this effect.

IV

Currently, the effective financial instruments in macroeconomic regulation in China can be summarized as follows.

First, given the low interest elasticity or inelasticity of investment, direct control of investment credit and its growth rate should be the main financial instrument for aggregate investment regulation.

Second, the consumer funds could be out of control if the growth of wage and bonus in disposable income exceeds the limits allowed by the net growth of national product. Therefore, the main solution that should be taken on the financial side is to tame the growth rate of money supply in relation to the net growth rate of national products.

Third, given the high elasticity of consumption (along with savings), the interest rate on savings can be adjusted to regulate the share of the various components of disposable income (consumption spending, savings deposit, and cash holdings). However, it should be noted that this only affects the proportion of consumption expenditure, savings deposit and cash holdings. It is not likely to directly influence the growth of total disposable income, and thus the growth of total consumption funds. This point again manifests the limitations of the role of interest rate in macroeconomic regulation.

In sum, my argument is that, for current macroeconomic regulation in China, the control of investment credit and that of money supply are more effective measures in financial regulation. And for the former, I emphasize the total amount of investment rather than the growth rate of investment.

—*Social Sciences in China*, issue No. 4, 1985

Chapter 10
1986: Reform of Ownership and Management of Shareholding Enterprises

I

The traditional socialist economic model does not recognize that a socialist economy includes a commodity economy and believes that enterprises in a socialist society have no independent economic interests and cannot be commercial producers or operators. In addition, it is considered that production and distribution should follow the government's mandatory plan. Precisely based on this argument, socialist ownership is characterized by pure public ownership, which only includes two forms: state ownership and collective ownership. The former is considered to be superior to the latter. As for the latter, the large-size collectives are considered to be superior to the smaller ones. It is generally believed that the higher the level of public ownership, the better. Therefore, according to these views, if there is a need to reform the ownership, it could only be a transition from a small-sized collective to a large-sized one, or from collective ownership to state ownership, i.e., to go for "large" or "public." Therefore, when we criticize the traditional socialist economic model, we must reject these views on ownership and its reform. The discussion below on ownership reform will be based on the notion that "socialist economy is commodity economy."

To be brief, the ownership reform includes four aspects.

First, pure public ownership does not conform to the requirements of developing a commodity economy in a socialist society. There should be diversified ownership, including public and non-public ownership.

Second, we should reform traditional state ownership to enhance productivity.

Third, we should also reform the traditional collective ownership to increase productivity.

Fourth, we can establish a new type of diverse ownership structure, representing a new economic system that accommodates state, collective, and private ownerships.

Based on these discussions, the ownership reform here neither transforms public ownership to private ownership nor abolishes state ownership all together. Instead, it refers to one that is compatible with the traditional socialist economic model as well as a commodity economy, i.e., to reform the traditional state ownership collective

Y. Li, *China's Economy Since 1978*, China Academic Library,
https://doi.org/10.1007/978-981-95-5733-2_10

ownership, and reform the ownership structure that is not suitable for the development of a socialist commodity economy.

In other words, the ownership reform precisely aims to adjust the ownership that does not fit the development of commodity economy, given the current situation and characteristics of social product development and socialist development. Moreover, such reform aims to adjust human relationships from the perspective of ownership relations and to mobilize the initiative and enthusiasm of all parties to realize rapid growth of the socialist economy.

As we know, the reform of the economic system can adapt to the socialist relations of production, meet the requirements of productivity, and provide possibilities and conditions for rationally organizing various production factors, to increase labor productivity and accelerate the development of a commodity economy. Therefore, only through ownership reform can we meet the requirements of overall economic system reform. This reform is essential to address key issues such as interest, responsibility, incentives, and motivation in the economy. Moreover, without ownership reform, other economic reforms could only have limited effect. All these problems manifest the significance of ownership reforms.

The ownership reform played a big role in accelerating the development of a socialist commodity economy and mobilizing the initiative and enthusiasm of all parties, which has been evident in the rural economic reforms over the past several years. The reason why the rural economic reform has achieved remarkable results so far lies not merely in the change of management form but the ownership reform. Implementing the rural household responsibility system has transformed the traditional public ownership that featured a three-tiered ownership based on production teams, and the integration of rural governments and rural communes. As a production unit with independent economic interests, a farmer contractor could separate an administrative organization from an economic organization to establish a new economic relationship of equality, mutual assistance, and mutual benefit. In addition, the extension of the land contracting period has led to farmer contractors' long-term and rational economic behaviors.

The rural reforms tore apart the unified management model in traditional collective ownership and implemented a decentralized management based on land nationalization and land contracts. As independent production units, farmer contractors possess autonomy, initiative, and resilience, which allows them to adapt to the unique characteristics of current rural production. Of course, the scope of public ownership includes land and water, underground mineral resources, farmland water facilities, and some agricultural machinery. Farmer contractors own another part of agricultural machinery. Besides, some capital goods, such as farm animals, tractors, and cars, can either be owned by the collective and used by individual contractors or owned by private individuals and used by the collective for a fee. Farmers own part of capital goods and adopt a new form of combined public and private ownership of capital goods, which is significant to bring great vitality to the rural economy.

The above analyses do not neglect the impact of rural reform in organizational forms. Undoubtedly, such changes occur in the countryside, i.e., the previous centralized form of labor with a uniform workforce was decentralized with households being the basic units. Moreover, this was also associated with various other organizational forms of production. However, the key to the development of rural commodity economy lies not merely in the reform of production organization, but more importantly, in establishing a new ownership structure that was adapted to the production promotion.

We also need to clarify another misunderstanding. It is common knowledge that the rural economic change lies in ownership, and such ownership reform is from public to private ownership. However, this is not the actual situation. The household responsibility system has not changed the public ownership of capital goods, such as land. Rural land is still a collective asset, and is managed by rural households based on contracts. In other words, the decentralization of land management does not mean the privatization of land. On the contrary, the socialization of essential capital goods is the basis for decentralized production and farmer contractors' management. It is a shift from traditional public ownership to a new type of public ownership, but not from public ownership to private ownership.

As to cities, how should we reform the traditional state ownership there? According to China's actual situation, the following measures could be considered.

Some SOEs (referring to large enterprises in the lifeline sectors of the national economy) can maintain the pattern of state ownership and state management. We should focus primarily on improving enterprise management and the system of economic responsibility.

Another part of the SOEs, namely small enterprises in various sectors, can be leased, contracted, auctioned, or transformed into cooperative economic institutions.

Some other SOEs, including large and medium-sized enterprises in general industries, can adopt a shareholding system that replaces traditional state ownership and form a model that combines government, enterprises, and workers to jointly run the enterprise. This approach does not change the nature of socialist public ownership but aims to establish a new type of state-owned shareholding enterprise.

By reforming traditional state ownership, China will develop a new socialist ownership system that better adapts to the development of the socialist market economy. It refers to a kind of ownership that can defines diversified ownership systems in the national economy and their reasonable proportions according to the actual development of productivity. Due to China's uneven productivity development and considerable differences among regions, sectors, and enterprises, the proportion of different ownerships should reflect the national conditions and the socialist commodity economy's development. Under China's current conditions of productivity, shareholding economy and cooperative economy that are widely in place as a result of the ownership reform belong to public ownership economy and are the main body of socialist commodity economy. Therefore, they are indispensable, and there is no need for transition between them. In the future, they can also evolve into a new economic union as a result of the development of a socialist commodity economy, or lead to new forms of public ownership. The previous path of ownership reform, which progressed from small collectives to large collectives and then to state ownership, is not only theoretically indefensible but also potentially harmful in practice. Hence, we should abandon it radically.

II

In a socialist society, the shareholding system for large and medium-sized enterprises in general industries is very fundamental in the overall design of ownership reform. First, we should emphasize that the shareholding system of enterprises in a socialist society is inseparable from the public ownership economy. Because the shareholding economy can have different forms and levels of socialist public ownership, we could combine different ownerships (including state, collective, and private ownership) to form economic units (shareholding enterprises) of varying structures, which do not contradict with public ownership. Moreover, the shareholding system of enterprises not only refers to the establishment of new shareholding enterprises but also involves the old SOEs, which is a primary way to undertake the ownership reform.

The shareholding economy is characterized by the separation of ownership and management, a feature that also exists under socialism. The shareholding economy reflects the objective existence of diversified ownership of capital goods. It was widely believed that the shareholding economy was a unique phenomenon to capitalism. It is OK to compare capitalist and the pre-capitalist economy because although shareholding enterprises had already existed in pre-capitalist society, it was only after the capitalist system was established that the shareholding economy developed dramatically. However, the shareholding economy is not equal to a capitalist economy. It is not an independent economic form; rather, its nature is determined by the nature of the shareholders. In a socialist society, government departments, SOEs, collective enterprises, and individual workers can all be shareholders. Enterprises formed through the pooling of capital from these shareholders differ in nature from those in a capitalist societies. In addition, the management of socialist enterprises must abide by the laws and be under the supervision of a socialist state's administrative departments. These fundamental differences highlight the unique characteristics of the socialist shareholding economy compared to its capitalist counterpart.

There are two important processes for an enterprise to become a shareholding one during ownership reform. The former is the demutualization of capital increment, i.e., the newly founded enterprise raises capital in shares, or the old enterprise issues shares when it scales up operation. The latter is the demutualization of capital stock, i.e., the approved value of the fixed assets of the old enterprise is converted into shares to become a shareholding enterprise.

It is relatively easier to establish a new enterprise by raising capital in shares. If the enterprise founders want to establish a new shareholding enterprise, they must follow specific approval procedures before issuing shares. The equity determines the ownership of this new enterprise. Under the condition of decentralized equity, whoever can hold a certain number of shares can be in control of the enterprise.

According to China's current situation, when the newly established enterprise issues shares, it may consider finding an investment bank or a trust investment company serving as an agency. The enterprise and the agency enter into a stock underwriting contract according to the share types, the enterprise conditions, and other circumstances. Then the enterprise pays commission for the issuance of shares. At the time of issuance, the par value is the price in the transaction of stocks. As for the future transfer of shares, business performance and market conditions will influence the rise and fall of their market value, and thus the price of the stock.

Meanwhile, at the current stage in China, dividends and bonuses on shares issued by newly established enterprises can generally follow these principles. A fixed dividend on shares is paid periodically as a cost item, and a certain percentage of the dividend is extracted from the after-tax profit and distributed according to investors' shares. Dividend per share fluctuates up and down with enterprises' retained profits. This practice can encourage investors to buy shares and facilitate enterprises' economic accounting. Of course, we accept the practice of some new shareholding enterprises to combine dividends and bonuses initially so that the interests of the enterprises and investors can be integrated into each other tightly. However, this should be limited to a few enterprises with more significant profit potential; otherwise, it is not suitable to attract investors to invest in shares at present.

The demutualization of capital increment also includes capital raised in shares by the old enterprise when it expands its operation. There are two parts in an enterprise's assets: the original assets and the new ones. The original assets are temporarily not part of the shareholding system, while shares capitalize the new assets. This measure is transitional and necessary for the SOEs at the current stage in China.

When a SOE initially issues share during the expansion of operation, it can follow the way that newly established enterprises take. However, the calculation and issuance of dividends and bonuses are rather complicated. Dividends are calculated on a fixed per-share basis and are part of the costs. However, dividends would not be appropriate if the original fixed assets of the enterprise and other conditions are not considered. Otherwise, the benefits of the state-owned economy would be damaged. Therefore, the proportion between the newly raised funds and the original funds should be justified, and then a portion of the retained profits can be set aside as a dividend fund for new shareholders after an expansion of operation.

Even if the proportion between the new shares and the original assets is the basis for allocating the dividend fund from the enterprise's after-tax profits and determining the dividend for the new shares, it may still be unreasonable to some extent because it is difficult to assess the contribution of the original assets and new shares to the enterprise's total profits. Regarding different production factors, in some cases, the original assets of the enterprise play a less significant role than their proportion of the total assets, but in other cases, the opposite may be true. Furthermore, let us consider non-monetary assets (such as reputation, trademark, geographical location, and connection with customers of the old enterprise, the social connection of the new shareholders, and the change in the enterprise's image in society after raising capital, etc.). Then, it becomes more difficult to assess the respective contributions of the original and new assets to the enterprise's total profits.

Therefore, another feasible approach is to pay dividends based on the newly raised capital rather than on a per-share basis when the old enterprise expands production. As a result, the dividend yield ratio can be slightly higher with a floating range. In terms of management decisions, when the old enterprise expands its production by raising capital in shares, it would not hold a shareholders' meeting (or a shareholders' representatives meeting) and elect the board of directors as a newly established shareholding enterprise would because the new capital only constitutes part of the total assets. However, there are more flexible approaches as follows. First, there is still the board of directors, in which the ratio between the original and new assets determines the composition of the board. The directors from the old enterprise will represent the original assets, and the directors elected by the new shareholders will represent the new share capital. Of course, such a board is not the ultimate one for a shareholding enterprise but a transitional institution. Second, there is no board of directors, with the organizational form and decision-making mechanisms in management remain unchanged. In addition, the meeting of new shareholders' representatives will consider opinions and suggestions on the enterprise management.

When the old enterprise expands its production, it can issue shares to its employees or the public. Issuing shares to the employees could better integrate their interests with those of the enterprise. However, if the enterprise is of a large scale, the total amount of funds that can be raised from the employees would be limited compared to the original assets, and these funds from the employees could only have some effect on enterprise development. Therefore, when an enterprise needs to increase its capital, it usually issues stocks to the society.

III

The demutualization of the old enterprise's capital stock is the most important and complicated process in implementing the shareholding system, which involves large and medium-sized SOEs. The original assets of the collective enterprises are relatively easy to be converted into shares. As for the small SOEs, leasing, contracting, or transforming to the cooperative economy is feasible in ownership reform without converting capital stock into shares.

What is the scope of the demutualization of the capital stock of the SOEs? This type of demutualization can be implemented except for some sectors and enterprises (such as railroads, large power stations, posts, telecommunications, etc.) that play a decisive role in the national economy and the people's livelihood. Consequently, reformed enterprises would have full management autonomy, take full responsibilities for their profits and losses, and distribute a specific part of the after-tax profits to their shareholders.

Various measures can be taken to implement the demutualization of capital stock according to different industries, regions, and scales of the SOEs. First, the total investment amount should include the original state investment in these enterprises over the years. Then the amount of the enterprises' retained profits in recent years is deemed their investment. These two parts are added together as a base figure, which form the respective proportions of state investment and the enterprises' investment in the total investment. For convenience, the calculation does not consider inflation and interest rates. Finally, with a certain proportion between these two figures, we can determine the valuation of the existing net assets of the enterprises.

The valuation of the existing net assets of an enterprise is quite complex. Nevertheless, since the ratio of state investment and enterprise investment from retained profits has been determined, any inaccuracy in the valuation would not be a major problem.

For example, assuming that the ratio of state investment to enterprise investment is nine to one, the equity is divided according to this ratio, regardless of the valuation of the enterprise's existing assets. However, there is a constraint on the valuation of the existing assets, which are the interests of shares. If there is undervaluation for the assets, then it would be a loss in the benefits of the original shareholders when issuing new shares in the future. If there is an overvaluation of the assets, it will be damaging to new issuance of shares, which impacts the future development of the enterprises. Moreover, the interests of the original shareholders will also be affected when enterprises are required to pay regulatory taxes on their net assets. Therefore, it tends to lead to a relatively moderate valuation of the net assets. In the process of ownership reform in China, we should gradually carry out the old enterprises' capital stock demutualization. It is essential to understand that shareholding enterprises represent a truly voluntary integration of interests. Apportionment of shares is incompatible with the nature of shareholding enterprises. Therefore, it is not advisable to be too hasty in the demutualization process, which needs gradual attempts and experiments. We can promote it with enough experience and demonstration effects of other enterprises.

It is conceivable that in the early stages of ownership reform in China, only a few enterprises may voluntarily pilot the shareholding system, and they are in different provinces and cities. Then more and more enterprises will learn from these experiences and follow, naturally accelerating the process. During this course, we should always follow the principle of voluntariness. Artificially creating a "demutualization campaign" can only have the opposite effect. There were many similar lessons in the past.

After demutualization, the state does not necessarily need to hold so many shares in each enterprise. It can determine the proportion of its shares in the total capital in accordance with different regions and industries and the different nature and scale of enterprises. Then the state can retain this proportion of shares and sell the excess shares in installments. The shares can be sold publicly to individuals or transferred to enterprises, which will pay cash or interests to the state to repay the debts in succession.

The funds received from selling out the enterprise shares may be used as a specific fund for the government's capital in a new shareholding enterprise, or as an investment for additional shares when the government deems it necessary to expand its share in the enterprise, or as funds for other governmental production and construction projects. However, the state should not use this fund as fiscal expenditure or cover the fiscal deficits for the current year.

We should point out that reducing the government share does not weaken public ownership. First, the government needs a certain number of shares to ensure a position in the enterprise, but it is not necessary to hold too many shares. Reducing government shares can still guarantee the government's largest shareholder status in the enterprise. Second, it is unnecessary for the government to be the most prominent shareholder or shareholders in each enterprise. It does not affect the public nature of the enterprise. If the government is not the largest shareholder in some enterprises, it will be the enterprise itself or others. Then, these enterprises remain public-owned ones. Third, by reducing its shares in some enterprises, the government can divert funds to more conducive fields for economic development.

IV

In implementing the enterprise shareholding system, *State-owned Assets Supervision and Administration Commission* should be established at all levels as soon as possible. Their task is to manage government shares. Since government shares are either those owned by central government or those by all levels of local governments, the Commissions should include the central, provincial, municipal, or county levels of organizations, which are not in a vertical leadership relationship with each other. For example, the Central Commission is the core, directly under the management of the State Council. Those at the provincial, municipal, and county levels are subject to the management of relevant local governments.

The Commissions manage government shares and dispatch government directors based on public equity interests. If there are shares of both the central government and the local governments (provincial, municipal, and county governments) in an enterprise after the demutualization, different levels of government will dispatch directors according to their respective equities. In this case, the directors from each Commission, i.e., the directors of the central and local governments (provincial, municipal, and county), have no leadership relationship. If the central government wishes to increase its shares, the Central Commission would need to invest in additional shares. Conversely, any funds received also go to the Commission. If the local governments determine to change their shares in the enterprise, then the expenditure and revenue could be treated similarly.

It is crucial to understand that the previous professional ministries, departments, and bureaus no longer manage the government shares. Due to corporatization, the government and enterprises become independent entities to each other. The professional ministries, departments, and bureaus are mainly responsible for formulating development plans and policies, coordinating relations among enterprises, and supervising the implementation of policies and regulations. They cannot intervene in the affairs of shareholding enterprises. On the other hand, the Commissions have the responsibility to manage their equity and dispatch government directors. Their role is to influence corporate decisions and activities, rather than to specifically manage the enterprises' affairs.

The Central Commission should not decentralize the central government's shares. In other words, the central government only holds shares in large enterprises that can significantly impact the national economy. Similarly, for provincial and municipal Commissions, the government shares are also concentrated in essential and large enterprises. In contrast, sub-provincial municipalities will likely hold more shares in large and medium-sized enterprises. As for the county Commissions, they can appropriately hold shares of enterprises in accordance with their original foundation and current financial conditions. Therefore, all of the above are commensurate with entirely playing the role of sub-provincial municipalities in the regional economy.

The Commissions at all levels manage government shares and receive relevant revenue (dividends and bonuses). The government can set a specific rate of income tax on share revenue, and the after-tax revenue from government shares remain in the enterprises as capital, which can be helpful for the development of government shares (investment in new shares), incentive compensation for government directors, daily expenses, and so on.

V

Shareholding enterprises should formulate more complete articles of association with the following principles. First, these principles include ones on independent accounting, self-financing, and external economic transactions according to contracts. Second, the factory directors (manager) under the board of directors' leadership need to be responsible for the enterprise, and the board of supervisors should supervise the enterprise. In terms of organizational structure, the highest authority of a shareholding enterprise is the general meeting of shareholders. It elects the directors and supervisors to form the board of directors and the board of supervisors. As the decision-maker for the enterprise's business policies and significant issues, the board of directors is responsible to all shareholders. As the supervisor of the enterprise's business policies and major issues, the board of supervisors is also accountable to all shareholders.

The actual percentage of shares held by shareholders determines their voting rights at shareholders' meetings, which in turn influences corporate governance and decision-making. Regular shareholders' meetings (or shareholders representatives' meetings) are to debrief, examine, and approve the work reports of the board of directors and the board of supervisors. Given that the equity division is clear, the state cannot interfere with the lawful activities of shareholders' meetings and the board of directors if the state does not hold any shares in the enterprise. However, if the state holds shares in an enterprise, it can influence the enterprise's decisions based on its equity stake, thereby ensuring alignment with broader economic policies and objectives.

The government's shareholdings demonstrate its participation in shareholding enterprises. However, government control does not necessarily mean holding more than fifty percent of the shares. In fact, due to equity decentralization, the government's share only needs to be one third or two fifth in general, or even lower. Moreover, even in shareholding enterprises, government ownership is not always necessary. As mentioned above, there are significant differences among sectors and enterprises. Government management will be necessary if some sectors or enterprises are very important in the national economy. While for sectors or enterprises that are relatively less important, the government may control shares or not. There is no fixed pattern here, i.e., there is no need to specify the percentage of shares that the government must hold.

If the government is controlling, it will have greater decision-making power in the board of directors. This power belongs to the government directors, who represent the interests of the state. Since the government controls a certain percentage of the enterprise's total shares, the interests of the state are in line with those of the enterprise. In this way, government directors also represent the interests of the enterprise at the same time.

Through the purchase and transfer of stocks, an enterprise can invest in equities in its enterprises or other enterprises with retained profits. Assuming that an enterprise has investments from the government, the enterprise itself, and other enterprises, all have reached a certain amount of capital. Therefore, all three parties can assign directors based on their equities. Furthermore, the enterprise's board of directors will at least have the directors from three parties, namely, government directors and enterprise directors (including those appointed by the enterprise and those dispatched by other enterprises). The board of directors' decision-making power is thus in proportion to the individual equity of these three parties and the number of directors.

Since shareholding enterprises in a socialist economy are a new type of public-owned enterprises, the directors of the enterprises that hold shares are also dispatched by the public economy and represent the latter's interests. In some enterprises, the government-controlled shares only account for a relatively small percentage of the total shares, and thus the government cannot hold the decision-making power of the board of directors. Alternatively, the government does not hold a controlling stake in other enterprises; nor does it appoint government officials as directors. However, since the enterprise directors (including those appointed by this enterprise and those dispatched by other enterprises who have certain shares in this enterprise) also represent the interests of the public economy, then the decision-making power of the board of directors is still in the public's hands.

The workers' congress has the right to elect the directors for their enterprise or other enterprises. These directors all represent the interests of their enterprise, regardless of where they are assigned.

As mentioned above, shareholding enterprises appoint directors according to equity. Government directors and enterprise directors (including those appointed by the enterprise and those dispatched by other enterprises) are all directly related to equity and are collectively called directors of equity interest. Employees of the enterprise can take shares, as can individuals in society. However, in the current situation in China, given the presence of the shareholding system in large and medium-sized enterprises, the shares owned by individual employees or individuals in society are insufficient to warrant equity directors representing individual investors.

Considering this circumstance, the board can add non-equity directors, who, although representing a relatively small percentage of the board, can effectively represent the interests of employees and individual shareholders in society, which helps the board to take a wide range of advice in decision-making. Non-equity directors generally include candidates from the following categories. The first is employee representatives from the labor union system. The second is social representatives sent by consumer groups, environmental protection groups, and social security groups. The third is expert representatives from academic groups related to the enterprise's production, operation, and technology. Assuming that the employees generally have shares and the total shares are large, the directors representing employees may also be equity directors rather than non-equity directors.

VI

The board of directors appoints the managers of a shareholding enterprise. Under the board's leadership, the managers are mainly in charge of the enterprise's daily management and production.

Under managers' leadership, the enterprise, as a whole, maintains a centralized and unified chain of command internally from top to bottom. The managers and other leaders in the enterprise have a leadership relationship with the latter appointed and dismissed by the former. According to the principle of hierarchical management, subordinates follow the command and are accountable to their superiors. Whose interests do the managers represent? This question needs analysis in terms of the nature of the shareholding enterprise.

The manager of a shareholding enterprise represents the interests of shareholders. Here we are talking about shareholding enterprises under a socialist public ownership. Therefore, in the enterprise with state shares, the manager represents the interests of shareholders and those of the state, the enterprise, and the employees. It means that the manager, as the head of a public-owned enterprise, must implement the state's policies, abide by the law, and safeguard the state's macro interests. In addition, the manager should also protect the interests of shareholders in the state-owned economy. The manager must adhere to the socialist direction of the enterprise, make the enterprise dynamic so that the interests of employees can be effectively protected in various systems, and grow together with those of the enterprise and the state.

What role does the Party organization play in an enterprise after the implementation of the manager responsibility system under a board of directors? Socialist enterprises must adhere to the leadership of the Party in order to ensure the socialist direction of the enterprise, but it does not mean that the Party organization can replace the board or the secretary of the Party committee can take over the duties of the manager. The Party's leadership of the enterprise is not limited to the leadership of the Party organization, but more importantly, it involves strategic guidance and the implementation of central government policies. The main task of the enterprise's Party organization should be the political and ideological work in the enterprise, and it plays a role in supervising the production and administration of the enterprise. If the Party organization finds that the enterprise has acted against the policy, it should criticize, supervise, and correct it. The enterprise's Party organization should actively support the Workers' Union in exercising its power of democratic management. It should also support the manager in exercising decision-making rights within the enterprise and guide staff representatives to adhere to the socialist direction. Additionally, it should care about the overall interests of the country and correctly balance the interests of the state, the enterprise, and the employees.

In the future, the income of the employees who hold shares in a shareholding enterprise should consist of wages, awards, and benefits derived from shares (dividends and bonuses). The interests of the employees are represented by the directors of the enterprise from the Workers' Union and by non-equity directors elected by the labor union system, who influence the decisions and supervise the board of directors. Although the number of shares owned by each employee is insignificant in the total number of shares, it allows the employees' interests to be more closely related to those of the enterprise. Of course, the employees in the shareholding enterprise cannot be incentivized because they are holders of few shares. It is a limitation of both shareholding and cooperative enterprises because each member's shares account for only a small part of the cooperative enterprise. More importantly, the shareholding system will put large and medium-sized enterprises on the big stage of market competition and self-sufficiency. Shareholding enterprises must create credibility for themselves, fight for survival, adjust their behaviors, and mobilize the employees from all sides. Survival of the fittest applies to business as well. The enterprises will be under the threat of merger or acquisition if they are not operating well. The merger of enterprises is just a reorganization of production factors, which is not negative for the socialist economy because both parties in a merger transaction are new public-owned enterprises.

In order to ensure that the board of directors decides the general policy for the enterprise and the manager exercises the right to direct production and operation, the directors cannot serve as the managers simultaneously and vice versa. The manager directs production and operation as an appointee of the board of directors.

All external directors (government directors, directors dispatched by other enterprises, directors serving as social representatives, and directors serving as expert representatives) are not "residents" in the enterprise. They come to the enterprise only when they attend the board of directors' meetings or when the board entrusts them for official duties. Their responsibilities are to make decisions on business policies and significant issues during the meetings and learn about the enterprise from various aspects to ensure that the decisions made by the board are in line with reality. They are not included in the establishment of the enterprise and do not receive remunerations from the enterprise.

Internal directors (directors of the enterprise and directors as employee representatives) are employees of the enterprise (except for the manager and main assistants). They do not receive extra remunerations on top of their salaries. Their duties are the same as those of external directors.

All directors may have some allowances during the board meetings. In addition, if the enterprise is profitable at the end of the year, each shareholding unit may take a certain amount of the share revenue as incentive compensation for equity directors after share-based distribution.

For example, the State-owned Assets Supervision and Administration Commission may use a portion of government share revenue to reward government directors. Likewise, the enterprise may use a portion of its share revenue as an incentive to reward its directors. Moreover, other enterprises similarly can draw a portion of their share revenue as rewards for the directors they dispatch. In addition, the enterprise only needs to pay incentive compensation to a small number of non-equity directors at a level approximately equal to that received by the enterprise's directors.

The Commissions appoint government directors. It may select government directors from the cadres, the professional ministries, departments, and bureaus to which the old enterprise belongs or appoint appropriate public officials from external departments as government directors. Since these public officials serve as directors who represent government equity, they are not obligated to report the enterprise's performances to their department while serving as directors.

Under the conditions of hierarchical control and a system involving parent enterprises, subsidiaries, and second-tier subsidiaries, directors generally do not serve concurrently with each other. If it is necessary to serve concurrently, one director could only serve two enterprises.

All directors have a term of office and are limited to one re-election only. The board of directors could vote by open ballot on significant issues such as corporate development strategies and production and management policies, ensuring transparency in each director's vote. It may also vote by secret ballot on issues related to personnel arrangements.

All of these provisions can prevent the bureaucratization of the board, i.e., prevent directors from being merely titular and irresponsible for the enterprise's future and from grabbing personal power or seeking gains for themselves in the name of the directors.

It is conceivable that through the management reforms mentioned above, shareholding enterprises will be more and more dynamic. As a result, these enterprises will also gradually become socialist shareholding enterprises with Chinese characteristics.

—*China's Economic System Reform*, issue No. 12, 1984 & issue No. 1–2, 1987

Chapter 11
1987: A Tentative Study of Socialist Ownership Structure

I

Ownership reform stems, in the final analysis, from the requirement for developing a commodity economy in this nation. It also arises from the unchangeable position of companies as commodity producers. Whatever its form, ownership structure should contribute to the promotion of production. A monomorphic ownership structure is detrimental to the growth of the commodity economy, to the motivation of firms as commodity producers, and to the effort to make the most of the superiority of socialism. All this gives rise to the mission of hammering out a post-reform ownership structure.

Will the post-reform ownership structure include public ownership? The answer is in the affirmative: Public ownership will be included. However, the reformed public ownership will no longer be the same as it is today. There will be differences between the two.

Under the influence of the traditional economic mode, people believed that the only workable way to run public companies was to put them directly into the hands of government institutions. In the reality of socialist economic development, however, the drawbacks of this practice were becoming pronounced. Companies became appendages of the government, which held all the power over human resources, finance and materials, and kept a tight rein on them. A company's performance thus had no direct bearing on its economic gains, nor was it held accountable for its own economic losses. Such was the inevitable outcome of the direct government intervention of business management, in which public ownership was synonymous with the direct involvement of government institutions in corporate activity. This is why the main thrust of ownership reform should be directed at public ownership.

We should know that in a public company, both capital goods and products belong to the public. The public attributes of such institutions represent the people's fundamental, overall, and long-term interests. Recognition of the public ownership of such companies means that they are engaged in production and management in the

Y. Li, *China's Economy Since 1978*, China Academic Library,
https://doi.org/10.1007/978-981-95-5733-2_11

common interest of the entire citizenry. The issue here is: How can public companies manifest their public nature in production and management, and go about their economic activity truly in the interests of all the people? It should be noted that public companies are not an empty concept but entities in the thick of economic activity. Their public nature is embodied in the fact that both their managers and workers are responsible for the interest of the whole population in such activity. However, this responsibility does not mean that public companies can only be run by the government. Moreover, it should be noted unequivocally that, supposing the public nature of these companies could be manifested only under government management, those companies that are malfunctioning and riddled with malpractice cannot honor their commitment—rather, they can only betray the basic interest of the entire state and citizenry. Thus, in transforming public firms, we must understand their public nature in a new light. That is to say, their public nature should be reflected in the results of their economic activity rather than in being state-managed. To reform public ownership is neither to negate this form of ownership nor to change the nature of public companies. To reform public ownership is precisely to emphasize these firms' public nature through effective and fruitful economic activity.

II

An essential task of the socialist ownership structure is to meet the requirement of the developing socialist commodity economy that forms of ownership should be diversified. Ownership diversity means that a socialist society may have more than one form of ownership, both public and non-public. Moreover, capital goods need not come solely under public ownership but under a mixture of state, collective, and private ownership. In this mixed-ownership system, public, collective, and private ownership are intertwined and infiltrate each other in a "you in me, me in you" situation. That is to say, the capital goods in a company may come under a mixture of ownership. The need for ownership diversity, including ownership mixtures, arises from the nature of labor in our nation at the present stage of development. Workers still care about their labor input—which differs in quality and quantity—and its economic returns out of the concern for their own interests. Furthermore, due to differences in working conditions, companies also vary in managerial performance and economic returns. Some may be more productive than others. The earnings from such extra output should be put at these firms' own disposal so as to spur their managers on to improve management. Diverse, mixed forms of ownership enable firms and workers to align themselves with production and management performance because this is where their own interests are at stake.

The existence of diverse and mixed forms of ownership is also relevant to our nation's present level of labor productivity. We know that a certain form of ownership of capital goods is determined by the development level of society's labor productivity. What forms of ownership should be adopted or allowed in a socialist commodity economy is circumscribed by the law governing labor productivity improvement. As things stand in our nation, productivity is relatively low and its development is uneven. This implies that, independent of man's will, diverse forms of ownership will be around for a long time to come while infiltrating or integrating each other inside a business.

In all, when designing a new national ownership structure, we should decide what kind of corporate ownership system is really needed. Such a decision cannot be detached from the requirements of the commodity economy and the restraints arising from the nature of labor and the level of productivity at the current stage of development. To advance the commodity economy, every company must organize its production and business as a producer, have the final say on production, supply, and marketing, and strive to survive and grow through competition. The issue here is not so much "decentralizing power to companies" as "returning power to companies." Companies should have the decision-making autonomy that they deserve as commodity producers. The same is true with public companies. After ownership restructuring is completed, the government should put capital goods at these companies' disposal and allow them to handle the fruits of their economic activity. As to what form of ownership a company should adopt, it should be decided according to the merits of individual cases.

III

It is both necessary and workable to establish and develop shareholding companies in a socialist society. Socialist construction cannot do without colossal sums of money. Dispersed capital should be pooled, and the financial potential of all sectors tapped. To allow companies to issue stock shares helps pool money and meet the funding needs of production expansion. Public ownership of capital goods is the foundation stone of the socialist economy. Shareholding companies should be built on the same foundation. If a collectively owned company sells shares to its workers, its collectiveness will remain intact because it is formed with money raised from and by its workers. The fact that the shareholding system can operate for collective companies should not be a cause of concern. The issue here, rather, is whether public firms should be allowed to issue stock shares, and whether doing so will change their public nature. We must see it in perspective. It is wrong to insist that only collective firms can issue shares and to forbid public companies from doing so. The adoption of the shareholding system by public companies should not be judged from a traditional viewpoint.

If a public firm becomes a shareholding company, its shareholders may fall into three categories judging from the current structure of capital goods ownership: central government agencies, local government agencies, and the company itself. If all its shareholders are in the public category, the company's public nature will not be affected. If the public firm raises funds from all walks of life, its new shareholders will roughly fall into three categories, excluding foreign investors: other local government agencies and other public firms, collective firms and workers. If all the new shares are sold to the first category of shareholders, the firm's public nature remains. If the new shares are also sold to the second and third categories of shareholders, the firm's public nature will acquire a collective element. No matter what happens, the enterprise remains publicly owned.

To determine who controls the use of capital goods, it is necessary to find out who are running the shareholding company, because the right to own capital goods and the right to use them are separated. The operation of such a company is controlled by its managers. Given that the shareholders of a socialist shareholding enterprise are workers or organizations that represent the workers' interests, then the managers elected by shareholders' representatives should also be regarded as the workers' representatives. In a shareholding company under public ownership, if the second and third categories of new shareholders have contributed more money than the old shareholders and the first category of new shareholders, the company is still in the hands of those representing public ownership. If the second and third categories of newcomers have bought more shares than the others but such shares are scattered rather than concentrated, the company is still under public ownership. In all cases, the company's public nature remains basically unchanged.

Even if a shareholding company is controlled by the second and third categories of new shareholders who have contributed more money while the shares held by the second category of new shareholders are not scattered, isn't the enterprise still a public socialist enterprise? Isn't the management of the company still in the hands of those representing workers' interests? Is there anything to be concerned about?

Now, a look at the superiority of the enterprise shareholding system. As the best option available for invigorating our companies, the shareholding system has at least three advantages.

Firstly, the shareholding system can fundamentally change the situation in which government administration is confounded with business management, and thereby turn companies into purely economic entities. Under this system, the general manager is held accountable to the Board of Directors, and the Board of Directors is responsible to shareholders, and thus the company can no longer be an appendage to a government department. The shareholding company makes its own decisions in compliance with government policy and economic legislation. In other words, the government can no longer interfere in the company's business, but can influence its economic activity by holding its stock shares. The economic relationship between enterprises and the government becomes one between paying and levying taxes, and the enterprises will have no problem in making their own business decisions.

Secondly, a shareholding economy works relatively more effectively in meeting the need to allocate production factors efficiently. The profit level of such a company is a signal that guides the shift of capital to high-profit fields, thereby rationally allocating capital and workforce, and raising capital utilization efficiency. The shareholding company can find a foothold in market competition and develop itself only if it can put its capital to best use, utilize it sensibly, and avoid decision-making errors and waste of money. Government departments may, through legislative and compensatory measures, attract share capital to the national economy's weak links and backward sectors in a well-planned fashion, and promote the rational allocation of productive resources from a macroeconomic perspective.

Thirdly, raising funds by selling shares helps pool idle money from nongovernmental sources to meet financing purposes. Under the prerequisite that funds are raised from nongovernmental sources and workers are allowed to buy shares individually, the surplus of personal consumption fund comes in the form of newly added share capital that cannot be withdrawn arbitrarily. For this reason, after the surplus fund for personal consumption is absorbed to buy company shares, it is unlikely for such money to be withdrawn from a shareholding company and spent in the consumer-goods market. Apart from allowing individuals to buy shares, the shareholding economy can also use part of the profit at a company's dispensation as a major fund-raising source. By pooling idle money from localities and companies and spending it on construction projects that have a close bearing on the immediate interest of these localities and companies, the shareholding economy can also speed up development, and effectively create jobs for society, rural areas in particular.

IV

The practice of companies buying each other's stocks gives rise to a corporate stock-holding system under socialism. As an inevitable result of economic development, this system, also known as "participatory system," originated in an economic organizational form that emerged from the monopolist stage of capitalism, when a big corporation infiltrated other companies by buying their majority shares and getting them under control. The control through stock-holding and penetration into multiple companies eventually brought about a corporate system in which the general company branched into one level of subsidiaries after another. Under capitalism, therefore, the corporate stock-holding system is a tool with which large capital controls and manipulates small capital.

As a form of business management in society's large-scale production, the stock-holding system can be made to work for the socialist shareholding economy on account of the dual attributes of business management: Its natural attribute is determined by society's large-scale production, and its social attribute is determined by the social system. In terms of society's large-scale production, socialism is identical to capitalism; in terms of social system, socialism is categorically different from capitalism. Thus, a socialist society can adopt the stock-holding system by retaining its natural attribute and altering its social attribute.

In a socialist economy, a competitive and highly efficient company may use its after-tax profit to buy another company's stock shares. When it has become the other company's majority shareholder and thus taken control of it, it will run or reshuffle that company according to its own will. Because of the role of equity and equity-related interests, the scramble between companies for majority holding rights is bound to intensify. When that happens, it is a boon, instead of a bane, for every shareholding company on the scene, because it gives them a good opportunity to improve their economic efficiency. When products become highly substitutable, when the prices of consumer goods show a large degree of elasticity, and when the profits from those products that are being upgraded become unstable, ill-managed businesses will be in danger of being "taken over" by others if they fail to cope with the situation. When such a business is taken over, the buying company may buy its stock in a large amount by taking advantage of its declining profit rate and its shareholders' hasty disposal of their shares. In this way the new CEO turns it into a subsidiary, and goes further to overhaul its production, management, and technology. This happens even in a monopolistic industry, where failing companies are in danger of a "takeover."

A small business that does not perform well may be taken over by its employees. These employees are scattered stockholders with a shared desire for their business to make a profit and grow, and their personal interests are tied to its gains and losses. When and where possible, they may pool their equities and act collectively to take over the business and reshuffle its management. When this happens, it is definitely conducive to the future success of the business.

V

A powerful large socialist enterprise under the shareholding system may organize trans-sectoral and trans-regional business, and, through multi-level share-controlling actions, establish multiple layers of subsidiaries to form a socialist corporate consortium or enterprise group. Several large socialist enterprises can foster different economic ties and combine themselves into a consortium or enterprise group. At the center of a socialist corporate consortium is the decision-making matrix—or holding—company. Under the parent company there are first- and second-layer subsidiaries which, rather than being mere branches or appendages, do business independently, make their own decisions, and bear the responsibility for their losses and gains. The matrix company exerts its influence through its control of stock shares. That is to say, the parent company carries out its business principle through its equity, thereby fending off the drawbacks of administrative intervention. This corporate management system, in which rights are both centralized and decentralized, helps set a company's business activity on a rational and efficient footing.

Some giant socialist enterprises may rise, and some others may fall in market competition. To put it another way, one giant socialist corporate consortium may grow in strength while another may fall into a decline. There is nothing odd in this phenomenon. A giant enterprise can stay competitive and at the top of the ranking chart only with sensible and effective development strategies, wise leadership and fine workforce quality. Companies or consortia are doomed, no matter how large they are, if they are no longer competitive, if their development stratagems are wrong, or their leaders and workforce are low in quality and proficiency. The shareholding system and the controlling shareholder system compel a company to readjust and save itself. Without such readjustment and self-rejuvenation, a waning company can only watch helplessly as its stock dwindles in value and its property rights become vulnerable to a takeover. Such a takeover, however, may give the company a new lease of life and return it to the ranks of competent competitors.

Under the stock-holding system, the relationship between banks and enterprises may change in one of two ways. First, specialized banks may convert themselves into commercial corporations under shareholding management, and allow businesses to purchase their stock shares to become their shareholders. Judging from the prospects of ownership reform in this country, it is not unlikely that businesses will hold stock shares of specialized banks and join their management. Second, demutualized banks may also participate in managing other businesses; and, as things stand at the present stage of development, the relationship between banks and businesses is more likely to change this way. We can assume that banks are not just loan providers. They are also stockholders of businesses and can run their own companies. After a bank gains control of a business' stock, the common interest resulting from this will bring the two sides closer. A bank that holds the stock of a large business can send representatives to join the latter in managing its funding, production, and business operation.

Banks can also convert themselves into socialist banking consortia through their involvement in business. Such a banking consortium may work alongside a socialist corporate consortium to do business that transcends departmental and regional boundaries. At the core of this banking consortium is a central bank that functions as the holding company. The first and second tiers of subsidiaries to such a central bank are not its branches or affiliates; rather, they are economic entities that make their own business decisions and are liable for their own gains and losses. The holding central bank needs to influence the production and management of these subsidiaries by way of its equity. Moreover, the bank's involvement in business also helps improve its credit management because if a business applying for a loan has no idea about the risks involved, the bank providing the loan is liable for such risks. If the bank cannot recoup the loan it has issued in due time, or if the project invested with the loan falls through, the bank will bear the financial loss thus incurred. In a shareholding company established with a bank's participation, the outcome of business failures is borne by all partners, a fact that can galvanize the bank into improving its management.

VI

Mixed-ownership companies, as the name suggests, are economic entities invested jointly by public, collective, and private partners. Firms of this type allow for joint business activity under different types of ownership even in the absence of the shareholding system. However, demutualization of firms inevitably produces a large number of companies under mixed ownership. Enterprises under a single type of ownership will go on as usual, but the emergence of many mixed-ownership economic entities will be an inevitable trend in a socialist economy.

How to define the nature of such mixed-ownership companies in a socialist society? If a public or collective enterprise has increased its capital by raising funds through stock share sales, and thus obtained a certain portion of share capital from a mixed-ownership firm and controlled its management, this company should be regarded as a public enterprise. If such a mixed-ownership firm is not deemed public, what else should it be? Let us look into this matter more closely. If, say, an enterprise has been set up with funds raised by selling stock shares to both companies and individuals, such a mixed economic structure should be regarded as an economic conglomerate under a new form of public ownership, which is different from traditional types of public or collective ownership.

We regard this type of economic conglomerates as public enterprises because they are similar to collectives whose partners buy stock shares with capital goods or cash. They represent a brand-new type of public ownership enterprise, which not only identifies workers as masters of capital goods but also energizes itself by becoming an independent commodity producer that makes its own business decisions and bears responsibility for its own gains and losses. Such economic conglomerates are most likely to become the mainstay in China's future corporate ownership structure.

The emergence of mixed-ownership companies meets the demand to boost productivity in socialist economic development, corresponds with the reality of the country, and promotes the commodity economy. Such firms can grow in both rural and urban areas. Flexible in business operation, they can adjust their corporate sizes according to circumstances to accommodate the idle and the jobless and better connect rural and urban areas. The presence of such mixed-ownership firms challenges old public enterprises to improve their management and start ownership reform at an early date.

VII

Like mixed-ownership companies, small cooperatives represent another nascent form of ownership. Convenient and flexible, these small cooperatives differ from mixed-ownership firms in two ways:

First, the shareholders of a mixed-ownership company are enterprises and individuals, and state-owned companies may buy their way into it. By contrast, small cooperatives are formed entirely by individual shareholders.

Second, mixed-ownership companies vary in size, whereas cooperatives are generally small, even though it is possible for them to grow bigger and evolve into mixed-ownership companies. Nevertheless, cooperatives tend to remain small, at least in the formative stage.

Small cooperatives, being organized by individuals who buy their way into them, identify their workers as masters of capital goods. That is why they are seen as a new form of socialist public ownership. Their members own the capital goods, join in collective labor and management, and distribute their after-tax profit among themselves. Such earnings may be used to cover daily expenses or be converted into new stock shares. Members of such a small collective get paid for their labor as employees while earning a certain percentage of the tax-paid profit as shareholders.

Small cooperatives are especially suitable for businesses in retailing, handicrafts, community services and farm produce processing. Their members are engaged in collective labor, make economic decisions and share gains and losses. Whenever funds need to be raised, they put their heads together to decide the ceiling and floor for the money to be paid by every member according to a ratio between labor and fund. This way of doing things is entirely agreeable to the nature of small cooperatives.

It does not matter whether or not a small collective company calls itself a "shareholding company." They represent the collective sector in the true sense of the term. They differ from shareholding companies precisely in that, instead of turning to society for financial help, they raise money exclusively among their members. They can become mixed-ownership firms if, someday, they start to raise money by issuing stock shares to the public.

To encourage individual workers to form their own small cooperatives by buying shares or converting their contribution of capital goods into shares, and to confirm the collective—i.e., public—nature of such cooperatives, is to respect both theory and practice. To accept the small cooperatives as public enterprises is for no other purpose than to recognize an established social fact that has to be accepted as such.

Small cooperative enterprises are often called "small collectives" or "collectives run by individuals." People may name such firms any way they want. However, when you choose to call them "small collectives," you are wrong if you think that small collectives are not as good as large collectives or that small collectives should be turned into large ones. When you choose to call them "collectives run by individuals," you are wrong if you believe that they are "informal collectives" or that they should be converted into public collectives. We must see cooperatives exactly as a form of collective economy as well as a form of socialist ownership that is highly flexible and adaptable to different levels of productivity and corporate scales. The cooperative economy does not necessarily need to develop itself into other forms of collective ownership, and there is absolutely no such inevitability either. The cooperative economy, other forms of collective economy, and the mixed-ownership economy each have their own strengths and applicable scopes, and should be allowed to exist side by side and develop together in the long run.

VIII

We may regard the adoption of the household responsibility system that links remuneration with output as the first step toward rural ownership reform. In this chapter, let me make some tentative study of the next stage of ownership reform in rural areas from the perspective of the national ownership structure.

Let us start with some background information about the next stage of rural ownership reform. We have to understand that, on the basis of initiating the household responsibility system, the rural economy is being restructured in transition to a large-scale commodity economy. Rural areas will adapt their production and processing undertakings to market demand, and provide large quantities of farm and sideline products. The advance of the commodity economy enables every farming household to enter the commodity market as both producers and business operators. Rural ownership reform should keep up with the burgeoning commodity economy.

According to the requirements of the commodity economy, the rural household responsibility system will be maintained for a long time in agriculture, forestry, fishery, and animal husbandry. However, rural production and businesses are bound to develop along specialized lines. That means some fields of production will operate independently and be specialized. On the basis of a division of labor and collaboration, farming households can freely collaborate with one another in different forms. The assets of such voluntary economic cooperation will be owned by the members, who will distribute the earnings among themselves according to work done. Part of such earnings, however, may also be distributed according to shares of capital or of capital goods. This will give rise to a large number of small cooperative farms (forest, fishing and animal farms included) similar to the small cooperatives described in the previous chapter. A creation of the broad masses of farmers in their production activity, these cooperative farms will play a major role in the future development of the rural economy. They represent a new type of collective economy, and a breakthrough from the old agricultural collective economy in which capital goods and labor are centralized. On the basis of household management, these farms can bring farmers' funds and production factors under cooperative management. The emergence of such farms is nothing short of another round of rural ownership reform that can fire the enthusiasm of the rural population for production and development.

In the course of developing a commodity economy, the issue of revamping the ownership of old rural enterprises will be put on the agenda. These rural enterprises, according to common sense, represent a form of cooperative economy run by farmers (and townspeople) with their own money, labor and technology. Although many of them are dependent on loans, they are supposed to repay such loans with nothing but their profits. However, in actual fact, these enterprises have changed their collective economic nature and evolved, to a certain extent, into local government-run businesses. Some local officials, holding the power to appoint or dismiss the managers of these businesses, are given to interfering in their business activity. Farmers can hardly benefit from such businesses because their profits are often manipulated by these officials. Such problems with the old rural enterprises can only be redressed through ownership restructuring—that is, to put an end to government interference in them and let farmers be their true masters.

I do not here deny the fact that many rural enterprises are doing perfectly well and that, in many places, local farmers are benefiting from them. Rural enterprise ownership reform is not directed merely at mismanaged enterprises. Of course, enterprises that do not perform well should be straightened out, and the best way to do so is to restructure their ownership. However, well-run rural firms need ownership restructuring as well. Now that rural firms are collective economic entities, they should not become appendages to grassroots governments and muddle along under government administration that is entangled in business management. We have got to restore them to their true beings as collective firms. If we limit ownership reform to poorly run enterprises, we must answer the question: If, someday, a local government comes into the hands of a new leader who has changed the old way of doing things, will well-run enterprises start going downhill? Is there any way to prevent this scenario from materializing? Clearly, all rural firms, large or small, good or bad, should have their ownership restructured. Only by starting from ownership reform can these companies' business problems be fundamentally addressed. As to which enterprises should be the first to engage in such a reform, this should be decided in light of actual production and management situations.

How, then, should rural enterprise ownership be reformed? The guideline is to liquidate the assets and check the accounts, and to distribute the stock to every member household. In this way, farmers can become shareholders who can impose their will on their companies through voting in elections and exercising their management rights. Major issues on income distribution will be settled by consensus. Apart from getting paid for work done, shareholders are also entitled to dividends allotted according to shares. Township governments are not allowed to run enterprises, and their power should be limited to guiding and helping farmers in business activity. New rural firms and cooperatives established by rural workers with their own money, and mixed-ownership firms are, without exception, new types of public enterprises. Farming households should also be allowed to run wholly owned enterprises that belong in the private sector.

Rural supply and marketing cooperatives should have their ownership revamped in two ways. First, large numbers of rural supply and marketing cooperatives at the grassroots level should be converted into independent cooperative firms. Only thus can they truly become supply and marketing cooperatives that make their own business decisions, function as independent accounting units, and take responsibility for their gains and losses. Their after-tax profit will be dispensed among members according to shares after a certain amount has been set aside as public accumulation fund and welfare fund. Second, supply and marketing cooperatives at and above the county level, including specialized companies and industrial and commercial businesses, should be transformed into mixed-ownership, shareholding companies that make their own business decisions as independent accounting units and are accountable for their own gains and losses. They will have the same organizational setup as other shareholding companies.

By putting the rural ownership system through the above-mentioned reform steps, the relationship between township governments and rural businesses will undergo another round of profound changes comparable to those taking place upon the adoption of the household responsibility system linking remuneration to output. The mode of rural economic activity born of the Movement of Agricultural Cooperation (1954–1956) and particularly of the Movement of the People's Communes that began in 1958, should be totally abolished. Grassroots governments will become pure administrative institutions detached from everyday production and business. Institutions that subject the broad masses of farmers to centralized administration, that allow a tiny number of township and town government officials to impose their will on people's economic activity, and that have hindered the growth of rural commodity economy and kept the monolithic rural economic structure unchanged for long years, will eventually be consigned to the dustpan of history.

The economic role of grassroots township governments will be limited to guiding the rural commodity economy. Land management is part of that role. The principle that land is public property shall never be changed, but it should not prevent land from being used with compensation. It is also the mission of grassroots governments to prevent arbitrary requisitioning of farmland and bar the selling and buying of land. These governments should also find ways and means to help local farmers beat poverty, organize them in running businesses, and help these businesses solve problems. They will also have a "matchmaking" role to play, that is, to bring enterprises together for technological and economic collaboration. "Serving the people" should be the motto for local governments in steering the advancement of the rural commodity economy. The purpose of their administration is specifically to serve farmers' business activities.

IX

Proprietorship over capital goods is at the core of ownership. However, to interpret ownership merely as proprietorship over capital goods is a narrow-minded understanding of the substance of ownership. In a broad sense, ownership also encompasses the organizational form of production and the administration and management of production, apart from proprietorship over capital goods. This being the case, the ownership reform discussed in the foregoing involves not only changes in ownership of capital goods before and after the reform, but also changes in the organizational form of administration over production. The new socialist ownership born of the reform effort refers precisely to proprietorship over capital goods, to new organizational forms of production, and to new administrative and managerial systems over production.

The reformed socialist ownership system will not be singular but plural. It will constitute multiple forms of ownership and can be understood from the following perspectives:

In terms of capital goods proprietorship, it will encompass diverse forms of non-public ownership in the service of the socialist economy, with socialist public ownership taking the lead. Under public ownership, there will be enterprises owned by all the people, enterprises under mixed ownership, and cooperatives. Under non-public ownership, there will be private firms, foreign-invested companies, and equity joint ventures with Chinese and foreign investment.

Concerning the organizational form of production and the administrative and managerial system over production, enterprises owned by all the people and enterprises under mixed ownership can be run on their own or rented or contracted out to cooperative enterprises or individuals. Likewise, cooperatives can also be run by themselves or rented or contracted out by individuals.

This socialist ownership system is born of the need of the burgeoning socialist commodity economy. In a shareholding company under public ownership, dividends are dispensed among shareholders according to their shares of capital (or money paid for stock shares), and shareholders are investors who contribute to production through the shares they have bought. The money they have spent on shares is similar in nature to bank savings, and therefore, they also deserve remuneration in the form of stock interest. The stock shares invested in the economy contribute a lot more to the growth and overall interest of the socialist economy than to the shareholder's individual interest. Leased and contracted management serves to adapt public enterprises to the demand for boosting productivity, allocating production factors effectively under the current circumstances, minimizing waste in human, material, and financial resources, and promoting production.

I deem it unnecessary to say anything here about the presence of private economy that does not belong in the public sector of the socialist ownership system. This is because the private sector exists to supplement the socialist economy and help create jobs and tax revenues. Self-employed workers rely on themselves in business activity. It is only normal for them to make more money through diligence and shrewd management. Given correct government policy, effective administration, and sensible education and guidance, the private sector can grow in the course of serving socialism.

To sum up, ownership reform will bring about a dual economic system. On the one hand, the national economy will contain hundreds of large enterprises that will grow into corporate consortia (enterprise groups), which, through multi-level investment, will bring about a network of second- and third-tier subsidiaries. These consortia will point out the way for the national drive for industrialization and technological progress. On the other hand, the national economy will have numerous small enterprises under cooperative, private, or mixed ownership, which will form a close-knit network of collaboration while competing with one another. Their shared mission will be to address the problems arising from the reallocation of surplus rural workforce, farm and sideline product production and processing, from the efforts to raise rural residents' income and build small towns, and from everyday services for urban and rural residents. These two groups of economic entities will each follow a different course of development and coexist in a mutually complementary relationship.

—*Hebei Academic Journal*, issue No. 1, 1987

Chapter 12
1988: The Overall Design of Economic Reform: Making Approach to Economic Reform Policy-Oriented

The primary approach to economic system reform only expresses one aspect on the direction of the reform, which has a strong theoretical nature and is largely normative, i.e., according to this primary approach, we can have a clear understanding of the direction and prospect of the reform, and understand what we should do and why we should do it. However, there is still a great distance between this and the actual economic reform. The approaches to economic reform must be changed into policies and be realized in practice. Policy design of economic reform is necessary because only a combination of normative and empirical research can better serve the reform. In other words, by making the approaches to economic reform policy-oriented, we can learn more about "how we should do it, how we can do it better, and how we can turn what is theoretical into what is practical."

There are more than one or two measures for economic reform but a series of policy measures that constitute a complete system. In this system, there are primary and secondary policies, key and non-key policies, and different policy measures must be coordinated. Moreover, the whole reform process is necessarily staged, and different stages have different central tasks. Thus, in terms of policy coordination, it is also necessary to adjust the relationship among policy measures according to the central task of each stage: the government could highlight certain policy measures at one stage, and emphasize other ones at another stage. All these are better in formulating the primary approach to the economic reform.

The policies to be carried out in the economic reform should not only be theoretically sound but also feasible, as impractical policies will inevitably be replaced by more viable alternatives. Therefore, the policy design may be much more difficult than formulating primary approaches to the reform. Therefore, when proposing the primary approaches to the economic reform, we mainly consider the issue from the perspective of economic theorists, but when designing a policy system for the economic reform, we should mainly think from the perspective of the economic practitioners.

Y. Li, *China's Economy Since 1978*, China Academic Library,
https://doi.org/10.1007/978-981-95-5733-2_12

This paper intends to elaborate on the policy design of the economic reform in general, which is divided into the following four parts: the guiding ideology of an overall design of economic policy; the division of the medium-term and short-term stages and the central tasks of each stage; the composition of the policy system; and the policy gradient and preferential differentiation.

12.1 The Guiding Ideology of the Overall Design of Economic Policy

The economic policy mentioned here refers to the policy that needs to be formulated and implemented in the economic reform. For the overall design, it is necessary to start from the current economic reality in China.

China is currently in a state of imperfect markets, unreasonable parity rate of commodities, and enterprises without independent status. Given this circumstance, we place our hopes on a decisive role for price reform, and think that as long as the price mechanism is rationalized, the economy could be on track of a virtuous cycle. Unfortunately, this kind of opinion is unrealistic. As a signal, price still has some crucial limitations. For example, whether can enterprises accurately receive the price signal or adjust their production and business activities according to the price signal? Under the condition that the market is imperfect and the enterprises have not yet become independent economic entities, the answer is uncertain. It can be said with certainty that even if the price mechanism is reformed and rationalized, due to a lack of vitality of enterprises, we will still fail to achieve the purpose of rational allocation of resources and promotion of economic development as initially required by economic reform.

Then, among the three issues of imperfect markets, unreasonable parity rate of commodities, and non-independent enterprises, what kind of economic policies should be adopted, and which issue should be addressed first to make the other two solved smoothly? According to current approach to the economic reform, it is necessary to highlight a series of the progress of the enterprise reform determines economic policies that promote the reform of the enterprise system, making these policies the priorities in the overall design of the policy system. The market will gradually improve as enterprises gain independent economic status, i.e., enterprises are truly independent producers of goods. In this process, the government should undertake corresponding price reform measures according to specific situations, then the issue of unreasonable parity rate of commodities will gradually disappear. Therefore, we should formulate and implement such reform policies, enabling full vitality to enterprises. Then the market would be formed with countless dynamic enterprises (including individual producers and farmers) and become perfect, and then it can gradually determine prices. Such economic policies are the ones that meet our national conditions at this stage.

In the policy design of economic reform, it should also be clear that if we confirm the core status of enterprise reform in the overall economic reform, the progress of enterprise reform determines the process of market perfection and price rationalization. If the policy to promote enterprise reform should take a major position in the policy system, then it is necessary to further clarify the core of enterprise reform. Which policies are key measures, and which are subordinate and supportive for promoting the enterprise reform? What is the theoretical basis to determine this primary-subordinate relationship?

We know that economic development and resource allocation are closely associated. There are two levels of resource allocation. One is the lower level, that is, how the production factors can be effectively utilized in a single production unit to achieve a reasonable allocation of resources; the other is the higher level, that is, how the production factors can be effectively utilized society-wide to achieve a reasonable allocation of resources. Accordingly, the enterprise reform also has a lower and a higher level. The lower level of the reform improves a single enterprise's operation mechanisms to utilize its resources effectively. The higher-level reform is to clarify the ownership relations and increase the social mobility of production factors, so that resources can be rearranged in the social scope and realize a reasonable distribution of resources among different units. Comparing these two levels, it is clear that the higher-level reform and resource allocation are much more important than the lower-level one.

Reform measures to solve the lower-level resource allocation problems mainly rely on the contract system. After the implementation of the contract system, enterprises can increase output, then increase income and state revenue, which is undoubtedly the advantage of the system. The contract system is a feasible approach, but it is not ideal; it has apparent issues. Generally speaking, the contract system may promote short-termism. This could cause tension in the distribution of income among enterprises, or the contractors may focus too much on their partial interests and ignore social interests. Indeed, these are the flaws of a contract system, but they can be overcome or alleviated by a continuous improvement of the system itself. In terms of policy design, we can develop several measures to overcome or alleviate the above issues of the contracting system, making it more perfect. However, it should not be overlooked that the contract system has a fatal flaw that cannot be eliminated through system improvements alone. The contract system cannot address higher-level resource allocation problems because it does not involve clarifying and adjusting ownership relations. In some ways, the contract system restricts a reasonable flow of production factors in the society, and it may fix what should not be fixed and strengthen what should not be strengthened. The higher-level enterprise reform is, in a certain sense, to precisely address this fatal problem of the contract system.

The higher-level enterprise reform measures are mainly to clarify ownership relations. Only when such relations are determined can enterprises become commodity producers with independent economic status that boasts a separation of government and enterprise, independent operation, self-finance, self-restraint, and self-growth. Enterprises that rely solely on a contract system cannot really form a market. Therefore, if undertaking the enterprise reform is the core and promoting the reform is the primary goal, clarifying ownership relations should be in the leading position in the policy design for the enterprise reform in order to smooth out the progress of the overall economic reform.

How to clarify ownership relations? For small SOEs, the transfer of ownership with compensation is a suitable method. By auctioning them through bidding, the enterprises could address issues in relation to the management and ownership relations, which can be seen as a dual benefit. If the small SOEs are originally unprofitable, this method could also be used to eliminate the burden and recoup government investment to develop the economy. Although the implementation of a rental system for small SOEs is not as straightforward and effective as that of paid transfer of ownership, it is still a feasible measure. As for large and medium-sized SOEs, it can be said that the shareholding system is by far the best way we know in terms of ownership relations. The shareholding system is the basis for the development of enterprise groups and is one of the effective ways for corporate mergers and acquisitions. The development of enterprise groups and the implementation of corporate mergers will lead to a rational flow of resources and promote optimal configuration of production factors. During the process of policy design, we must consider the timing and steps of introducing various measures conducive to the advancement of a joint-stock system, the establishment of enterprise groups, and the promotion of corporate mergers.

12.2 The Division of the Medium-Term and Short-Term Stages and the Central Tasks for Each Stage

From now on, there are about eight years until 1995. We may divide this period into three stages. The first stage is about three years (1988–1990), the second stage spans two years (1991–1992), and the third stage covers three years (1993–1995). According to the guiding framework that situates the deepening of the enterprise reform as the core and focuses on the clarification of ownership relations, the central tasks for these three stages can generally be considered as follows.

The first stage: developing and improving the contract system, implementing pilot projects of a shareholding system.

The second stage: clarifying ownership relations, distinguishing the state's role as an owner of capital from its role as an economic manager, and progressing from a contract to a shareholding system.

The third stage: finalizing the corporatization of enterprises, i.e., the promotion of a shareholding system, making stock companies the leading form of large and medium-sized enterprises.

All other economic reforms should be carried out around the enterprise reform, which is the central task. They are subordinated to and serve the enterprise reform. These three stages of economic reform, in general, should be arranged as follows.

12.2.1 The First Stage (1988–1990)

Since the central task is to develop and improve a contract system, measures such as maintaining basic price stability should be taken during the first stage. Hence, the enterprises that have implemented the contract system can devote themselves to improving efficiency and increasing production and income under the premise of stable prices, instead of distorting their behaviors due to the expected increase of price and costs. At the same time, if prices fluctuate significantly at this stage, households living burden will increase. They can hardly bear the pressure of inflation, then their enthusiasm for reform will undoubtedly be discouraged, and the social resistance against the reform will be on the rise, all of which will be highly unfavorable to the reform process in the future.

How to maintain overall price stability? From the perspective of fiscal reform, at this stage a contract system is feasible, although either the incremental or fixed contract system is not the ideal fiscal arrangement. As long as the fiscal revenue can be increased and fiscal expenditure can be controlled, the purpose will be served.

From the perspective of price reform, this is not the right time to overhaul the price system. This is because price reform, in its original sense, means liberalizing prices and letting the market set prices, with the government playing only an indirect role in regulation. Therefore, the adjustment of the price parity cannot be regarded as price reform in the original sense. Otherwise, we could say that we have been implementing the price reform for a long time, which is, of course, incorrect. At this stage, we should maintain a basic stability of prices. And it is necessary to restrain demand properly to achieve this goal. More importantly, we should try to increase supply. Seriously unreasonable prices are obstacles to an increase in supply. Therefore, while maintaining a basic stability of prices at the first stage, it is essential to make local adjustments against seriously unreasonable prices, such as adjusting the prices of certain agricultural products. Expectations for such local adjustments should not be high, because even if the adjustment can be done, price irrationality will still exist. After a local adjustment, it is inevitable that "price parity reversion" will occur (i.e., after some time, the price parity returns to the original irrational state). However, at least for a certain period of time, these adjustments can promote the growth of the supply of certain products.

At the first stage, financial subsidies for prices remain indispensable. Explicit subsidies are better than implicit ones, but explicit subsidies are still not ideal. However, as already explained in the section on the guiding approach to policy design for the reform, both fiscal and price reforms must be subordinated to and serve the enterprise reform in order for the latter to proceed smoothly. As long as the contract system advances smoothly and enterprise efficiency improves, the conditions for subsequent reforms will be ready in place.

12.2.2 The Second Stage (1991–1992)

At the second stage, the central task is to clarify ownership relations. The function of the state as an owner of capital should be distinguished from that as an economic manager. The management institutions for state assets should generally be established to ensure the effective management and maintenance of state-owned resources. In contrast, the roles of managing and regulating the economy, as well as adjusting the relationship between total social demand and total social supply, should be assigned to the comprehensive economic management departments. Moreover, it is necessary to upgrade the contract system to the shareholding system, making the latter as the normative form of enterprises with clear ownership structures. At this stage, therefore, in designing other economic policies associated with this central task, it is necessary to implement a large-scale adjustment to commodity price parity, including that of industrial and agricultural products, and the price ratio of raw materials to manufactured goods, in order to increase the vitality and resilience of the enterprises. These adjustments will not only reduce the resistance in the process of transformation from a distorted contract system to a normal shareholding system, help promote the transfer and merger of enterprises, and the development of enterprise groups, but also prepare the conditions for a thorough price reform in the future.

At this stage, the implementation of the financial lump-sum can improve the financial situation, which also increases financial support for the wide range of commodity price adjustments. The "explicit subsidy" policy cannot be abolished at this time, but it could be changed with the increase of enterprise income and the close link between the workers income and enterprise efficiency. The latter refers to the fact that workers income would include all or part of the price subsidy, and the government would no longer bear it. The implementation scope of the "explicit subsidy" can be limited to the staff of state departments. This is also necessary to prepare the conditions for the next stage of price reform.

It should be noted that at the second stage, the shock to the social economy would be relatively large. On the one hand, the widespread adjustment of commodity price parity requires substantial financial support as it involves significant changes to the existing pricing structure. On the other hand, with the transition of enterprises from a contract system to a shareholding system, and with the promotion of enterprise transfer and merger transactions based on clear ownerships, the way of absorbing labor by enterprises would be different compared with the past. There will be a group of redundant labor laid off from enterprises. For them, there would be problems of placement, retraining, and transferring jobs and workplaces. If these problems cannot be reasonably solved, social instability will surge. Therefore, it is also necessary for the financial sector to share the responsibility with the society. Even though the unemployment problem will be solved mainly by social coordination, it's still difficult to eliminate social instability if there is no specific financial capacity to assist the society.

It can be said that in the process of deepening the enterprise reform, after completing the transition from the contracting system, as long as the enterprises implement the shareholding system and have the autonomy to choose employees based on independent operation and self-financing, there will be unemployment problem in the society. This kind of unemployment belongs to frictional unemployment or structural unemployment. Financial support is not the fundamental way to solve this kind of problem, but its role in reducing the shock suffered by the social economy cannot be ignored.

12.2.3 The Third Stage (1993–1995)

At the third stage, the central task would be to corporatize the enterprises and make the stock company the predominant form for large and medium-sized enterprises. For this central task to be realized, it is necessary to adopt reform measures in both price and finance that are compatible with this central task.

After the second stage of a wide range adjustments of commodity price parity, with the further increase in the vitality of enterprises and resilience to the price reform, a thorough price reform can be introduced at this stage, which would involve liberalizing prices and allowing market to set prices, and the government only playing an indirect role in price regulation. Price liberalization here refers to the abolition of the dual-track system of prices to establish a single pricing regime in the market. However, it does not mean the government would give up its role as an economic manager. According to the relationship between government regulation and market regulation, it can be concluded that market regulation is the primary regulation, and government regulation is secondary. The secondary regulation is a higher-level regulation that makes up for the failures of market regulation. Wherever the market can do, there is no need for a government. The government intervenes only when the market cannot do. The purpose of price reform is to establish the principle of market pricing. Therefore, the government will act as the secondary regulator, and use indirect control measures to adjust prices.

Market pricing doesn't only refer to pricing in perfectly competitive markets. In an imperfect competitive market, market pricing refers to imperfectly competitive market pricing with the prices often higher than those in a perfectly competitive market. However, this is still normal for goods in imperfectly competitive markets. Moreover, the indirect regulatory role of the government is more significant in imperfectly competitive markets than in perfectly competitive markets.

Considering that the gap between supply and demand for some products remains large at the third stage, and it is not yet possible to realize a basic balance between supply and demand by increasing supply in a short period of time due to the resource constraints. Under this circumstance, the quota system can still be retained, i.e., the quota system and the market pricing can temporarily coexist, but this should be limited to a very small number of essential production materials that are related to the national economy and the people's livelihood. Although this is a peculiar situation, its existence does not hinder price liberalization of general significance at the third stage.

At this stage, a significant reform measure in fiscal reform would be a transition from a lump-sum system to a distributive system between central and local governments, in which direct taxes belong to the central government and indirect taxes mainly belong to the local governments. The progress of enterprise corporatization is conducive to the implementation of the tax distribution system. The operational result of the system will significantly incentivize the local governments while ensuring stable growth of revenue for the central government.

At the third stage, the reform of the wage system should be adapted to liberalized prices, i.e., price liberalization and wage reform must be synchronized and closely linked. Enterprise corporatization prepares good conditions for the reform of the enterprise wage system, i.e., enterprises would implement an efficiency-based wage system, and the state would no longer interfere with wage standard and total wage amount. Under the premise that the labor force can be fluid, wage would fluctuate with the efficiency of the enterprises. As for the national public servants, they are subject to the "high-salary-for-clean government" and the "pegging" policies. The former means that national public servants are paid relatively generously, but they are not allowed to have any illegal income. If these rules are violated, they will face severe punishment. The "pegging policy" means that the salaries of national public servants should be pegged to the cost-of-living index to ensure that their real income does not decline. In terms of the choice between "explicit peg" (which means that salaries fluctuate according to the index) and "implicit peg" (which means that the index is the basis for timely adjustments to the salary base), the experience of other countries around the world suggests that "implicit peg" is better than "explicit peg."

12.3 The Composition of the Policy System

During the economic reform, various economic policies should be coordinated with each other. At present, since the enterprise reform is on the center stage and the policy measures to promote high-level enterprise reform are the focus, all other related economic policies should be formulated around enterprise reform. This is how the policy systems for the above three stages are structured as follows.

12.3.1 The First Stage (1988–1990)

As mentioned above, at the first stage, the enterprise reform is based on the development and improvement of the contract system, and the public finance sector also implements the contract system. As for prices, the goal is to maintain overall stability and make local adjustments to the prices of certain products. Accordingly, the following policies can be adopted in four areas: finance, investment, foreign trade, and agriculture.

In terms of finance, the pace of reform should be accelerated, the corporatization of the banks should be gradually implemented, and the capital market should be developed and improved. Because of the increasingly important role of finance in the overall economy, financial reforms should be slightly faster, rather than slower, than that of enterprises. This can be demonstrated in the following situation. When enterprises are still at the stage of developing and perfecting the contract system, banks can move toward corporatization and separate the link with the government to a greater extent. When it is difficult to perfect the commodity market due to the severely distorted price parity, the capital market can be more open so that capital prices (interest rates) determined by the market can regulate the supply and demand of funds. This reflects the supportive role of financial reforms in enterprise reform.

In terms of investment, the fixed asset investment fund system should be improved, and investment should be arranged according to the funding situation. The funds provided by the state treasury should play as yeast, i.e., a part of government funds should be used as interest payment for social funds to attract more funds. As a high-level macroeconomic planning and coordinating agency, the State Development Planning Commission does not handle specific operations over investment projects. Instead, the projects are operated and managed by entrepreneurial investment companies. After the projects are completed, the investment companies can transfer them for benefits, lease them out, contract them out, or hold the controlling share and make them a subsidiary. Doing so is compatible with the progress of the enterprise contract system and can also promote the development of the capital market.

In terms of foreign trade, reform is also needed to implement a contract system, which is conducive to the principle of independent operation and the increase of foreign exchange earnings. Moreover, in the distribution of foreign exchange revenues, we should implement a regime in which "who earns foreign exchange, who retains and uses more foreign exchange." Therefore, increasing the proportion of the retained foreign exchange is an essential measure.

In terms of agriculture, the first stage of agricultural reform should increase the mobility of production factors. Although the household contract system has many advantages, it has some shortcomings. One of them is that it is not conducive to moderate scale management in agriculture, and thus to agricultural intensification and stable increase in the agricultural supply. While we are partially adjusting prices (including those for major agricultural products), financial organizations should be used to support agriculture, promote commercial transfer of land utilization, develop scale operation, and establish an agricultural price stabilization fund to maintain the stability of agricultural production. The implementation of agricultural reform will facilitate the task of maintaining overall price stability as required at the first stage to ensure the smooth implementation of enterprise reform.

12.3.2 The Second Stage (1991–1992)

At the second stage, enterprises will transition from the contract system to the shareholding system on the basis of clarifying ownership relations. Accordingly, prices will undergo extensive adjustments, with which reforms in finance, investment, foreign trade, and agriculture would need to be taken in conjunction, respectively.

In terms of finance, the infiltration between banks and industries should be accelerated at this stage. A vital step should be taken toward a shareholding system and a consortium system of financial institutions, while the scope of the capital market should be further expanded to allow active stock trading.

In terms of investment, with the transition of enterprises from a contract to a shareholding system and the interpenetration between banks and industrial sectors, investment banks should also implement capital financing for enterprises, and they will become the center of financial-industrial consortium.

In terms of foreign trade, we should allow more enterprises to directly participate in foreign trade activities, and foreign trade enterprises should be developed into cross-sectoral and multi-industrial shareholding enterprises.

In terms of agriculture, we should support socialist household farms based on commercial transfer of land-use, to fully play their roles in agricultural production, transportation, and marketing. Furthermore, through the support of financial institutions, household farms can voluntarily raise funds to organize transportation and marketing cooperatives to increase their income.

12.3.3 The Third Stage (1993–1995)

At the third stage, price liberalization is one of the most notable measures centered on corporatization. Therefore, reforms in finance, investment, foreign trade, and agriculture should be in accordance with this.

In terms of finance, interest rates should be liberalized, and the state plays an indirect role in regulating supply and demand in the capital market. The regulation of credit scale shall be mostly eliminated, i.e., it is used only on essential occasions.

In terms of investment, the subject of investment is changed to enterprises (including investment banks and investment companies), and investment is regulated by market mechanisms, which should be profit-oriented after price liberalization. On the one hand, the government plays an indirect role in adjusting investment regulated by the market. On the other hand, the government arranges non-active investment projects according to its financial resources.

In terms of foreign trade, the exchange rate should be liberalized, and the country should implement a managed floating exchange rate system through the reform. The balance of payments in foreign trade can be regulated by expanding exports, tariff rates, and import quota system.

In terms of agriculture, in addition to the price liberalization of agricultural products, the rural labor market, real estate market and capital market should also be liberalized successively. The cooperation of production, transportation, and marketing of household farms will be further developed in the open and liberalized market.

12.4 The Policy Gradient and Preferential Differentiation

The above economic reform policy designs are for the whole nation. However, considering the unevenness of socio-economic development in various regions and the fact that certain coastal regions were a step ahead in terms of opening-up and enjoyed benefits from preferential policies on varying degrees, it is important to note the following two points in the design of economic policies on a national scale.

First, how to avoid the impact of the coastal areas that are one step ahead of proximate areas in terms of prices and wages, i.e., to attract the inflow of goods and talents from proximate areas with higher prices and wages, thus hindering the latter's economic development? If we let this situation develop, even if we follow the three stages of reform measures designed above, the effectiveness of these policy measures will be significantly weakened in the relevant provinces, cities, and regions adjacent to the coastal areas.

Second, how to avoid an excessive widening of the income gap between wealthier regions (including coastal areas) and poorer regions (mainly the inland remote and mountainous areas)? Again, this would affect social stability.

In order to solve these two problems, or at least not to make them more acute, the concepts of policy gradient and preferential differentiation should be introduced in the overall design of economic reform policies and be reflected in specific measures.

The policy gradient corresponds to the gradient in national development and opening-up. The development gradient of the country is an objective existence. If we consider the relatively most developed regions and the least developed regions as two extremes, several intermediate regions should exist in between, such as more and less developed regions, etc. There are disparities in industrial structure, product structure, income level, and cultural and technical levels of workers in regions with different degrees of development. Moreover, the opening-up is almost on two levels at present, i.e., one is the coastal area and the other is the mainland. Degrees in policy preference are not on a scale of more to less, but of "existence" and "nonexistence." Therefore, the objective and actual gradients in development and opening-up are not in sync. To change this disproportionate situation, there should be a differentiation in policy, that is, a formation of a policy gradient. This should be reflected in the differences between the development policies and the opening-up policies, and makes several transitional stages between the two extremes, so that the gap between the two extremes can be reduced in several steps, without disruptive confrontations.

The preferential differentiation is precisely the reflection of the policy gradient. This is because policy differentiation is ultimately reflected in the varying degrees of policy preferences granted. For example, when the favorable policies given to some coastal regions are calculated as one hundred, then the policy gradient that corresponds to the gradient of opening-up manifested in the favorable policies given to several transitional stages should be roughly eighty, sixty, forty, and so on. At this stage, it is apparent that all regions of a country cannot enjoy the same kind of favorable policies (in fact, if all regions enjoy the same kind of policies, actual favorable degree would be equal to zero). Therefore, we must allow some regions to enjoy more favorable policies. Then with the extension from the coastal to the inland, it is possible to make a series of differences, from the most preferential to sub-preferential, and then to no preferential. This is beneficial to moderate the impact of the open, coastal areas on the inland's economy, and accelerate the development of the areas adjacent to the coast.

Considering from such a development strategy, the following arrangements can be made in the design of the policy system at different stages of economic reform.

First, in terms of prices, according to the policy gradient and the imperative of preferential differentiation, most of the product prices in coastal areas can be liberalized (that is, without first going through local price adjustment and extensive adjustment on commodity price parity). The prices of some products in adjacent areas can also be handled in accordance with this approach. This can avoid an unreasonable flow of certain commodities in these areas, which is instrumental in ensuring economic stability and development.

On a national scale, it should be noted that we should implement a principle that first vitalize the enterprises to be able to afford and digest the impact of price reforms, then liberalize prices generally, so that prices can be determined by the market. However, for coastal areas and adjacent regions, enterprise reform and price reform can be implemented simultaneously, mainly because these reforms have been implemented in the coastal areas (such as Guangdong Province), it is impossible to stop the pace of the reforms or reverse the situation there. In order to reduce the economic impact of the coastal areas on the adjacent regions, it is feasible for the latter to selectively relax price controls on some products, following the practice of coastal areas. Besides, even if the coastal areas and their adjacent regions are included in price liberalization, they still occupy only a tiny part of the national population and production, thus will not cause a significant nationwide economic shock, and will not hinder the central task of a nationwide enterprise reform.

Second, in terms of public finance, the coastal and adjacent areas can adopt practices different from those of the mainland provinces. For example, in the case of the fiscal contract system, in order to accelerate the development of these regions, a fixed contract system, or a more preferential incremental contract system can be adopted based on policy gradient and preferential differentiation, and the degree of preferences can be decreasing. Moreover, on a national scale, the third stage will be the period of shifting from the fiscal contract system to a central-local tax sharing system. However, in the coastal and the adjacent areas, the transition period to the new tax system can be appropriately shortened according to the actual situation of each region. This is in accordance with the economic reform and development in these regions.

Third, in terms of agriculture, the situation is different between coastal and their adjacent areas. It can even be said that the situation along the coastline in the coastal provinces is quite different from that in the rest of the provinces (especially the mountainous areas). Therefore, while agriculture is still at a nationwide stage where household farms are the primary production unit and production tends to be diversified to maintain stable income and output, the coastal provinces can take the lead in certain areas, such as specializing in relatively centralized land management intermediated by financial institutions, developing single-household farms, and raising funds to establish cooperative organizations in production, transportation, and marketing. Institutional innovations such as farming and harvesting companies, "land savings banks" or "land savings cooperatives" that are conducive to scaled management can be initiated in the coastline and then extended to the interior of coastal provinces and adjacent areas in the more developed counties to promote. The farming and harvesting companies here refer to enterprises that specialize in farming and harvesting for farmers who have contracted land. For some rural households, as their main labor force has been transferred to non-agricultural areas, the contracted land has a meager yield per unit area. However, they do not want to give up the land, so they can subcontract to these companies that specialize in agricultural production, or be charged for fees by the companies according to the quantity and quality of labor, or share profits based on the harvest. The contract period can be as short as one year, to as long as several years, sometimes even more than ten years. The role of "land savings banks" or "land savings cooperatives" are entities that accept contracted land and the right to use the land as deposits by farmers who can then earn a certain amount of interest. The land-use rights are centrally disposed of by the banks or the cooperatives for one year or longer, and the longer the period, the higher the interest rates. At maturity, farmers can take back the land-use right or deposit it again. Where a "land savings bank" or "land savings cooperative" cannot be established for various reasons, a "land savings fund association" can be in place by a joint venture of farmers or other investors in a given area, which is an entity that absorbs farmers' land savings.

This is also a suitable arrangement for the coastal and adjacent areas in agriculture reform. Later, when the conditions are mature, the vast areas of the interior provinces can follow this practice.

Fourth, in terms of foreign trade, the coastal areas and adjacent areas can also adopt the principle of policy gradient and preferential differentiation to facilitate opening-up, in areas such as direct foreign trade rights and foreign exchange retention by foreign trade enterprises. Differentiated measures can be adopted, or a step ahead from the mainland in the process of implementation.

What's more, in the reform of wages, social security and employment, considering the characteristics of coastal areas and adjacent areas, and the implementation status of other measures, specific policy differentiation can also be considered according to such principle. These measures will not hinder the progress of nationwide reforms but instead promote the economic development of coastal and the adjacent areas. This cannot be ignored in the overall design of the economic reform.

—*Finance & Trade Economics*, issue No. 7, 1988

Chapter 13
1989: The Markets for Agricultural Products and Macro-Regulation

To understand the characteristics of China's agriculture at present, we must first understand the current situation of the supply and demand of agricultural products and the market. Moreover, we must start by analyzing the current imbalances in China's economy. Only in this way can we identify the key of the current agricultural issues in China and find out the primary path to revitalize agriculture that suits the national conditions.

When we regard imperfect markets and limited resources as the essential characters of economic imbalance, agriculture has a more prominent nature, especially given the fixed quantity of land and the restrictions on resource transfer. Specifically, the current imbalances are primarily manifested in three key areas.

First, under the condition of limited supply, free transfer of resources is greatly restricted due to ill-defined property rights. It refers to the restriction on the free transfer of resources within agriculture, as well as that between agriculture and non-agriculture, and between rural and urban areas.

Second, primary agricultural supply is insufficient, and there is a gap between the supply and demand of these products. The main agricultural products markets are correspondingly restricted: There are both government quotas and market supplies. The coexistence of dual-track prices reflects the imperfect competitive nature in primary agricultural transactions.

Third, even in the transaction of agricultural markets without government quota restrictions, there are insufficient information, tangible or intangible restrictions on sales among regions, the immaturity of intermediaries and a lack of critical systems, resulting in high transaction costs and insufficient competition.

All the above show that to solve China's agricultural problems, we should take measures from the perspectives of price and market, and take other measures according to such imbalances. Moreover, as far as the actual situation is concerned, measures other than price and market should be the main ones, which relates to the role of macro-regulation in the supply and demand of agricultural products.

Y. Li, *China's Economy Since 1978*, China Academic Library,
https://doi.org/10.1007/978-981-95-5733-2_13

Alternative measures for governments to increase the supply of agricultural products beyond price and market include:

1. Establishing an Agricultural Products Stabilization Fund. The government determines the main types of agricultural products. It then sets support prices to guarantee output and ensure farmers' income. When the prices of these agricultural products fall below the support prices, the Fund will be used to purchase them at the support prices. This Fund is primarily supported by fiscal allocations. The income of the Fund, obtained from the acquisition and sales of agricultural products, can also be a supplementary source. The support prices should be announced in advance and remain stable over a certain period of time, stabilizing producers' expectations and avoiding the ups and downs of the outputs of major agricultural products. At present, the initial level of support prices could be slightly higher. In the future, if the supply of agricultural products has increased, and the gap between supply and demand has narrowed, it should be kept in operation for a long time. However, the support prices can be adjusted according to the situation of market supply and demand.
2. Developing farming agencies that help farmers cultivate and harvest to promote the relative concentration of land by the help of financial intermediaries. Given a lack of enthusiasm on the part of the agricultural producers for planting and management, and restricted flow of agriculture resources, there needs to be a stable labor force to be engaged in agricultural production to increase the supply. Therefore, the government should support the rapid establishment and development of farming agencies. Farming agencies would be established by social fund-raising. They sign sub-contracts with land contractors for helping in farming and harvest, charging fees based on their services or sharing the profits according to the actual harvests. The farming agencies often have relatively stable labor force and higher productivity. Therefore, they can significantly increase the outputs with the entire land area, improving the land's utilization rate.

Promoting a relative concentration of land through financial intermediaries means establishing financial institutions, such as land savings banks (or land savings credit cooperatives, farmers' land savings foundations), setting up land deposit businesses, and paying interests for land contractors. On the one hand, these institutions can loan the land deposited by land contractors to farming experts or agencies. On the other hand, they can sign contracts with the farming agencies and adopt a profit-sharing system or remunerating the agencies according to their services. These financial institutions can be formed through social fund-raising, and make profits through the interest margin of land deposits and loans and their land management income. Through these financial institutions, land concentration will be significantly accelerated. In addition, farming experts can operate at scale based on renting land and developing it into family ranchers.

3. Establishing exclusive acquisition systems and cooperative supply networks of agricultural materials. Given a shortage in agricultural materials and an imperfect market, the government quota system for essential agricultural materials (such

as chemical fertilizer, pesticide, agricultural machinery, fuel, and film) should be reinforced rather than abolished. The exclusive acquisition system is feasible at the present stage. The government's quota should be based on a targeted approach that takes account of average and historical proportions. When determining the quota target of the primary agricultural materials, the government should put grain in the first place. However, it is not enough to solely rely on the government's quota and exclusive acquisition system. Cooperative supply networks should be established as soon as possible to replace the current supply and marketing cooperatives. The latter tends to have a wide range of commodities and businesses, which makes it impossible to concentrate on the supply of the primary means of production under the government quota. In addition, supply and marketing cooperatives have been in place for a long time. Although they are called collective economic institutions, they are not close to agricultural producers. Therefore, producers should raise funds to reorganize the supply network to be specialized in managing the primary means of production. They are easy to be supervised and managed by agricultural producers, and better help them complete sales target.

In addition, given the imbalance in China's economy, the government should take appropriate measures to adjust demand for agricultural products, and focus should be placed outside price and market. This does not mean that measures such as the government's adjustment on agricultural prices do not help narrow the supply gap. They cannot be the main measures in effectively reducing the gap between agricultural supply and demand under non-equilibrium conditions. The government quota for certain essential agricultural products can still be used in cases of severe shortage, but this is not a primary measure to do so from the perspective of demand.

Among the measures to regulate demand beyond price and market, the following three options are mainly available for the government:

1. The demand for agricultural products from users of raw materials should be adjusted by measures such as differential tax rates, interest rates, and credit amount. There are three main types of consumers for agricultural products. One is enterprises and other production units that use agricultural products as raw materials. Where there is a severe shortage of agricultural products, users of the agricultural raw materials should be encouraged to reduce their demand and adjust the structure of their demand. Although the government can do this by adjusting the price or adopting a quota of raw materials, the adjustment of price could fluctuate widely, and the implementation of quotas is detrimental to the enthusiasm of enterprises and other production units that use these materials. Government quota also does not guarantee more efficiency in the production of raw materials. Therefore, one measure the government could adopt is to guide enterprises and other production and business units to adjust the structure of raw materials and reduce the use of agricultural products in shortage by implementing differentiated tax rates, interest rates, and credit amounts. Of course, the adjustment of a raw material structure needs additional investment. However, if the government can award actual benefits to the enterprises and other units that for adjusting their raw material structure, therefore using less raw materials, this

will increase their positive expectation and prospect. In this case, it will benefit the society and the users of raw materials.

2. To adjust the structure of export commodities and reduce export volume of agricultural products, measures can be taken by the government such as differential tax rates, interest rates, credit amount, and proportions of foreign exchange. Among the three categories of agricultural product consumers, the second category includes agricultural export enterprises. When a shortage of some agricultural products is severe, these exporters can reduce the export volume of these products. When necessary, the government can achieve this goal through more restrictive measures, such as export quotas, although this may dampen the enthusiasm of exporters. Therefore, better options would be differential tax rates, interest rates, credit amount, and foreign exchange retention ratio to motivate exporters to adjust the volume and structure of agriculture exports according to supply and demand. On the one hand, it is easier to stimulate the enthusiasm of enterprises engaged in export business; on the other hand, these measures are more flexible, enabling export enterprises more initiatives in adjusting the structure of export commodities.
3. To change the household's savings-consumption ratio in various ways. Changing household's consumption structure could lead to less consumption of agricultural products in short supply. Among the three categories of agricultural product consumers, the third category is residents. They directly or indirectly buy agricultural products. For example, food is mainly the agricultural product directly purchased by residents. In terms of cotton, hemp, cocoon, and wool, the primary market demand comes from enterprises, while clothing materials or clothing purchased by residents are produced by enterprises using these raw materials. Therefore, cotton, hemp, cocoon, wool, etc., can be regarded as the indirect purchase of agricultural products by residents (residents' purchase of processed food can also be regarded as residents' indirect purchase of agricultural products). For these direct and indirect purchases, in addition to price adjustment measures and quotas, the government can also try to change residents' savings-consumption ratio and consumption structure, including their food structure. In this regard, the government has a series of measures to choose from, such as (1) changing existing tax rates or interest rates to adjust the savings-consumption ratio; (2) levying a new tax to change the ratio and the structure of consumption (including the structure of food); (3) facilitating transactions in real estate or gold and silver jewelries to change the consumption structure of residents. Additionally, considering to sell assets of SOEs, to issue shares of SOEs and government bonds; (4) encouraging residents to increase service-consumption ratio (including tourism expenditure, and cultural and educational expenditure, etc.) to reduce their direct or indirect purchase of agricultural products; (5) reducing the total social demand when it is greater than the total supply through measures such as fiscal and credit policies, thus reducing the demand for agricultural products. These adjustment measures can also be combined with the adjustment of the agricultural prices or the quotas, and can also be used in conjunction with the adjustment of agricultural supply.

However, the above adjustments to the supply and demand of agricultural products are not easy. The difficulty lies in the fact that the adjustment measures here all target external prices and markets. They either change the supply and demand ratio of agricultural products through government's fiscal policy, credit policy, and the adjustment of the stock assets, or make certain institutional changes (such as the establishment of the land savings system, the implementation of the stock system, etc.) as the preconditions to change the supply and demand ratio of agricultural products. If the agricultural producers are not willing to expand the scale of production and operation, or if the consumers of agricultural products are not interested in changing the structure of raw materials and consumption, the costs of these changes are too high and their profits would be too low. Then no matter how the government adjusts the supply and demand, it is not easy to achieve the policy goal. In other words, if both the suppliers and consumers of agricultural products eye for short-term benefits, and they believe that the measures taken by the government to regulate the supply and demand are not clear with their short-term interests, they are not likely to arrange their future economic activities according to the government's predetermined regulatory goals. As for the long-term benefits, they may care little, so it is clear why government regulation is not entirely effective. It can be seen that the government's macro-control of the supply and demand of agricultural products is obviously in conflict with the short-term behavior of both sides.

An important question is: What kind of government regulatory measures can be used to make agricultural suppliers and consumers overcome the tendency of short-termism and promote their long-term interests? Fundamentally, the long-term behavior of a microeconomic unit (whether it is an enterprise or an individual) depends on three conditions. First, the microeconomic units should have a clear development goal when engaging in economic activities. Second, they should have internal motivation in pursuing these development goals. Third, while working toward the predetermined development goals through efforts, they should feel confident about achieving these goals through efforts. Therefore, when discussing the current situation and development trajectory of China's agriculture, let us first analyze the actual situation of agricultural product suppliers in combination with these three conditions for the long-term behavior of microeconomic units.

The first is about the development goals of economic activities. Determining the development goals for agricultural suppliers is crucial. Providing agricultural products by agricultural producers can only be seen as a necessary means to achieve their own development goals. It cannot be simply understood that the development goals of agricultural producers are to farm the land, raise poultry and livestock, and provide agricultural products to the market. If they see that providing agricultural products is a contribution to society, they will set a goal to make more contributions. If they believe that providing more agricultural products can increase their income, improve their living conditions, and make themselves rich, they take material interests as their development goals. If social responsibilities and material benefits are combined, the resulting development goals will be more substantial. In any case, as long as there is a development goal, agricultural producers will know the direction they should work toward. However, at this stage, such a goal has become ambiguous.

As a development goal, social responsibility is considered too vague, and material interests are considered unrealistic because the material benefits of many economic activities other than the agricultural products' supply are likely to outweigh the material benefits of providing agricultural products in reality significantly. As a result, for many agricultural producers, development goals are becoming increasingly murky.

The second is about the motivation to achieve predetermined goals. Without development goals, there would be no motivation. Under the premise that the development goals of agricultural producers are becoming more and more uncertain, their motivation to provide agricultural products (especially the additional investment to increase the supply) is insufficient. Of course, this does not mean that agricultural producers have no incentive to engage in any economic activities. However, if they are not interested in increasing the supply, they lack the motivation to do so. Although their pursuit of immediate benefits can also be regarded as the "goal" they would like to achieve, this is not the same as the development goals in economic activity. Due to this lack of motivation, agricultural producers cannot align their economic activities to the government's wishes, even if the latter takes fiscal, credit, or other regulatory measures.

The third is about confidence in achieving development goals through efforts. This problem is similar to the issue of motivation mentioned above. If the development goals are not clear and motivation is insufficient, how can one have confidence in achieving the development goals? It is not difficult to explain the short-term behavior of agricultural producers. It is worth noting that even if some of them have their own development goals and are ready to achieve them in increasing the supply of agricultural products, can they succeed by their efforts? Most likely, the confidence would be lacking. In the case of an imperfect market and shortage of resources, agricultural producers may not be able to make their efforts to achieve corresponding results. In this way, as their confidence weakens, their efforts to increase the supply of agricultural products will also weaken. Then it is difficult for the government to realize its target of promoting agricultural supply through various regulatory measures.

The above discussions are all analyzed from the perspective of short-term behaviors of agricultural producers. Next, let us discuss it from the perspective of the consumers of agricultural products. The latter could be classified into two categories: enterprises and residents. Under poor market conditions, lack of profits, and budget constraints, enterprises cannot have their own development goals, as well as the motivation and confidence to achieve them. Therefore, it would be difficult for enterprises to reduce the purchase of agricultural raw materials by adjusting the structure and cutting the costs. Therefore, the short-term behavior of the enterprise determines its short-term behavior as a consumer of agricultural products. On the other hand, when residents are the consumers of agricultural products, they have significant limitations in changing their consumption structure, especially in changing the food structure when the general income level is still low. Besides, due to the imperfections of the market and the shortage of resources, residents' expectations are volatile, therefore they may not change their direct or indirect purchases of agricultural products in the manner predetermined by the government's regulatory measures. In other words, the disorder in residents' expectations determines their short-term behavior as consumers of agricultural products.

The above can be understood as the incompatibility of the relationship between supply and demand of agricultural products and government regulation in China. Therefore, it is urgent to further reform the agricultural system.

Where to start for the further reform of the agricultural system? It is not only an urgent issue to be addressed, but also a complex issue in theoretical research. From the above analysis, we can see clearly that the key is to address the short-term behavior of both supply and demand sides of agricultural products. Although the short-term behavior of the consumers is closely related to an ease of the gap between supply and demand of agricultural products, it is not the main problem in the agricultural system. Further reform of the agricultural system should be mainly to improve the short-term behavior of agricultural suppliers, that is, how to make the behavior of agricultural suppliers (agricultural producers) long-term-oriented through further reform of the agricultural system. According to the previous discussion, to overcome the short-term behavior and increase the supply of agricultural products, they must have a clear set of development goals, the essential motivation, and the confidence to achieve the predetermined goals through their efforts. It seems that this should be the starting point for the further reform of the agricultural system.

For most agricultural producers, the issue of land ownership is directly linked to the goal, motivation, and confidence. Suppose the rural land reform suitable for the primary stage of socialism can be formulated according to China's actual situation and the ownership expectations of most agricultural producers, it will be most beneficial to reverse the weak enthusiasm of agricultural producers and turn their behavior into a long-term one. Then, how should the land system be reformed? Can private ownership of land be established? In my opinion, based on the public ownership of land that has been implemented for many years, it would do more harm than good to establish private ownership of land again. On the positive side, private ownership of land may enable agricultural producers to increase their willingness of investment on land, taking care of their property and performance, cherishing the land and expanding production. However, the negative side may be more significant, because the land has been publicly owned for many years, and the concept of public ownership has been rooted in all social sectors. If public ownership is abolished, the ensuing social turmoil may bring very negative consequences. In addition, private ownership of land would inevitably involve the issue that the private land owners can sell and transfer the ownership according to their own will. Under current circumstances, it is likely to destroy agricultural productivity and increase social conflicts. Therefore, weighing the pros and cons, I disagree with land privatization as the key to further reform of the agricultural system.

In this way, we must discuss how to overcome the short-term behavior of agricultural producers operating under public ownership of land. First, what kind of public ownership should we adhere to? Is it like what has been in practice so far? No. The practice so far is a kind of public ownership with ambiguous concepts, unclear boundaries, and underutilized advantages. It can be called the traditional public ownership of land. The task at hand is to transform this traditional public ownership of land. The specific design is as follows:

1. Implementing land nationalization. All land within the territory of the People's Republic of China belongs to the state. The State Land Commission would be established under the Standing Committee of the National People's Congress. Its role would be to oversee and manage state-owned land on behalf of the people. Land, the resources belonging to people, is not allowed to be encroached upon.
2. Implementing individual land possession system under nationalization of land. "All the lands belong to the state," but every piece of farmland for agricultural production has a specific occupant, i.e., the microeconomic units (farmers or agricultural enterprise organizations) who are contractors of land and engaged in agricultural production. The meaning of an individual land possession system based on land nationalization is a system that ensures the state has the absolute ownership of agricultural land. Although the microeconomic unit that owns a piece of agricultural land can farm, transfer, rent, and pass it on to their successor as a property, the absolute ownership of the land belongs to the state. Therefore, the microeconomic units have no right to decide on their own to use agricultural land for non-agricultural purpose, and to transfer or lease the land to non-agricultural users and foreigners. In addition, when they transfer their land to other agricultural land users, they have to go through transfer procedures and pay specific fees (land transfer fees, etc.) in the land management institutions under the State Land Commission, which is the representative of the state as the land owner (ultimate owner).

With the state's ownership of land established, the property rights are clearly defined at the level of absolute ownership. As individual possession of farmland is recognized, all microeconomic units have the right to use and inherit their land as long as they do not infringe on the absolute ownership of the state, and their willingness to take care of the land will be greatly increased. However, a question may arise. Is it a contradiction if a piece of land is owned by the state and possessed by the individual farmers simultaneously? This problem can be solved. State ownership refers to the ultimate ownership, which is in line with the nature of public ownership of land. Individual possession refers to the possession of land by individuals without violating or infringing upon the ultimate ownership of land by the state. There is only one ultimate owner land, which is the state. Suppose an individual sells a piece of land to another person, the absolute ownership will remain unchanged, which shows that the confirmation of the absolute ownership is helpful to determine the nature of land ownership. Therefore, the coexistence of the state's absolute ownership and individual possession is conducive to the improvement of land-use efficiency and the long-term behavior of agricultural producers.

Another related problem is that, after the nationalization of land and the individual possession of land are confirmed, will it be regarded as deprivation of the collective ownership? It might. So, this needs to be considered before further reform of the agricultural system. This problem is, however, solvable. We should know that the collective indeed represents the agricultural producers and is composed of households. What should be implemented is the state ownership of land, and the individual possession of the land. The two coexist, and the former is a prerequisite for existence of the latter. Meanwhile, the latter is what the collective economy hope to achieve. Compared with the simple nationalization of land, this scheme is more realistic. Farmers would think, "the collective ownership of land in the past was unrealistic, and now the individual land possession is more practical." In addition, although the collective ownership of the land has been replaced by the state ownership and individual possession of the land, when it comes to the disposal of construction projects previously invested by collectives, both the state and the individual should compensate the collective, which can significantly reduce the resistance of the collective.

Assuming that the agricultural system is reconfigured according to the above strategy, the state, as the ultimate land owner, will collect the appropriate rent from the individual as the owner of the land. At the same time, the state, as the manager, will also collect taxes from agricultural producers. Theoretically, the natures of rent and tax differ, but they can be integrated from the authentic way of collection. In addition, based on individual land possession, it is also feasible for individual agricultural producers to voluntarily form cooperative economic organizations. After the land possessed by individuals becomes shared properties, the individual and state ownership of the land will remain unchanged. However, if individuals form cooperative economic organizations by raising funds, the newly established cooperative institutions can either rent or purchase land from individuals, making it a shared property of the cooperatives. Even so, the land is ultimately owned by the state and the cooperative, the latter still having to pay taxes and rents to the state.

In short, to promote the long-term behavior of agricultural producers, further reform of the agricultural system (mainly reform of the land system) has become more and more urgent. There are also several alternative ideas on land reforms, such as "land privatization," "collective ownership of land, individual contract, and transferable land-use right," "collective ownership of land, individual long-term or even permanent tenancy," simple "nationalization of land," and so on. The assumption of "individual possession based on state ownership" is only one option. It cannot be denied that this option is imperfect, but is more feasible.

—*Agricultural Economy*, issue No. 2, 1989.

Chapter 14
1990: Discussions on Social Mobility

I have always been deeply interested in ethical issues in economics. Not long ago, when Xu Chongzheng sent a proof copy of his book, *Comprehensive Human Development and Social Economy: An Introduction to Ethics*, and asked me to write a preface for the book, I agreed. But what to write about? On a second thought, I would like to address the issues of the relationship between social mobility and comprehensive human development, and the ethical judgment on social mobility. We often encounter these two issues but seldom talk about them in our lives.

Social mobility refers to people changing their places of accommodation, occupation, social class, etc. It usually includes two kinds of mobility. One is horizontal, which means that people change their residence or occupation without changing their social classes. The other is vertical, which refers to a change in people's social classes. In a hierarchical society, such as the feudal and the capitalist societies, the movement of people from a lower to a higher social class, or from a higher to a lower one, are regarded as upward social mobility or downward social mobility respectively. Assuming there is no longer a hierarchical distinction in society but an objective hierarchy of positions in government agencies or business organizations, then the movement of people from a lower to a higher position or from a higher to a lower one can still be seen as a vertical (upward or downward) social mobility. However, it is not the same as social mobility in its original sense (changes of the social class to which people belong).

If social mobility is highly restricted, i.e., it is difficult to change their place of residence, occupation, and social class no matter how hard they try, such a society is usually called a closed society. On the contrary, if there are few restrictions on social mobility, people can change their places of residence. Then can also change their occupations and social classes with effort. Such a society is usually called an open society. In this sense, the degree to which a society is closed or open largely depends on the ease of social mobility. In a socialist society, institutional restrictions and mobility qualifications are still influential factors that hinder social mobility when analyzed objectively. For example, institutional barriers to social mobility may make

Y. Li, *China's Economy Since 1978*, China Academic Library,
https://doi.org/10.1007/978-981-95-5733-2_14

it difficult for people to move horizontally and vertically; overly restrictive qualifications or conditions of social mobility may be hard for people to obtain, thus making social mobility unattainable. Barriers to social mobility arise from both objective and subjective aspects, i.e., whether people are competitive, ambitious, confident, determined, and diligent, or whether people are indolent, complacent, and more risk-averse. This subjective aspect may make some give up social mobility opportunities even if the conditions exist. Or it may make some create conditions for social mobility through their efforts and achieve social mobility under certain objectively adverse conditions. Although the institutions that could hinder social mobility can be changed by reforms, and the restrictions on qualification eligibilities that hinder social mobility can be reduced both by the adjustment of these qualifications and by individual efforts and favorable conditions, the negative effects of subjective barriers to social mobility cannot be ignored. Can people claim the objective conditions to be disadvantageous if they lose the opportunities objectively available on their own? Regarding qualification restrictions that could be overcome with individual efforts, can objective disadvantages be blamed for making social mobility unachievable when individuals are unwilling to act? Thus, it can be seen that the subjective inertia can often pose a greater barrier to social mobility than objective constraints.

In general, there are four kinds of relationships between social mobility and comprehensive development for human beings: (a) Why social mobility is desirable, and what exactly is its relationship with human development? (b) Why might individuals exhibit greater subjective resistance to social mobility, and how does this reflect the need for comprehensive human development? (c) If social mobility were to be achieved, what impact would it have on comprehensive development of human beings? Under what circumstances is social mobility conducive or detrimental to such development? (d) If societies make greater progress in promoting comprehensive development, what impact will this have on social mobility? What are the prospects for social mobility in this context? The following is a discussion of these four relationships.

Let us begin with the first relationship, i.e., the relationship between our quest for social mobility and the desire for comprehensive social development. It should be understood that the fundamental purpose of the demand for social mobility is twofold: to increase income and improve situation, and to seize the opportunity to utilize talents and expertise for a greater contribution to the society. Some prefer the former, some the latter, and the rest, both. Under certain circumstances, the first purpose clashes with the second. For example, some jobs may be well paid, but the nature of the jobs may not be suited to the individual's talents and expertise, so that they are not fit for personal development, and may even be a waste of it. Therefore, social mobility in this context, in which people would rather give up jobs where they could develop their talents and expertise in order to increase their income, is not in line with the requirements of comprehensive human development. In other words, social mobility can be reconciled with the requirements of comprehensive human development only in the following two contexts. The first is that people cannot fully utilize their talents and expertise in their current jobs due to certain restrictions, but these can be brought into full play after job changes (including changes in place of residence, occupation, position, etc.). Then social mobility can be in line with the requirements of social development. The second is to consider that comprehensive human development means not only the full development of one's talents and expertise, but also a gradual disappearance of all kinds of discriminations (such as those against ethnic minorities and women) and differences (such as urban-rural and labor-intellectual differences) inherited from the old society. Therefore, any social mobility that contributes to eliminating such discriminations and differences can be seen as being in line with the requirements of comprehensive human development. Adaptation of social mobility to the requirements in the first case can be called adaptation in a narrow sense, while that in the second case can be called adaptation in a broad sense. However, there is a potential problem here. Suppose someone moves merely for increasing his/her income to take up an occupation irrelevant to talents and expertise, but then argues that "this is a detour toward human development because an increase in income provides a material basis for the full development of talents and expertise," then how this is accounted for? This is indeed a more complex issue. Let us discuss it further below.

Turning to the second type of relationship: the relationship between the subjective aspects of resistance to social mobility and comprehensive human development. As noted earlier, if individuals choose to give up opportunities for social mobility which could increase their income or develop their talents and expertise because of factors of inertia, the latter would constitute a resistance to social mobility. The inertia can be expressed as complacency, lack of ambition, fear of taking risks, and even unwillingness to create conditions for social mobility (e.g., learning skills). The existence of inertia as an impediment to social mobility highlights the importance of human development in at least two different ways. First, a comprehensive human development includes growing and forming the entrepreneur, creative, and innovative spirits. An all-round person must be constantly creative and innovative, and comprehensive development is incompatible with inertia. The process of such development is in fact a process of overcoming inertia. Second, changing jobs through social mobility makes it possible to develop one's talents and expertise and then contribute to the society. When considering whether to change jobs or not, some know that they can contribute more to the society. It is important to understand that comprehensive human development includes the cultivation and formation of a sense of responsibility and dedication to society, which are essential for an all-round person. People are often governed by inertia and reluctant to change, although there could be more contribution to the society. We can see the importance of overcoming inertia here. Of course, it does not mean any person who is willing to move has associated his/her mobility with the idea of social contribution. As mentioned earlier, some move purely for higher income. However, we can conclude that when inertia does not prevent an individual from moving, they can contribute more to society through social mobility.

The third relationship is the question about under what circumstances the realization of social mobility would be conducive to the comprehensive human development. This question has already been mentioned earlier. It can be said that mobility purely for higher income and private interests instead of personal development in talents and expertise and the contribution to society, would be hardly compatible with, and likely unconducive to the comprehensive human development. What, then, are the conditions in which social mobility can be conducive to such development? This issue needs to be analyzed at two different levels: the individual level and the social level. The individual level of analysis means that if mobility is conducive to the development of one's talents and expertise, the growth of ambition and creativity, and the strengthening of social responsibility, then such mobility will be beneficial to the overall human development. The social level of analysis means that everyone is a member of the society, so the impact of his/her mobility cannot be denied, although the latter is usually very small. If one's mobility is positive, whether materially or spiritually, then it will more or less bring benefits to the society and social development. Of course, although an individual's mobility may have a limited impact on society, widespread socially beneficial mobility could positively influence the society greatly.

Finally, we turn to the fourth type of relationship, namely, how will the greater social progress in promoting the comprehensive human development impact on social mobility? That is to say, the influence between social mobility and social development is mutual and reciprocal, and social mobility can be either beneficial or detrimental to such development, which in turn has corresponding effects on social mobility. It is the latter one that will be illustrated now. On this point, it is appropriate to begin with the changes in people's perceptions of social mobility, that is, about their deep understanding of the meaning of social mobility. As mentioned above, the comprehensive human development refers to a proper understanding of how to utilize one's talents and expertise, and better fulfill their social responsibilities. If the society has made greater progress in promoting social development, i.e., people have more capability in overcoming inertia, and have a deeper understanding of social mobility in utilizing their talents and expertise and realizing their social responsibility and contribution, it is undoubtful that social mobility, both from a quantitative and qualitative perspectives, will be upgraded to a new level.

The general trend of social development is to transition from a closed society with many restrictions on social mobility to an open one with fewer such restrictions. However, can we simply assert that freedom is necessarily preferable to restrictions on social mobility? It is not easy to conclude without a specific analysis.

An example may be illustrative, i.e., the restrictions on the mobility of urban residents in early medieval Western Europe. How to evaluate it? It is known that there had been strict restrictions on the social mobility of the inhabitants. In some cities, guilds dominated social and economic life. Guilds usually stipulated that no inter-guild operations were allowed. Strict regulations were imposed on the number and qualifications of craftsmen. Craftsmen were forbidden to peddle and serve door to door; various restrictions were imposed on the movement of craftsmen among cities. Various measures were used to maintain the inherited nature of craftsmen's occupations, and so on. If the restrictions mentioned above are viewed by the social evaluation standards that have been in place since industrialization, they were unreasonable. But it is not a simple problem. These restrictions should be assessed in the context of the urban socio-economy of early medieval Western Europe. In other words, a historical analysis on such an issue is necessary. At the beginning of a feudal society in Western Europe, the cities were emerging. Craftsmen were just getting a foothold in the cities. Commodity-money relations had not yet been developed, and the market was few. The city authorities and the craftsmen's organizations adopted these restrictive measures to maintain socio-economic stability and prevent the intensification of internal competition. These restrictive measures were actually progressive in the historical context, as they maintained socio-economic stability and guaranteed the development of social productivity. It was only in late medieval Western Europe, with the development of the urban economy and the expansion of commodity-currency relations, did these measures increasingly hinder the creativity of craftsmen and limit technological progress. Thus, they turned into an obstacle to social development so that they must necessarily be denied and rejected. This is an example of the scientific evaluation of social mobility. I believe this example is instructive.

The evaluation of social mobility is based on its practice, but not the emotions of the practitioners and researchers of social mobility. The significance of practice is sufficiently illustrated by the example of the severe restrictions on the social mobility of urban dwellers in the early medieval Western Europe mentioned earlier. This is because in the local feudal society, the primary task with the rise of cities was to maintain its socio-economic stability, and the various measures taken by the guilds at that time to restrict the movement of craftsmen were suitable for social stability and productivity development. And the stable and sustained development of the urban economy of the Western Europe in the long period since then justified the measures taken at the beginning to restrict the movement of craftsmen.

As for social mobility in a socialist society, we must likewise proceed from the situation and tasks of each particular stage. Social mobility in a socialist society can only be assessed by practice. Only by unifying the ethical assessment of social mobility with the practical test can we clarify exactly what kind of social mobility should be affirmed for a particular stage of the socialist society. In my book *Socialist Political Economy*, I once wrote: Realizing the goals of socialist production and building a modern socialist society that embodies a high degree of material and spiritual civilization aligns with the common aspirations of Chinese workers and serves their best interests. Therefore, we can adopt "the best interests of the workers" as the ethical criterion for economic actions. In other words, actions that are in "the best interests of the workers" are considered right or good, while those that are not are deemed wrong or evil (Li 1986). Hence, in a socialist society, social mobility should be assessed based on whether it aligns with the best interests of the workers.

In reality, people's movement in urban and rural areas, especially those in the workforce, is subject to certain restrictions. Some restrictions on social mobility (or the regulation of social mobility) might be necessary according to our current situation. If people could move into cities, especially large cities, without restrictions, if employees could leave their existing jobs and move to new one at will without approval, and if corresponding qualifications were not set for certain positions, then our society and economy would be more chaotic. The necessary restrictions or regulations on social mobility are based on the interests of the society. The criterion that simply states that "social mobility without restrictions is 'good' and one with restrictions is 'evil'" is untenable, precisely because it separates the ethical judgment of social mobility from the practical test, and social mobility from the interests of the society.

The degree of restriction, scope, and methods of managing and facilitating social mobility is not always static. At different stages of socialist society's development, the management scope and methods of facilitating social mobility should be adjusted in line with changes in the objective situation. Nonetheless, unrestricted social mobility is still impossible. In fact, unrestricted social mobility (often referred to as entirely free social mobility) cannot exist in the reality of any country, but is at most an assumption in theoretical analysis.

In making ethical judgments of social mobility, it is important to remember that certain restrictions at a given time create the conditions for removing them in the future. Without the restrictions in the previous period, there would be no lifting of them in the subsequent period. There are many examples in the economy. For instance, a country initially implements a policy of protective tariffs (restrictions on free trade) to protect and accelerate the development of an emerging industrial sector. When this new sector becomes more substantial and internationally competitive, the protections can be gradually reduced (relaxation of restrictions on free trade) until their final removal (no restrictions on free trade). It is fair to say that the initial protection of this sector and the subsequent removal of restrictions on free trade are both necessary and reasonable. The same is true about the enforcement of foreign exchange controls. A country must impose exchange control when it has a poor balance of payments and limited foreign exchange reserves. The purpose of the control is to increase foreign exchange earnings and effectively use the scarce foreign exchange resources. Moreover, after the balance of payments has been improved considerably and foreign exchange reserves have become abundant, foreign exchange control could be relaxed. This kind of tightening and loosening, strictness and tolerance are interrelated. Without the tightening and strictness in the previous stage, the loosening and tolerance in the later stage would be out of the question. In making an ethical judgment on foreign exchange control, can one simply affirm the approach of loosening and deny the approach of tightening? Obviously, it is not appropriate to see things that way. How can the same logic not apply to the evaluation of restrictions on social mobility? In the process of developing a socialist society, the initial imposition of strict restrictions on social mobility is by no means an end by itself, but merely the creation of conditions for socio-economic development. Without such strict restrictions on social mobility, it will be challenging to improve the socio-economic situation, and it will be impossible to adopt a more liberal social mobility policy in the future. I believe that every economic researcher who understands our national conditions will agree with this argument.

Now, let us return to the question posed earlier, that is: If someone moves for the sole motive of increasing the income and takes up an occupation that does not involve talents and expertise, but justifies it because "increasing personal income first, and then there will be a material basis for the full development of talents and expertise," how should this be evaluated? It cannot be denied that there are such cases in real life, but social mobility should be evaluated based on actual social gains or losses, not based on hypothetical ones. Meanwhile, gains or losses here are not for individuals. An increase in personal income due to mobility is only a personal gain and does not necessarily equate to a social gain.

—*DUSHU/Reading*, issue No. 11, 1990.

Reference

Li Y-N (1986) *Socialist Political Economics*, The Commercial Press, Beijing, pp. 438–439.

Chapter 15
1991: Development Environment for Chinese Enterprises and Qualities of Chinese Entrepreneurs

A hot debate is raging among Chinese industries and academia on how to enhance the vitality of large and medium-sized SOEs, improve their economic efficiency, and overcome the short-term nature of their behavior. Like human beings, enterprises are living entities that need to survive, develop, and adapt to various environments. For a human being, besides surviving and developing under normal conditions, one also needs the capacity to survive and develop under abnormal conditions. Otherwise, life would be too fragile to withstand setbacks or blows. The same is true for an enterprise. If an enterprise can only operate under normal conditions but cannot survive and develop under abnormal conditions, then such an enterprise is too vulnerable. The so-called "adaptive capacity" refers to the ability to adapt to abnormal conditions rather than normal conditions. In other words, both a person and a company must have the ability to adapt to abnormal conditions under which they can live and achieve sustainable development. It is also an important indicator of vitality of a person or a company.

Here we focus on the situation of enterprises, especially the Chinese ones. It is arguably the case that the current conditions for enterprises are mostly abnormal. Although it doesn't mean there are no normal conditions for survival and development, they can at best be considered as exceptions or temporary phenomena. This point is questionable, however, especially in terms of the economic situation in recent years. For example, a normal condition for the survival and development of enterprises is a normal trade credit environment. However, in reality, the trade credit of some enterprises can be so poor that accounts receivable cannot be collected. The resultant defaults and payments in arrears among enterprises result in chains of debt that occupy a large number of enterprises' working capital. Another example of a normal condition is that enterprises should compete on a level playing field with equal opportunities. However, in reality, there is no such objective environment. Some enterprises may have access to resources for production at planned prices while others have to pay at market prices; some have to sell their products at planned prices while others may sell all or part of their products at market prices; some are taxed at

Y. Li, *China's Economy Since 1978*, China Academic Library,
https://doi.org/10.1007/978-981-95-5733-2_15

one rate while others at another, and so on. Under these conditions, many enterprises have to operate under abnormal conditions. Another example is also obvious. Under normal conditions, enterprises should have the discretion to decide the number of staffs according to production tasks and profitability; they have the right to control wage costs. However, in reality, wages and bonuses are rigid, which can only rise and cannot fall. The same is true for the scale of the labor force. Thus, redundant staff are not laid off but have to be assigned within various departments within the enterprise. As a result, enterprises can neither control wage costs nor increase the production efficiency. Such examples can be named for quite a few, which well explains that China's enterprises are still operating under abnormal conditions.

However, it is notable that, although most enterprises are operating under abnormal conditions, why can some of them still make a profit, develop, and expand? Even if they only account for a fraction of the total, it is still intriguing why they can develop under abnormal conditions while others cannot. This is a question that cannot be ignored. Of course, we should leave aside the favorable treatments by the government and focus on the adaptive ability to abnormal conditions of those enterprises. Only in this way can a study make sense.

Further analysis can be explored on this issue. If conditions that are considered abnormal are common in China, what would be considered as an "extremely abnormal condition"? Let's explain it with an example. Enterprises could be faced with difficult situations of tight working capital and poor sales, or they may not be able to decide the prices by themselves and lay off redundant staff. Even though these are abnormal production and operating conditions, they have become normal for enterprises if all of them have to operate in and adapt to the same system. Considering all enterprises have more or less accustomed to the abnormal conditions, a new problem emerges: How can enterprises survive and develop under "super-abnormal conditions"?

We all know that the following questions are studied by the theory of disequilibrium: What are the differences between normal unemployment and abnormal unemployment? What are the differences between normal and abnormal inflation, normal and abnormal shortage, normal and abnormal surplus, and so forth? According to the disequilibrium theory, if the equilibrium under zero unemployment or zero inflation is nonexistent, such equilibrium would be one of excess or shortage, i.e., under normal unemployment or normal inflation. Therefore, in the economy of non-equilibrium, unemployment, inflation, shortage, and surplus at certain ranges can be regarded as normal, while indicators out of these ranges can be regarded as abnormal. (For instance, unemployment beyond normal unemployment is excessive unemployment, inflation beyond normal inflation is excessive inflation, shortage beyond normal shortage is an excessive shortage, and surplus beyond normal surplus is over surplus.) That's to say, in the economy of non-equilibrium, unemployment, inflation, shortage, and surplus can be divided into two categories by nature, normal and abnormal. Therefore, approaches in national economic management adopted under non-equilibrium conditions should mainly target the abnormal conditions of unemployment, inflation, shortage, and surplus.

If we use similar methods to analyze the objective conditions of production and operation of Chinese enterprises at the current stage, we can also make a similar distinction. In reality, enterprises operate under abnormal conditions. However, if these abnormal conditions are institutionalized to which enterprises have already become accustomed, the environment will become similar to normal conditions under non-equilibrium conditions. The so-called "super-abnormal" conditions refer to the special conditions encountered by enterprises in the process of production and operation, and they are more than the general abnormal conditions that have already been accustomed to by enterprises. For example, a dual-track price system is an abnormal condition for enterprises, but since enterprises have been used to the system, it won't be unbearable for them as long as they have relatively stable expectations on prices, costs, sales, and profitability. Nevertheless, once the dual-track system is combined with local protectionism and regional segregation, the market will be divided into several small and isolated units. Accordingly, the planned price in the dual-track system will evolve into one that reflects local protectionism, and the bargained price in the dual-track system will evolve into discriminatory prices in the regional areas. Then the company's expectations on prices, costs, sales, and profitability will all be disrupted. If these happen, the production and operation conditions will become "super-abnormal conditions," making it hard for enterprises to adapt to and cope with what can be addressed under general normal conditions.

Many more similar examples can be made. Enterprises that have become accustomed to the abnormal conditions have more or less developed the capability to adapt to such conditions in practice. For example, some enterprises in China are good at tapping into their potentials, mobilizing the morale of employees, launching new products according to changes in external conditions and coordinating various internal and external relationships. It should be acknowledged that this is an "internal capacity" developed by Chinese companies over the years. Sometimes we hear people say that Chinese business leaders are not as capable as their foreign counterparts, which is unfair. Perhaps many of them may not as capable in terms of management skills and modern management know-how. However, in terms of the adaptability to abnormal conditions, quite a few of them certainly outperform their foreign counterparts. If you don't believe it, imagine that they swap positions. Under the abnormal conditions faced by Chinese enterprises (for example, their relations with superior authorities, suppliers, communities, staff wages and bonuses, competitors, etc.), it must be impossible for any foreign expert in business management to cope with the various relations without any special background, channels or preferential conditions given their lack of the ability possessed by Chinese business leaders to adapt to abnormal conditions. Even if one is patient enough, it might take a few years to develop the adaptive capability. Only in this way can the enterprises survive and develop under abnormal conditions.

The situation faced by Chinese enterprises and their leaders can be seen like this: They have developed the adaptability to general abnormal conditions so that they can undertake operations and even seek expansion under those conditions. However, what is worried most is the deterioration of general abnormal conditions into "super-abnormal conditions." If this happens, it would become hard for enterprises to maintain simple reproduction, let alone seek development. This is exactly what has happened. Enterprises can manage under the dual-track system, but they are worried about the combination of the dual-track system and regional market segregations arising out of local protectionism. They can adapt to the dual-track system, but they are afraid of apportion and any covert act of apportion. They can work around a shortage of working capital, but they are afraid of a pervasive chain of debt that is often too messy to untangle. It is not a big issue for factories to have certain redundancy, but it can be a problem if wages and bonuses are rigid that can only rise but not fall. All in all, it is the super-abnormal conditions that worry Chinese enterprises and business leaders most at present.

For people who study the development of Chinese enterprises, it is not enough to focus research on enterprise behaviors under normal conditions or general abnormal conditions. Given the realities Chinese enterprises face, it is necessary to study enterprises' production, operation, and development under the super-abnormal conditions: The causes and characteristics of "super-abnormal condition," its influences on enterprises and how enterprises cope with such conditions. If the "super-abnormal conditions" are unavoidable in reality, can businesses adapt to them just like they do to general abnormal conditions? Enterprises of various natures are bound by the same "super-abnormal condition," then the question becomes why some of them still make profits while others suffer losses in various degrees? This is a problem that is worth studying.

As mentioned earlier, enterprises and business leaders gradually developed the ability to cope with general abnormal conditions in real economic activities. Then for enterprises that can make profits or only suffer small losses under super-abnormal production and operating conditions, they must have developed the adaptive ability in daily operations. If the adaptability of enterprises or business leaders to general abnormal conditions is an "internal capacity," then the ability to adapt to "super-abnormal condition" must be a more powerful "internal capacity," with which they can manage under any situation. Since the adaptability of these enterprises is so strong that they can survive super-abnormal conditions, they have nothing to be afraid of under general abnormal conditions and normal conditions (they have nothing to be afraid of once the production and operating conditions of the enterprise transforming from "super-abnormal state" into general abnormal state or normal state).

In summary, there are at least three important and closely related topics in the theoretical and empirical studies of the development of Chinese enterprises. First, how can enterprises develop the ability to adapt to "super-abnormal conditions"? Second, how can China's production and operating conditions gradually improve from the super-abnormal mode to the general abnormal mode, and then to the normal mode? Third, for enterprises that have developed the ability to adapt to the "super-normal conditions," how can they fully unleash their potential for further growth and development if the situation transforms from a super-abnormal mode to a general abnormal mode or normal mode? The first of the three topics can be more convincing if we add more examples on theoretical analysis. The second topic clearly goes beyond the scope of the enterprise development theory because it is directly related to the study of national economic management and theories of economic reform and development. The third topic is ahead of time to some degree, but it is necessary to conduct advanced research on the development of Chinese enterprises. Since the "super-abnormal condition" is making it hard for most enterprises to survive and develop, it won't last long in the future. Therefore, it can be expected that the production and operating conditions of enterprises will sooner or later transform from the super-abnormal mode to the general abnormal mode.

—*Reform*, issue No. 5, 1991.

Chapter 16
1992: Market Regulating the Economy, and Government Managing the Market

There is not much difference between market economy and commodity economy. In a book published in 1988, I wrote: "It is generally believed that market economy exists only in capitalist society or under the condition of private ownership. But this view is not exactly correct. Is it possible to produce and exchange commodities without markets? Can commodity economy become a reality without the market? In fact, the existence of the market is a precondition for the production and exchange of commodities, as they provide the necessary mechanisms for transactions. What it is called is another matter. Indeed, there is not much difference in features between commodity economy and market economy (Li 1988)."

The laissez-faire market economy is merely a theoretical assumption. In real life, market economy always adopts two kinds of regulation measures simultaneously: market regulation and government regulation. The essence of market economy is that resources are allocated according to market laws. The market system is centered on competition rather than directives, choices rather than quotas. On the contrary, within the traditional planned economic system, directives replace competitions and quotas replace choices.

For a market economy, it is crucial to differentiate the primary and the secondary regulation. The primary or the basic regulation is market regulation. It refers to the regulation of the economy by the market, which exists anywhere and anytime. The secondary or higher-level regulation is government regulation which involves government formulating competition rules, managing the market, and re-regulating the economy. Anything that the market could do needs no intervention from the government. The government steps in only when the market fails. This highlights the critical points of the primary and secondary regulation. So, this kind of economic system can be characterized as "market regulating the economy" and "government managing the market." This is a system that has yet to be realized in a socialist society. In general, these two aspects are integrated. The former is about the primary regulation which means the market regulates the economy in the first place, and

Y. Li, *China's Economy Since 1978*, China Academic Library,
https://doi.org/10.1007/978-981-95-5733-2_16

the latter is to function in the secondary regulation, i.e., government manages and re-regulates the market.

Why is the market economy mentioned above still yet to be realized in a socialist society? And how should we understand this term "to be realized"?

First, we can understand the term "to be realized" from the perspective of empirical economics. It means that there has not been such an economic system so far in China. This is consistent with the actual situation of our economy. The socialist economic system can be distinguished into three types: the traditional planned economy, the dual-track economy, and the market economy. Although the production and exchange of commodities exist within the traditional planned economy, the scope is minimal. It only included necessities and capital goods, the production and exchange of which only take place between two kinds of public ownerships (state ownership and collective ownership). Market regulation does not exist in this kind of economic system, while government's mandatory plan and quota system control the economy tightly, leaving it no space of autonomy. Within the dual-track economy, the scope of commodity production and exchange have expanded; market regulation on the economy has strengthened; and government regulation on the market has begun to change its scope, significance, or function. However, since this is the transition period from the traditional economic system to a new one, the traditional one has gradually withdrawn from the stage of economic activities but has not disappeared yet. With the remnants of the mandatory plan and quota system still in place, market mechanisms have just emerged, yet to function well. Therefore, there is neither an objective environment that allows the market to assume the task of the primary regulation, nor a condition for the government to assume that of the secondary regulation. "Market regulating the economy" and "government managing the market" are still the economic system that has yet to be realized. Obviously, such an economic environment can only be formed after the market economy replaces the dual-track system. Then the new economic system can become the one in which socialist economic activities prevail.

Second, we can understand the notion "to be realized" from the perspective of the normative economics. That is to say, it can be put aside whether "market regulates the economy" and "government manages the market" have been realized so far, or whatever conditions are required to achieve such an economic system and how these conditions can be in place. Solely from a normative perspective, the notion "to be realized" reflects a target system that is worth striving for and being made a reality. "To be realized" implies the direction of our efforts. The reason for this is quite apparent. "Market-regulated economy" and "government-managed market" can not only give full play to the initiatives and enthusiasms of all microeconomic units that participate in economic activities, but also enable the government to perform in the secondary regulation, allowing resource allocation in a reasonable direction.

The economic system that has yet to be realized is a socialist market economy, a new "small government, big market" system. "Small government" here refers to a capable and efficient government. The government only undertakes what it should do, and leaves everything that the market can do to the market, so there is no need for the government to manage the enterprises, interfere with their production and operation, and make specific arrangements for their supply and demand of general products (including capital goods and necessities). In the past, no matter within the traditional planned economic system or the dual-track system, the government undertook what could have been done by the market, so there had to be many kinds of government institutions, and their efficiency was difficult to be improved. Within the new system, "small government" refers not only to a capable government, but also a high-efficiency one. The number of government institutions would not necessarily be large, but their work could be carried out orderly.

"Big market" here refers to a complete market system, including commodity market, capital market, labor market, technologies market, information market, property rights exchange market, real estate market, etc. After shifting to a market economy, the gap of resource supply and demand would only be gradually reduced rather than disappear immediately. The system would also not be perfect soon while there is a gradual elimination in market defects. However, since there already forms a complete market system in the economy, the supply and demand of commodities, capital, and labor can all be regulated respectively by the specific market. "Big market" does not mean that the market has been complete enough to enable perfect competition in the economy. Instead, the market would regulate all relations between supply and demand. And the government only functions in the secondary regulation.

"Small government" and "big market" are integrated. Without "big market," there cannot be "small government" and vice versa. Assuming that a "big government" needs to be maintained, which means the government would take over a lot of things that it doesn't need to do, then the market must be shrinking and strictly restricted.

In short, for a market economy, there is no doubt over the choice of *she* (socialism) vs. *zi* (capitalism). Capitalism is not synonymous with a market economy, and neither is socialism. Socialist market economy refers to a market economy in a socialist society, while capitalist market economy refers to that in a capitalist society. Market economy is essentially about allocating resources according to market laws and is characterized by competition and choice. It's the same in a capitalist society as it is in a socialist society. If there must exist any difference, it lies in whether to allocate resources according to the market laws in a socialist society or in a capitalist society.

To briefly describe the market economy with "market-regulated economy" and "government-managed market" or "small government, big market," the difference between socialist market economy and capitalist market economy can be easily distinguished.

"Market-regulated economy" indicates that the market plays a part in the primary regulation, which is dominated by public ownership in a socialist society or private ownership in a capitalist society. "Government-managed market" suggests that the government functions in the secondary regulation, which is led by the proletarian party in a socialist society or the capitalist party in a capitalist society.

"Small government" means a capable and efficient government. Similarly, it refers to the government led by the proletarian party in a socialist society or the capitalist party in a capitalist society. "Big market" manifests a complete market system. It is based on public ownership in socialist society while on private ownership in capitalist society.

After elaborating all these above, we can further understand that the transition of socialist economy from the traditional planned economic system to the new market economy is the development and improvement of the socialist economic system itself. It doesn't fundamentally involve following a capitalist road.

—*Economic Research Journal*, issue No. 11, 1992.

Reference

Li Y-N (1988) *National Economic Management*, Hebei People's Publishing House, Shijiazhuang, pp. 47-48.

Chapter 17
1993: Growth and Fluctuations in Economic Disequilibrium

17.1 Restraints of Disequilibrium on Growth and Fluctuations

The late 1960s witnessed a great stride made in disequilibrium theory. In his two papers, "The Keynesian counter-revolution: A theoretical appraisal (in Hahn FH & Brechling FPR ed. *The Theory of Interest Rates*, Macmillan, London, 1965)" and "A reconsideration of the micro-foundations of monetary theory (*Western Economic Journal*, issue No. 6, 1967)," American economist Robert Wayne Clower came up with a notable argument on disequilibrium theory: Economic instability comes not from a specific market but from discordance between markets, a discordance that stems from the incompleteness of these markets, and of the information transmission mechanism between them. If this argument on disequilibrium is applied to analysis of economic growth and fluctuations, the result will be obvious: Not only will the *equilibrium equation* of *growth predicated on the complete conversion of savings into investment and the full utilization of the production capacities thus yielded become void*, but the supposition about fluctuations that lists the restrictions of income and its changes on effective demand as a major destabilizing factor in an economic system will also be considered as having major limitations.

Shortly afterwards, Swedish economist Axel Leijonhufvud published *On Keynesian Economics and the Economics of Keynes*: A Study in Monetary Theory (New York: Oxford University Press, 1968), among other books. Like Clower, Leijonhufvud reinterpreted the Keynesian economic theory with a disequilibrium approach, and made his own analysis of the causes behind economic stability and instability. He maintains that between labor supply and commodity sales on the economic chain in real life, there are intermediary links, including employers hiring workers, workers producing commodities, employers paying workers, workers buying commodities with their wages, and employers selling commodities. Nevertheless, price rigidity, incomplete markets, and flawed information transmission may disconnect any one of these links, thereby severing the economic chain and inevitably destabilizing the

Y. Li, *China's Economy Since 1978*, China Academic Library,
https://doi.org/10.1007/978-981-95-5733-2_17

economy. This is precisely a manifestation of economic disequilibrium. If this analytical method based on disequilibrium is applied to economic growth and fluctuations, it can likewise prove that it is neither possible for the economy to follow the road of balanced growth as designed by those who subscribe to the equilibrium theory of growth, nor can economic fluctuations be overcome by negotiating the balance between aggregate demand and aggregate supply on the basis of the equilibrium equation for national income.

From the 1970s onward, French economist Jean-Pascal Benassy and Hungarian economist János Kornai probed deeply into the theory of disequilibrium from different points of view. They have made quite a few breakthroughs in disequilibrium studies, which is evident in Benassy's *the Economics of Market Disequilibrium* (New York: Academic Press, 1982), *Macroeconomics and Imperfect Competition* (Paris,1984), and *Macroeconomics: An Introduction to the Non-Walrasian Approach* (New York: Academic Press, 1986), and Kornai's *Anti-Equilibrium* (North-Holland Pub. Co. 1971), *Economics of Shortage* and *Growth* (Amsterdam: North-Holland Pub. Co., 1980), *Shortage and Efficiency* (Oxford: Basil Blackwell, 1982). Their studies on macroeconomic operation contribute greatly to studies of economic growth and fluctuations.

Benassy's contribution to the theoretical study of disequilibrium lies mainly in his analyses of the restraining factors in economic disequilibrium and of the effects of quantitative quotas. According to him, when prices are rigid, traders ought to adjust demand and supply according to both market price and quantity signals. That is to say, traders are restrained by both prices and quantity.

The quantity constraint is embodied in quantitative quotas of various forms. That is to say, the market rations the limited supply among demanders when supply falls short of demand, and apportions the limited demand among suppliers when supply outstrips demand. The equilibrium achieved through quantitative quotas is called "rationed equilibrium," which is actually a kind of disequilibrium or, in a certain sense, temporary, ex post equilibrium. The position of this kind of equilibrium is determined by the shortest side in demand and supply. Benassy maintains that, when observing an economy in disequilibrium, not only should the presumption of price flexibility be abandoned, but price rigidity and asymmetric price elasticity should be taken into consideration as well. Although price rigidity is somewhat relevant to asymmetry in price elasticity, the two factors are different in their impact on actual economic activity. Asymmetry in price elasticity tends to complicate resource allocation in economic disequilibrium, and to further hold back the effectiveness of government policy. If the concept of expectation—that is, individual traders' expectations of uncertain behaviors in economic disequilibrium—is factored in, stabilizing the economy in disequilibrium will become a tougher proposition.

Kornai's analytical approach to the disequilibrium theory is distinctly his own. His study is focused on economic disequilibrium under repressed inflation, that is, disequilibrium characterized by supply shortfalls, where limited commodity supplies are rationed out to demanders by way of quantitative quotas. In that scenario, any increase in fiscal expenditure can further boost the demand on the commodity market, and further strain the distribution of the already limited supplies, thereby worsening the repressed inflation. If, on the contrary, the government attempts to curtail demand by tightening up expenditure, supply and demand will shrink simultaneously, thereby defeating the purpose of making up for supply shortages. Kornai's study of economic disequilibrium is valuable in that he focuses discussions on both hard and soft budget restraints, because the existence of firms' soft budget constraint can keep the economy in long-run disequilibrium and make it hard to eradicate supply shortfalls.

The studies by Western economists drive home clearly that both economic growth and fluctuation are inevitably restrained by economic disequilibrium.

The influence of the equilibrium theory runs deeply in the economic growth theories represented by the Harrod-Domar model, Neoclassical model and Neo-Cambridge model that came in vogue in the 1950s and 1960s. What sets the Neo-Cambridge model far apart from the other two models is that it incorporates two different kinds of income and the restraints of income distribution on economic growth. However, even with this legitimate contribution to growth theories, the Neo-Cambridge model still fails to eschew explicit or implicit assumptions of a complete market, flexible prices, and smooth information transmission. As a result, this model ascribes the difficulties encountered in the process of economic growth mainly to income distribution problems rather than to market imperfections and the incompatibilities between markets. In this way, the Neo-Cambridge model falls short of accounting for the restraining impact of persistent supply shortages on economic growth.

One thing that should be noted is that Joan Robinson and other major advocates of the Neo-Cambridge model were, theoretically speaking, against assumptions of economic equilibrium. Proceeding from Keynes' viewpoints on economic disequilibrium, they raised a series of arguments against mainstream post-Keynesian theorists. But why was it that they could not shake off the influence of the equilibrium theory in their analysis of economic growth? It was because their microeconomic theory was inadequate and weak, and because their neglect of analyses of market transaction behaviors, corporate operational mechanisms, and information transmission mechanisms determined the inherent drawbacks in their model of economic growth.

In economic fluctuation studies, the relevant theory represented by the IS-LM (investment savings—liquidity preference money supply) and Multiplier-Accelerator models that were popular in the 1950s and 1960s is preconditioned by equilibrium and equilibrium growth assumptions. According to these models, economic fluctuations are caused by over-investment, over-saving, over-supply, or inefficient money supply, and by the inherent law of technology and equipment upgrading, and are not directly associated with market imperfections, price rigidity, and informational frictions. What is more, the IS-LM model also ignores the analysis of the microeconomic basis of the macro-economy, while the Multiplier-Accelerator model does the same by leaning heavily on the economy's technical factors. Such oversight determines the serious flaw in the fluctuation theory that was current in the 1950s and 1960s.

The progress made in the late 1960s in researches on the disequilibrium theory provided no small inspiration for studies of economic growth and fluctuations. And the restraining effects of the imbalanced nature of the economy on growth and fluctuations were increasingly accepted in academic and economic circles thanks to constructive explorations made by researchers in the disequilibrium theory. These explorations were made without totally disallowing the significance and reference value of either the Harrod-Domar, Neoclassical, and Neo-Cambridge models in the realm of theoretical research on economic growth, or the IS–LM and Multiplier-Accelerator models in their studies of the fluctuation theory. Such explorations were important in that they approached growth and fluctuations from a unique perspective, thereby putting their studies on a new and more realistic footing. That is why some of their conclusions are closer to reality than those derived from the theories popular in the 1950s and 1960s.

The studies of disequilibrium analyses of growth and fluctuations so far can be summarized in the following four major conclusions:

First, with incomplete markets, inflexible prices, and inefficient information transmission, the conversion of savings into investment will be held back, and the imbalance between supply and demand, once it occurs, cannot be easily corrected. Shortages in supply and demand can be mitigated by the function of market to a certain extent, but will not disappear totally. The equilibrium thus achieved under a non-zero unemployment rate or a non-zero inflation rate can restrain economic growth or cause major fluctuations.

Second, disequilibrium makes it harder for markets (commodity market, capital market, labor market, etc.) to function in a coordinative way. Once supply or demand shortages occur in one market, they cannot possibly disappear and will go on to cause new shortages and exacerbate existing ones in other markets. This may become a restraint on growth or an importance cause behind major fluctuations.

Third, disequilibrium is characterized by price rigidity. The major impact of price rigidity on growth and fluctuations is manifested in that economic agents have to make supply-demand decisions based on imprecise signals. However, price rigidity does not mean that a price will hold forever. On the contrary, it may entail sudden, large-scale, and asymmetric price changes. This is detrimental to economic growth, to be sure, and more importantly, it may cause or aggravate fluctuations.

Fourth, the presence of disequilibrium or equilibrium under non-zero rates of unemployment and inflation is bound to alter the expectations of market participants, which in turn gives rise to irregular and short-sighted economic behaviors. Such behaviors are likely to become not only a major cause behind intensified fluctuations, but also a stubborn retardant on steady and sustained economic growth.

17.2 Telling Two Kinds of Disequilibrium Apart, a Study of Growth and Fluctuations

Using disequilibrium analysis, and combining it with the country's actual economic situation, we will be able to get a better understanding of the guidelines for the ongoing economic reform and the way the economy develops.

Given that disequilibrium is caused by incomplete markets, inflexible prices, and inefficient information transmission, either of the following arguments will make sense in theory:

Argument A. To avoid volatile fluctuations and stabilize the growth rate, it is necessary to remove price restraints and improve market conditions, and to put economic agents on equal competitive footings. Economic growth will be realized in a relatively complete market with flexible prices.

Argument B. With market mechanism flaws such as incomplete markets, inflexible prices, and inefficient information transmission, it is necessary to tighten up macroeconomic management to make up for market deficiencies and rectify economic deviations with government regulation of quotas and prices. Steady and sustainable economic growth will be achieved mainly by allocating capital, labor, and production materials via quantitative quota. To put it another way, economic growth under disequilibrium can be achieved mainly through quantitative quota implementation.

Both arguments stem from analyses of economic disequilibrium. In fact, Argument A is a succinct interpretation of the theory on "price reform as the centerpiece of economic reform," while Argument B emphasizes "macroeconomic stabilization as the centerpiece of economic reform." Insofar as economic growth and fluctuations are concerned, Argument A attributes economic fluctuations in disequilibrium to incomplete markets and inflexible prices, so that flexible prices and better market conditions are the first steps to take to avoid fluctuations or maintain stable economic growth; while Argument B ascribes fluctuations to incomplete markets or limitations in the market mechanism itself, so the inevitable reform step is to strengthen macroeconomic management through government quota and price regulation.

However, a study of the actual performance of the Chinese economy proves that neither price reform nor macroeconomic stabilization, if chosen as the centerpiece of economic reform, can ward off wild fluctuations or maintain steady economic growth. This means that neither Argument A nor Argument B tallies with the current Chinese economic situation.

Given that both arguments are based on studies of disequilibrium assumptions and therefore inappropriate, one may wonder what really went wrong. Isn't it that the disequilibrium theory itself is wrong, or that analysis of this theory is not thorough enough to account for such complex issues as economic restructuring, growth, and fluctuations in this country? The disequilibrium theory is, without a doubt, an advance in economics. Equilibrium assumptions are unwarranted in the absence of complete markets, flexible prices, and efficient information transmission. In reality, however, economies are always in disequilibrium; therefore, they can be observed only with disequilibrium analytical methods. For this reason, we cannot make light of the disequilibrium theory simply because the above two arguments do not fit. The problem does not lie in disequilibrium analysis itself.

What really went wrong? The problem dwells in the flaws of general disequilibrium analysis, so much so that it falls short of explaining such complicated issues as economic restructuring, growth, and fluctuation in China.

What merits attention is that general disequilibrium analysis does not take into account the dynamics of firms as microeconomic units. Instead, its assumption is that firms are dynamic enough. It thus follows that analysts attribute disequilibrium to incomplete markets, inflexible prices, and inefficient information transmission. This is how Arguments A and B are drawn, and why disequilibrium analysis is flawed.

In my book *Disequilibrium in the Chinese Economy* (Li 1990), I propose to divide disequilibrium into two categories, one with incomplete markets, and the other with both incomplete markets and enfeebled firms. The current Chinese economy falls into the second category. This being the case, economic restructuring in this nation should proceed in two stages: Firstly, to transform firms more deeply until they become dynamic and profit-maximizing entities that enjoy decision-making autonomy and are liable for their profits and losses, so that the Chinese economy can complete its transition from the second category of disequilibrium to the first category of it; and secondly, to center economic restructuring on building a complete market and decentralizing prices, so that the economy can edge its way toward equilibrium. My book differs from the general studies of the disequilibrium theory in that I have differentiated between two categories of economic disequilibrium and observed the attributes of the second category of disequilibrium.

It makes sense to distinguish between these two kinds of disequilibrium, because it helps analyze Chinese economic growth and fluctuations. Economic growth is restricted to a larger extent and more vulnerable to fluctuations in the second category of disequilibrium. In the same vein, it is more difficult to maintain steady economic growth and avoid wild fluctuations under the second category of disequilibrium than under the first category of it. Without clarifying the difference between the two categories of disequilibrium, we may mistake incomplete markets, inflexible prices, and inefficient information transmission for the main restraints on economic growth and the basic causes behind fluctuations. We will miss the point if we adopt economic policies in light of these judgments. It is like a doctor who, acting on a false diagnosis, writes out an inappropriate prescription and leaves an illness untreated.

If, instead of telling the two kinds of economic disequilibrium apart and seeing that China is in the second kind of it, we set improving market conditions and decentralizing prices or intensifying macroeconomic management as our major policy decisions to stabilize economic growth and avert fluctuations, we are ignoring the most forceful restraints on economic growth and fluctuations imposed by weak firms that, as investors and consumption fund issuers, are not responsible for their management decisions, profits and losses. Under the second category of disequilibrium, firms are yet to become independent commodity producers liable for their management decisions, profits, and losses, so their status as investors and consumption fund issuers is nominal and unrestrained. In that scenario, the following problems will occur:

1. Owing to their lack of autonomy, firms may not be able to make investment even when it is profitable to do so, thus making it hard to keep overall economic growth in pace with these firms' increasing economic returns.
2. Having no self-restraints on investment and bearing no investment, production, and management risks, firms in the process of expanding investment will be susceptible to repetitive construction and fail to realize economies of scale. In

that case, economic growth is likely to be a process of ballooning overstock and financial losses for such firms.

3. Myopic economic decisions such as allocating the consumption fund to serve immediate interests will impair firms' growth potentials and leave them with outdated equipment and technology. Economic growth will be held back as a result.
4. Firms with no self-restraints may issue more consumption fund than is allowed by their economic returns, and such economic returns are often adulterated even though they are pegged to wages and bonuses. Under these circumstances, the more tightly wages and bonuses are pegged to economic returns, the bigger the losses will become for firms and the state. Economic growth will invariably be held back as a result.
5. The negative macroeconomic impact of the lack of self-restraints on investment and consumption fund cannot be underestimated. Over-investment and runaway growth in consumption fund are one of the manifestations of this negative impact. In that case, even if the economic growth rate is increased, such an increase will be short lived and sow the seed for future economic disorder. Extended losses on firms and stressed fiscal balance are another manifestation of this negative impact, with stressed fiscal balance becoming a major cause behind economic instability and a huge obstacle to sustained economic growth.
6. The fact that firms take no responsibility for their own profits and losses and, in particular, cannot stop production or be closed down, merged, or transferred because of government-business collusion, deprives the flow of corporate capital stock of proper channels and makes it impossible to optimize the reallocation of production factors. With bottlenecks like these, industrial restructuring can never go smoothly, and sustained economic growth is hamstrung as well.
7. When firms have no decision-making autonomy and bear no responsibility for their profits and losses, neither can their capital stock be made to flow, nor can the purpose of industrial restructuring through reinvestment be served. Increases in investment are limited, and limited increases in investment can hardly put an end to the disproportionate industrial structure. The problem, however, does not stop here. If we liken corporate capital stock to a pool of stagnant water, and reinvestment to flowing water, the real problem is that when year's increased amount of investment is reinvested in a firm, it becomes part of the firm's capital stock the next year. If this cycle is made to last, it is tantamount to constantly turning running water into stagnant water—no amount of running water can put an end to the situation. Consequently, bottlenecks persist and economic growth is greatly held back.
8. Under the second category of economic disequilibrium, because firms, as microeconomic units, remain as government appendages, whenever the government takes macroeconomic regulation steps, they either find it difficult to adapt their business activity to macroeconomic changes or cannot respond properly for lack of self-restraints. As a result, the government regulation steps fail to yield the desired results. The lack of elasticity—in the investment interest rate, the import and export exchange rate, and output prices—is exactly a telltale sign of the

undesirable results of government regulation steps. In the absence of stability-oriented internal adjustment mechanisms, once economic fluctuations occur, the situation can only be tackled with government intervention. However, under the second category of disequilibrium, government intervention from top on down to the grassroots level often comes seriously belatedly. The higher-up leadership (or decision-making authorities) will not take action until problems become serious enough. Furthermore, the negative impact of inappropriate government intervention on economy stability should never be overlooked.

These eight problems illustrate what is so unique about the growth and fluctuations in the Chinese economy in the second category of disequilibrium. Therefore, our studies of Chinese economic growth and fluctuations should proceed from the relevant factors, with the second category of disequilibrium as the precondition.

17.3 Understanding the Wooden Barrel Principle in Disequilibrium

An important principle in the disequilibrium theory is the "law of the shortest side," which is believed to be the key restraint on economic growth and the essential cause behind fluctuations. The "law of the shortest side" is tenable in this regard. This is because in a disequilibrium economy, the market cannot play a complete role in regulating the relationship between supply and demand, and therefore the existence of the shortest side becomes an inevitability, which forces production factors to be reallocated in compliance with the minimum demand. This is like a barrel composed of planks of different lengths. The capacity of the barrel is determined by the shortest plank rather than the longest one. If more water than the shortest plank allows is poured into the barrel, the water will spill out. This is what the "law of the shortest side" entails.

When applying the "law of the shortest side" to the study of growth and fluctuations in economic disequilibrium, the following problems are worth our further consideration:

1. Why can the shortest side persist for a long time? Despite years of economic growth, the shortest side of previous years remains to this day or becomes even shorter. That is, the shortest plank of the barrel becomes still shorter. What has gone wrong?
2. In theory, production factors are mutually replaceable and supplementary to a certain extent. This means that the shortest side could be replaced or made up for by certain longer sides. In reality, however, the ability of longer-side production factors to replace or supplement shorter ones is very limited, a fact that has a considerable influence on economic growth and fluctuations. The issue here is: Why mutual replacement and complementation between production factors can be so difficult as to allow the "law of the shortest side" to become the key factor in inhibiting economic growth and causing fluctuations?

3. Reallocation of production factors can address economic problems caused by shortest-side factors, boost economic growth, and curtail fluctuations. Take, again, the barrel for example. Since how much water a barrel can contain is determined by its shortest plank, the situation can be remedied in two ways. One is to saw a certain length off the longest plank and nail it onto the shortest one, so that the two new planks are level with each other. This can happen only when production factors are mutually supplementary. The other is to dismantle the barrel and put the old planks together to make a new one, hopefully a larger one. This is tantamount to the aforementioned reallocation of production factors. Nevertheless, in reality, such reallocation is an unrealistic proposition probably because the barrel is too solid to be torn apart for reassembling. Then we should ask why the barrel is so solid. Why can't we break it apart? Is it really difficult to reallocate production factors?

All these problems are relevant to the characteristics of growth and fluctuations under economic disequilibrium. Bearing in mind the differentiation between the two types of disequilibrium, and combing it with the fact that the Chinese economy is in the second category of disequilibrium, let us proceed from the "law of the shortest side" to observe these three problems, so as to better understand the "law of the shortest side."

17.3.1 Problem One: The Shortest-Side Syndrome in the Second Category of Disequilibrium

The shortest-side syndrome refers to the situation where shortest-side factors remain, or are growing even shorter in spite of years of economic growth and restructuring. Where is the problem? In economic equilibrium, shortest-side factors will disappear when the market mechanism promotes the free flow of production factors and resources are reallocated in response to price signals. In this way, even if new shortest-side factors emerge in the process of economic growth, the economy is immune to the shortest-side syndrome. Apparently, the shortest-side syndrome tends to occur when production factor is stagnant and resources cannot be reallocated smoothly.

Supposing our economy is in the first category of disequilibrium, which is characterized by incomplete markets, inflexible prices and incomplete information, production factors can flow more freely by improving the markets and decentralizing the prices, and resource reallocation can take place in response to price signals. In this way, the shortest-side syndrome may disappear gradually. Though scarcity in some resources may make it difficult to reallocate resources and overcome the shortest sides, the syndrome can be avoided if this scarcity can be eased with replacements or imports.

However, the situation is more complicated in the second category of disequilibrium, which is peculiarly prone to the shortest-side syndrome. In this category of economic disequilibrium, clogged production factor flow and troubles in industrial restructuring and resource reallocation can be imputed respectively to the "lack of information, incentive and channel."

"Lack of information" means that when faltering firms operate in an incomplete market, their access to price signals is bound to be inappropriate, untimely, and incomplete. At the same time, because these firms, as microeconomic units, are under the strict control of their leadership authorities, the government cannot obtain timely and accurate information from both the market and these firms. Therefore, government quota adjustments are often at odds with market needs, and resources can only be reallocated in the absence of accurate information. As a result, shortest-side factors are mistaken for longest-side ones, and vice versa; and ineffective supply is regarded as being effective.

"Lack of incentive" means that the lopsided industrial structure is a solid fact, and firms have obtained adequate information about shortest- and longest-side factors and can respond accordingly, but they are not motivated enough to act and run the risks. This is because, as government appendages that have not the final say in management and are not liable for profits, losses, and production and management risks, these forms are neither motivated to restructure their products and nor willing to run such risks.

"Lack of channels" means that even if firms as microeconomic units and the government as macroeconomic authorities have both received adequate information about shortest- and longest-side factors and are willing to restructure the economy, there are no channels to facilitate the free flow of production factors. This is because firms are mere government appendages while the economy has been sectioned by a labyrinth of ownership boundaries, making it difficult to reallocate resources, let alone optimize them. All this bears out the unavoidability of the shortest-side syndrome.

17.3.2 Problem Two: Difficulties in Mutual Replacement Between Production Factors in the Second Category of Disequilibrium

As mentioned above, as long as production factors are able to replace each other, shortest-side factors can be eased with the help of longest-side ones. This is not to say, however, that such replacement is absolute; rather, it is relative, and cannot work under all circumstances. Moreover, the replacement of one factor by another can either improve or reduce efficiency. Only when the margin of drop in efficiency caused by such replacement is narrower than that caused by the scarcity of the factors in question can such replacement be deemed feasible.

In an economy in equilibrium, whenever production factor replacement is possible, the price and cost-benefit ratio will motivate firms to alleviate the shortest-side syndrome by choosing effective methods for such replacement. In the first category of economic disequilibrium, replacement difficulties caused by inflexible prices and distorted price signals can be overcome by improving the market conditions and decontrolling the prices.

However, the situation is worlds apart in the second category of economic disequilibrium, where the problem is not limited to the incomplete production factor market. The fact that production factor suppliers and demanders are government appendages is more of a problem. For instance, when human resources are controlled by government quotas and sectioned to different departments, localities, and firms, they are unable to make up for capital shortages even if replacement is possible. It is also necessary to make reinvestment and upgrade technology and equipment when there is a possibility of replacement between material production factors. On the one hand, because material production factors are supplied by some departments and localities, and demanded by others, it is hard to achieve supply-demand balance under intersected government administration. On the other, reinvestment involves problems concerning the investment system. If the old system continues, production factor replacement cannot take place. In a word, it is not easy for production factor replacement to be realized.

17.3.3 Problem Three: Hindrance to Production Factor Reallocation in the Second Category of Disequilibrium

We have noted that shortest-side factors can be compensated for through reallocating production factors. However, why is it so difficult to reallocate production factors in the second category of disequilibrium? Take the barrel again. Why is it so sturdy that it refuses to be torn apart and re-assembled? Herein lays the key to studies in the ongoing Chinese economic growth and fluctuations.

Production factor reallocation calls for at least three conditions: first, well-defined property rights; second, smooth flow of production factors; and third, competence of the organizer of such reallocation. The biggest reason why reallocation of production factors under the second category of disequilibrium is so difficult is that the first two conditions are not available. To be more specific, the second kind of disequilibrium is subject to ill-defined property rights under public ownership, business-government collusion, lack of responsibility for management, gains, and losses, and lack of internal and external restraints on the part of firms. All these result in inefficient production factor flow, indeterminate beneficiaries of reallocation gains, and undefined risk bearers in such reallocation. These obstacles to reallocation arise when the first two conditions are not satisfied.

Judging from the third condition, the success of production factor reallocation lies in the organizer's proficiency for the task and ability to secure potential benefit from it. Who, then, is the eligible organizer in the second category of economic disequilibrium? As government appendages, firms have yet to become autonomous commodity producers, and are therefore not qualified.

If firms cannot organize the reallocation of production factors, how about the government? It is not that the government cannot to do the job, but that it may not be able to fulfill the task in the absence of the first two conditions. Let me explain. If what is referred to here is the central government, it is powerful enough and in the possession of the means for such reallocation, but, as a macroeconomic regulatory institution, it cannot possibly be directly engaged in reallocating production factors. In fact, the government here refers to local authorities. Supposing a local government has difficulty in reallocating production factors due to institutional obstacles, to what extent can it break through those obstacles? Is it authoritative enough to overcome those obstacles? What's more, can a local government be highly efficient in directly organizing the reallocation of production factors? In any case, it is difficult for any local government to be fully competent in the second category of economic disequilibrium. Thus, the third condition is not available either. Furthermore, whether the organizer is a firm or a government, reallocation of production factors can succeed only when it is handled by someone who is highly innovative and capable of organizing modern production. In fact, innovators and organizers of this type are rare, a fact that also accounts for what a difficult task allocating production factors can be in this nation.

17.4 Production and Circulation in Economic Growth

The relationship between production and circulation merits due attention. In analyzing economic growth factors, some authors tend to emphasize elements in the production field, such as investment quantity and its proportion in national income, the input-output ratio, the contribution of production factors (technology, and human resources included) to economic growth, different combinations of production factors, and their impact on corporate and macroeconomic returns. They tend to give a second seat to the circulation factor in economic growth in general and sustainable economic growth in particular. Three reasons may account for this analytical approach. First, they stress the decisive role of production in circulation to the neglect of the reaction of circulation to production. Second, they base their calculation of the economic growth rate on output value, as if increases in output value are equal to economic growth, regardless of the fact that the percentage of ineffective supply in output value cannot be counted as part of real economic growth. Third, insufficient attention to circulation and misunderstanding in the role of markets lead to inadequate understanding of circulation. Small wonder that circulation is held in a secondary seat in economic growth in these authors' analyses of economic fluctuations.

In the Chinese economy, however, the importance of circulation and consumption to production and distribution is becoming increasingly more pronounced in the traditional economic system's transition to a new one. It is because people's freedom and motivation in economic life are growing steadily. They are engaged in production to meet their needs. Those needs are satisfied on a daily basis through market transactions, and more and more commodities are reaching people through the market.

Commerce promotes production, coordinates distribution, ensures circulation, and guides consumption. As to all the consumer goods, most of the public goods, and a fair quantity of capital goods, the effectiveness of their supplies hinges on whether circulation can go smoothly. Poor circulation leads to ineffective supply, and goes further to hold back economic growth and give rise to major fluctuations.

The importance of circulation to economic growth is also evident in the flow and reallocation of production factors. Production factors fall into two categories: real ones and latent ones. The production factors that flow and reallocate through circulation are real ones, which is bound to activate latent ones. For instance, the full employment, free flow, and reallocation of real labor resources will inevitably bring latent labor resources to the market to augment the real labor resources. The same is true with capital. If real capital is put to full use of and flows freely to effectively combine with other production factors, more latent capital will be brought forth. This is the way latent production factors are converted into real ones, to the benefit of economic growth. The role of circulation figures prominently in this regard in the current period of development in the Chinese economy. To maintain sustained economic growth in this country, which abounds in latent production factors but falls short in the supply of absolutely and relatively real ones, it is necessary to turn latent production factors into real ones through reform and hard work on circulation.

So much for the paramount importance of circulation to the Chinese economic life. In recent years, however, there has appeared an abnormal "debt chain" in circulation. Although this "debt chain" is directly related to economic austerity, overstocked inventory, shortage in capital investment, and the ensuing overdue obligations to suppliers, however, we can understand it more profoundly and in a new light if we turn our attention to economic disequilibrium, the second category of it in particular.

The "debt chain" is not to be perceived merely as a result of an inordinate industrial or product structure. It is understood that this inordinateness can lead to sluggish sales, overstocked inventory, and overdue obligations to suppliers, but it is unfair to regard it as the fundamental cause behind the "debt chain." Inordinate industrial or product structure is nothing new, but why this "debt chain" has surfaced only in the last couple of years? What is more, why haven't we done anything about it? What has thrown the industrial or product structures off balancc, or, in other words, what is the deep-seated cause behind the "debt chain"? Obviously, the answers cannot be found from structural inordinateness alone.

It is equally superficial to impute the "debt chain" to economic austerity. Austerity is nothing but a government policy, whereas the "debt chain" is deeply rooted in the economic system. It is thus unfair to blame the "debt chain" on a certain government policy, not to mention the fact that after this chain appeared, government policy has never stopped its move from austerity to relaxation, such as major increases in credit and loan grants. However, the loans issued to undo the "debt chain" never worked. It is all too obvious that austerity is not the culprit for the "debt chain."

In light of a study of the attributes of the second category of economic disequilibrium, the "debt chain" may be explained in this way: The development of a commodity economy is in direct conflict with government-business collusion, which is a hallmark of this category of disequilibrium. Therefore, the "debt chain" was born of the contradiction between government-business collusion and the burgeoning commodity economy. To be more exact, without the commodity economy, government-business collusion would not have resulted in overdue obligations to suppliers, let alone a "debt chain." If government were detached from business, the "debt chain" would not appear no matter how fast the economic economy grows, not even when a temporary slump appeared. This is because when a creditor asks for repayment according to law, the debtor may liquidate his assets to honor the debt until he files for bankruptcy.

However, this is not the case with present-day China. On the one hand, a commodity economy is emerging; and on the other, the second category of disequilibrium persists. That is to say, the longstanding government-business collusion is yet to give way. When transactions between firms are taking place in increased frequency, if A is overdue in payment to B, and B to C, the debtor-creditor relationship can be very complicated. In government-business collusion, debtors are always backed by the government, so that creditors are not in a position to ask for due repayment, let alone demand for liquidating the assets. It is another story when a debtor is responsible for its own benefits and losses. This indicates that liability disputes between firms come down to disputes between government departments when the "debt chain" involves firms that are government appendages. Because such disputes cannot be settled by bankruptcies, the debts will be piled up, and the chain will grow in length with each passing day. Fundamentally speaking, the "debt chain" can never be eradicated if we fail to deepen corporate reform, detach government from business, and turn firms into commodity producers making their own business decisions and bearing their own profits and losses. In other words, the transition from the second category of disequilibrium to the first category of it must be accomplished at an early date to get rid of the "debt chain."

The nature of economic disequilibrium also sheds light on another major issue in the field of circulation, the issue of the outsourcing of circulation. Stable and sustained economic growth is determined not only by production, but also by circulation. Production bottlenecks, clogged circulation channels, and ineffective supply all play a part in volatile economic fluctuations. Therefore, the outsourcing of circulation should become an indispensable part in our study of economic growth and fluctuations, the growth and fluctuations in the Chinese economy in particular.

At the first glance, clogged circulation channels bring about an overstock of some commodities and shortages of others, and strain supply. These problems merit attention, but they cannot be addressed by improving circulation alone. The outsourcing of circulation takes on a different meaning in economic disequilibrium from in economic equilibrium.

In economic equilibrium, where the market is complete, prices are flexible, information transmission is smooth and firms are liable for their management decisions, benefits, and losses, the outsourcing of circulation is inevitably characterized by free circulation of commodities at flexible prices and by production and sales in the interest of firms.

In the first category of disequilibrium, firms are responsible for their own business management, benefits, and losses. However, the market is incomplete, prices are inflexible, and information transmission is clogged. As a result, free circulation will run up against obstacles. Firms will find it hard to organize production and sell their products on their own. In addition, supply or demand shortfalls will make it hard for market prices to play a due role in economic adjustment, so much so that such shortfalls must be eased, to some extent, with quantitative adjustment either by the government or by the market.

The situation is much more complicated in the second category of disequilibrium. Apart from an incomplete market, inflexible prices, and clogged information transmission, firms are failing and yet to become autonomous. The disparity between supply and demand is more acute in capital goods than in consumption goods, and therefore, it is more pressing to develop capital goods than to procure more consumer goods. According to this interpretation, the outsourcing of circulation in the second category of disequilibrium should be interpreted in this way: We should develop all sorts of markets, capital goods markets in particular, while combining quantity regulation with price regulation in relevant markets, particularly in the markets for pivotal capital goods. Only thus can obstacles to circulation be lifted, and the effective combination of production factors optimized nationwide. The percentage of quantity quotas and that of price regulation should be decided in light of the degree of economic disequilibrium, because we can always make do with the second-best choice where and when the first best choice is hard to come by.

It is in accord with the principle of the second-best choice to understand the outsourcing of circulation in economic disequilibrium from the perspective of combining quantity and price regulation. What merits attention here is that the replacement of price regulation with quantity regulation in economic disequilibrium is not the same as replacing complete competition with incomplete competition. Rather, it is the replacement of one kind of incomplete competition with another. In economic disequilibrium, there will never be a complete market, and therefore the effort to improve the market is invariably in conflict with quantity regulation. It is unrealistic to deny the existence of such a conflict and its effect on economic growth and fluctuations. In the current stage of economic development, what we should and can do is to improve the management of circulation as much as possible, dredge up the circulation channels, further the commercial reform to minimize obstacles to the outsourcing of circulation. In the meanwhile, we should also mitigate economic disequilibrium in multiple ways to ease the conflict between market improvement and quantity regulation.

We have elaborated on the restraining impact of circulation on economic growth and fluctuations, probed into the deep-seated causes behind the "debt chain," and elucidated the need to outsource circulation in economic disequilibrium. Thus, we are able to better understand the economic growth and fluctuations in China in two ways.

Firstly, observed from the viewpoint of circulation alone, the profound impact of the second category of disequilibrium on the realm of circulation has clearly become a potent restraint on economic growth and an essential cause behind fluctuations. Only by taking into consideration the effect of the second category of disequilibrium on both production and circulation can the economic growth and fluctuations in this country be better interpreted.

Secondly, from our observations of circulation we can arrive at this conclusion: If, instead of proceeding from invigorating our companies to push economic restructuring, we allow government-business collusion to persist in the long run, sustained economic growth will be out of the question, and major fluctuations will become unavoidable. This fully bears out what economic restructuring is all about in the second category of disequilibrium.

17.5 Thoughts on Normal and Abnormal Fluctuations

The topic of this study being fluctuations in economic disequilibrium rather than in equilibrium, we are confronted with the issue of normal and abnormal fluctuations. Fluctuations are always deemed abnormal in economic equilibrium, where normal fluctuations are nonexistent. However, it is the other way around in disequilibrium, where gaps in either supply or demand are a common occurrence, and the market can bridge such gaps but cannot root them out. That is to say, disequilibrium is essentially balance with non-zero unemployment rate and non-zero inflation rate. To put it differently, disequilibrium is a kind of equilibrium that is accompanied by a certain unemployment rate or a certain inflation rate (or a balance between certain demand shortfalls and certain supply shortfalls).

Any economic gap can be interpreted as "shortage." For instance, a rise in prices, which means that excess money is chasing commodities that are in short supply, can be termed as "commodity shortage." Unemployment, which indicates that many workers are hunting for a few jobs, can be expressed as "job shortage." Similarly, undercapitalization denotes a "fund shortage," while overcapitalization points to "shortage in investment outlets." A bottleneck in resource supply indicates "shortage of a certain resource," while idle resources indicate "shortage of resource users." Since any gap can be regarded as a shortage, there must be two kinds of shortages in economic disequilibrium—normal shortages and abnormal shortages.

As stated above, normal shortages are common and inevitable in economic disequilibrium. However, it does not mean that a certain shortage cannot be eliminated by any means, but that one shortage can be eliminated probably at the cost of another shortage that causes even a greater loss in efficiency. For instance, a 2 percent unemployment rate is an indicator of a normal shortage of jobs, but someone insists to eliminate this normal unemployment rate. We are not saying that he has no way of accomplishing it, but that in doing so, some firms may be overstaffed and suffer major efficiency losses. In other words, the normal job shortage is eradicated in return for a higher disguised unemployment rate and a greater loss in efficiency. We may follow a similar line of thinking to prove how a visible inflation rate that is within a normal range of shortage in economic disequilibrium is made to disappear in return for an increased disguised inflation rate and a major efficiency loss.

From this analysis, we can see that the alert line for macroeconomic operation in disequilibrium cannot be marked with zero shortages (zero unemployment rate, zero inflation rate, etc.). The alert line in question is designed to guide government regulation. When the economy runs below this line, there is no need to act. Only when the economy surges above the line should the government take appropriate steps to regulate it. Under disequilibrium, the position of the alert line is directly relevant to the extent of normal shortages. Assuming there is a zero shortage level in the economy (zero unemployment rate, zero inflation rate, etc.), the alert line must be somewhere above this level. The space between the two lines represents normal shortage; the space above the alert line is abnormal shortage, as is shown in Fig 17.1:

In the book *Strategic Choice for Prosperity* by Li Yining et al, the concept of "alert line" is explained in Chapter 8, "The integration of planning and market mechanism in resource allocation": There are two alert lines—the first alert line and the second alert line. The first line sets the boundary between market regulation and government-planned regulation. The second line runs above the first one. Whether the government should give priority to direct regulation or indirect regulation depends on the space above the first alert line. When the economy operates between the two lines, it comes mainly under indirect government regulation. When it runs above the second alert line, it is evidence that indirect regulation has not achieved desired results and, therefore, it is time to shift the emphasis to direct regulation in place (Li 1991).

With a second alert line added to Fig 17.1, Fig 17.2 is drawn. The alert line featured in Fig 17.1 is presented as the "first line" in Fig 17.2

In *Strategic Choice for Prosperity*, an additional explanation is made: "Whether it is indirect regulation or direct regulation that prevails, the adoption of planned quotas should not be excluded when restraints on resource become strong and shortages run high, and changes in market prices and supply and demand must be followed (Li 1991)."

As shown in Fig 17.2, the second alert line divides abnormal shortages into two sections. Let us call the section between the second and first alert lines "abnormal shortage I," where the government gives priority to indirect regulation. The section above the second alert line is dubbed "abnormal shortage II," where the government gives priority to direct regulation. If abnormal shortage in the economy is serious enough to necessitate forceful intervention, the government can turn to the "last resort," unconventional intervention in the economy. The reservation of this "last

Fig. 17.1 xxx

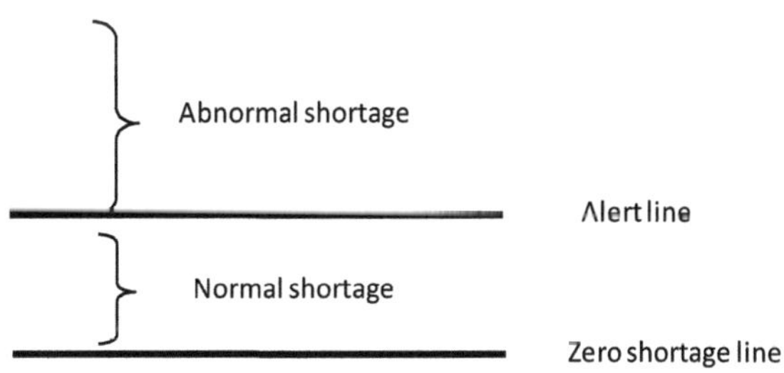

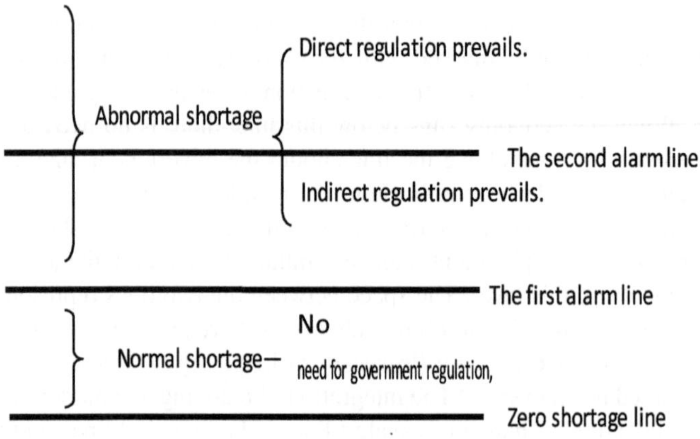

Fig. 17.2 xxx

resort" testifies to the government's resolve and strength to regulate the economy—it will never look on with folded arms as the economy goes from bad to worse (Li 1990). This can be shown in Fig 17.3:

With these concepts in mind—zero shortage line, normal shortage, abnormal shortage I, abnormal shortage II, the first alert line, and the second alert line—we gain a better understanding of what normal fluctuations and abnormal fluctuations are all about.

What are normal fluctuations in economic disequilibrium? We can reach this preliminary conclusion: when the economy operates above the zero shortage line and below the first alert line—that is, within the scope of normal shortage—fluctuations are normal.

What about abnormal fluctuations in economic disequilibrium? We can also arrive at the following preliminary conclusion: When the economy operates above the

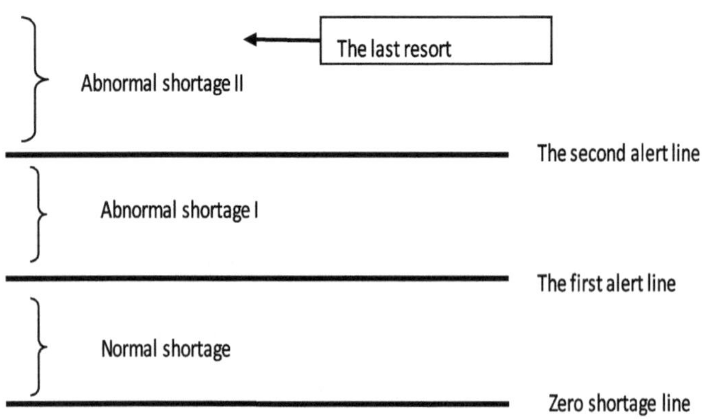

Fig. 17.3 xxx

second alert line but is still within the scope of abnormal shortage II, fluctuations are abnormal.

Figure 3 indicates that the section between the zero shortage line and the first alert line represents normal shortage. When the economy runs within this range, normal fluctuations in economic disequilibrium occur; what happens in the section above the second alert line is abnormal shortage II, in which abnormal fluctuations in disequilibrium take place. This poses the question: Are fluctuations normal or abnormal when the economy operates between the first and second alert lines? Further analysis is needed to give a reasonable answer.

Fluctuations are usually indicated with changes in the economic growth rate. However, the economic growth rate cannot accurately reflect shortages. A high growth rate can be achieved under both normal and abnormal shortages, and so can a low growth rate. Therefore, when studying the economy's performance in a specific year or a period of years, we find it hard to discover the close ties between economic growth rate and the degree of shortages. In addition, changes in the degree of shortages are concealed when fluctuations are measured by economic growth rate. Therefore, if we judge whether fluctuations are normal or not merely by changes in economic growth rate, we are courting two mistakes.

First, fluctuations seem to have nothing to do with economic disequilibrium. The difference between normal and abnormal fluctuations under disequilibrium conditions is concealed in the changes of economic rate. Thus, we cannot see through fluctuations and predict their future course of development.

Second, a high economic growth rate can be achieved in the presence of abnormal shortages, whereas a low growth rate may happen amidst normal shortages. This being the case, if we judge fluctuations on the basis of growth rate changes, we will probably go astray in attempting to maintain a high economic growth rate by expanding abnormal shortages instead of maintaining a low growth rate by curtailing such shortages.

Obviously, we cannot jump to a conclusion on normal or abnormal fluctuations in economic disequilibrium simply according to changes in economic growth rate. Rather, we should base our observation on changes in the degree of shortages. We will get a clearer picture of this if we observe the economy for a longer period of time. This is because, supposing the economy operates within the range of abnormal shortages under disequilibrium conditions, problems caused by such shortages will definitely affect economic growth rate and betray themselves in the form of marked fluctuations.

Now let us return to the previous question: Is it normal or abnormal fluctuation under disequilibrium when the economy operates between the first and second alert lines? The answer should be based on changes in shortages during an extended period of economic growth. There are two scenarios.

The first scenario: The economy has been operating within a normal shortage range, and economic growth has been achieved on this basis. If the economy runs above the first alert line and fluctuates between the two alert lines, such fluctuations are deemed abnormal.

The second scenario: The economy has been operating within abnormal shortage II, that is, above the second alert line, and economic growth has been achieved on that basis. If the economy operates between the two alert lines and fluctuates within abnormal shortage I, it is considered a normal fluctuation, because compared to the previous period, the economic fluctuations are moving toward normalcy.

—*A Speech at a Meeting to Summarize the "Growth Theories and Mathematical Models of the Chinese Economy," a Research Project of the National Natural Science Foundation of China, March 21, 1993*

References

Li Y-N (1990) *Disequilibrium in the Chinese Economy*. Economic Daily Press, Beijing, pp. 70-71.
Li Y-N et al (1991a) *Strategic Choice for Prosperity*. Economic Daily Press, Beijing, p. 204.
Li Y-N et al (1991b) *Strategic Choice for Prosperity*. Economic Daily Press, Beijing, pp. 204-205.

Chapter 18
1994: Property Rights Reform of Rural Enterprises

I

More and more people are coming to terms with the importance of rural enterprises to the Chinese economy, an importance that has been borne out by reality. The reform of large and medium-sized state enterprises and the development of rural enterprises are part and parcel of the effort to reshape the microeconomic foundation of the socialist market economy being developed in this nation. Academic discussions are elaborate and thorough concerning the property rights reform of large and medium-sized state enterprises, but somewhat lacking on the significance of similar reform of rural enterprises and the approaches to it. Indeed, discussions about the latter have merely touched upon the development of the "joint-stock cooperative system." In truth, the property rights reform of rural enterprises is no less important and difficult than that of state enterprises. Moreover, the term "joint-stock cooperative system" is yet to be clarified. All this necessitates some in-depth study.

To begin with, we should not take the burgeoning development of rural enterprises over the recent years for granted. Rather, we should contemplate the role of the market in the survival and development of these enterprises, and look at the question of what is to be done to adapt them further to the market.

Rural enterprises have no lack of competitors. On the home market, they compete with each other, but their competition comes mainly from state enterprises, large urban collectives,[1] private businesses, equity joint ventures with Chinese and foreign investment, and imported commodities. After a rural enterprise is built or expanded, its managers must think about where its market is, how to carve out a niche in the market for its products, and how to expand its market shares.

Rural enterprises cannot count on local governments for incentives or fringe benefits. They are mistaken if they believe that local governments can help them secure

[1] Large urban collective, a term dating back to the Big Leap Forward of 1958, referring to firms in which capital is owned collectively while workers are accorded the same wages and welfare benefits as state enterprise employees.

Y. Li, *China's Economy Since 1978*, China Academic Library,
https://doi.org/10.1007/978-981-95-5733-2_18

local markets, bar the entry of outsiders, monopolize local supply of raw materials, and prevent local raw materials from being shipped to other areas. This is because local protectionism runs counter to market economy principles, and, judging from the requirements of either the planned economy or the market economy, is bound to be ditched. From the perspective of the planned economy, the practice of monopolizing the supply of raw materials and carving up local markets among local businesses flies in the face of the principle of centralization and of quota-based distribution. From the perspective of the market economy, local protectionism violates the principle of fair and square market competition and market unification. In the short run, this protectionist practice may benefit rural enterprises, but in the long run, it is wrong in that it protects backwardness, strangles businesses, and can backfire on rural enterprises themselves. Enterprises must grow in strength through market competition, because their survival hinges on product quality, profitability, and creativity.

If flexible business mechanisms can stand rural enterprises in good stead when competing with state enterprises and big urban collectives under the planned economy, that competitive edge can do them little good when they are pitted against equity joint ventures and private enterprises. Competition between rural enterprises themselves can be tough, too, as their competitiveness is neutralized by the common business mechanisms they employ and the common incentives they receive from local governments. Market competition is merciless; its result is always the same: In the course of it, some rural enterprises collapse, some grow in strength, and new ones keep appearing.

Therefore, it is reasonable to conclude that market conditions are the test of rural enterprises. Today, such enterprises are burgeoning everywhere in the country. Will this robust development grow to disastrous proportions? Under central planning, fast proliferation of rural businesses would have been the undoing of the national economy. However, that was then, this is now. The rural enterprises we have today are worlds apart from their predecessors in that they must face the market and be tested by it. The underdogs in market competition are doomed. Their predecessors might have still been muddling along under central planning and gone on consuming all sorts of resources no matter how inefficient they were and how deeply they sank into debt. The test of the market was always there, but under central planning, businesses could ignore such a test or stay impervious to it. Not so for the rural enterprises of today. They are sensitive to the test of the market because their survival is on the line. They must strive to raise economic efficiency and produce nothing but what the market needs. In other words, under central planning, the existence of too many losing companies was a disaster to the national economy because they could be established but were not allowed to die, they were allowed to hang around but not allowed to disappear. By contrast, rural enterprises today are allowed to rise or fall of their own accord; those doing poorly are phased out without mercy; the national economy is immune to fluctuations caused by drastic increases in the number of rural enterprises; and society is in no danger of turmoil when large numbers of such enterprises collapse. This being the case, if people are saying there are too many enterprises, that is because too many ill-managed enterprises are still dragging along under old-fashioned central planning and because too few enterprises can measure up to market economic requirements and stand the test of the market. If people are saying enterprises are growing too fast, we know they are complaining about the unbridled development of enterprises that are insensitive to market changes and never bother to cater their production to market demand, while enterprises that produce only for the market and whose products sell briskly on the market are not growing fast enough. Rural enterprises of today belong in the latter category.

II

I deem it necessary to say something about repetitious construction. Should repetitious construction be discontinued? Generally speaking, it should be disallowed. This is because with a given supply of resources, repetitious production is synonymous with waste, or unwarranted use of resources that serves nothing but to aggravate the already strained supply. With a given level of market purchase power, repetitious construction or production often means that, for lack of demand, some products become a drag on the market or are stockpiled, which again is tantamount to wasting or abusing resources. This double waste or abuse of resources is a cost or a menace that repetitious construction poses for the economy.

When censuring repetitious production, people tend to lump rural enterprises in with it, as if there were an indissoluble bond between the rise and expansion of these enterprises and repetitious production. Yet they have forgotten what really matters with such production is not whether an enterprise is rural or state-owned, but whether it has changed its operational mechanisms and whether its investment system is new or old. Rural enterprises are flexible in management, and they make their own business decisions while bearing their own gains and losses. Common sense tells us that repetitious production is a losing cause because it inevitably strains resource supply, inflates production costs, and inhibits sales because of the market's limited purchasing power. Rural enterprises do not meddle in repetitious production in the same way that a man never bangs his head against a wall, knowing perfectly well that such an action spells nothing but headache. By contrast, enterprises that do not have to bear the consequence of investment risks under central planning may willingly go after large production scales and as many production projects as possible at all costs, even if such investment brings no returns at all. The crux of the issue is precisely whether an investing enterprise is accountable for the investment risks it chooses to run. Rural enterprises do not embrace redundant production because they can, of their own accord, shun investment and redundant production projects that bring no economic returns.

From a macroeconomic point of view, we should go a little further in our observation of what people really want out of repetitious production. The term generally refers to building a new factory to make a product that someone else is already making. It is a typical behavior of waste. But the question here is: Does banning repetitious production protect monopoly and backwardness? Is repetitious construction detrimental to the national economy on all occasions? Should competition be allowed between manufacturers of the same product? Take, for instance, a certain product being manufactured by a factory, which is in short supply and leaves a considerable market share to be filled. The dilemma here is whether to allow the factory to expand production or to build a new one to make up for the shortage. In this case, construction of a new a factory should obviously not be regarded as repetitious. Again, if the factory already in existence can meet market demand for the product in question but its price is too high and its quality leaves something to be desired, whereas the same product to be made by the factory to be built will be better in quality and lower in price, is it wise to allow the existing factory to monopolize the product and bar the participation of the new factory? It simply does not make sense to tolerate one factory making an inferior product and reject another factory that can offer the same product with a lower price and better quality. In all, repetitious construction should not be used as an excuse to justify protecting monopoly and backwardness.

Now, a look at the waste of resources associated with repetitious construction. It should be pointed out in the first place that it is a waste or abuse of resources to allow a factory to go on making a product at high price and with poor quality while banning the construction of a new factory to produce the same product more competitively. If, under the pretext of sanctioning repetitious construction, we choose to ban the construction of the new factory that can use the same number of resources to produce a superior product, and tolerate the existing factory's poor performance, isn't that an abuse of resources? Moreover, it should be reiterated that the market is the test of all enterprises, rural enterprises included. As long as the principle of "survival of the fittest" is followed in economic affairs, those making expensive and shabby products will be eliminated and those making cheaper and better products will survive even if both the amount of capital goods and the market purchasing power are limited. The limited supply of capital goods and market share should be awarded to the latter and denied to the former. Through a period of competition, the fittest survive, and the least fit are phased out. The waste of resources is naturally taken care of through market competition. Isn't there any reason for us to insist that repetitious production is bad? Overlapping production of expensive and shabby commodities should be banned, and so should the overlapping construction of factories produce such commodities, whether the factories involved are owned by the state or farmers.

A profound lesson to be drawn from practice is that rural enterprises can never measure up to the requirements of the market economy if they fail to speed up property rights reform, organize production according to market needs, give precedence to profitability, and establish a managerial system that fuses incentives with restraints. We dare say that the good days are numbered for those rural enterprises that are doing well despite their ill-defined property rights. The market economy is pressing them to overhaul and transform themselves before it is too late.

III

This justifies the need to elaborate on the importance of rural enterprise property rights reform. This reform is designed to standardize the organization and behavior of market participants. At the present stage of development in this nation, its mission is to revamp those enterprises in which government administration is entangled with business management and property rights are ill defined, and which cannot make their own management decisions and bear responsibility for their gains and losses. Only when management is free from government intervention and property rights well defined can enterprises have the final say in economic activity, and account for their own profits and losses. The property rights reform entails transforming old enterprises and establishing new ones. According to the reform guideline, new enterprises should, from day one, have their management detached from government patronage and their property rights clarified, make their own decisions and be liable for their own gains and losses.

As is mentioned above, the market is the test for enterprises, and "survival of the fittest" the rule of market competition. To root out repetitious production, enterprises must be overhauled and new ones set up according to the guidelines for property rights reform. Only thus can they restructure their products in light of market changes, phase out unneeded products and turn out products that are needed and can elbow out competitors' high-priced shabby products. More importantly, property rights reform puts all enterprises on the same scratch line and detaches their management from government administration. Abiding by law and paying taxes according to rules, they are not directly under government administration and their production and business activity are immune from direct government intervention. Through property rights reform, every company bears investment risks and is liable for their gains and losses, instead of living off the government's egalitarian system of distribution and preferential treatments. The significance of property rights reform as a fundamental step toward a modern market economy is self-evident.

People are still wondering if property rights reform is as much needed by rural enterprises as by state enterprises or large urban collectives. The answer is in the positive: Rural enterprises need property rights reform. Such enterprises' survival and further growth are predicated on changing their operational mechanisms, making independent business decisions, bearing responsibility for their gains and losses, and ceasing to be government appendages. If they do not have the final say on business decisions and cannot take responsibility for their own profits and losses, how can it be said they have stood the test of the market and followed the "survival of the fittest" rule to compete for all their worth? If they are still subject to stringent government restrictions and intervention the way state enterprises and large urban collectives used to be, how can it be said they are a force powerful enough to breach the dyke of central planning? The saying that rural enterprises are following a different property right system than the state enterprises and urban collectives is a vague statement. It does not tally with reality in two ways.

On the one hand, only a fraction of rural enterprises has radically changed their business mechanisms to qualify as independent commodity producers. Many others are not qualified as such because they are still following the beaten track of central planning—they are rural enterprises in name but "rural-owned" or "town-owned" enterprises in reality. In other words, they are still appendages of local governments at the grassroots level. For them, property rights reform is yet to begin, and local rural or town governments are yet to come to terms with the necessity and importance of such reform. That is why it is absolutely wrong to believe property rights reform is not a requisite for rural enterprises.

On the other hand, even those rural enterprises said to have changed their operational mechanisms have, in fact, only begun to do so. Their property right structure is yet to be standardized, and their relationship with rural governments is yet to be readjusted before they can qualify as one hundred percent independent commodity producers.

Therefore, the pressing task for rural enterprises today is to push property rights reform, standardize their property right configurations, and put their property right structure on a sound footing. To believe their immediate task is expanding production and increasing investment is to overlook the key to their development. It matters, of course, for rural enterprises to expand production and increase investment. But that should come as an inevitable result of property rights reform rather than a substitute for such reform.

The impact of rural enterprise property rights reform does not stop just there. There are other aspects where its impact is apparent. Firstly, it enhances farmers' awareness of their status as owners of their enterprises and thereby fortifies their resolve to boost production and transform their homeland; secondly, it improves farmers' cultural endowment and business acumen and puts rural socio-economic development on a fast track; thirdly, it promotes rural government reform and shores up the nation's political power at the grassroots level; and fourthly, it improves farmer income and livelihood and furnishes beneficial conditions for the achievement of common prosperity in rural areas. The following is a further elaboration of the impact of rural enterprise property rights reform in these four aspects.

(1) Enhancing farmers' awareness of their status as owners of rural enterprises.

It should be noted that without genuine property rights reform, the property rights of rural enterprises can remain vague and ill defined, and farmers' self-respect as owners—even if they are just partial owners—of rural enterprises will be hurt, and this will further shake their commitment to production and investment. If, on the contrary, property rights reform has been carried out in all seriousness so that every farmer investor in such an enterprise becomes clear about his or her share of property right, their awareness of themselves as owners of their enterprise will be vastly enhanced. They will become more attentive to the incremental value of the assets in their enterprise, and be personally concerned with their business performance and more enthusiastic for production and investment. When rural enterprises are energized by property rights reform to increase their profits and output, they can open the eyes of their farmer-owners and investors to the prospects of rural development and the impact of their economic growth on rural development. Their resolve to turn their villages into brand-new ones will be greatly fortified as a result. It is often reported that, bored or disheartened by village life, able-bodied farmers are quitting farming and leaving their country homes, causing a drain on the rural workforce. True, this is what happens in some rural areas. However, it is equally true that in areas where rural enterprises have grown to a sizeable scale, and particularly where such enterprises are using part of their profits to improve rural cultural and living conditions, farmers are in a peaceful frame of mind and live a contented life. Not only are local able-bodied farmers staying put, but farmers are coming from elsewhere to join them as well. Therefore, there is every reason to believe that once property rights reform has boosted farmers' awareness as owners of rural enterprises and vastly energized their enterprises, tremendous changes are bound to take place in the rural economic and cultural landscape, and local farmers will become more committed to building up their homeland than ever before.

(2) Improving farmers' cultural and technical proficiency and management acumen.

Farmers' cultural and technical proficiency and business acumen can be improved in many ways. An important way is property rights reform of rural enterprises, which is meant to turn farmers into true owners and investors of such enterprises, give them the opportunity to attend enterprise meetings, and open up new avenues for them to improve their cultural endowment, skills, and business acumen. This is because without such a reform, farmers are just nominal owners of their enterprises, and have no opportunities to attend these enterprises' meetings and make their voice heard, to say nothing of improving themselves through the activities of these enterprises. Under these circumstances, farmers' relationship with their rural enterprise is reduced to the point where they are mere workers or people who have spent some money on them—no enterprise would regard them as its masters. That situation can change dramatically through property rights reform, which serves to clarify farmers' status as owners and investors as well as their share of property rights to rural enterprises. As owners and investors, they can take part in the decision-making process or send representatives to meetings. In this way they gain a gradual understanding of their enterprise's business and financial situation, and get to know the causes behind their successes or failures behind the rise and fall of the value of their assets. If a farmer happens to be working in the enterprise he owns or invests in, he is entitled to participate, directly or indirectly, in the making of production and business decisions. If several rural enterprises are presented to him as investment options, he may compare them, and upgrade his technological and economic know-how through such comparisons. The market economy is often said to be a great school in which people can learn a lot of things that cannot be learned from books. However, farmers can learn a lot more from the market economy as rural business owners and investors than if they are mere workers. The more they come to know the market economy, the more smoothly the market economy can grow. To help farmers understand the market economy deeply, it is necessary for them to participate not just as consumers, workers, or bank-savings depositors but as investors and managers as well.

(3) Bolstering up rural governments at the grassroots level.

The building of governments at the township level involves a number of issues, such as promotion of democracy in rural government elections, the building of Party organizations at the grassroots level, and the character building of rural government officials. It also involves readjusting the relationship between grassroots governments and rural enterprises. Rural government reform is intimately related to the property rights reform of rural enterprises, and the key to the success of both reforms lies in unfettering businesses from government intervention and turning rural enterprises into independent commodity producers with well-defined property rights and decision-making autonomy and bearing their own gains and losses. When rural enterprises cease to be government appendages, rural governments can no longer regard them as their own businesses, let alone turn them into their slush funds. This is something that can never be achieved without genuine property rights reform. As a matter of fact, there is no lack of local governments which, by capitalizing on rural enterprises' ill-defined property rights, put these enterprises under their control and turn them into their slush funds even if they are not making a profit. This inevitably saps the energy of these enterprises and dampens their farmer-owners' ardor for production and investment. As a hotbed for corruption among rural government officials, these illegal "off-book coffers" also spoil the image of grassroots political power, rob local governments of popular support, and destabilize local political and economic life.

The dire consequences of the wanton behaviors of rural government officials in this regard have been borne out by a series of legal cases that have been cracked in recent years. As de facto bosses of some rural enterprises with political and economic power in their control, these people have wantonly violated the norms of the market economy by willfully withdrawing money, extorting reimbursement for personal expenses, and practicing nepotism in enrolling workers. Shouldn't these behaviors be sternly sanctioned in the course of reforming the property rights of rural enterprises?

Obviously, it is not just a paramount economic issue, but also a political issue with a close bearing on whether rural political power can be consolidated and whether rural social stability can be maintained. We have got to follow the principle of defining property rights and separating administration from management when we readjust the relationship of rural enterprises with grassroots governments and turn them into independent commodity producers that enjoy well-defined property rights and decision-making autonomy, and bear their own gains and losses. On no account should this task be taken lightly.

(4) Raising farmer income and striving for common prosperity in rural areas.

Improved rural livelihood is a fruit of increased farmer income. The issue here is how farmers can increase their income quickly. Simply put, there are two ways to achieve this. First, developing farm production (animal husbandry, fishery, forestry, sideline occupations included), and boosting labor productivity by a large margin. Second, striving for fast growth in rural enterprises in the primary, secondary, and tertiary industries and for major growth in labor productivity, so that farmers can make more money immediately as laborers and investors. In addition, rural enterprises may also use part of their profits to support agriculture, improve rural cultural and living facilities, and ameliorate farmers' livelihood.

Some farmers have left their home villages for somewhere else, but many of them end up working in rural enterprises away from home. It is thus clear that the property rights reform of rural enterprises and the effort to revive rural enterprises for further development are conducive to increasing farmer income and improving rural material and cultural lives.

What is to be done to help the rural poor to beat poverty? What is the relationship between the development of rural enterprises and the drive to help the rural poor? First of all, helping the rural poor is a social issue that can be addressed only by the concerted efforts of the entire society. This calls for special policies addressed to impoverished areas and households, aid from urban businesses and institutions for economic, technological, and educational and Medicare development of underdeveloped areas, as well as help from families that have become affluent earlier than others to poor families. Another method that works is to enlist help from rural enterprises for poverty-stricken areas and underprivileged households. For instance, enrolling workers from poor areas and investing in these areas for developmental purposes helps tap local resources and boost local income. Rural enterprises in relatively more developed regions may pair up with counterparts in less developed regions. In all, the enthusiastic participation of rural enterprises can vastly accelerate increases in the income level of households and regions in financial difficulties. Such actions are an embodiment of the fruits of property rights reform.

IV

Now look at the goals target model for rural enterprise property rights reform. That the contract responsibility system cannot become a target model for enterprises under the market economy is a foregone conclusion among many accomplished economists, and therefore does not need further elaboration. Instead, what target model should be set for this field of property rights reform merits further study.

The cooperative system can be a target model for rural enterprise property rights reform, as it defines the economic nature and organizational form of enterprise properties. What this goal can achieve can be summarized in four points.

First, when adopted to establish or transform rural enterprises, the cooperative system helps separate government administration from business management, clarify property rights, and enable enterprises to enjoy business autonomy and hand gains and losses on their own.

Second, when employed to establish or transform rural enterprises, the cooperative system helps combine farmer investors and farmer workers into one, thereby motivating farmers as both investors and workers.

Third, when used to establish or transform rural enterprises, the cooperative system can foster a congenial internal environment, thereby enhancing internal cohesion, and promoting labor productivity.

Fourth, when applied to establish or transform rural enterprises, the cooperative system enables them to tighten up their management system under a standard corporate constitution, restrain their leaders, and protect the lawful rights of workers and investors, thereby paving the way for their smooth development.

With the aforementioned strengths, the cooperative system for rural enterprises should not be overlooked as an organizational form for corporate properties. The notion that cooperative enterprises are outdated does not tally with reality. It need be stressed that the rural enterprises established or transformed according to a standard principle are different from their counterparts that existed under central planning or still exist nowadays. Ill-defined property rights make it hard for those rural enterprises that are known as collectives in name only to identify who their investors are. Some of these firms are established with money raised by individuals, but they do not treat their investors as owners, and the investors themselves do not regard themselves as owners, either. By contrast, the rural enterprises that have adopted the cooperative system take on a new look that distinguishes themselves categorically from firms under collective ownership. The cooperative system may also be a form of collective ownership, but it is a new form of collective ownership adapted to the socialist market economic system.

The cooperative system, nevertheless, is just one of the target models for rural enterprise property rights reform. Compared with joint-stock rural enterprises, cooperative rural enterprises have five limits.

First, the cooperative system works smoothly when rural enterprises are small, but it falls somewhat short when they grow larger. When it is adopted to set up or transform a small rural enterprise, its investors are also its workers, thereby creating a congenial corporate atmosphere in which the "one man, one vote" decision-making system—the slogan of the cooperative system—works perfectly. But if the enterprise is big and has a lot of people on its payroll, the same decision-making system is likely to dwindle into a mere formality if it is put in place, for it cannot work as effectively in coordinating the enterprise's internal relationships as it does in a small enterprise.

Second, from a financing and fund-raising point of view, a cooperative rural enterprise compares unfavorably with a joint-stock one. A joint-stock rural enterprise can raise funds from a wide spectrum of public avenues, whereas a cooperative rural enterprise may have trouble raising more money than its internal fund-raising mechanism allows, especially under its "one man, one vote" decision-making system. This limit of the cooperative rural enterprise becomes more pronounced when it grows in size or when it lets a major profit-making opportunity slip through its fingers because of lack of money.

Third, when a rural enterprise sets about redefining its property rights, it is often harassed by the issue of converting its capital stock into stock shares. The same problem can be easily addressed under the joint-stock system. Yet under the cooperative system, it can be solved only by selling the capital stock evenly among members, something that is easy for a small enterprise but becomes unwieldy for a large enterprise.

Fourth, an enterprise in the course of development sometimes needs to acquire another enterprise's stock, or take control of it through such acquisition. Sometimes it needs to sell its stock shares to other enterprises. It may also grow into an enterprise group through mergers. These normal economic behaviors can go smoothly if rural enterprises are regrouped or transformed under the joint-stock system, but may hit some snags under the cooperative system.

Fifth, the cooperative system differs from the joint-stock system in that the stock shares of such a rural firm can be withdrawn freely, which can be a destabilizing factor for its production and business scale, whereas in a joint-stock rural enterprise, shares can change hands only among colleagues, which helps maintain its production and business scale. Moreover, under the joint-stock system, stock shares are transferred at the current price instead of the original price, which puts investors at a relative advantage. Under the cooperative system, it is hard to price the withdrawn shares—if the original price is applied, the man withdrawing his stock will find himself at the losing end of the deal, but if a higher price is set on the basis of reevaluating the assets, it may trigger off an exodus of stockholders. If that happens, how can the enterprise go on with its production? However, if a cooperative rural enterprise bans such withdrawal altogether, doesn't this violate the cooperative principle? Herein are some operational snags for such an enterprise in dealing with voluntary withdrawal of stock shares.

Cooperative rural enterprises are also confronted with the quandary of whether or not to admit new participants. If they do not accept new members while allowing those on the payroll to withdraw freely, won't they shrink in size constantly? At least their membership will keep diminishing. If new participants are welcome, what price should they pay for admittance? If the original price is used, it will do a great favor to newcomers and attract more new arrivals, leaving old members to feel cheated. Thus, the conflict between old and new members will go from bad to worse. If newcomers are asked to pay at a price based on a reevaluation of the assets, the going will be tough for the enterprise. For joint-stock rural enterprises, where stock can only be transferred internally, the problem becomes a lot simpler.

V

Despite all that has been said, the beauty of the cooperative system for rural enterprises can hardly be gainsaid. It works as effectively as the joint-stock system in helping rural enterprises meet their goals by reforming their business mechanisms, keeping government administration from interfering in business management, defining their property rights, making their own business decisions and bearing responsibility for their gains and losses. The problem, however, is that the cooperative system works perfectly in small rural enterprises, but not as effectively as the joint-stock system in large rural enterprises, particularly where large and medium-sized enterprises are established or transformed. In other words, the cooperative system is appropriate for the property rights reform of small rural enterprises, while the joint-stock system should be pursued where the property rights of large and medium-sized enterprises are reformed.

This brings forth another topic for our discussion: the joint-stock cooperative system. What is the "joint-stock cooperative system" all about? Most of the rural enterprises that claim to be under this system are small companies under joint partnership. The others are irregular joint-stock enterprises. Rural enterprises that follow the textbook-perfect cooperative or joint-stock system are few and far between. For this reason, not just those rural enterprises that have not reformed their property rights should carry out such reform—those already passing themselves off as "joint-stock cooperative" enterprises should also undertake this reform in earnest, so as to standardize their operational system. They may either be transformed into cooperatives or joint-stock firms, or, in the light of their property right situations, become private firms under either single ownership or partnership.

The term "joint-stock cooperative system" is somewhat off the mark. The cooperative system and the joint-stock system entail different organizational forms of corporate assets. An enterprise may or may not choose either system. It is impossible for a firm to adopt both at the same time, or combine them in one. Nevertheless, the "joint-stock cooperative system" catches the fancy of many a rural enterprise out of three probable considerations.

First, concern over being dubbed "capitalist," a term that may cause some raised eyebrows in socialist China. Out of the belief that the cooperative system is socialist and the joint-stock system capitalist, some enterprises choose to call themselves a "joint-stock cooperative enterprise" when regrouping or transforming themselves to measure up to the requirements of the joint-stock system. They do this to avoid unnecessary controversy and enhance their sense of security even though the name bears little meaning for a joint-stock company. Such concern is uncalled for today. The joint-stock system is, if anything, an organizational form of corporate assets. It is therefore contentious to call it either socialist or capitalist. The joint-stock system can stand on its own. There is no need to pass it off under the ill-fitting title of "joint-stock cooperative system."

Second, the belief that the adjective "cooperative" can help attract government policy incentives. This again is unnecessary. Government policy incentives may be granted in two ways. Firstly, an enterprise that meets national or local policy requirements for industrial restructuring naturally qualifies for such incentives whether or not its name contains the word "cooperative." It is the industrial nature of the enterprise's investment and production that counts. Secondly, cooperative enterprises deserve certain policy incentives in compliance with relevant national and local legislation. An enterprise must be regrouped or transformed under the cooperative system to qualify for such incentives. It won't do to add "cooperative" to the name of an enterprise that is not really a cooperative one. If a "joint-stock cooperative" is truly cooperative, why don't they simply call themselves "cooperative"? It is useless to gild the lily.

Third, mistaking the "joint-stock cooperative" system for a corporate property organizational form with Chinese characteristics, which is different from both the cooperative system and the joint-stock system. It so happens that some enterprises have divided their stock into "collective shares" and "corporate shares." Believing that this division does not accord with the standard joint-stock system, and that "collective shares" and "corporate shares" smack of the cooperative system, they have renamed themselves "joint-stock cooperative enterprises." It also happened that some people—on the ground that the cooperative system allows investors to withdraw their shares but the joint-stock system does not, and that in a cooperative enterprise under the "one man, one vote" decision-making system, votes are decided by the number of stock shares—have coined the term "joint-stock cooperative" system in the hope of incorporating the strengths of both systems, so that old investors can withdraw their shares while new investors, individuals and legal entities included, can be attracted. They assert this "joint-stock cooperative system" is distinctively Chinese. This way of thinking, however, is misleading. For their tremendous role in Chinese economic development, rural enterprises are "distinctively Chinese" enough. There is absolutely no need to concoct an ill-fitting joint-stock or cooperative system. Such irregular systems, if allowed to exist, can only hold back the growth of rural enterprises.

VI

Property rights reform is under way among rural enterprises. The rise of the "joint-stock cooperative" rural enterprises are a nascent phenomenon no matter how you look at them. They deserve help and guidance to meet established business norms. They should not be discriminated against, still less rebuked or disbanded. Their rise is spontaneous to a large extent. Rural government officials and local farmers have embraced them with great gusto. Some of these enterprises, though looking somewhat outlandish, are the brainchild of local people. If the rise and development of rural enterprises had played a positive role in the development of China in the 1980s, part of that contribution came from the "joint-stock cooperatives." If, with their presence and growth, rural enterprises are a powerful onslaught on central planning, the contributions of "joint-stock cooperative" rural enterprises cannot be denied. Practice proves that in comparison with the "orthodox" enterprises which are collective in name but centralized in deed, the "joint-stock cooperative" rural enterprises may well qualify as "heterodoxy." However, to unshackle the national economy from central planning, we would do better to have more of such "heterodoxy." Property rights reform should be carried out variously in light of specific circumstances, and different measures are called for to institutionalize the property right configuration of rural enterprises. Such reform should also be allowed to go at different speeds. The general trend is that the cooperative system will be the target model for property rights reform in small rural enterprises, and the joint-stock system for this reform in large and medium-sized rural enterprises. Having made this point previously, I will not labor it further.

Joint-stock rural enterprises need not be listed on the stock market. Under the joint-stock system, only a few companies eventually become listed. Someday, however, some rural enterprises may qualify for it, a likelihood that should never be excluded. Most joint-stock rural enterprises, however, may be converted into limited liability companies, which I believe is a property organizational form universally applicable for rural enterprises. A certain number of them may be transformed into limited liability companies with internal stock shares. It should be noted that the joint-stock system cannot be divided into "urban enterprise joint-stock system" and "rural enterprise joint-stock system," nor can it be split into "joint-stock system for regrouped state enterprises" or "joint-stock system for regrouped rural enterprises." The joint-stock system applies to all manner of shareholding companies.

Some enterprises, out of one consideration or another, choose to stay with the name "joint-stock cooperative enterprise." What is to be done about this? In this case, impetuosity gets us nowhere. The goal of property rights reform is to prevent the government from interfering in business management, to define property rights, and delegate enterprises with autonomy to make business decisions and handle their own gains and losses. A rural enterprise may still be known as a "joint-stock cooperative enterprise" provided it has reached the goals of property rights reform, adopted effective business operational mechanisms, and has already been organized and operated under a standard joint-stock or cooperative system. Someday, it may awaken to the need to change its name to "joint-stock enterprise" or "cooperative enterprise."

The "joint-stock cooperative system" is a transitional corporate property organization form. The "rural enterprise" is transitional, too, and many firms have stuck to this name since its debut for two reasons: first, to differentiate them from enterprises under the dominant central planning, such as state enterprises and large urban collectives; and second, to take into consideration the fact that they are located in villages and towns, with their workforce coming mainly from among local villagers. What will become of these "rural enterprises" in the future? Will there be any more "urban enterprises" in contrast with "rural enterprises"? Can "rural enterprises" be established only in villages or towns, and can their workforce come only from local villages? If, in these early days, it is necessary to use the term "rural enterprise" to highlight their differences in business operational mechanisms from those under central planning and their identity as "above-norm" commodity producers, is there any need to differentiate "above-norm" commodity producers from "planned" commodity producers in a future market economic environment? As mentioned in the foregoing, enterprises are enterprises, joint-stock enterprises are joint-stock enterprises. There is absolutely no need to divide them into "urban" and "rural" enterprises, still less "urban" and "rural" joint-stock enterprises. "Rural enterprise," as a transitional name, will disappear at last, and so will "rural joint-stock enterprise."

This, however, will not happen anytime soon. Returning to reality, we should pursue joint-stock reform among rural enterprises and devise proper ways and means to establish and operate them. Moreover, to repeat once again, even though the notion of "joint-stock cooperative system" is inaccurate, and the establishment and operation of such enterprises can be very difficult, we may as well let such a title stay, considering the fact that it has been widely accepted by rural officials and farmers. The use of the name "joint-stock cooperative" system, or simply the "joint-stock system," represents a departure from the status quo. In property rights reform, instead of haggling over names endlessly, we should set our eye on the essence of things. If an enterprise is traveling down the road of property rights reform, it will not reach its goal in just a single leap. A more realistic approach is to go step by step toward the final destination.

—Study & Exploration, issue No. 3, 1994

Chapter 19
1995: Accelerating Economic Legislation and Eradicating Corruption

I

China has suffered a severe loss of state-owned assets. Some assets have fallen into the hands of the leaders or officials of government departments; some have gone to the pockets of the heads or staff of enterprises and institutions. Both circumstances are directly related to corruption.

There are five main channels through which state-owned assets can be embezzled. First, after accepting bribes, officials in government lease state-owned land at lower-than-normal rental prices or transfer state assets at low prices, both of which incur losses to state-owned assets. The same applies to state-owned banks that grant unsecured loans. Second, some officials may acquire private shares or take bribes in the process of SOE restructuring. Third, they collude with contractors or leaseholders of SOEs, then accept bribes or benefits. Fourth, they turn public property into private property in the process of setting up economic entities. Fifth, they exploit loose management to register private accounts for national investment overseas, effectively converting public investments into private ones; or they embezzle state property on the occasions of transferring, buying, and holding shares.

II

At present, there is not only a huge loss of state-owned assets in the society, but also a large number of other forms of exploitation of power for personal gains. These corruption phenomena are closely related to the lag of China's legal system.

Building an incorrupt government mainly relies on the law. The law is normative and binding, and no one is permitted to have privileges to transgress it. Whoever takes bribes and embezzles state-owned assets must be punished by the law. However, as far as China has adopted legal means to eradicate corruption, there is not only a delay in enforcement and administration of justice under the existing laws, but more importantly a lack of certain anti-corruption laws which are directly related to the construction of an honest administration. This inevitably affects the progress of striving for a clean government and restricts our anti-corruption efforts.

Y. Li, *China's Economy Since 1978*, China Academic Library,
https://doi.org/10.1007/978-981-95-5733-2_19

The following laws should be enacted as soon as possible to accelerate the legislation related to building a clean government and combating corruption.

i Anti-Corruption and Bribery Law

The guiding principle of the law should be to punish crimes such as corruption, bribery, and embezzlement of state property committed by staff of state institutions and public-owned enterprises and institutions. Same standards should be applied to all and no privileges should be granted to any person. At the same time, the spirit of integrating punishment and leniency should be embodied in this guiding principle so as to divide and disintegrate the offenders. The law should clearly define corruption, bribery, and embezzlement of state property to enhance its operability.

ii Asset Declaration Law for Public Officials

The guiding principle of this law should be to increase transparency by making the incomes and asset of staff of state organs and public-owned enterprises and institutions subject to the supervision of the public and the authorities concerned. Furthermore, the law should also be applicable to all public officials, irrespective of their positions and merits, who should declare their assets in accordance with the provisions of the law. The law serves to prevent corruption by not only binding the behavior of public officials, but also strengthening their self-discipline.

iii. Law on Citizens' Right to Report

The guiding principle of this law should be to mobilize the general public to supervise the conduct of staff of state organs and public-owned enterprises and institutions, and to guarantee citizens' right to report. This is an important legislation to curb corruption and ensure the construction of a clean government, as well as an effective measure to combat various kinds of crime. When there is a broad mass base, it would be easier to build up an incorrupt government.

iv. Supervision Law

The guiding principle of this law should be to supervise the compliance and enforcement of the law by the staff of state organs, particularly in cases where public officials fail to observe and strictly enforce the law or fail to punish the law-breakers. At present, there is still a lack of effective supervision on whether public officials comply with the laws, whether their behaviors are regulated in accordance with the laws, and whether the laws are strictly enforced to ensure the normal operation of social and economic activities. Supervision comes from various parties. Only when such supervision is integrated into the legal system can it be effective.

III

Among the economic laws to eradicate corruption, the enactment of state-owned assets law is particularly urgent. According to the legislative plan of the Standing Committee of the National People's Congress (NPC), the Finance and Economics Committee of the NPC is in charge of drafting laws on state-owned assets.

The drafting work is progressing smoothly, but there are also many difficulties encountered.

One of the controversial issues is whether the scope of state-owned assets law should be adjusted to target the state-owned commercial assets or all types of state-owned assets. The main reason for advocating the inclusion of the state-owned commercial assets is that current problems such as irrational resource allocation, dysfunctional industrial structure, and low enterprise efficiency are mainly due to a lack of strict management of the state-owned commercial assets. Moreover, the institutional reform of state-owned asset management is progressing slowly, and SOEs have not yet achieved the separation between government intervention and independent operation. Thus, it is better to enact laws on the state-owned commercial assets first. A different opinion is that, besides these assets, there are non-commercial ones, which might also be subject to inefficient use and continuous loss. Since this problem has not been paid much attention to, it needs to be regulated by a state-owned assets law. Therefore, all types of state-owned assets should be included in the law.

Of the above two views, the latter deserves more attention. In fact, there is no absolute boundary between commercial and non-commercial assets. They overlap to some extent and can be interconverted in some cases. For example, canteens, guesthouses, and theaters in public-owned enterprises and institutions can be converted into commercial assets under certain circumstances, even if they are currently non-commercial assets. If state-owned non-commercial assets are not included in this law, their continuous loss will consequently cause damage to the country.

Another controversial issue is whether state-owned assets should be distinguished between the ownership of the central government and the ownership of local governments at all levels. There are mainly two different propositions here. One is that any investment made by the government should be owned by the state. In fact, national assets are assets owned by the state as a whole, and local governments at all levels are only responsible for supervision and management. The other is that since both the central government and local governments at all levels have made investments, there naturally comes a system of assets formed by the central government's investments and assets formed by the investments of local governments at a certain level, that is, a system of hierarchical ownership of state-owned assets.

In the former view, only unified state ownership is recognized, which may undermine the incentives of local governments at all levels to operate and manage state-owned assets and detrimental to the further development of the local economy. However, it is more reasonable. State-owned assets are, by definition, owned by the state. State-owned assets are uniformly owned by the state and are supervised and managed by the central government or a certain level of local government. The ownership issue is indeed not involved here.

Under the premise that state-owned assets are owned by the state and managed by the government at different levels, what is the difference between centrally managed assets and locally managed ones? Law should be clarified as soon as possible to prevent state-owned assets from being neglected and continuously depleted.

The law may support the establishment of state-owned asset management companies that operate across different regions and industries, potentially holding controlling stakes in the companies they manage and appointing representatives to oversee operations. State-owned asset management companies may compete with each other and may make decisions on the transfer of state-owned property rights. In this way, although some state-owned asset management companies are under the jurisdiction of the central government and others under that of the local management, once the relationship is clarified in law and operated in the above manner, the allocation between hierarchical government management and unified state ownership can be coordinated.

How should the relevant state department deal with the transfer of state-owned property rights? This issue is related to the authority of state-owned asset management companies. Assume that such companies are required to observe the following provisions with regard to the transfer of state-owned property rights. Firstly, companies may independently conduct property rights transactions below a specified threshold, while those exceeding this amount require state agency approval. Secondly, transactions in designated industries and enterprises must be approved by the agency, whereas others can be determined by the asset management company. Thirdly, any transaction that results in a loss of controlling rights in an enterprise should be subject to agency approval. In this manner, the authority of management companies to transfer property rights can be clearly defined, and the operation and management of state-owned assets be put on a standardized track. The issue of value maintenance and appreciation of state-owned assets can also be addressed through effective management and oversight.

In addition, the supervision and management of state-owned assets must be strengthened, and various loopholes must be plugged. Specific measures should include improving asset evaluation, implementing strict audit supervision, and setting up certain procedures and approval systems for the transaction of state-owned assets.

IV

In ancient China, there was a saying that "honesty and integrity through high remuneration." In modern times, some countries have also regarded this as a guideline, connecting the building of an incorrupt government with generous salaries of civil servants. At the same time, this is also regarded as an important measure to stabilize the national civil service, so that the talented are more willing to work in the public sectors. Of course, some countries, while offering favorable living conditions, emphasize heavy penalties for corruption and bribery. The combination of "high salaries" and "heavy penalties" is the essential way to motivate civil servants to assess whether the benefits of using their power for personal gains outweigh the costs, so that they can work diligently and conscientiously.

It should be admitted that this practice of "high salaries for integrity" is reasonable. At the present stage of China, the low salaries of civil servants not only restrain government institutions from attracting and retaining talented people, but also may cause the staff members to deviate from their proper jobs and to work part-time in their spare time for the improvement of livelihood. Moreover, it is also possible that some staff of government organs may go astray, abusing their power or taking advantage of their positions for personal gains. However, the role of "high salaries for integrity" should be properly recognized rather than overestimated. It is not appropriate to consider that only high level of salaries can lead to high integrity, that is to say, there would be no way to build an incorrupt government without a high remunerative system.

For civil servants, three mechanisms are necessary: the screening mechanism, the guarantee and motivation mechanism, and the restriction and supervision mechanism.

The screening mechanism means that appointments and promotions of civil servants should be made through competition, which is merit-based. The positions should be open and so be the competition. This mechanism makes it possible to appoint and promote anyone who meets the requirements.

The guarantee and motivation mechanism refers to the fact that, after a civil servant is appointed, his/her living condition should not be lower than that of other professionals with the same educational background and experience, which could ensure the stability of the national civil servant team and relieve their worries about livelihood. After regular reviews, there should also be a standardized system for promotion and income increments.

The restriction and supervision mechanism means that the conduct and work ethics of civil servants should be supervised by all parties. They must abide by the code of practice for civil servants, and offenders shall be punished. At the same time, civil servants must strengthen their self-discipline with high standard.

Undoubtedly, the screening mechanism, the guarantee and motivation mechanism, and the restriction and supervision mechanism of national civil servants need to be legislated and institutionalized. The anti-corruption and bribery law and supervision law that need to be enacted in the future will focus on the legislation on the restraint and supervision mechanisms. On top of this, the laws related to civil servants, will also concentrate on the legislation of the screening mechanism and the guarantee and motivation mechanism.

— *People's Procuratorial Semimonthly*, issue No. 11, 1995

Chapter 20
1996: Relying on the Working Class to Deepen the Enterprise Reform

Deepening the enterprise reform is not only the focus but also a difficult part of current system transition. However, how to transform the operation mechanisms of enterprises effectively and make significant breakthroughs in enterprise reform? This is a hot issue in the economic field at present. Although there are some different ideas on deepening the enterprise reform, and various ways to transform the management mechanisms of enterprises, relying on the working class to deepen the reform is undoubtedly a principle we must adhere to. As Comrade Jiang Zemin pointed out: "Our enterprises and modern industries would not be successful without the initiative and enthusiasm of the working class"; "Without the support of the broad masses of workers, the enterprise reform cannot be successful." These words highly summarize the role of the enthusiasm, creativity, and initiatives of vast workers in deepening the enterprise reform.

20.1 The Status of the Employees in Shareholding Companies

Joint-stock limited companies and limited liability companies are the basic forms of shareholding companies, which are adopted in the reform by most large and medium-sized SOEs, except those in special industries. According to different situations of industries and enterprises, joint-stock limited companies and limited liability companies that can be state-controlled with or without government shares. Their formation should be carried out strictly in accordance with the Company Law of the People's Republic of China.

To form a shareholding company, the following two points should be considered. On the one hand, a joint-stock limited company or a limited liability company should meet the requirements of market economy and be compatible with international practices. On the other hand, the management system of these companies should

Y. Li, *China's Economy Since 1978*, China Academic Library,
https://doi.org/10.1007/978-981-95-5733-2_20

not only be accepted by the broad masses of workers, but also be helpful to the mobilization of their enthusiasm and the promotion of economic development. One of the main issues involved here is to confirm the participation of employees in the democratic management of the shareholding companies and to give full play to the role of the employees.

First of all, for any shareholding companies including joint-stock limited companies and limited liability companies, and regardless of whether the employees have invested in shares or how many shares they hold, we need to make it clear that both relying on employees to run the company well and ensuring employees' democratic management and effective supervision of the company are indispensable. Although the shareholding system has its own characteristics in the property right structure, it is not contradictory to the fact that the employees have the rights to participate in the management of the enterprise.

The Company Law of the People's Republic of China (Article 16) has such a provision: "Wholly State-owned companies and limited liability companies invested in and established by two or more SOEs or by two or more other State-owned investment entities shall, through staff and workers congresses or other forms, practice democratic management in accordance with the provisions of the Constitution and relevant laws." It is pointed out here that wholly state-owned companies and limited liability companies entirely composed of state enterprises or state-owned investment entities implement democratic management through the workers congress, which will help them improve management and economic efficiency, and give full play to the positive role of the employees.

The Company Law stipulates: "Companies must protect the lawful rights and interests of their staff, and strengthen labor protection to achieve safety in production (Article 15)"; "Company staff and workers shall, in accordance with the Law, organize trade unions to carry out relevant activities and protect their lawful rights and interests (Article 16)."

The Law also stipulates: "A company shall, in studying and deciding on issues involving the personal interests of its staff and workers such as their salaries, welfare, safety in production, labor protection and labor insurance, solicit in advance the opinions of the trade union and the staff and workers of the company. And representatives of the trade union or the staff and workers shall be invited to attend relevant meetings (Article 55 and Article 121)." "A Company shall solicit the opinions and suggestions of the trade union and the staff and workers of the company when studying and deciding on major issues concerning production and operation, and formulating important rules and regulations (Articles 56 and 122)." "The supervisory board shall be composed of representatives of the shareholders and an appropriate proportion of company staff. The representatives of the staff and workers in the supervisory board shall be democratically elected by the staff and workers of the company (Articles 52 and 124)."

The above statutes apply to all shareholding companies. They show that the status of the employees in shareholding companies wouldn't be diminished by the position of the shareholders as an authority. According to the Company Law, not only are the legitimate rights and interests of employees protected, but also the employees have rights to elect supervisors to exercise supervision over the company and convey their opinions and suggestions through the labor union. There is no doubt that if the employees are to buy shares, then they will enjoy all the rights of shareholders, and the directors elected from the employee representatives will participate in decision-making in the board of directors.

Relying on the working class to deepen the enterprise reform and improve the management of shareholding companies is precisely related with giving a full play to the initiatives from the employees. The leading group of a joint-stock limited company or a limited liability company must understand that the improvement of management and market expansion is inseparable from improving efficiency and product quality. And the key to improving efficiency and product quality is to arouse employees' morale and solicit the creativity from the employees in technical and management work. At the same time, for the healthy development of enterprises, democratic supervision of the enterprise leadership is necessary. In shareholding companies, in addition to democratic supervision through the board of supervisors attended by employee representatives, institutions such as the trade union representative assembly or the employee representative assembly should be used to effectively supervise the enterprise leadership by the employees. Only in this way can shareholding companies get better and better.

The notion that shareholder companies should depend on capital raised from their investors and neglect the importance of their employees is misguided. Even if employees do not take equity stakes, it does not mean that the companies do not need to rely on their initiatives and participation in corporate management. The realization of the investors' interests is inseparable from employees' efforts, so that the interests of investors are consistent with those of the employees. A shareholding company that can continuously develop in the market competition must have strong internal cohesion. It can greatly induce employees' initiatives and has an effective supervision system of employees over the company's leadership. In the past few years, the practice of China's enterprise reform has fully proved this.

20.2 The Role of Labor Union under the Modern Enterprise System

The role of labor unions in shareholding companies has been mentioned above. In order to fully understand the status of employees in the enterprise reform, let's further discuss the role of labor unions under the modern enterprise system.

Under the modern enterprise system, labor unions in enterprises carry out their work independently according to the law, protecting and mobilizing employees' initiatives and creativity. It goes without saying that the role of labor unions in Chinese enterprises should be regarded differently from that in the Western countries. If we make a more detailed analysis, we can draw the following conclusions: In socialist China, the role of labor unions in enterprises under the planned system is somewhat different from that under a market economic system. They can't be taken simply as the same.

At present, there are many types of enterprises in China. In joint ventures of Chinese and foreign investment, foreign-invested companies and private enterprises, the existence of labor-capital relations makes the labor union's role as a prominent labor representative, which can generally be accepted. However, the problem is that in a wholly state-owned company or a limited liability company entirely owned by state investment entities, does the work union play a role in representing the employees? And in a township & village enterprise (TVE) with a collective ownership, does the labor union have a similar role? The answers to the above questions should be positive.

Labor unions represent employees. Under the modern enterprise system, to make the relationship between enterprises and employees coordinated and encourage two parties to work together to develop the enterprises, the role of labor unions is undeniable. Even for a wholly state-owned company, the enterprise should be an independent legal entity since the government and the enterprise are no longer integrated. Thus, the existence of labor unions is necessary, whether from the perspective of coordinating the relationship between enterprises and employees or improving the management, facilitating the development and promoting the efficiency. This situation will not change even if the government is the sole investor of the enterprise, which is the same in a TVE with a collective ownership. Although many individuals may fund this kind of enterprises, and employees themselves are both workers and investors, as long as the enterprises are established and the employees are in place, it is also necessary to establish labor unions and make them work.

The concerns about the role of labor unions in SOEs and collective enterprises are mainly as the following:

In a SOE, assuming there is a dispute between the enterprise and the employees, and both sides hold different propositions, should the labor union speak for the interests of the employees or those of the government (enterprise)? If the labor union represents the employees, wouldn't that be bad for the government? If the labor union represents the enterprise, is it still necessary to form a labor union?

In a TVE, assuming that there is a dispute between the enterprise and the employees with differing accounts, which side should the labor union be with? The employees of an enterprise are both workers and investors. No matter which sides the labor union stands with, it has its own difficulties. Therefore, is it necessary for labor unions to be established and undertake activities?

In fact, these two kinds of concerns are unnecessary. They mainly result from a lack of understanding of the relationship between the modern enterprise system and labor unions, or the role of labor unions under the modern enterprise system.

First of all, as pointed out earlier, under the modern enterprise system, the government and enterprises are separated, and the SOEs are no exception. Therefore, when a dispute arises between an enterprise and its employees, one cannot simply equate a specific SOE with the government, and the interests of a certain SOE cannot be equated with those of the government, either. Since the labor union is an organization of employees, it should indeed act as a representative of the employees and speak for them. But this does not mean that the labor union does not need to understand the dispute in advance and make judgments on it. Labor unions should act legally, carry out activities legally, and protect the legitimate rights and interests of employees. In this sense, labor unions cannot be simply regarded as speaking only on behalf of enterprises or employees. Labor unions in SOEs safeguard legitimate rights and interests of employees in accordance with the law. This is to maintain the credibility of the law, that is, to maintain the interests of the country and society.

In the TVEs, although the employees are also investors, disputes between enterprises and employees cannot be simply regarded as ones between investors. Issues about business policies and business decision-making should be resolved by investors. As for the problem that the legitimate rights and interests of employees are not protected, the labor union should represent the employees, negotiate with the enterprise, and assist in solving such problems. This role of labor union cannot be replaced by the discussion of investors.

Relying on the working class to deepen the reform of enterprises involves the reforms of both SOEs and TVEs. In the process of these reforms, it is necessary to establish labor unions, enable a full play to their role, and ensure that they can work independently and legally.

Here, it is essential to enable a full play to the role of labor unions in guiding and assisting employees in signing labor contracts, undertaking the duties of the director of *the labor dispute mediation committee* of the enterprise, and participating in labor dispute mediation. We must recognize that China's collective bargaining and collective contracts are playing an increasingly important role in enterprises under the new situation of the transition to a socialist market economic system. At present, it is generally confirmed that collective bargaining and collective contract systems are implemented in joint ventures of Chinese and foreign investment, foreign-invested companies, private enterprises, and shareholding companies. Enterprises and employees are two sides. In order to coordinate the relationship between them, it is indeed necessary to implement collective bargaining and collective contract system. But sometimes one may doubt the necessity in state enterprises. And in the TVEs, is it necessary or even feasible?

The answer is clear. No matter in a SOE or a TVE, it is necessary and possible to implement a collective bargaining and collective contract system.

Within a market economy, the government and enterprises are separated. Even the state-owned enterprises are not integrated with the government. It is the state-owned enterprises that are hiring workers, not the government. These enterprises have the right to recruit employees, while the employees have the right to select jobs. Therefore, the relationship between the two parties should be established and confirmed in the form of labor contracts, and disputes should be resolved through negotiation. In this way, the government shall not intervene in any of them, and should handle the problem fairly and legally.

The situation in the TVEs is similar. Although the TVE employees may be both workers and farmers, as long as they work in these enterprises, their legal rights and interests as workers should be protected. It is not allowed to deduct their wages, illegally extend their working hours, downgrade their working conditions, etc. From this point of view, collective bargaining and collective contracts are equally necessary and feasible for TVEs.

In order to carry out collective bargaining and reach collective contracts, all enterprises should establish labor unions. Labor unions appear as the representatives of collective bargaining and the main body of collective contracts. Employees recognize the qualifications of the labor unions as the bargaining representative and the subject of collective contracts. Labor unions represent the interests of employees and express their opinions.

The content of the collective contract is clearly stipulated in the Labor Law of the People's Republic of China. Article 33 of the Law states that the employees of an enterprise as one party may reach a collective contract with the enterprise as the counter party on remunerations, work hours, breaks and leaves, workplace health and safety, insurance, welfare, and other matters. After the collective contract is signed, it is binding on the enterprise and all the employees. In a labor contract signed by individual employees and the enterprise, the relevant standards on working conditions and labor remuneration shall not be lower than the provisions of collective contracts.

A collective contract does not specify the type of the enterprises and management. This is because the corporate system and operation management are the adjusted contents of the Company Law, while the labor relations are subject to the Labor Law. Therefore, the collective contract does not involve the enterprise system and operation management, and it will be more conducive to the development and independent operation of the enterprise. At the same time, it will not exclude the employees from democratic management of the enterprise.

There are also explicit provisions in the Labor Law regarding potential disputes over collective contracts. Article 84 of the Labor Law states that where a dispute arises from a collective contract and no settlement can be made through consultation by the parties concerned, the labor administrative department of the local government may organize the relevant departments to handle the case in coordination. Furthermore, where a dispute arises from implementing a collective contract and no settlement can be reached through consultation by the parties concerned, the dispute may be submitted to the labor dispute arbitration committee for arbitration. Any party that is not satisfied with the adjudication of arbitration may bring a lawsuit to a people's court. These regulations are very important, otherwise the collective bargaining and collective contract system may become merely a formality and fail to function as expected.

In economic reforms, regulations on collective bargaining and collective contracts are novel developments. Compared with the era of the planned economy, this is undoubtedly a great progress. Although the current experience is still limited, collective bargaining and collective contracts would indeed play an increasingly important role in the economy with the progress of the enterprise reform.

20.3 Pay Attention to Some Employees in Difficulties in the Process of the Enterprise Reform

It has been pointed out earlier that in the course of the enterprise reform, some companies with poor efficiency and no competitiveness are facing severe situations of adjustment and reorganization, and even suspension of production and bankruptcy. This is an inevitable phenomenon in the process of shifting from a planned economy to a socialist market economy. Nevertheless, we must pay attention to the difficulties some employees may encounter in the enterprise reform, and we must take effective measures to help them find more opportunities. Two sayings have recently been popular. One is "market does not protect the weak," and the other is "market is ruthless." These two assertions may reflect the reality, but it doesn't mean we should do nothing. Market does not protect the weak, but society has the responsibility to do so. Market is ruthless, while the society should be merciful. The society can take various measures to help employees with difficulties. This is an important aspect that cannot be ignored in the process of deepening the enterprise reform.

When it comes to social assistance to employees in need, it is often regarded as a protective shield. This view is somewhat correct. However, it would be unrealistic to push all the employees in difficulties to the society for relief. First, social relief usually has specific targets, which mainly refer to the poor who lose working capability, have no kith and kin, suffer from disasters, or face redundancy due to under-capacity or factory shutdown. Second, the funding for social relief mainly comes from the state's fiscal revenue. However, at present, since China's state financial resources are limited, it is impossible to cover all employees in difficulties as the objects of social relief. Certainly, poor employees can receive a certain amount of social relief subsidies if they are unemployed when the companies go bankrupt or they cannot earn a living from work.

Obviously, it is beyond our capacity to solve the livelihood security of employees in difficulties. Social insurance and unemployment insurance alone are insufficient for this purpose. But the problem is that the reform of the social security system is gradually advancing, and it is expected that after several years of hard work, by the end of the twentieth century, a basic social insurance and unemployment insurance system adapted to the market economy would be established. Once this is done, the livelihood security for employees can be more or less guaranteed. However, the reform of the social security system is still gradually progressing, and raising a sufficient amount of social security funds needs a period of time. Therefore, the idea of the reform is sound, but it does not mean that we are able to solve this issue in accordance with the requirements of the new social security system. At present, in the cities and enterprises in good conditions, employees suffering from bankruptcy are in a better position with the help of social insurance, but not all employees of the SOEs are included, let alone those in other types of enterprises.

Thus, how should we look after the employees in difficulties at present, especially for those low-income workers who are not really unemployed (mainly due to the economic difficulties of the enterprise and cannot receive full wages)? This is a typical issue during the period of a systemic transition, which must draw our attention.

According to the different situations of enterprises in various regions, several methods can be used to alleviate the difficulties of the employees.

1. As for the couples who both work in the enterprises in difficulties, the government should try to help one of them get a job with stable income, or provide technical training. As long as one of a couple can have a certain income, the family's living difficulties can be partially alleviated, because the biggest difficulty is that neither one of the couples can receive a full salary or even no money.
2. If both of the couple are working in the enterprises in difficulties, we can try to get one of them handle procedures of resignation or early retirement, and guarantee a certain resettlement fee for him or her to engage in self-employment or freelance work. Then they can obtain a certain amount of income and family difficulties could be alleviated.
3. Enterprises in difficulties can organize employees to engage in a wide range of self-help work under the conditions of production suspension, reduction, and under-capacity operation, so that employees' income can be increased and family difficulties can be alleviated.
4. The enterprises in difficulties shall truthfully inform relevant schools of the actual situations of the difficult employees' families, so that the children of these families could be able to obtain grants and scholarships, or the tuition fees may be reduced or waived.
5. Local governments should give proper care to families of employees in difficult situations in terms of medical treatment and housing.

In short, these are all ways that could alleviate the difficulties. But in order to truly get the employees from difficult enterprises out of the predicament, deepening the enterprise reform, adjusting the industrial structure and establishing a new social security system are still in need.

From a positive perspective, offering laid-off workers re-employment opportunities is an important way to alleviate their difficulties. Therefore, the society should actively create conditions to enable employees from bankrupt companies to find new employment opportunities based on a recombination of production factors through methods such as property rights reorganization. In this regard, the following measures can be taken at present. First, to establish and improve on the property rights trading market, and formulate policies to promote the auction of fixed assets of bankrupt companies. Second, to encourage domestic and foreign investors to purchase and lease bankrupt companies, and then realize resource reorganization. Third, some skilled workers and managers can transfer with enterprises' fixed assets, which is suitable for forming new production capacity as soon as possible. In addition, the society should also provide employment information, carry out vocational training for employees of bankrupt enterprises, and guide them to engage in appropriate work in new positions. The government can allocate special funds to establish re-employment training bases, enabling laid-off workers to receive training or improve their literacy and technical levels. Meanwhile, information should be provided to employers so that laid-off workers can obtain re-employment opportunities under the premise of a "two-way choice."

At the same time, laid-off workers should be encouraged to seek jobs themselves, including self-employed businesses or household services. And it is necessary for laid-off workers to change their attitudes toward employment, that is, employment does not solely mean working in an enterprise or institution. Both individual businesses and even family services are occupations.

The re-employment of laid-off workers is a huge project that requires the attention of the entire society. If this issue cannot be properly resolved, it won't be easy to deepen the enterprise reform.

Finally, it should be pointed out that the construction of roads, large-scale afforestation, and canals can also absorb a lot of unemployment. Although these mainly absorb surplus labor from rural areas under current conditions, if laid-off workers in cities can change their attitudes toward employment, some of them would also be able to engage in these public projects. Even though public projects are not very effective in alleviating the employment issue of laid-off workers in cities, this can release the employment pressure of redundant labor in rural areas, thereby indirectly helping laid-off urban workers to find suitable work opportunities nearby.

In conclusion, when talking about relying on the working class to deepen the enterprise reforms on the one hand, we should form joint-stock limited companies and limited liability companies (including wholly state-owned companies) in accordance with the requirements of the Company Law to mobilize the initiatives of a vast mass of employees, and give full play to the role of trade unions, trade union representative assemblies or employee representative assemblies. On the other hand, we should mobilize all sectors of the society to properly solve the life security problems for employees in difficulty, including promoting the reform of the social security system and realizing the re-employment project. These two aspects of work are equally important. Without any of them, it would be difficult for the enterprise reform to make greater progress.

— *Chinese Workers' Movement*, issue No. 9, 1996.

Chapter 21
1997: Meshing Fiscal Policy with Monetary Policy

21.1 Limitations of Fiscal Policy in an Incomplete Market

21.1.1 Policy Effectiveness in Relation to Economic Growth

The interaction between fiscal and monetary policies was a much-debated issue between Keynesians and Monetarists. According to post-Keynesian mainstream economics, in macroeconomic regulation the government should, except in times of crisis, avoid adopting fiscal and monetary policies that are tight or loose at the same time. A better choice is to pair tight fiscal policy with loose monetary policy, or loose fiscal policy with tight monetary policy. Monetarists, in principle, are not opposed to the interaction between fiscal and monetary policies, but they maintain that fiscal policy has great limitations. For example, a loose fiscal policy may not achieve the expected goals because fiscal expansion tends to partially "crowd out" private consumption and private investment, but if fiscal policy is tight, it cuts into the economic growth rate, resulting in fiscal expenditure cutbacks that invariably bring down fiscal revenue, thereby diverting the fiscal policy from its prescribed goals. Consequently, they believe that monetary policy is more effective than fiscal policy. Such is the basic policy preference of Monetarists.

In a policy debate with Monetarists, Keynesians further argue that the coordination between fiscal and monetary policies should be discussed in combination with economic policy goals. To be specific, they argue that it is necessary to observe the effects of the coordination between these two policies from the perspective of whether it is conducive to economic stability and sustainable growth.

A loose fiscal policy is supportive of economic growth and plays a positive part in GNP growth. But can it "crowd out" private consumption and private investment? Sweeping generalizations should be avoided in answering that question. The key to the answer lies in whether the market is restrained or not, that is, whether the market can expand in time with GNP growth. If the market expands constantly, a loose fiscal policy in interaction with an equally loose monetary policy in the course of economic

Y. Li, *China's Economy Since 1978*, China Academic Library,
https://doi.org/10.1007/978-981-95-5733-2_21

growth will squeeze out neither private consumption nor private investment. To put it another way, the "crowding out" effect can happen only when a loose fiscal policy interacts with a tight monetary policy. Only in that scenario can the Monetarist hypothesis make sense.

Nevertheless, to pair a loose fiscal policy with a loose monetary policy is bound to aggravate inflation. But this consequence can be forestalled if, on the one hand, the monetary policy is loosened only to a certain extent, and on the other, inflation is kept within bounds by boosting economic growth and aggregate supply. If this condition prevails, it broaches the topic of to what extent should monetary policy be loosened to avoid inflation resulting from increased money supply without allowing increased fiscal expenditure to suppress private consumption and private investment. Research on this topic has yet to be fully completed.

Whether the pairing is between a loose fiscal policy and a tight monetary policy or between a tight fiscal policy and a loose monetary policy, it calls for a comparison of effectiveness between the two parings, as well as that between a tight policy and a loose one. Without such a comparison it is hard to decide how the two should be paired.

21.1.2 Impact of Market Completeness on Policy Effectiveness

The above summary of Keynesian and Monetarist viewpoints about coordinating fiscal and monetary policies makes a valuable reference. It is hard to judge which school is correct, because it involves the margin of economic growth and the margin of growth in aggregate supply. If the economic growth rate is too low while aggregate supply grows too slowly, neither fiscal policy nor monetary policy can work whether they are tight or loose, because fiscal expenditure will crowd out private expenditure or decline along with financial revenue. In that way, coordination between fiscal and monetary policies is out of the question. The analysis of monetarists may be warranted in this case. Otherwise, the Keynesian position may sound even more reasonable.

However, the experience of China and that of some other developing nations indicate that the effectiveness of fiscal and monetary policies is associated with the degree of market completeness. To be specific, both fiscal and monetary policies work most effectively if the market is fairly complete. By comparison, a tight fiscal policy tends to meet more impediments than a tight monetary policy in the course of enforcement, and, as a result, its effectiveness will be more or less curtailed.

The situation will be different if the market—capital market, securities market, foreign exchange market, property rights market, and so on—is less than complete. In this scenario, monetary policy may come across more obstacles in the course of implementation than fiscal policy, and its effectiveness may be limited to a larger extent. By the same token, a tight monetary policy may face more hindrance than a tight fiscal policy. This is because monetary policy works through the capital market, securities market, foreign exchange market, property rights market, and so on, whose incompleteness can deprive the monetary market of its transmission mechanism or make its transmission mechanism less effective.

Fiscal policy differs from monetary policy in that it impacts the commodities market directly. If the general market is incomplete, the commodity market is usually less incomplete than the other markets, while the capital, securities, foreign exchange, and property rights markets tend to be most incomplete. This is exactly true of the Chinese experience, where fiscal policy works relatively more effectively even though a tight fiscal policy may still encounter a lot of obstructions.

This point may be illustrated with the effect of fiscal policy on economic growth. Because fiscal policy has a direct bearing on the commodities market and can change GNP through the extension and contraction, or ebb and flow of that market, it can either restrain or stimulate the rate of economic growth. Even if the commodity market is incomplete, fiscal policy can still act on GNP through corresponding changes in that market, which is ultimately indicated in changes of economic growth rate. This is something monetary policy cannot do, as its impact on the economic growth rate can be considerably lessened—and therefore cannot be as pronounced and direct as the impact of fiscal policy—as long as the capital, securities, foreign exchange, and property rights market remain incomplete. In China, a loosened-up fiscal policy works better than a loosened-up monetary policy in stimulating economic growth, but conversely, it is also more likely to play a larger part in aggravating inflation.

The effects of a loose policy and a tight policy are asymmetrical in an incomplete market. Given the same money market tightness benchmark, a relaxed policy is more effective than a tight policy. This is particularly true of monetary policy in an incomplete market. This is because—under the assumption that the capital, securities, foreign exchange and property rights markets are incomplete while the monetary policy lacks a transmission mechanism—the impact of a tight money market is different than that of a loose one even though the effect of monetary policy is restricted to a certain extent. When the money market is loosened up, investors can always obtain credit from different channels, and the economy will be animated correspondingly even if the market remains incomplete. When the loose money market is tightened up, however, some investors will still act on prescribed plans, because market incompleteness has made them oblivious to the pressure of a rising interest rate or a rising reserve requirement ratio. This is because the more incomplete the market is and the bigger the informational restraints are, the more unfair competition becomes. As a result, some privileged investors can still obtain credit and make investment. They may gradually feel the pressure, but generally speaking, the effect of a tightened-up monetary policy on them always comes belatedly.

21.1.3 Pairings of Loose and Tight Policies in an Incomplete Market

This gives rise to the issue of how to pair a loose policy with a tight one in macroeconomic regulation of an incomplete market. Such pairings are different from those in a complete market in two ways.

Firstly, in a complete market, the effects of both fiscal and monetary policies are keenly felt. Even though a tight fiscal policy tends to hit more snags than a tight monetary policy, it works reasonably well, when and where necessary, to coordinate a loose fiscal policy with a tight monetary policy, or to pair a tight fiscal policy with a loose monetary policy. Yet, for reasons mentioned above, things are different in an incomplete market: Fiscal policy is more effective than monetary policy. To meet the goal of macroeconomic regulation, fiscal policy is preferred over monetary policy, whose role can be very limited unless robustly enforced. Therefore, it is impractical to count on monetary policy in this regard. Such is one of the salient features of macroeconomic regulation under conditions of an incomplete market.

Secondly, a tight fiscal or monetary policy will strain money supply, bring down the economic growth rate, and curtail the inflation rate, whereas a relaxed fiscal or monetary policy will loosen up money supply, boost economic growth, and reduce unemployment. However, all this can happen only in a complete market. In an incomplete market, macroeconomic regulation will be slow to take effect, and worse, the results might be unexpectedly distorted. This is because the securities, foreign exchange, and property rights markets are more incomplete than other markets, and therefore the transmission mechanism of monetary policy becomes even more flawed. If curtailing inflation is the goal of government policy regulation, the adoption of a tight fiscal policy can quickly cool down the economy and reduce inflation because this policy works especially well in this field when it is tightened up. However, the tight fiscal policy needs to be paired with a loose monetary policy if we are to prevent the economy from being cooled to such an extent as to thwart economic growth. Furthermore, because of the incompleteness of the market, and the flaws in monetary policy's transmission mechanism, a loosened monetary policy cannot work properly in the course of enforcing a tight fiscal policy, thereby defeating the purpose of maintaining the economy's momentum. As a result, with the tight fiscal policy having a strong effect and the loose monetary policy having a weak effect under incomplete market conditions, the economy is likely to be over cooled or even bogged down in stagnation. That echoes the saying, "It is easier to stop a car than rev it up."

Similarly, when raising economic growth is the goal of government policy regulation, a relaxed fiscal policy can be adopted in interaction with a tight monetary policy because this is where the relaxed fiscal policy works particularly well. Stimulated by expanded fiscal expenditure or tax reduction or exemption, the economy achieves rapid growth, but it is necessary for the relaxed fiscal policy to be accompanied by a tight monetary policy to curb inflation in this process of accelerated economic growth. However, the incompleteness of the market and the flaws in its own transmission mechanism prevent the tight monetary policy from working properly in the course of enforcing the relaxed fiscal policy, thereby failing to achieve the goal of keeping economic growth and inflation from running too high. Thus, under incomplete market conditions, the strong effects of the relaxed fiscal policy, coupled with the weak effects of the tight monetary policy, can result in excessive economic expansion, and make it hard to contain hyperinflation.

Therefore, the troubles met in the coordinated application of fiscal and monetary policies in an incomplete market are attributed to the "limping status" of both policies. In other words, the pairing of an effective policy with a less effective one makes it hard to achieve the goals.

This, however, does not preclude the combined use of fiscal policy and monetary policy in an incomplete market. Rather, it means that the forcefulness of both policies should be considered when pairing them up. For instance, given the strong effect of fiscal policy and the weak effect of monetary policy, we can implement the latter with more impetus than the former, so as to maximize the outcome of the combination.

21.1.4 Conclusion: It Is Easier to Stop a Car Than to Rev It up Again

In the previous chapters I have made a tentative study of the coordinated adoption of fiscal and monetary policies. What does this mean for the Chinese economy in the present stage of development? As I have stated in the foregoing, the effectiveness of monetary policy is considerably restrained in an incomplete market, which makes it even harder to be coordinated with fiscal policy. For this reason, I would like to draw attention to the following two points:

First, in the current stage of economic development in this nation, it is inappropriate to adopt a relaxed fiscal policy alongside a relaxed monetary policy, or a tight fiscal policy together with a tight monetary policy, because the former tends to lead to runaway inflation and the latter a stifled economy. The only option is to couple a tight fiscal policy with a relaxed monetary policy, or vice versa. Given the different attributes of the effects of the fiscal and monetary policies under incomplete market conditions, I would suggest a relatively tight fiscal policy alongside a relaxed monetary policy.

Secondly, under incomplete market conditions, the Chinese economy is typical of the saying, "It is easier to stop a car than to rev it up again." It is also where the asymmetrical nature of the effects of macroeconomic regulation is most pronounced. That is to say, when macroeconomic regulation tightens up, its effect is quickly felt and the economy retrenches as a result. By contrast, if macroeconomic regulation slackens only slightly, it can hardly serve the purpose, because the economy can only revive slowly or stay stagnant for a considerable time before it comes back to its own. Why? Because the economy can be dynamic, the purchasing power stay strong and the market thrive only when businesses and investors are optimistic about the prospects of good profits and consumers are confident in anticipation of higher income. Nevertheless, it takes time to boost optimism and confidence. Expansionary policies cannot make people sanguine about market prospects right away, while the "limping state" in which fiscal policy outplays monetary policy can land macroeconomic regulation in an impasse. It will be even harder to rev up the economy with a tight fiscal policy in the absence of a relaxed monetary policy.

Hence the foregone conclusion: At the present stage of development, China can only slightly tighten up its fiscal policy while loosening up its monetary policy a little. Otherwise, the economy can never be delivered from the dilemma in which "it is easier to stop the car than to start it up again."

21.2 Be Prudent with Unconventional Monetary Policy Tools

21.2.1 Three Basic Monetary Policy Tools Predicated on Market Completeness

Monetary policy impacts GNP through its effects on the capital, securities, foreign exchange and property rights markets. If changing GNP is the policy's ultimate goal, a series of intermediary goals are needed. If changing inflation and GNP are the dual ultimate goals, they cannot be fulfilled before the intermediary goals are attained. Therefore, in our research on the impact of monetary policy on the economy, we should study this policy's transmission mechanism, and observe, through its different tools, the policy's impact on the intermediary goals, for the purpose of finding the ways and means with which to attain the ultimate goals through these intermediary goals.

Interest rate is one of the intermediary goals of monetary policy. Under complete market conditions, the central bank applies a rediscount policy to influence the interest rate. When the rediscount rate is readjusted, it will change commercial banks' cost of borrowed funds, thereby precipitating readjustments in the interest rate on the market, and compelling investors to raise or reduce their monetary demand. Money supply thus becomes the most important of all intermediate goals that, alongside the interest rate, influences society's monetary demand, aggregate demand, and GNP. If the monetary policy's transmission mechanism is effective, it can exert its impact, through the central bank's rediscount policy, to attain both the intermediate goals and the ultimate goals. This, however, also has something to do with the economic environment as a whole. If the market is incomplete, changing the rediscount rate cannot work as a monetary policy step on money demand the way it does in a complete market, nor can it work effectively for the attainment of another intermediate goal, the volume of money flow. Unless the rediscount policy is executed with government intervention, changing the rediscount rate cannot work on the increases or reductions in money flow.

We may take a further look at the impact of the rediscount rate policy. For the changing rate to exert a desired influence on interest rate, there needs be full competition among commercial banks that are supposed to grant loans to clients strictly in line with the norms of market competition and selection, while the clients are likewise expected to compete on an equal footing. Otherwise, the impact of rediscount rate readjustments on interest rate will be much confined.

Adjusting reserve requirement ratio is another monetary policy tool to influence commercial banks' derived deposit, restrain their lending behavior, and ultimately to affect money supply. Here, another intermediate goal—the volume of money supply—can be attained through adjusting the central bank's reserve requirement ratio. This, however, can materialize only when this ratio stays at a high level. Otherwise, even though the reserve requirement ratio can work as a monetary policy tool, it cannot serve the purpose of forestalling any financial crisis. Furthermore, the reserve requirement ratio cannot function as a policy tool without two preconditions. For one thing, commercial banks should set maximum profits as their goal, for without such a goal, the effectiveness of readjustments in the reserve requirement ratio and of the reserve requirement system itself will be greatly blunted. This precondition is hinged on the soundness of the commercial banking system. For another, central bank's adjustment of the reserve requirement ratio should be compulsory rather than elastic; otherwise, it could defeat the purpose of this monetary policy tool to intervene in money supply. Although the adjustment of reserve requirement ratio is not a frequent monetary policy tool, the effectiveness of its transmission mechanism still rests on the degree of market completion.

The central bank's open market operation is yet another monetary policy tool that should also be observed from an economic environment perspective. In comparison with other monetary policy tools, open market operation calls for more stringent market conditions—a complete and mature securities market over and above a rational market interest rate and sensible investors. Pitfalls in the transmission mechanism of open market operation can not only make it hard to achieve the intermediate goal of adjusting money supply but also frustrate open market operation as a monetary policy tool.

The rediscount rate, the reserve requirement ratio, and open market operation discussed here are three essential monetary policy tools. Their transmission mechanisms are, without exception, associated with the soundness of the market and the commercial banking system. They invariably become crippled or totally ineffective under incomplete market conditions or a flawed commercial banking system.

21.2.2 *Unconventional Policy Also Depending on Market Completeness*

Now a look at two unconventional policy tools besides the three aforementioned monetary policy tools: (1) credit scale control or credit rationing and (2) rediscount quotas and relending quotas. The central bank uses the former to control the lending scale of commercial banks, and the latter as a supplement to rediscount rate readjustments. Both are adopted under incomplete market conditions or under a flawed commercial banking system, but each uses a different transmission mechanism.

The central bank decides credit scale on the basis of its judgments of the economic situation. Differences in the grounds and perspectives for such judgment, and errors in evaluating credit scale effectiveness invariably led to considerable arbitrariness in the central bank's credit scale control. The will of the government plays a big role therein as well. Controlled credit scale can change the money supply volume directly and rapidly, and in that sense, the transmission mechanism of the credit scale control policy is effective. However, prompt response and an effective transmission mechanism are not necessarily conducive to the attainment of the monetary policy's ultimate goal. This is mainly because resource allocation must be optimized constantly if economic growth is to be sustained and inflation is to remain low. Optimized resource allocation indicates improved efficiency. However, the effectiveness of credit scale control is a different story. The problem with credit scale control is that money supply may change the way policymakers want in the short run, but in the long run, with the will of policymakers imposed on it, this monetary policy tool is detrimental to optimizing resource allocation, and will inevitably derail the monetary policy's ultimate goal.

Rediscount and relending quotas are adopted as another unconventional policy tool to make up for the limitations of rediscount rate readjustments. Rediscount quotas may enable the central bank to manipulate commercial banks' money-lending capacities by increasing or decreasing such quotas, and starting from there to further control overall money supply. The same purpose can be achieved by increasing or decreasing the relending quotas. However, the central bank's rediscount quotas and relending quotas, being arbitrarily decided by the government, are so subjective that they do not necessarily fit the reality of money supply. Therefore, whether such quotas are beneficial or detrimental to the realization of the monetary policy's ultimate goal is open to question. On the other hand, these unconventional tools may impair the optimization of resource allocation, and, in the long run, which will hold back the attainment of the ultimate goal of the monetary policy.

21.2.3 Using Credit Scale Control and Other Unconventional Measures with Prudence

From our study of monetary policy's transmission mechanisms, we may conclude that if the market is complete and the commercial banking system sound, these transmission mechanisms may work effectively. If the market is incomplete and the commercial banking system flawed, it is impossible for conventional monetary policy tools to achieve expected results. As to such unconventional monetary policy tools as credit scale control, rediscount quotas and relending quotas, although their transmission mechanisms may remain effective in such a scenario, they are, in the long run, detrimental to the optimization of resource allocation and the attainment of the monetary policy's ultimate goal.

The question at hand to be answered is: What is to be done to re-activate the economy after a period of economic retrenchment? As is noted in the previous section, the adoption of a relatively tight fiscal policy in coordination with a loosened monetary policy under these circumstances is better than the pairing of a loosened fiscal policy with a tightened monetary policy, and even better than coupling fiscal and monetary policies that are both rigid or both relaxed. Our analysis of monetary policy's transmission mechanisms is further proof that this conclusion tallies with the reality of our nation.

Unconventional monetary policy tools—credit scale control, rediscount quotas, and relending quotas included—are often resorted to under incomplete market conditions. Worse, the trend is to regard these unconventional measures as conventional ones, as if the ultimate goal of the monetary policy can never be attained without doing so. In fact, this is sheer misunderstanding. Just as is discussed in the foregoing, despite being somewhat effective, these unconventional measures are harmful to optimizing resource allocation, and, corrupted by government will, cannot satisfactorily fit the money supply situation in economic operation.

To rejuvenate the economy after a period of retrenchment, it is imperative to loosen up the monetary policy more forcefully along with a relatively tight fiscal policy. Thus, prudence must be applied when employing such unconventional policy measures as credit scale control, and for three reasons:

First, the transition from economic entrenchment to economic revival hinges on restoring and enhancing public confidence in market prospects, but confidence can be built up only through a cumulative process. The adoption of unconventional monetary policy tools can engender nothing but uncertainty whether they are relaxed or rigid. If the government can employ relaxed measures, it can also choose rigid ones. In either case there are no norms to go by, because things are at the mercy of those who adopt such measures. The result can be the same: People feel their confidence draining away. That being the case, little or no use should be made of unconventional measures. We would rather adopt conventional monetary policy tools that are sure to help boost people's confidence. Although incomplete market conditions may somewhat tarnish such measures' effectiveness, that can be remedied with redoubled enforcement efforts.

Second, because unconventional monetary policy tools are often misleading to investors, and thus of great disservice to optimizing resource allocation even if a relaxed monetary policy has been adopted to activate the economy, the ultimate goal still cannot be attained due to the failure of these tools to optimize resource allocation. To rejuvenate the economy and keep it primed after a period of retrenchment, it is really important to focus on optimizing resource allocation so that production factors can be grouped and resource use efficiency increased according to market demand. In this regard, unconventional monetary policy measures compare unfavorably with conventional ones. It must be pointed out that, the restraints imposed on conventional measures by an incomplete market can always be overcome through redoubled implementation efforts.

Third, monetary policy can be loosened up a little more than usual, but this should be done on condition that commercial banks issue loans only according to the redeemability of such loans and the borrowers' fund use efficiency. Otherwise, bad debts will pile up, and economic vitality will suffer. What, then, is to be done to avoid the accumulation of debts under a relaxed monetary policy? What kind of monetary policy measures—conventional or unconventional—should be employed in this regard? Obviously, unconventional monetary policy measures are susceptible to arbitrariness and government intervention, making it hard to curtail bad debts, let alone achieve the anticipated results of the relaxed monetary policy.

21.3 The Eclipse of Monetary Policy's Effectiveness

21.3.1 What Makes Monetary Policy Increasingly Less Effective

The eclipse of monetary policy's effectiveness becomes an issue when our study comes to the position and impact on objective economic regulation of such policy. This refers to the fact that after a monetary policy has been executed for some time, its positive impact on attaining the ultimate goals of economic growth and monetary stability will ebb steadily while its negative impact on the economy will increase.

The waning of a monetary policy's effectiveness may be a universal occurrence. It happens whether the market and commercial banking system are flawless or not. Naturally, the decline in policy effectiveness becomes more serious when the market is incomplete and the commercial banking system faulty.

The decreasing effectiveness of monetary policy is attributed mainly to the fact that market participants—commercial banks, other monetary institutions, and nongovernmental investors—are sensible economic agents that react rationally to the monetary policy adopted by the central bank. Even if the market is complete and the commercial banking system healthy, these agents will take countermeasures against the changing economic landscape and policy if their overriding thought is to maximize their own interests. Such countermeasures may cause the effectiveness of a certain monetary policy measure to decrease correspondingly, or force the central bank to reconsider its policy's effectiveness and readjust it. This phenomenon is undoubtedly more pronounced under incomplete market conditions and a flawed commercial banking system.

Monetary policy's waning effectiveness has also something to do with the limitations of its transmission mechanisms. The policy attains the ultimate goal through intermediate goals. However, the economy is in a state of constant restructuring that constantly updates money demand. That is to say, the relationship between money supply and demand always changes in pace with economic restructuring. The monetary policy tools taken are, without exception, focused on changing money supply, to the neglect of the new money demand of economic restructuring. As a matter of fact, this means the central bank's monetary policy should be designed to adapt such demand to money supply, not the other way around. Changing the money supply is an intermediate goal of monetary policy; changing the demand for money is not. To put it another way, the monetary policy impacts directly on money supply, and indirectly on money demand by changing money supply. Thus, it can be said the monetary policy does not have a transmission mechanism that directly impacts money demand. Precisely because of this missing point in the transmission mechanism, investors in the chain of money demand inevitably seek to meet their demand for money or influence the aggregate demand for money through other channels, which are beyond the reach of policymakers. Thus, the steady decline in the monetary policy's effectiveness becomes inevitable even if the market is complete and the commercial banking system perfect. The achievement of this policy's ultimate goal, observed from a monetary point of view, is predicated on changes not only in money supply but also in money demand. Only by coordinating such supply and demand can a monetary policy be effective in the attainment of the ultimate goal.

21.3.2 The Eclipse of Monetary Policy's Effectiveness Under Incomplete Market Conditions

The unstoppable ebb of a monetary policy's effectiveness under incomplete market conditions and an imperfect commercial banking system is also ascribed to the following causes that are perhaps more important than the aforementioned ones.

First, in an incomplete market and under a flawed commercial banking system, the central bank habitually resorts to unconventional monetary policy tools like credit scale control, rediscount quotas, and relending quotas. However, because the design and use of such tools smack of government intervention, the central bank is actually not in a position to adjust regarding to the changing economy. As a result, these tools become rigid policy measures that can only defeat the purposes. Moreover, because these policy measures are usually introduced and backed by the administration, their effectiveness is invariably whittled down because they are rejected, openly or covertly, by commercial banks and other monetary institutions.

Second, under incomplete market conditions and an unhealthy commercial banking system, the central bank's quantitative monetary control over the entire economy is limited. The more incomplete the market and the commercial banking system are, the more likely that firms and investors choose to obtain money beyond the central bank's control. Similarly, under the same conditions, the more the central bank tightens up its quantitative money control, the more firms and investors will try to dodge such control and seek money in areas beyond the reach of the central bank, resulting in a reduction in the effectiveness of the monetary policy.

Third, under incomplete market conditions and a flawed commercial banking system, the activity of the central bank and commercial banks may be interfered with by government at all levels that demand, including the demand for more loans and—in extreme cases—bank overdrafts. This manner of government intervention inevitably cuts deeply into the monetary policy's effectiveness and makes it difficult to reach its prescribed goals. To unshackle them from such intervention, not only should the commercial banking system and the market be straightened out, but the central banking system itself should be rectified as well. This calls for normalizing the relationship between the Ministry of Finance and the Central Bank, and between local governments and the Central Bank's local branches.

21.3.3 Monetary Policy Needing to Be More Loosened and Forceful—Judging from Its Eclipsed Effectiveness

Now let us return to the issue of coordinating fiscal and monetary policies in the post-retrenchment years. Now that we have seen that the eclipse of a monetary policy's effectiveness is unavoidable and even more so under incomplete market conditions, we have every reason to believe that, to re-activate the economy in the wake of the retrenchment action, it is necessary to adopt a slightly tightened-up fiscal policy in coordination with a monetary policy that is loosened up more forcefully. Such a necessity is justified from three aspects:

First, the countermeasures taken by those under the impact of a monetary policy—commercial banks, other monetary institutions, and nongovernmental investors—against the changing situation brought about by that policy can keep eroding its effectiveness. As a result, the monetary policy may not work as it should on a relaxed money market if it is not loosened up with appropriate forcefulness. Sensible investors always take countermeasures according to experience and government behavior, and are especially cautious in action after going through the retrenchment years. They will tend to hold back and bide their time, lest an ill-advised investment move put them at a disadvantage. This being the case, the monetary policy has to be relaxed a little more vigorously if its effectiveness is to stop its decline, and if its prescribed goals are to be achieved.

Second, as illustrated above, to rebuild and enhance public confidence in market and investment prospects is vital to post-retrenchment economic revival. Because this calls for a cumulative process, to loosen up the monetary policy more forcefully in coordination with a relatively tight fiscal policy is a sensible recourse for the government to prevent the monetary policy's effectiveness from diminishing endlessly and to boost people's confidence in market and investment prospects. Whether or not a consumer chooses to buy something he can do without is a conventional benchmark of his confidence or the lack of it. The consumer may make that decision on the spur of the moment, but its impact on the market cannot be underestimated. If the monetary policy is tight, people tend not to buy things they can dispense with, and thus the hope for a revived market is dashed. That tendency will remain unchanged if the monetary policy is not loosened up enough. People will not be confident enough to buy commodities in the gray zone between necessity and non-necessity, and the economy and market will not come back to their own unless the monetary policy is loosened up adequately.

Third, it should be noted that a booming stock market alone is not enough to put the economy back on track right after a period of retrenchment. On the contrary, if the stock market is the only thing that is thriving, it may be evidence that the economy is still in a quandary, as dim investment prospects in many other fields are channeling large sums of money into the stock market. Furthermore, a bustling stock market may most likely be built on a flimsy foundation when investment prospects are grim in other fields. Under these circumstances, we should go out of our way to boost the other investment fields, at least those industries that can bolster up the economy. In conjunction with this, the monetary policy must be loosened up more emphatically to give precedence to the indispensability of its structural nature. That is to say, the policy must not be loosened up in a disorderly fashion and regardless of the industrial and investment structures. Rather, it should be designed, in the first place, to revive selected industries that can bring the economy to life and cause a chain reaction in other industries. To loosen up the monetary policy a little more liberally for these industries helps increase effective supply to the extent where inflation will not be aggravated. Growth in effective supply means true economic growth. In addition, we have got to realize that economic growth at the present stage is not without bubbles. Of all the bubbles foaming in the economy, those in economic growth are the most obvious. To get rid of such bubbles, ineffective supply must be eradicated. This can be done by liberalizing the structural monetary policy a little more.

All in all, to shift the economy back on boom conditions in these post-retrenchment years, we should not only coordinate a relatively tightened fiscal policy with a relaxed monetary policy, but also step up our effort to loosen up the latter. In the meantime, we should apply unconventional monetary policy measures with prudence, and make more use of conventional monetary policy measures. Such is the keynote of this thesis, entitled "Pairing fiscal policy with monetary policy."

—Carried in Excerpts in *Asia Pacific Economic Times*, May 29, June 5 and June 12, 1997 monetary policy is tight, people tend not to buy things they can dispense with, and thus the hope for a revived market is dashed. That tendency will remain unchanged if the monetary policy is not loosened up enough. People will not be confident enough to buy commodities in the gray zone between necessity and non-necessity, and the economy and market will not come back to their own unless the monetary policy is loosened up adequately.

Third, it should be seen that a booming stock market alone is not enough to put the economy back on track right after a period of retrenchment. On the contrary, if the stock market is the only thing that is thriving, it may be evidence that the economy is still in a quandary, as when investment prospects in many other fields are channeling large sums of money into the stock market. Furthermore, a bustling stock market may most likely be built on a flimsy foundation when investment prospects are grim in other fields. Under these circumstances, we should go out of our way to boost the other investment fields, as it is these industries that can bolster up the economy. In conjunction with this, the monetary policy must be loosened up more emphatically to give precedence to the indispensability of economic recovery. That is to say, the [illegible]

Chapter 22
1998: The Dual Foundations of Efficiency

22.1 The Human Factor in Efficiency Studies

In a market economy efficiency is regulated by market, as economic activity is driven by interests. To gain interest, every resource investor must group his production factors in light of supply and demand and prices, and raise his efficiency. Therefore, the mechanism behind efficiency in the market economy is none other than the interest mechanism, or market mechanism, and the investor's goal is to maximize his interest. Thus, motivation for interest and the lure of goals are unified insofar as efficiency is concerned.

Where there is government regulation besides market regulation, there will be the impact of government regulation on efficiency. The lure of goals is by and large a manifestation of such impact. Government goals are multiple rather than single. To meet its goals, the government needs to influence resource investors by way of regulatory means, and compel them to choose investment fields and forms of investment in line with government goals. Efficiency is affected as a result.

Because market regulation works hand in hand with government regulation, efficiency, whether high or low, is under their combined influence. Our study of this issue, however, does not stop just here. We need to probe deeper into it, because those engaged in market activity are individual traders, each being a resource investor. Market participants are subject to government regulation. As resource investors, they are concerned with both their own interests and the impact of government regulatory steps on their interests. This raises the questions: What is on the minds of resource investors? What factors are affecting their behaviors? Apart from market and government regulation, are there any other factors?

Take, for example, any normal firm. The relations in such a firm fall into two categories: relationships between people and materials, and interpersonal relationships. The relationship between people and materials finds expression mainly in the relationship between the means of production and those who use them. The condition and average quantity of the means of production per worker are basic indicators of

Y. Li, *China's Economy Since 1978*, China Academic Library,
https://doi.org/10.1007/978-981-95-5733-2_22

a firm's technological level, which in turn determines its efficiency level. The interpersonal relationship is a lot more complicated. It can be broken up into a number of relations such as the relation between the firm's leadership and workers, between members of the leadership, between the leadership and the managerial body, between members of the managerial body and between workers. Some of these interpersonal relations are congenial, others are not. Some interpersonal relations are agreeable under one condition, but disagreeable under another. The agreeability of these interpersonal relations impacts efficiency in ways different from the impact of technology. If the technological level is low, it may be upgraded as a sine qua non for efficiency growth by increasing investment, adding new equipment, constructing new factory buildings, putting workers through training, or encouraging them to hone their skills. If interpersonal relations are disagreeable, can reinvestment be effective? How can it send efficiency skyrocketing?

Supposing the technological level of a company is fixed, the human factor—managers and workers included—will become so prominent as to determine the efficiency level. In this human factor, every employee's work hour, cultural attainment and skill adeptness, and how well-defined is work-post responsibility are observable factors, but there are also unobservable factors. For one thing, people's diligence level is elusive, for it is hard to tell exactly how hardworking everyone is. For another, employees are under the effect of a certain level of inertia. Those who are less affected by it are more motivated and aggressive in work; those affected more by it are lethargic. To what extent they can overcome inertia is another unknown factor. Moreover, efficiency grows when employees' goals match their firm's goals, and drops when their goals are at odds with each other, but whether or not these two kinds of goals can match each other is anyone's guess. The impact of these unobservable factors on firm efficiency merits careful study, for it is a hard nut to crack for both market and government regulation.

Therefore, the study of efficiency needs to go beyond the scope of market and government regulation. This is not to say that market regulation and government regulation mean little to the rise and fall of efficiency. It only shows the limits of their impact, limits that, in particular, can affect our analysis of the sources of efficiency. For instance, in our research on a firm's interpersonal relationships, the impact of unobservable factors such as diligence and inertia on employees should be probed. Work ethics affect human behavior and go on to affect efficiency in many ways. What is the true source of efficiency? It is the human factor. Efficiency hinges on people's motivation and innovativeness, so work ethics should never be overlooked. Efficiency improves greatly when full scope is given to people's potentials, and when they are highly motivated and innovative under the influence of work ethics.

It should be noted that the above analysis is predicated on a given technological level. Technological level, judged from the perspective of the relationship between people and the means of production, is relevant to efficiency level. If the technological level of a country, region, or firm is a lot higher than that of another country, region, or firm, it makes comparing the impact of work ethics very difficult. Only by accurately reading the impact of work ethics on efficiency at a given technological level can such comparison make sense.

22.2 Efficiency Stems from Organizational and Social Cohesion

As illustrated in the previous chapter, the source of efficiency at a given technological level lies in people's motivation and innovativeness. To make the most of such motivation and innovativeness, it is essential to develop rational economic operational mechanisms and agreeable interpersonal relationships.

The cohesion parameter of the agreeability of interpersonal relationship falls into two categories: cohesion of an organization, and cohesion of society. The cohesion of an organization or society hinges on the agreeability of its interpersonal relationships. Cohesion generates efficiency. Organizational cohesion delivers efficiency inside an organization, and social cohesion endows efficiency on society.

The organization in this context refers in general to businesses, institutions, communities, villages, households, and others. Organizations may vary in size, but each has its own cohesion. Organizations may be structurally loose or tight. Tight structure is not synonymous with high cohesion, while loose structure does not always mean a lack of cohesion. The structural looseness or tightness of an organization is irrelevant to cohesion or the lack of it, but is directly relevant to the agreeability of the relationship between the organization and its members and between its members. If the members of an organization are given to scheming against each other or are in discord with their leaders, this organization will be devoid of cohesion no matter how close-knit its organizational structure is. By contrast, if members of a community are in an amicable relationship with one another and with their leaders and work with one mind to make progress, such a community will enjoy cohesion, and a strong cohesion at that, even if it is loosely organized.

A firm consists of workers and managers. Its cohesion is one of many kinds of organizational cohesion. To foster corporate culture helps cultivate corporate cohesion. A highly cohesive firm can not only improve its efficiency steadily but also overcome difficulties and tide over adversities.

Some questions come to mind at this point of this study: How does society's cohesion come about? What is the relationship between organizational cohesion and social cohesion? How should such a relationship be handled to achieve both organizational and social cohesion?

Social cohesion is the force that rallies members of society together as one to achieve common goals. There is no lack of outstanding examples in this regard, such as the concerted effort, hard work, and self-sacrifices of people rallying against foreign invaders or natural disasters. Under such unusual circumstances, this kind of cohesion can generate high social efficiency and work wonders. Under normal circumstances, a society with harmonious interpersonal relationship and strong cohesion invariably enjoys an agreeable social environment that is a boon to the growth of efficiency.

As to the relationship between organizational cohesion and social cohesion, they may either promote or circumscribe each other, depending on what the organization's nature and goals are. There are all sorts of organizations in society that differ in nature and pursue different goals. If separatism is a political organization's overriding call, then the more cohesive it is, the more destructive it becomes to society. Of course this is an extreme example that can be excluded from my discussion. Generally speaking, an organization and society can get along if they have compatible goals, and consequently the cohesion of the organization and that of society are complementary. Below let me take firms for example again.

In a market economy, maximization of interest is the primary goal of firms that function as commodity producers making their own business decisions and being accountable for their profits and losses. To meet that goal, they must beat competition by constantly adjusting their production and business directions, improving their management, and enhancing their internal cohesion.

Competition on a level playing field is essential to the proper handling of the relationship between firms, in which their shared interest lies in the belief that the more stable society is and the more the economy thrives, the better off the firms become. The rise of one firm does not necessarily mean the downfall of another. In an environment of social stability and economic prosperity, every firm has the opportunity to grow and convert their good intentions into reality. However, even in such a friendly environment there are still firms that have to downscale production, go bankrupt, or be annexed due to decision-making errors or failure to keep pace with technological development. These occurrences are a normal reflection of the regrouping of resources. As long as such regrouping proves salubrious to efficiency of the economy as a whole and brings new opportunities to investors, the common interest of the business world will not be hurt by the aforementioned production cuts, bankruptcies, or mergers.

Organizational cohesion and social cohesion, however, are not the same thing. Whether the former can be unified with the latter, or whether enhanced organizational cohesion can strengthen social cohesion, is determined by the substance and efficacy of advancement in culture—corporate culture, community culture, campus culture, etc.—as a major element in the promotion of organizational cohesion. If a firm's corporate culture emphasizes not only its own goals but also the goals of society, and aims not only at cultivating its own corporate spirit but also at fostering fine social mores, the achievement of such a corporate culture will be reflected in the improved cohesion of both the firm and society. The unification of corporate and social cohesion precisely embodies the social function and value of a sound corporate culture. Conversely, if a firm is bent on pursuing its own corporate and workforce interests at the expense of its corporate culture's social function and value, it will have no way of coordinating its cohesion with that of society, nor can its improved corporate cohesion result in improved social cohesion. This point should not be overlooked when analyzing the sources of efficiency.

A more nuanced understanding of the issue enables us to see that growth in national wealth is connected with society's economic prosperity and development in culture and education. A prosperous society with advanced culture and education is better endowed to promote cultural development and coordinate its own cohesion with organizational cohesion. Moral values also play an outstanding role in enhancing social and organizational cohesion, a role that cannot be superseded by market or government regulation. This is because only moral values can demonstrate to members of organizations that their own organizations' goals are in line with those of society and that the interests of individuals and organizations are, fundamentally speaking, compatible with the interests of society. That realization enables them to identify themselves completely with society's goals, thereby bolstering both organizational and social cohesion. Both organizational and social cohesion can be steadily enhanced under the impact of moral force.

Hence my conclusion: In the past, researchers of the source of efficiency have often stressed economic and technological factors to the neglect of non-economic and non-technological factors, emphasized the impact of interests at the expense of public goals and a sense of social responsibility, and reiterated material values regardless of human values. Under the sway of such outdated ideological and methodological approaches, researchers could neither probe into the deep-seated issue concerning changes in efficiency, nor explain that the human factor and interpersonal relations—rather than the material factor and the relationship between people and materials—are the true fountainhead for efficiency. Organizational cohesion generates organizational efficiency, and social cohesion brings forth social efficiency. This being the case, the source of efficiency and its enhancement lies not in market mechanisms or government interventional behavior, but in the force of morality and its impact on people.

22.3 Where Super Efficiency Comes from

It is generally acknowledged that efficiency rests on a material foundation. Such a foundation encompasses production equipment, raw materials, technological conditions, workers with a certain level of technical proficiency, and social infrastructure (including means of communications and transportation, telecommunications facilities, water and heat and energy utilities). The importance of the material foundation is common knowledge. Efficiency suffers when the material foundation stops improving itself.

Does efficiency have only one foundation, the material foundation? Is it true that where there is a material foundation, there will be growing efficiency? As noted previously, a material foundation alone is not enough to account for the ebb and flow in efficiency. Due consideration must be given to the other foundation—the moral foundation. Manufacturing equipment and raw materials are used by people. The efficacy of technology cannot operate without man's proficiency, motivation, and creativity. In other words, workers with a certain level of proficiency are an integral part of the material foundation of efficiency. However, workers are not robots. They are human beings who think, feel, and pursue ideas and goals. They may take one attitude or another toward life, and be either devoted to or uncaring about work. In addition, they are not isolated, but interact with one another to form all sorts of interpersonal relations with varying degrees of coordination. All this constitutes the other foundation for efficiency, the moral foundation.

The material and moral foundations of efficiency exist alongside each other. Neither of them can stand alone to account for a rise or fall in efficiency. Let us imagine that two firms have the same material and technological conditions and make the same product needed by consumers: How is it that one firm is more efficient than the other? The answer can be found by comparing the differences in the moral foundation of their efficiency.

Thus, it makes sense to say that efficiency has dual foundations, material and moral.

Organizations—as small as families, companies, or villages or as large as communities or nations—cannot survive without spiritual cohesion, norms of conduct, and moral values in the same way as they cannot dispense with science and technology. In handling interpersonal relations, morality comes to assist when and where science and technology are helpless. Once interpersonal relations are finely tuned, once full scope is given to people's initiative and creativity, efficiency grows as a matter of course. This shows that efficiency does indeed have a moral foundation.

Efficiency's material foundation changes constantly with economic growth, technological advancement, and the renewal of knowledge on the part of those who use the means of production. Moreover, its changes are unstoppable. Does efficiency's moral foundation ever stop changing itself? Is there any unalterable moral principle that forms this foundation? Given that the material foundation is ever-changing, can the moral foundation stay intact alongside it? If the answer is in the positive, does the moral foundation ever change on its own or only in unison with circumstances? If it changes on its own, this refers to changes in moral values, rules of conduct, and evaluation criteria. If it changes in unison with circumstances, this means that it can adapt itself to the material foundation. However, it is difficult to distinguish between these two kinds of changes, which, in fact, are often intertwined with each other.

Now consider this question: Where does super efficiency come from? While the material foundation usually offers conventional efficiency, the moral foundation not only ensures conventional efficiency but also provides super efficiency.

The super efficiency of the immigrant societies of yore has been a topic of perennial academic interest. During the millennium-long war and turmoil following the demise of the Han dynasty (206 BC-220 AD), immigrants from central China hacked their way through brambles and throngs and settled in what are today's Guangdong and Fujian provinces, where they dredged rivers and converted barren land into fertile farmland. Beginning from the twelfth century, immigrants into the Western European region now known as the Netherlands reclaimed the land, built water conservancy projects, and developed farming and animal husbandry. What these immigrants embodied was precisely a kind of super efficiency. How did they achieve such efficiency with medieval tools, limited manpower, and harsh environment? There was neither market force nor government intervention during the process of immigration and the rise of the immigrant society, so what had motivated these people to toil with such high efficiency? This can only be attributed to the magical forces of morality, cohesion, and creativity. We may as well say that given the historical circumstances, these immigrants performed pioneering feats with extraordinary strength under extraordinary conditions. Even their social organizations were extraordinary. These factors combined to work miracles in human history. In the absence of a commensurate moral foundation, there could not have been such extraordinary immigrant social organizations, the immigrants could not have mustered such extraordinary strength as individuals, and such super efficiency would have been out of the question.

The achievement of super efficiency fully testifies to what potential efficiency growth can do. Such potentials can be tapped by relying on the moral foundation of efficiency. Examples in this regard are aplenty, besides the aforementioned immigrant societies. The role of morality, confidence, and faith in stimulating human willpower and abilities can be seen in people's death-defying behaviors in resistance against foreign invaders, in combating natural disasters, and even in the effort of members of an organization—as small as a family or clan and as large as a nation or region—in attaining their goals or in safeguarding dignity and honor. Super efficiency arises precisely from among these people. Can the material foundation also contribute to the rise of super efficiency? Efficiency can certainly not do without its material condition. For instance, our forefathers would not have accomplished their pioneering cause without certain means of production in their possession no matter how motivated they were. We cannot combat natural adversities empty-handed. However, without the tremendous impact of morality and faith under these circumstances, material conditions can only yield mediocre efficiency. We must admit to ourselves that in the absence of a moral foundation, our efficiency may still be inadequate, low, or even negative despite the provision of an efficient material foundation.

The longstanding controversy about the conflict between the efficiency standard and the moral standard is settled through our analysis of super efficiency. The conflict between these two standards is about judging economic behavior with two criteria. One is a standard of efficiency, meaning that an economic behavior is good when it boosts efficiency and bad when it reduces efficiency. The other is a standard of morality: Efficiency is good if it accords with the moral principle and evil if it violates it. These two standards are often in discord because rising efficiency may run counter to the moral principle, whereas efficiency that accords with the moral principle may fall. This longstanding issue cannot be settled mainly because of uncertainty about which standard to use in judging the moral good or evil of efficiency.

The efficiency standard is an issue in economics, and so is efficiency judgment. However, neither the moral standard nor moral judgment is a subject or research task for any economists. Both belong in the realm of economics where and when an economic issue touches upon the relationship between moral standard and efficiency standard, and the need arises to determine whether or not a moral judgment corresponds with an efficiency judgment. In my *Socialist Political Economics* I put it this way, "The moral judgment of economic behavior should be tested in practice, otherwise the moral principle for the economy could become elusive... We may as well regard 'maximum workforce interests' as the moral standard for economic behavior. That is to say, an economic behavior is sound when it complies with 'maximum workforce interests', and is evil when it does not (Li 1986)." This approach to coordinating efficiency and moral standards may serve to support my judgment of certain economic behaviors.

After all, the conflict between efficiency and moral standards may still occur in evaluating some other economic behaviors, to the bewilderment of the economists of today. However, the emergence of super efficiency testifies to the accord between both standards. Extraordinary efficiency itself is evidence of an impressive boost in efficiency, and therefore, the efficiency standard is entirely applicable here. How, then, does super efficiency come about? It is directly related to the role of morality, as I have stated before. Without morality, super efficiency would have been out of the question in an immigrant society or in combating foreign invaders or major natural catastrophes. Thus, super efficiency that measures up to the efficiency standard is also up to the moral standard.

22.4 Tapping Potentials in Efficiency Growth

The mention of the moral foundation for efficiency brings the following question to mind: Under which condition is the potential greater for efficiency growth—the more the initiative is taken into the hands of individuals, or the less the initiative is taken into the hands of individuals while the more closely individuals are attached to their organization or society?

Why should I raise such a question? It has something to do with the moral foundation of efficiency. Given the technical nature of the means of production, given objective production conditions, and provided the cultural and technical proficiency of individuals as producers is fixed, individuals with more freedom of choice may become highly motivated and innovative, and thus have greater potential for efficiency improvement. That is to say, the larger the number is producers and workers with freedom of choice in economic activity, the more dynamic the economy becomes, the better the economy's capacity for growth is, and the easier the potentials of efficiency growth are to be tapped. Therefore, it is wrong to believe that the more autonomy is allowed for producers and workers, the more detrimental it is to the economy. On the other hand, however, given that the source of efficiency also lies in harmonious interpersonal relations and in people's compatibility with their organizations or society, it is more likely to coordinate these relations and enable individuals to adapt themselves to their organizations and society if they are subordinate to those organizations or society as a whole. Does this also point to greater potential for efficiency growth?

As a matter of fact, this question is not unanswerable. Individual autonomy and subordination to a particular organization or society can be mutually compatible instead of mutually exclusive. The moral foundation for efficiency entails not just making the most of people's enthusiasm and creativity; it also involves coordinating and harmonizing interpersonal relations. It is senseless to emphasize the former to the neglect of the latter, or vice versa. Nor can we believe that efficiency can grow continuously rather than temporarily when individuals are deprived of autonomy and lack enthusiasm and creativity as members of a particular organization or society, or when individuals enjoy a lot of autonomy while interpersonal relations are growing increasingly more inordinate and incompatible. Thus, it is ideal to have both individual autonomy and coordinated and compatible interpersonal relations, with neither aspect neglected. This being the case, there should be individuals subordinate to organizations and society on the one side, and organizations and society holding individuals in due respect on the other—the coexistence of both conditions can keep efficiency growing steadily. In other words, individuals' subordination to organizations and society should be genuine and voluntary. Instead of being imposed upon them, their subordination should be conditioned by coordinated interpersonal relations and mutual respect, but at the same time, individuals should also conduct themselves with dignity and self-respect.

That should be the way it is in reality. People living in society are inevitably its members. A member of society invariably participates in certain organizations or institutions. The family is the smallest cell of society, and everyone belongs to a particular family. If a man is a worker, he works in a factory, where he may also be a trade union member. If he is a farmer, he may become a member of a villagers' self-governing organization, if such an organization ever exists. If he is an urban dweller, he belongs to the local community or neighborhood. If he is a private or self-employed business owner, he must belong to a certain association in which he handles interpersonal relations the best he can in order to live and work in harmony with fellow members. Meanwhile, as an individual, he should have his own wishes and demands, follow his own principles in dealing with people and daily life, and take the initiative into his own hands to stay motivated and innovative. In all, he should be a dynamic human being. Self-dependence is the prerequisite for someone to be in good interpersonal relations and get along with his organization and society. Good personal and interpersonal relations can mean nothing, and there will be no coordination and compatibility to speak of, if people are deprived of self-dependence and personal initiative. Doesn't this mean that personal initiative should be put in the first place in comparison with harmonious interpersonal relationships?

Society consists of numerous individuals, and an organization or institution comprises a certain number of individuals. If these individuals enjoy self-dependence, are motivated, energetic, and innovative, and have the latitude to pursue their own goals while adapting themselves to organizational and social goals, interpersonal relations can be better handled, and efficiency can grow faster and by bigger margins. Isn't this exactly what society and organizations hope for?

Based on the above study, we know that the moral foundation of efficiency is an objective reality, but efficiency growth may either be real or potential, and the potential in efficiency growth is not necessarily tapped to capacity. To give full scope to such potential, we have to do two things: first, to respect people's self-dependence and give full scope to their motivation and innovativeness; and second, to coordinate interpersonal relations and adapt individuals to their organizations and society (Li 1986).

— *Journal of Peking University (Humanities and Social Sciences)*, issue No. 6, 1998.

Reference

Li Y-N (1986) *Socialist Political Economics*, The Commercial Press, Beijing, pp. 438–439.

Chapter 23
1999: Management, Self-Discipline, and Moral Motivation

23.1 Sources of Sustainable Individual Initiative and Motivation

Everyone needs self-discipline in economic activities. The conventional wisdom takes self-discipline as moral restraint for an individual, however, this understanding is somewhat narrow. Being self-disciplined has some up-and-coming effects. That is to say, one is supposed to be proactive and dedicated to work, making achievements regardless of the type of work or position. Spiritual vitality is essential. Moral motivation can be considered as the other side of self-discipline, which is complementary to and mutually reinforcing with moral restraints.

As for the relationship among moral motivation, professional dedication, and individual initiative, we might as well start with the dynamics of economic life. In economic analysis, the assumption that "motivations come from an individual's material interests" has some limitations. Individual interests are not confined to material interests. Human beings are "social beings," thus one's interests are broader than simple material or economic interests. That is exactly how the assumption that "motivations do not come solely from interests" is proposed. At any level of income, individual behavior is supposed to be affected by other factors apart from interests, which tend to be more prominent as personal income increases. That is to say, when personal income reaches a certain level, material motivation to individual initiative and motivation will be lessened. Individuals would consider more that is beyond interests, which may contribute to a part of, or a larger part of, their initiative and motivation in economic activities.

Just because of the non-interest factors, individual motivations often do not marginally diminish in economic activities. The term "diminishing motivation" refers to the fact that when one is engaged in economic activities, their initiative and proactivity tend to weaken as income increases. Under the premise that motivation is solely derived from individual's material interests, diminishing motivation is likely to occur. This is because the income is no longer an incentive it used to be. Here it

Y. Li, *China's Economy Since 1978*, China Academic Library,
https://doi.org/10.1007/978-981-95-5733-2_23

involves the substitution between income and efforts. For individuals, as the level of income rises, they tend to consider whether it is worthy of making as much effort to achieve a certain amount of income. For many, time and energy may become more valuable, thus leading to diminishing motivation of both personal income and material interests. However, as non-interest factors play a larger part in individual economic activities, motivation is not necessarily on the decline even if personal income increases. At this point, it is absolutely possible for people to be more proactive than before. Since the economic concerns are gone, one can devote most of the time and energy to careers motivated by non-interest factors.

If we consider from this perspective, the limitations of the material interest assumption are clear. It is from this premise that we can further explore the sources of sustained individual initiatives and proactivity in socio-economic activities.

Of course, we should examine sustained initiative and motivation not only by individual perspectives but also by incorporating objective conditions. Individual efforts no doubt play an important role in sustaining initiative and morale. However, it is also important for companies to instill and mobilize those spirits among their employees. Otherwise, it will be difficult for an individual to develop sustained initiative and proactivity. Furthermore, the economic system is also related to enterprises' mobilization capacity. In order to achieve that, we should let the market play a decisive role instead of the administrative instructions, provide a fair and competitive environment rather than providing differential treatment for enterprises, and allow enterprises, not the government, to be responsible for their own gains and losses. By implementing these strategies, enterprises can pay more attention to motivating their employees.

Assuming that both the economic system and the enterprise system have met the requirement of a market economy, how can individual initiative and motivation be generated and sustained? Let us turn to the discussion of moral motivation as the latter is the source of sustained individual initiatives.

23.2 The Compatibility of Moral Motivation and Material Incentives

Can one's moral motivation be compatible with his/her moral incentive at work? This is a question worth discussing. We cannot simply assume that once a person has a material incentive, moral motivation will disappear. Nor can we ignore the impact of material incentive just because sustained initiative is generated by moral motivation. One's initiative probably comes partly from material interests and partly from moral urges. The origin of sustained initiative and proactivity could be the same, except that moral motivation may play a more important role. In addition, even if an individual activity is motivated by interests, professional dedication is also essential. When an individual makes a transaction with others, credibility is important, which also involves moral motivation.

Most people in society are motivated by both personal interests and public purposes because the two are believed not to be exclusive. For example, if one starts up an enterprise with success, the enterprise's prosperity will not only increase one's personal interests but also benefit the society, i.e., a contribution to the public good. On the same token, if one works in an enterprise, the job can not only increase family income and improve life quality but it will also increase the profits of the enterprise, which will then benefit the whole society. In these terms, the motivations of personal interests and public good are in fact compatible. Although there are always people who devote themselves to the public rather than personal interests, they are only a small percentage after all.

When personal interests and public objectives are in conflict and the choice is exclusive, it will be a challenge for most people who care about both of them. The compatibility of these two makes it unnecessary for individuals to make exclusive choices, since the realization of personal interests can be beneficial to the realization of public interests and vice versa. However, not everyone can make the right decision when the choice has to be exclusive, and it is exactly when moral motivation asserts itself. When moral strength flinches, people will choose personal interests over public objectives. There are quite a few examples in history and real life. But there are still many who choose public objectives over personal interests, which is the result of self-discipline. Self-discipline provides them with both moral restraints and moral motivations. Moral restraint keeps them within the bounds of not violating public interests and objectives while not being sacrificed for the sake of personal gains. Moral motivation, on the other hand, inspires one's efforts toward the realization of public interests and objectives above personal interests when the two conflict. Here, moral restraint and motivation are of equal importance.

Moral motivation is sometimes misunderstood in socio-economic activities. For example, when an individual obtains gains out of material incentives, one tends to be regarded as being motivated by personal interests. In this case, moral restraint may still exist but moral motivation does not. This misunderstanding is popular because moral motivation and interest incentive are often understood as mutually exclusive. However, as discussed above, the following conclusions can be drawn.

When there is no need to make exclusive choices between personal interests and public objectives, for individuals, the realization of these two can be compatible. Moral motivation not only contributes to the realization of public objectives, but also benefits the realization of personal interests. In this regard, moral motivation is consistent with personal interest. In order to achieve personal interest, one will endeavor to provide products and services more welcomed by society under the inspiration of professional dedication, integrity, and credibility.

When people have to make a decisive and exclusive choice between personal interests and public goods, conflict arises. If one chooses personal interests over public objectives, it means that moral motivation does not work and it is inconsistent with one's interest incentive. If one chooses public objectives over personal interests, it suggests that moral motivation is at work and it is compatible with personal interests in making the appropriate choice. An individual who strives for personal interests without compromising public interests and objectives may give up his /her personal interests in the face of the conflict between personal interests and public objectives. All those behaviors can be influenced by moral motivation. These show that moral motivation and personal interests can be compatible in an inclusive relationship that public objectives contain personal interests.

Thus, it can be seen that moral motivation and personal interests can be compatible but are not necessarily in sync. When one must choose between the two and the choice is based on personal interests instead of public objectives, the incompatibility between moral motivation and personal interest incentive is exposed.

23.3 Self-Discipline as the Integration of Moral Restraint and Moral Motivation

The analyses above suggest that moral restraint is undoubtedly essential but moral motivation is equally important. In socio-economic life, if there is only moral restraint and no moral motivation, the society may lose its vitality and initiative, and people may be too cautious to make mistakes. If there is only moral motivation without moral restraint, people might become lax in their actions and fail to adhere to the ethical code. Only when moral restraint and moral motivation are integrated can we develop a dynamic and vigorous society and integrate both public objectives and personal interests into consideration. A worker who is good at self-discipline can be one with the spirit of devotion or ambition. One can also be a person with professional dedication and rising income. One's dedication, initiative, professionalism, career success, and income trajectory are all related to one's moral motivation and restraint.

A person who needs to survive under abnormal conditions needs not only moral restraint but also moral motivation. Putting historical conditions aside, in real-life experiences, one needs to survive, thrive, and adapt to a variety of living and working conditions in the society. Apart from the ability to survive and thrive under normal conditions, one must do so under various abnormal conditions. Otherwise, one will be too vulnerable to survive and withstand any adversities and strikes. It should be noted that the notion of adaptation is not primarily the ability to adapt to normal conditions, but rather the ability to adapt to abnormal ones. An important criterion to judge a person's strength and vitality is to see whether he/she can survive and adapt to all kinds of adversities under abnormal conditions.

However, among those under the same abnormal conditions, why are some of them lagging behind, while others are progressing? Some give up, while others carry on. These are in fact the result of the co-influence of moral restraint and motivation. If someone remains self-sufficient and proactive in abnormal conditions, they can identify the source of their adaptability from a spiritual standpoint. The role of moral motivation should be particularly mentioned here. Under the influence of moral motivation, one will try to deal with difficulties in a positive way, overcome them, and regard the challenging environment as a test for one's faith, dream, and goal. Moral motivation tends to enable one to learn how to adapt to abnormal conditions and thus develop oneself. In this sense, the more one is exposed to abnormal conditions, the more moral motivation is required, and the more prominent the function of moral strength can play.

No one can avoid inertia and its influence on individual behavior. How can inertia be overcome? On the one hand, the formation and influence of positive social customs are needed. On the other hand, sustained moral motivation is necessary. Under the influence of positive social customs, when people around you can overcome inertia and strive for progress constantly, there is more possibility that you will achieve the same. Moral motivation is more important when positive social customs have not yet been established for the following reason: Whether people around have overcome the inertia, whether they are creative or progressive, as long as we work hard under moral motivation, we can not only overcome the inertia but also influence the people around us, giving them confidence and perseverance to overcome their inertia.

In short, self-discipline, which is considered as the integration of moral restraint and moral motivation, always warrants the attention of the society and the administrative authorities. When people are motivated by moral restraint, they will be strict with themselves in socio-economic activities; they will not do anything against moral standards and resist any action detrimental to public interests and public objectives. When people are inspired by moral motivation, they tend to become more motivated, devoted, and professional; they will overcome their inertia and difficulties; they can successfully finish their work and be outstanding even in the face of adversities.

I hope all the discussions above can be informative in improving our administrative and managerial work.

— *Modern Management and Leadership*, issue No. 1–2, 1999.

Chapter 24
2000: China's Choice on the Reform Mode Correct

The ideological line of seeking truth from facts was re-established at the Third Plenary Session of the Eleventh Central Committee of the Communist Party of China (CPC), which opened the door for market-oriented reforms. Today, after twenty years of reform, in the review of this process, we do feel that the reform direction we have chosen is absolutely right.

It should be known that the planned economic system consisted of several sub-level systems, such as the planned enterprise system, planned fiscal and taxation system, planned financial system, planned price system, planned labor system, personnel system, etc. They are tightly integrated with each other. One sub-level system depends on another sub-level system, which in turn depends on the third one. All these systems are intertwined and inseparable. If one exists, then the others will work. If one fails, then the others will not. Therefore, it is simply impossible for any single enterprise or individual to break through the constraints of a planned system. This situation clearly shows that it is very difficult to replace the planned economic system with the socialist market economic system. Had an inappropriate reform path been chosen, for example, the "shock therapy" recommended by some foreign economists, i.e., a reform approach of liberalizing prices comprehensively in a concise period, the Chinese economy would only have been in a state of chaos, rather than the developments we have achieved.

The reform mode that China has chosen was to start with rural reforms and then urban reforms. The latter was a gradual process with the enterprise reform as the main line, and a series of supportive reforms undertaken simultaneously. The liberalization of prices was also gradual. The price reform is not necessarily the breakthrough for the entire reform, but a price system based on a free market must be its end point. Practices so far have proved that our choice on the reform mode was correct.

The household contract system was established in rural reforms. By the early 1980s, the appearance of the countryside had experienced dramatic changes. Farmers' lack of food and clothing had basically been solved. Instead, they began

Y. Li, *China's Economy Since 1978*, China Academic Library,
https://doi.org/10.1007/978-981-95-5733-2_24

to provide more agricultural products to the market, contributing to a more diversified commodities market. All these depended on the correct line formulated by the Third Plenary Session of the Eleventh Central Committee of the CPC. Because of the achievements made in rural reforms, the focus of the reform was shifted from the rural to the urban area starting from the Third Plenary Session of the Twelfth Central Committee of the CPC in October 1984.

In urban reforms, had the enterprise reform not been the main theme, the reform would not have made any real progress. Furthermore, it would have been a more likely continuous increase of prices, then eventually a suspension and abortion of the reform. This is because the core of the enterprise reform is to define property rights and separate government and enterprise. Various supporting reforms are connected to the reform of property rights. For example, if investors were required to bear investment risks without the property rights reform, how could they manage these risks and adapt to the market economy? As another example, an important part of the financial reform aims to transform professional banks into self-operated commercial banks with responsibility for their own gains and losses, which is also tightly connected to the property rights reform. The independent operation and self-financing of commercial banks are based on the premise of defining and clarifying property rights. In order to make commercial banks become real financial enterprises, they, as a legal person, must own all property rights of the capital raised from investors, including the state, and become legal entities that enjoy civil rights and bear civil liabilities. Isn't this about property rights reform? Finally, in terms of the social security reform, it is necessary to establish an enterprise pension and unemployment insurance system, enterprise work injury insurance system and a proper operation of social security funds. If the property rights reform was not carried out and the property rights relationship of enterprises were not straightened, how could insurance funds be operated in coordination within the entire society? How could social security funds be run within the scope of the society and increase their value? It can be seen that the property rights reform is indeed the key to advancing economic reforms.

However, it is not a smooth sailing for the enterprise reform, with the core of defining property rights and separating government and enterprise. There has been huge ideological resistance from time to time. Some believe that the property rights reform is to implement privatization and restore capitalism. The debate over the choice of *she* (socialism) versus *zi* (capitalism) and the *gong* (public) versus *si* (private) has been haunting for as long as ten years. Nonetheless, the reform has not stopped. The route chosen by the Third Plenary Session of the Eleventh Central Committee of the CPC has been deeply rooted in the idea of allowing experimentation and exploration, and deepening the enterprise reform gradually. Since then, it has been learned from reform practice that all reforms, including the property rights reform, should be undertaken under the principle of safeguarding the socialist system. These reforms will promote the development of productivity and help achieve the goal of common prosperity. If we had been hesitated on this issue, being plagued by disputes with the choice of *she* versus *zi*, and *gong* versus *si*, we would only have delayed the opportunity for reform.

When talking about the necessity of the reform, Comrade Deng Xiaoping pointed out many times that after the victory of the socialist revolution and the establishment of a socialist system, institutional reforms became the driving force for further economic development under socialist conditions. If reforms are ignored as the engine of socialist economic development, and the establishment of the socialist system had followed a stereotypical routine, it would have not only made it difficult for socialism to continue advancing, to achieve common prosperity based on the continuous development of productive forces, but also made the socialist society lose vitality and appeal. After the drastic disruptions in the Soviet Union and Eastern European countries, we have a deeper understanding of this and cannot miss the opportunity to reform. If we do not seize the moment to undertake the reforms, we will eventually lose the socialist system. The socialist economy will be full of vitality if the reforms are insisted. And people will keep desiring and supporting socialism only if the superiority of this institution can be realized to facilitate the increase of productivity. Then the socialist system will be maintained, and socialism can continue to advance. Nowadays, when we look back on the course of reforms that we have gone through in the past twenty years, we have more understanding of the great historical significance of the Third Plenary Session of the Eleventh Central Committee of the CPC and the correct reform mode that China has chosen.

The practice of China's twenty years of reform and opening-up has shown the world that, as long as we stick to reform and opening-up, China's economy will surely develop rapidly, and the people's living standards will also be gradually improved. Under the guidance of Comrade Deng Xiaoping's theory of socialism with Chinese characteristics, we need to accelerate the reform and development. In this way, by the end of the twentieth century and the beginning of the twenty-first century, a preliminary socialist market economy will be established in China. By the middle of the twenty-first century, namely at the centenary of the founding of the People's Republic of China, China will become a developed socialist country. We all believe this without a shadow of doubt.

— *Economic Information Daily*, on April 26th, 2000.

Chapter 25
2001: Views on the Scope of Economics Research

Since the early 1990s, I have served as the Chinese member of the China Council for International Cooperation on Environment and Development and the head of the environmental economic expert group for nearly ten years. During this period, the environment, resources, and sustainable development have essentially become my research fields. In the discussions with several Ph.D. candidates studying environment and resource economics at Guanghua School of Management, Peking University, I once asked them three questions. First, what is the research scope of economics? Second, what are the boundaries of economics? Third, how is this new branch of economics formed?

These are also what I often think about. I hope that more and more people in the economics community are interested in these issues and are willing to participate in the discussion. Recently, I was delighted to read a book titled *The Economics of Sustainable Development* written by Professors Hong Yinxing and other scholars of Nanjing University. Several theoretical issues involved in the manuscript are related to the first and the second questions I mentioned above, including the relationship between population growth, natural resources, ecology, environment, and sustainable development, the relationship between industrial coordination, regional coordination, property rights, technological progress, and sustainable development, as well as the relationship between culture, legal system, and sustainable development. Then the third question above is related to the exposition of sustainable development economics and its theoretical history in the manuscript. This book is a monograph with specific research objects and research scope. I do not want to state my views on the specific issues involved in this book, but sustainable development economics, as a new branch of economics, prompts me to think further. When Prof. Hong Yinxing invited me to write a preface for this book, I would like to start with some comments on the above three questions.

Y. Li, *China's Economy Since 1978*, China Academic Library,
https://doi.org/10.1007/978-981-95-5733-2_25

25.1 What is the Scope of Economics?

There are two questions here. First, what is the scope of pure economics? Second, what is the range of the research scope of all economic branches? The so-called pure economics means nothing more than basic economic theories. Moreover, its scope is mainly conclusive, covering basic economic theories in production, distribution, transactions, and consumption. From another perspective, theoretical research on macroeconomics, microeconomics, and institutional economics should fall within the scope of pure economics. According to the conventional view, economics is a science of resource allocation, so the research of pure economics involves the way to rationally and effectively allocate resources and adjust them to promote fairness and efficiency, and the coordination of the two aspects. Therefore, based on this definition, we can roughly assess whether the issues to be studied fall in pure economics or not. In short, the research scope of pure economics involves the fundamental theoretical issues of economics. As for the research scope of all economic branches, it is difficult to clarify because no one knows how many economic branches there are, and which new one will be identified in the future. For example, in the late nineteenth and early twentieth century, could masters of economics, like Alfred Marshall in the Britain, forecast the emergence of so many branches of economics in the following decades? Marshall, who once studied the issue of consumption, could not have expected the emergence of consumer economics afterwards. Is it for welfare issues? This subject also had not emerged when Marshall was alive but came into being soon after his pass-away. No one can accurately count the number of branches of economics. While the research scope of economics should include all branches, the range is only an unanswerable question.

However, we may answer this question in another way. As long as it is related to the economy, an issue could always be classified into certain branches of economics sooner or later. If a relevant branch of economics is not existing now with the in-depth and meticulous research work of other disciplines and the broadening horizons of people, it will gradually emerge. Is it true that a series of sub-disciplines of economics, such as academic economics, environmental economics, health economics, information economics, and tourism economics, have emerged one after another? What is more, the sub-disciplines mentioned here include both secondary and tertiary disciplines. Their emergence means the expansion of economics research. There will be some fourth-level subjects under the third level, regardless of how we call them. In this way, we can confirm that the research field of economics will be larger and larger, and within each specific one, the research will become more in-depth.

25.2 What Are the Boundaries of Economics?

The boundaries of economics research involve three related issues. First, does economics research spill over into (or “invade”) other disciplines? Second, where is the end of economics research? Third, if there is a boundary in economic research, do research subjects also allow other disciplines to intervene?

Of course, research in a specific discipline should have a boundary. Otherwise, any issue could become the research object, then the division of disciplines would be meaningless. Therefore, specific subjects always have boundaries in research. The question is: How we define the boundaries of one subject? In terms of economics, does economics research spill over into (or “invade”) other disciplines? Let us take two branches of education economics and health economics as examples. Education economics is a combination of the marginal disciplines of economics and pedagogy, while health economics is that of economics and medicine. Since these two economic sub fields are interdisciplinary or marginal disciplines, when researchers study related issues in these areas, they inevitably penetrate the fields of pedagogy or medicine. Such infiltration is expected. Otherwise, how can interdisciplinary or marginal disciplines emerge and develop? In other words, delineating the boundary between the two disciplines is difficult, because conducting research and debate at the intersection or edge is regular and meaningful. Therefore, there is no need to demarcate the boundaries between one subject and another at the intersection or edge. In this way, we can answer: The question “Where is the end of economics research?” lies in the intersection or edge of each branch of economics with other disciplines. Because of the wide range, it is difficult or even unnecessary to demarcate the boundaries of economics. Therefore, the end of economics research can only be defined in general terms, not in specific ones. Moreover, new branch disciplines will continue to emerge in the future. There would be a new intersection or marginal area every time a new branch of economics appears. The development of economics research needs to include this new intersection or marginal area. Thus, it is also an unstoppable trend in academic research.

“Endless” is only a general term for economics research, but there are always certain boundaries. It is impossible to include the study of all issues. Given this, can other disciplines intervene within the boundaries of economic research (even if it is ambiguous and indefinite)? Here, it is necessary to explain these two points.

First, if researchers in other disciplines study economic issues out of their own identities or personal interests, it is irrelevant to the boundary issue. For example, François Quesnay is a physician who studied economic issues in depth. However, it does not mean that medical research has penetrated economic research. Similarly, Nicholas Barben is a physician, an architect, and an economist, but we cannot say that Barben combined medicine, civil engineering, and economics. It is common for individuals to transcend the research of one discipline to that of the second or third discipline out of hobbies or interests.

Second, since there is an intersection or edge between economics and other disciplines, we believe that new branches of economics and their related subjects will continue to appear in economics and so do other disciplines. Therefore, the involvement of other disciplines in the field of economics is inevitable, and it is not an issue whether the economics community allows other disciplines to trespass. The study of economics can venture into other disciplines, which does not require the permission of the latter, either. Is it possible if the economics community does not allow other disciplines to trespass in economics research? Can it be stopped?

By clarifying these issues, we can also consider a general statement among some people. This statement is: "Economics is imperialistic in that it always invades the fields of other disciplines; Economics tends to be 'expansionist', and its fields has been extended too wide...." No doubt this statement is wrong. If a person who studies economics is interested in other disciplines, such as literary theories or mathematics, then this is purely one's private matter and has nothing to do with the research field of economics. Just as a chemist also explores some musical or historical issues in spare time, this has nothing to do with the research field of chemistry. If new branch disciplines in economics and a new intersection or marginal area between economics and other disciplines appear continuously, this should be a result from scientific progress instead of the "expansionist" tendency in economics. It should be a relatively common phenomenon, not just in economics that new branch disciplines and crossed or marginal areas are constantly emerging with the advancement of science. Isn't there more and more branches in sociology, law, and ethics? Each of them has a research field that intersects with economics. Can we say that sociology (or law, ethics) has invaded the field of economics and thus has a tendency toward "expansionism"? Such a judgment does not make sense.

25.3 How is a New Branch of Economics Formed?

Usually, three conditions are required to establish a new branch of economics.

The first condition is that some economics researchers have engaged in related issues before forming a new branch. They are either researching from economic theories or discussing the practical issues involved. They would come up with some valuable arguments from the study, which draws more people's interests and their willingness to invest in similar studies.

The second condition is that the upcoming new branch of economics has significant potential for development and can become a new and independent research field. In this way, people have progressively reached a consensus through research that it is necessary and possible to establish a new branch of economics. Otherwise, the research cannot be carried out in-depth.

The third condition is that the new branch of economics is always at the intersection or edge of economics and other disciplines. Therefore, besides the efforts of economics researchers, establishing a new branch of economics also depends on the efforts of related researchers in other disciplines. In other words, forming a new marginal discipline at the periphery requires researchers from both disciplines to work together because no a single party can succeed in this cause.

With these three conditions, new branches of economics would gradually take shape. It does not matter whether this sub-discipline is recognized by an authoritative academic classification institution or a document compilation institution in economics. Because academic research is a matter for the academia, it may take a long time to have it recognized in an authoritative subject classification catalog or listed in a literary journal. As long as this new economic discipline has a broad prospect for development, in-depth exploration, and debate, it will not obstruct the continued development of this new sub-discipline whenever it is identified by the relevant institutions or agencies.

Overall, I have elaborated my opinions for the three questions raised in this paper respectively. Now, let us turn to the topic of sustainable development economics.

Sustainable development economics is a new branch discipline in economics. It is a branch discipline formed at the intersection or periphery among economics and population, environment, resources, ecology, and other disciplines. Within economics, it also overlaps with disciplines such as development economics, demographic economics, education economics, environmental economics, resource economics, technical economics, regional economics, urban economics, industrial economics, etc. Issues on sustainable development are of common concern to all of these disciplines (both outside and inside the economics) and need to be discussed by researchers jointly. More and more people have recognized the importance of sustainable development, and examples of economic growth have increasingly proved the difficulty of sustainable development. Therefore, the task of establishing such a new branch of economics is urgent. Then, is there any overlap between the study of sustainable development and other branches of economics? Is it necessary to build another branch of the discipline, namely sustainable development economics? It should be admitted that the overlap is inevitable, which is the characteristic of interdisciplinary and marginal disciplines. However, it does not mean that establishing a new branch of sustainable development economics is unnecessary. For example, in the study of sustainable development economics, the issues of population, environment, and resources should be discussed. Thus, it is evident that there are overlapped areas in population economics, environmental economics, resource economics, and sustainable development economics on related issues. Therefore, we need to research population economics, environmental economics, resource economics, and economics of sustainable development. In the case of interdisciplinary and marginal areas, some repetitions in the research do not matter. Sustainable development economics is different from population economics, environmental economics, and resource economics on these issues. These differences lie in a comprehensive study of sustainable development issues and are not limited to population, environment, and resources. It also examines many issues that other disciplines do not. Therefore, it is necessary to establish economics of sustainable development just because there are already population economics, environmental economics, and resource economics.

Although some of the arguments remain to be explored in *The Economics of Sustainable Development* written by Prof. Hong Yinxing and his co-authors, they have made a perfect start in this field. I sincerely hope that they will continue to discuss on the existing basis and further contribute to the establishment and development of this new branch of economics.

—*Journal of Nanjing University (Philosophy, Humanities, and Social Sciences)*, issue No. 1, 2001.

Chapter 26
2002: Discussions on the Development of Local Industry

Upon joining the WTO, China made two major commitments on industry: the reduction of tariff rates; the opening and access to related domestic sectors. Given that these concessions will put relevant industries under more pressure, what should we do in response?

First, the transformation in government functions focuses on its regulation of enterprises. There is a simple analogy. Suppose you are given a pile of sand, rocks and cement, how to mix them together? The best way would be to put them in a mixer. When it turns, they can be evenly distributed. Similarly, the market is like a large-scale mixer, which spins with the input of various factors of production, and finally they can be allocated efficiently. The mixer needs a regulator that functions in three ways: to formulate rules and regulations, to deal with malfunctions during operation, and to fine-tune the rotating speed of the mixer to fit the requirement. Accordingly, like a large-scale mixer, the market also needs a regulator. The government is the regulator of the market, which is also responsible for three tasks: to formulate laws and regulations, to solve problems with regard to the market, and to fine-tune the macroeconomy. Only in this way can the government function well. China's automobile industry, for example, was established in 1958, but it has developed slowly for more than forty years. In contrast, China's home appliance industry was established only in the last decade, but it has experienced rapid development and the products have been exported abroad. Why? The main reason is that the automobile industry is under too much control of the government while the home appliance industry develops and competes mainly under market forces.

The second is about asset restructuring. We should revitalize the stock of the state-owned assets. China is a socialist country with three categories of SOEs in the national economy. The first category includes those in certain sectors that must be of sole state ownership, such as the production of cutting-edge weaponry, the mining of special minerals and money printing. The second category includes those in certain industries that play an essential role in the national economy, such as iron and steel, chemicals, petroleum, railways, banking, etc. These enterprises may be state-controlled rather

Y. Li, *China's Economy Since 1978*, China Academic Library,
https://doi.org/10.1007/978-981-95-5733-2_26

than sole state-owned. The third category is comprised of those in general industries. Based on the actual situation, the state shall not intervene if not necessary. In short, it is important to change the perception on asset restructuring.

Controlling shares does not mean "over 50 percent." Multiple investment entities with diversified ownerships are suggested. The state should try to make full use of less state investment to attract more social capital, thus revitalizing the stock of state-owned assets.

Concerning the transfer of state-owned assets, it's essential to dispel the misconception that transfer means loss. There are two forms of state-owned assets: physical and monetary. Through the process of open tendering, revenue from the sales of public assets can be deposited in the Treasury. If the transaction price is reasonable, this can be considered a normal conversion of physical assets into monetary assets. However, the monetary form of state-owned assets is temporary and can be reinvested to transform into a new physical form of assets in a certain way. Therefore, it is suggested to sell what should be sold, the earlier the better. Delays may lead to lower prices. State-owned assets would also be wasted if they are left idle.

It's a fallacy that enterprises with good performance cannot be reformed earlier. There is a saying that beautiful girls shouldn't marry early. However, the key is one's perception of marriage itself. If marriage is viewed negatively, then no one, regardless of their appearance, should consider it. But if marriage is seen as a positive, it benefits both to some extent. Similarly, reforms may benefit an enterprise in boosting performance, absorbing capital investment, increasing tax revenue for the state and promoting social employment. Therefore, both well-performing and ill-performing enterprises should "marry" whenever opportunities come. The difference only lies in that well-performing enterprises charge a higher price than ill-performing ones in asset restructuring.

As to the restructuring, we must be open-minded. Enterprises should not be arbitrarily arranged. In this process, the government acts as the bridge-builder, while enterprises are the protagonists, as mergers and reorganizations are fundamentally market-driven and corporate practices. The government formulates policies to allow foreign enterprises, Sino-foreign joint ventures, private enterprises, joint-stock enterprises, and TVEs to participate in the restructuring. With their free combination, the results would be efficient and viable. To sum up, asset restructuring is a vital measure for the industry.

The third is about industrial upgrade. On the one hand, high-tech enterprises are the main players; on the other hand, we should also pay attention to traditional industries. Traditional industries are the foundation of China's national economy. Upgrading them relies on the introduction of technology and innovation. There prevails a famous saying in economics: "no sunset industries, only sunset technologies." And is there a sunset enterprise? An enterprise that runs on sunset technologies is a sunset enterprise. Therefore, each enterprise needs to be aware who their competitors are and in which area they need to innovate. The key to increasing an enterprise's market shares in a market downturn is to upgrade the industry.

The fourth is about positioning in the market. China has a large population and a huge market. Since people are at different income levels, an enterprise should locate its target consumer group and produce what is suitable for different people. The above strategy is called market positioning. Some products made by Chinese enterprises are not as good as those produced by their foreign counterparts, but we do have advantages in some areas because we are most familiar with the situation. Therefore, with accurate positioning in the market and identification of target consumer groups, each Chinese enterprise can find the space for further development.

The fifth is about branding strategy. We should make great use of the brand effect and try to create our new brands. For example, a person from Wenzhou goes to Italy and produces the same leather shoes like those in the hometown, turning them into Italian-made products. Then the price of the shoes would increase tenfold from RMB 300 to RMB 3,000. However, in the process of creating a new brand, reputation matters a lot. So long as the reputation is hurt once, the brand may be tarnished, resulting in great losses.

The sixth is about reforming the private enterprises. Private enterprises have developed from the family form, which was effective at the beginning. But after they reached a large scale, the limitations gradually emerge. There are four limitations in general. First, the decisions of family enterprises are always made by founders based on their experiences. Second, finding a successor is not easy. Third, hiring employees is often based on family ties without the consideration of competency. The recruitment system does not work when an unsuitable person is in a key position. Fourth, property rights are controlled by families, so the benefits can be kept within the family. But the development of private enterprises might be restricted under this condition. How can the reform of private enterprises be carried out? Like that of the SOEs, it must follow the path of the modern enterprise system, transforming private ones into enterprises of limited liability. Then families can hold controlling shares in the enterprises, just like important enterprises are mainly owned by the state. Many private enterprises operated by Chinese in Hong Kong and overseas are basically family-run in the first generation, and after the second generation, most of them are transformed into modern family-controlled enterprises. The larger the scale of a family enterprises is, the more necessary it is to undertake reforms. However, some reforms are just pro forma. For example, the family-run enterprises are transformed into joint-stock enterprises, with shares divided into three parts: for the family, spouses, and children, respectively. This cannot be considered as real reforms.

The seventh is about nurturing entrepreneurs. An entrepreneur does not represent a position, but a sense of quality. The so-called quality means that an entrepreneur should possess the vision to make money, the courage to make decisions and the skills to organize. A person who corresponds with these three criteria can be considered as an entrepreneur. The above competencies are written in the textbooks of economics; however, they are not enough for the modern entrepreneurs of the twenty-first century. Now they should also pay attention to the following two things. The first one is to embrace the concept of lifelong learning. As knowledge is updated quickly, it is necessary to keep on learning. Methods of learning also deserve attention. For example, entrepreneurs can attend workshops and undergo training in famous colleges. By doing do, they can not only acquire abundant knowledge but also make new friends. The second one is to be skilled in financing and recruiting. In the New Year Forum of the MBA program at Guanghua School of Management, Peking University in 2001, I summarized four stages of making money. The first stage is "earn money," which means to start an entrepreneurship by working hard with our own hands through competition. At the second stage, more money can be generated with the help of a financial platform. Then enterprises can go public after transforming into joint-stock enterprises. With a bull market, capitalization could surge rapidly. The third stage is the further expansion of the enterprises through mergers and acquisitions. The fourth stage is to absorb a large number of talents into the enterprises. Then enterprises can develop further and more money may flow in.

Before the 1950s, when referring to efficiency in economics, it was exactly about production efficiency. The so-called production efficiency means that there must be input to produce output and more input can produce more output. After the 1930s, there was another concept of efficiency: resource allocation efficiency. It indicates that changing the allocation method with stable input can lead to different levels of efficiency. For example, with method A, N products are generated, and with method B of higher efficiency, N + 1 products can be generated. The concept of resource allocation efficiency brings two significant changes in economic theory. First, it addresses the fallacy that with the concept of production efficiency, anyone who engages in organization, personnel, publicity, and administration is considered non-productive and creates no efficiency. With the concept of resource allocation, entrepreneurs need to understand that those people also participate in the creation of efficiency. Second, the securities market facilitates resource allocation efficiency. It optimizes the combination of resources, adjusts the industrial structure, and guides capital flows. Hence, an ideal enterprise may raise funds in the securities market. At the same time, there should be a proper assessment of the Chinese stock market in the past ten years. The mainstream assessment is positive, and the suggestions about "reversing the inheritance" or "wait until it drops to 1,000 points" are harmful to the stockholders and the country. Entrepreneurs should understand the above statements.

An entrepreneur in the new era must be profit-oriented rather than crisis-oriented. How to understand profit-oriented? It means that, although an enterprise operates smoothly, makes money, and goes along the development path successfully at present, an entrepreneur still has to look further and strive to achieve greater profits in the future. In order to gain more profit, reforms must be undertaken. Then what does it mean to be crisis-oriented? Many SOEs in China are crisis-oriented. That is to say, as long as they can survive, the entrepreneurs will not think of reforms. Only when the enterprises almost go out of business will they consider reforms. Why? As the saying goes, "Reform is always mandated in times of crisis." Why do entrepreneurs merely carry out reforms when there is a crisis? Why are they crisis-oriented but not profit-oriented? Because for business leaders, their gains and losses are asymmetrical. They do not personally gain a lot when they carry out profit-oriented reforms. On the contrary, they may encounter trouble or offend superiors and colleagues during the reform. Sometimes they may experience a bad relationship with the employees during the reform. Then the superior may come to ask: "Why do you want to make a reform on a successful enterprise? It seems like messing around." Eventually, the leaders may be dismissed. Obviously, they gain nothing or even have to shoulder the fault on their own if the reform fails. That is why they are always unwilling to engage in a profit-oriented reform. In consequence, most of the reforms are crisis-oriented. They take place when the situation forces the leaders to change track. Besides, both the feasibility and necessity of the reform should be taken into consideration. When an enterprise operates smoothly, it seems that there is no need for reform, regardless of the feasibility at this time. When a crisis takes place, reforms become less feasible and more difficult. Therefore, the entrepreneurs in the new era should be profit-oriented rather than crisis-oriented.

Entrepreneurs in the new era also need to understand experts and compare the decisions. Any decision, feasibility study, or strategic development plan must be made by a group of experts. But can you easily reject it if you consider the decision made by experts is inappropriate? You have to consult another group of experts to prove that those experts have made the right decision. Assuming that the second group of experts agree with the first, that is fine. If not, then you might doubt their decision. What should you do? You need to find a third group of experts to assess the first two groups. In the end, it is the experts who make decisions. Then one may come up with a question, how can the enterprise hire so many experts? Currently, there are so many experts in the society, and the consulting industry has become a promising sector with great potential and bright prospects. They provide a variety of consulting services for enterprises, so there is no need for enterprises to hire too many experts, otherwise the costs would be high. Entrepreneurs should invite experts from universities and scientific research institutions to make plans and conduct demonstrations. In short, the consulting industry has boundless development prospects in China and it should be further utilized.

For modern entrepreneurs, another requirement is lifelong learning. Professor Zhang Weiying from Guanghua School of Management, Peking University has a famous saying: "Knowledge is like milk and fruit, and they all have a shelf life." With knowledge being constantly updated, especially in the era of technological innovation and fierce market competition, entrepreneurs must recognize the significance of lifelong learning. Learning comes with costs, but the benefits are much greater. Although entrepreneurs graduate from universities, they must keep on learning. And how to learn? Be sure to attend workshops and apply for the MBA or EMBA programs. As mentioned earlier, entrepreneurs can benefit from such workshops in two ways. One is to acquire knowledge, and the other is to make new friends. Since the workshops are composed of entrepreneurs from all walks of life and all over the world, this classmate relationship may benefit them for a lifetime.

What should also be emphasized here is that enterprises that value corporate culture tend to be competitive. The competitiveness of an enterprise mainly lies in its cohesion, and enterprises need to make innovations. Without consistent practice, commitments, and cohesion of the employees, there would be no way to succeed. Thus, the core issue is to enhance employees' cohesion and mobilize their enthusiasm.

Human enthusiasm matters most. It is considered as human capital in economics. Physical capital refers to mechanical equipment, raw materials, and factory buildings, while human capital includes talent, knowledge, motivation, and enthusiasm embodied in each person. In ancient Greek and Roman slave societies, slaves owned nothing, but some of them became extraordinary writers, or even merchants later. How could this happen? Although slaves had nothing left, they had human capital. They made the most out of their human capital, redeemed themselves, and finally succeeded in starting their own businesses. Who were the first group of entrepreneurs after the reform and opening-up in 1978? They were definitely not the former capitalists in China before 1949, but builders and construction workers. None of them had anything to do with those previous capitalists. So how could they become entrepreneurs? They were talented people from the countryside, educated youths returning from the countryside, and the convicts released from prison. At first, they had no physical capital left and couldn't find a job. The only thing they had was human capital. Obviously, the first group of entrepreneurs appeared with the help of human capital. Therefore, enterprises should fully explore the human capital of each employee. Once an enterprise can do this, it will embrace a bright future.

— *Minzu Tribune (Economy)*, issue No. 6, 2002.

Chapter 27
2003: Protecting Private Property Beneficial to Improving China's Basic Economic System

The current laws of China stipulate the protection of public property, but there is still no specific legislation for the protection of private property. Therefore, it is very detrimental to the development of the private economy. Thus, many private investors are afraid to increase investment and expand the scale, concerning the safety of their property. There have even been cases of "quitting while you are ahead" or transferring capital abroad. The report of the Sixteenth National People's Congress proposed improving the legal system for protecting private property, which would promote the development of the private economy and play a significant role in mobilizing the enthusiasm of private investors.

First, upholding and improving the basic economic regime requires a sound social environment and market order. In economic activities, to obtain the trust of peers and the public, enterprises must be honest and law-abiding. Protecting all legal investment and property formed by investment and the income generated is one of the necessary conditions for maintaining regular market order. Naturally, all legal property, whether public or private, should be protected by law. Thus, there must be laws to go by, laws must be strictly enforced, and law-breakers must be prosecuted. Assuming that the law only stipulates the protection of public property, and private property was not protected, then such as law would be incomplete and flawed, and the market order could not be normal and sound. For example, disappointing incidents might occur occasionally, such as arbitrarily appropriating the outcomes of private investment, violating the contracts signed with private enterprises, defaulting on debts owed to private enterprises, and stealing, embezzling, and peculating funds of private enterprises. One of the reasons is that the legal system for protecting private property is not yet perfect, leaving loopholes available for people to exploit. Under such circumstances, how can there be a sound market order? When there is chaos, all enterprises would suffer, not just private ones. It will also bc tough to uphold and improve the basic economic system under a chaotic market.

Y. Li, *China's Economy Since 1978*, China Academic Library,
https://doi.org/10.1007/978-981-95-5733-2_27

Second, China's basic economic system is that the public sector plays a dominant role, with joint development of economic entities with diverse forms of ownership. In terms of the forms of enterprise organization, apart from a tiny number of enterprises funded by the government, enterprises with mixed ownership generally exist. There are also enterprises funded solely by private investment. The mixed-ownership enterprise mentioned here is jointly established by public and non-public investment entities. For example, in the category of limited liability companies, joint-stock enterprises all belong to mixed-ownership enterprises, provided that public investment entities own shares (regardless of the proportion). If there are only legal provisions for the protection of public property but not for private property, public and private properties will be in an unfair position. Then it is hard to expect that a mixed-ownership enterprise with public and non-public investment entities would embark on a smooth development path. Finally, public investment entities that invest in mixed-ownership enterprises will suffer damage by the poor management, and the design for the development of the mixed-ownership economy will therefore fall apart.

Third, within the basic economic system, both the public and the non-public sectors play essential roles in the national economy. In the macro environment of the market economy, not only do both sectors have a competitive relationship, but more importantly, there exists a cooperative and complementary relationship. The cooperation and complementarity between the two sectors are a win–win situation, rather than one sector annexing the other. In terms of a specific enterprise, whether it is an SOE, a mixed-ownership enterprise, or a solely private enterprise, it may lose in competition or may go bankrupt, which are common phenomena in a market economy. The bankruptcy of an enterprise is nothing but the beginning of a recombination of production factors. Nevertheless, competition, cooperation, and joint supplement still exist between the public and non-public sectors. However, without improving the legal system for the protection of private property, it will undoubtedly be difficult for the non-public sector to develop healthily, and the development of the public sector will then be constrained and hindered. A socialist economy in a virtuous circle should not and cannot lie in a single public economy. History has fully proved that in a socialist economy, if we only strive for the development of the public economy, the national economy cannot grow continuously and steadily. The public economy itself cannot develop smoothly, either. Furthermore, under the situation that social employment pressure increases with population growth, the burden of the public economy will become heavier if there is no development of the private economy and mixed-ownership economy to absorb labor. Then it will eventually drag down the public economy. In this sense, the protection of private property promotes the development of the private and mixed-ownership economy and benefits the development of the public economy.

Fourth, improving the legal system to protect private property will help guide the SOEs into the right track of competition. Under socialism, the capital formation of the public economy is nothing more than two ways: One is through new investment from the government or public investment entities, the other is through additional investment from the surplus accumulation of the public enterprises. Every SOE and public investment entity must care about their investment outcomes and the property formed by investment, improve the efficiency of capital, and increase income in their operations. All levels of government and all SOEs must recognize that we cannot achieve the goal of strengthening the public economy by depriving, encroaching on, and dictating acquisitions to damage legitimate rights and interests of the private sector. It is illegal for any unit or individual to embezzle public or private property. The legislation should clarify that the law protects both public and private property. Therefore, improving the legal system of protecting private property could urge every enterprise to abide by the law and protect their accumulated wealth through legitimate competition and enhanced efficiency. Improving the legal system for the protection of private property will help guide all SOEs into legitimate competition, which ultimately helps to improve their core capacities.

— *Contemporary Economics*, issue No. 6, 2003.

Chapter 28
2004: Improving the Quality of Economic Growth, and Founding New Ways for Development

28.1 The Top Priority Is to Improve the Quality of Economic Growth

A variety of different views has emerged in the response to some new situations and problems in China's economic development since last year. In my view, improving the quality of economic growth by any means should be given the top priority. There are three criteria for assessing the quality of economic growth. The first one is the rate of resource degradation. Its continuous decrease in economic operations indicates an improvement in the quality of economic growth. The second one is the degree of damage to environment caused by economic development and environmental restoration. If economic growth comes at the expense of environmental destruction, with low restoration efforts and poor environmental awareness, it cannot be considered high-quality growth. The third one is the amount of independent intellectual property. The more, the better. Judged by these criteria, China's quality of economic growth hasn't performed up to the expectation despite the increased GDP. It is our urgent task for now and the future to take effective measures to improve the quality of economic growth with great efforts.

28.2 Assessment on the Current Economic Situation

The current economic situation has featured in a lot of discussions. At the beginning, there were arguments on the heatedness of the economy, and now different opinions emerge on macro-regulation methods. Criteria should be made clearly before these are assessed. The same is true for the analysis and assessment on the economic situation. The phenomenon of excessive investment in local industries does exist now, but it doesn't prove to be an overheated economy. A certain level of inflation is not worth causing a panic under the condition that the supply of most goods exceeds

Y. Li, *China's Economy Since 1978*, China Academic Library,
https://doi.org/10.1007/978-981-95-5733-2_28

their demand. Generally speaking, most central banks tend to consider inflation a very severe problem because their goal is to maintain price stability. In my view, the main reasons for the inflation since last year are as follows. First, the global economic recovery has been accompanied by rising prices of raw materials, fuel, and shipping. In such global background, our austerity policies fail to function well. Instead, we should increase the investment in related sectors. Second, lack of attention on agriculture over the years and reduction in grain output and cultivated land led to higher prices of agricultural products. In this regard, austerity policies are also ineffective. On one hand, land control should be reinforced; on the other hand, investment in agriculture should be further enhanced. Third, the restrictions to "bottleneck" sectors may account for inflation. Structural adjustment rather than austerity policies can only cause structural inflation. On the contrary, investment in related sectors should be increased. Fourth, some industries obtain excessive investment. Austerity policies may work for this situation, but the key is to speed up the reform of the investment and financial system, and to eliminate local protectionism. Therefore, in dealing with inflation, it should be emphasized to accelerate structural adjustments and systemic reform, rather than one that is "one-size-fits-all."

28.3 New Ideas for Industrialization, Urbanization, and Agricultural Industrialization

The first is about industrialization. Industrialization should focus on innovation to develop independent intellectual property rights. The gain will otherwise be outweighed by the loss if we just focus on import processing.

The second is about urbanization. Land must be utilized in the development of a city, and it's inadvisable to adopt the policy of not approving any land development. A certain proportion of revenue from land requisition should be invested in other lands, which is called "to support this land with other lands." The revenue from selling an acre of land can be used for improving a few acres of other lands to increase the output. Even if the total land were to be reduced to 1.2 billion acres in the future, one ton of grain produced by one acre of land would add up to 1.2 billion tons of grain. Even if the output per acre were to be reduced by half, 0.6 billion tons of grain would be produced. We must act in this way so that many problems can be solved quickly. This is not just a matter of management and restriction but an idea that needs to be practiced.

Last but not least is agricultural industrialization. At present the key is to adopt a new type of cooperative system. The latter is regarded as a combination of companies, production bases, and rural households, through the connection of agriculture contracts. Rural households can become members of a cooperative association as long as they sign the contracts. Agricultural cooperation in Western countries like Denmark and New Zealand is based on the principle of single-household production and then cooperation in the sphere of circulation. Through unified transportation and sales management, rural households can consequently share the profits. Such a path needs to be taken for agricultural industrialization to be consistent with modernization. And we can also avoid the type that each household produces, transports and sells goods simultaneously but respectively. But we can't depend only on large grain-production households since our land is quite limited. Even 150 acres of land (i.e., 10 hectares) can only be counted as a small farm abroad. Therefore, it is inadvisable to rely only on large grain-production households, and a new type of cooperative system should be implemented for agriculture. Production bases are responsible for promoting new technologies and products, companies oversee sales and investments, and rural households are engaged in the actual production. The three entities above can be combined to form a socialist cooperative.

—*Economic Committee and Communication*, issue No. 5, 2004.

Chapter 29
2005: Corporate Social Responsibility

As is known to all, China's economic growth cannot be achieved without Chinese entrepreneurs, and the growth of Chinese entrepreneurs is inseparable from Chinese and the global environment. Among the discussions about entrepreneurs, a traditional view is that entrepreneurs have vision, courage, and organizational skills. All these points are valid. But for Chinese entrepreneurs, there is one more point to be added: a sense of social responsibility. Based on the fact that China has developed from a state of backwardness and poverty, the sense of social responsibility is one of the qualities that a Chinese entrepreneur should possess.

What exactly is corporate social responsibility (CSR)? It can be perceived in the following three aspects.

Firstly, the most important aspect of the CSR for an enterprise is to provide the society with high-quality products and services, to grow talents and accumulate successful experiences. This is the most significant achievement of an enterprise. If China's enterprises provide high-quality products for the society, then they can go out to compete in the global market; if enterprises provide high-quality services, then China can attract customers from all over the world; if enterprises grow their talents, then business managers can be trained within our own enterprises; if enterprises provide successful experience, then it can be used as a reference by other enterprises for mutual development. This is the greatest contribution that enterprises can make to the society. As to employment, it is impossible for an enterprise to recruit too many people, but it needs to constantly improve the quality of its employees. The most important contribution is that to social employment, which could be increased once enterprises could fulfill their most important CSR. Good products result in a rise in purchasing power per capita, then the incremental demand creates more jobs. Thus, the development of an enterprise can not only increase its own employment, but also increase social employment.

To fulfill their social responsibilities, enterprises must be entrepreneurial and innovative. There is no limit to entrepreneurship, and innovation initiates a new beginning in every era. The enterprises have to possess independent intellectual

Y. Li, *China's Economy Since 1978*, China Academic Library,
https://doi.org/10.1007/978-981-95-5733-2_29

property rights as many as possible because they are of the most significance and reflect the contribution of the enterprises to the society. There prevails a popular joke, and I wonder if you've heard it before. I've ever told it and I'd like to repeat it here. Two guys were walking through a jungle. All of a sudden, with a roar, a tiger appeared from a distance, running toward them. What to do at this time? One guy hastened to crouch down, took his shoes off and put his sneakers on. The other guy was curious and asked: "Why do you put on your sneakers? Do you think you will run faster than the tiger?" The guy replied, "Of course I know the tiger runs faster than man, but I just have to run faster than you." He put on his sneakers and fled, while the other guy calmly took off his shoes and climbed up the tree. The tiger chased and ate the guy in sneakers. This joke tells us that one definitely cannot avoid facing harsh conditions in competition, and all you should do is to master extraordinary skills. You can climb a tree but the tiger can't, or it would be better if you were Wu Song, a fearless fighter who subdued the tiger (Translator's note: A famous story in *Water Margin*, one of the four classic novels of Chinese literature). Thus, enterprises must have their own independent intellectual property rights. In brief, entrepreneurship and innovation are quite necessary for the enterprises to fulfill their social responsibility as well.

Secondly, enterprises must focus on the quality of economic growth. For contemporary China, the quality of economic growth is more important than economic growth itself. At the current stage, there is no problem in maintaining high economic growth and there's always a way for an enterprise to increase production, but it's not enough unless the quality of economic growth is emphasized. The most important aspects of the quality of economic growth are the continuous reduction of resource consumption and the improvement in environmental quality. It is against our social responsibility to focus solely on increasing production by expanding resource consumption, because resources and the environment are shared over generations. Assume that there is an enterprise which produces and exports based on high energy consumption, it should still be blamed for its high consumption of resources, although it makes contributions to foreign exchange earnings. Has this enterprise considered the environment and resources? Shouldn't it be blamed? Therefore, enterprises need to focus not only on the output value and foreign exchange earnings, but also on resource degradation rate and environmental protection. An enterprise should at least dispose of its own wastewater, gas, and sewage, reduce pollution, and improve the ecological condition and the environment in its area. It is what an enterprise should be able to do. When they do so, they are fulfilling their social responsibilities in this regard.

Thirdly, the CSR also lies in the contributing to social harmony. Enterprises live in groups, in communities and the society. They need to care about social groups, and correspondingly, social harmony is the condition for sustainable and stable corporate growth. The idea of "people-orientation" is practiced by those enterprises that care not only for their current and retired employees, but also for their communities, in which everyone lives together. Here is a story that a little boy was walking along the road when he came across the Lord. He asked: "Lord, what is heaven and what is hell? I've always heard people talk about these words, but I've never understood them." The Lord replied: "Follow me and I will show you heaven and hell." The child followed the Lord to a large house with two rooms on both sides. The Lord said: "Let's go inside and have a look." They entered the room on the left where there was a buffet table in the center offering dishes of chicken, duck, fish, meat, and bread. Then there came a group of people, each of whom was skinny, desperate, and starving. Everyone held a pair of three-feet-long chopsticks, but the chopsticks were too long to be used to get the dishes into one's own mouth. All of them squatted on the ground crying. The Lord said this was hell. Then they entered the other room on the right, identical to the first: With the dishes, the group of people, the same long chopsticks. But there everyone was happy and satisfied because they were willing to feed each other. The Lord said it was heaven. Therefore, it seems that it will be hell if people only care about themselves, and it would be heaven if people help each other, love each other, and trust each other. Only in this way can social harmony be achieved.

—*China Business and Market*, issue No. 7, 2005.

Chapter 30
2006: A Comparative Study of Industrialization

30.1 Industrialization and Capital Supply

The main issue of industrialization is investment. Without investment, there cannot be industrialization. Before industrialization, the shared investment by each person was very little. For example, if a mine was to be exploited and a road was to be built, all we needed was a spade, which was very cheap. As industrialization continued, the average amount of investment required per capita increased. So, the first issue to be addressed by industrialization is where to get capital. Britain was the first country to industrialize, followed by France and Germany. It is generally believed that the capital for industrialization was plundered from abroad, but empirical studies in the economic field suggest that this view is wrong. The capital for industrialization came from home, not abroad.

Why? This is because British industrialization began in the mid- and late eighteenth century. At that time, West India was more important to Britain than East India. West India was mainly engaged in the slave trade and plantation production, such as sugarcane. But where did the money go? The West India Group mainly used the money to buy luxury houses in Britain, enjoy extravagant entertainment, and campaign for Parliament, but did not invest the money in industry. Then where did the initial industrial capital come from? According to economic history, the earliest factory owners in Britain mainly developed from artisans, small businessmen, and small business owners. The West Indian businessmen and the East Indian businessmen did not entirely neglect commerce, but they mainly invested in commercial shipping rather than industry, because in their views, industry, with a long investment cycle and an uncertain profit margin, was very troublesome. They looked down on the small businessmen and often thought, "how can I get involved with small shops and factories?" When did this situation change? By the late nineteenth century. Why? Mainly because the stock market had been developed. In the early stages of the stock market, they were engaged in overseas trade and investment, shipping, and railway construction. In the late nineteenth century, the stock market developed. By then, they

Y. Li, *China's Economy Since 1978*, China Academic Library,
https://doi.org/10.1007/978-981-95-5733-2_30

felt that they did not need to operate by themselves, and instead they bought industrial stocks, leading to the development in the industrial capital. In the late nineteenth century, the pace of industrialization was relatively fast. In the twentieth century, the situation completely changed so that industrial management mainly relied on the stock market.

Such was the process of the capital accumulation of industrialization, which was the case in France, Germany, and Britain. In fact, there are three important aspects in solving the problem of capital supply.

First, the stock market is most conducive to industrial development. Without the stock market, the industry itself would have accumulated and developed very slowly.

Second, in the process of industrialization, Britain was relatively slow, while Germany was faster. In the twentieth century, there was a process of mergers and reorganization of enterprises. Where did the capital come from? It also came from financing. The Chinese character for "earn" is composed of "financing" and "merger," which is also in line with economic development. The reason why Britain's industrialization was slow was that there was no merger. In the beginning, British enterprises did not rely on mergers, but on their own development. They did not start mergers until after the second great crisis.

Third, international trade existed far before the capital market in the process of industrialization. What was the role of international trade in this process? There were actually two main effects:

(1) Countries lacking raw materials obtained them through international trade. For example, the British textile industry needed cotton, so it imported cotton from Egypt, India, and the US. Without the import of raw materials, they could not promote the further development of industrialization.
(2) The most important thing in international trade is to export products to foreign countries. To which countries? In the past, it has been said that one country should import a large number of raw materials from undeveloped countries and sell manufactured products mainly to the developed countries. This view is wrong, at least not in line with the facts. The import side is correct, but the export side, especially the exporting countries of high-grade manufactured goods, are not mainly undeveloped countries, but industrializing or industrialized countries. Raw materials enter developed countries from undeveloped countries, and then return again to undeveloped countries after being made into manufactured products.

For the balance of payments deficit in the long run, it is the repayment of capital and interest after borrowing that needs to be paid attention to, but not foreign investment. The key to borrowing lies in what the borrowers do with the capital. Most countries borrow not to develop their economies, but engage in war or squander. Therefore, the key to the balance of payments deficit lies not in foreign trade or external investment, but in the fact that borrowed money was not well utilized. When the time comes for repayment of capital and interest, they blindly borrow more to repay the debt. The views on industrialization and capital supply have somewhat revised our previous impressions.

30.2 Industrialization and Talent Supply

Industrialization required capital and talent. Where did the talents for industrialization come from? Talents include two types: skilled workers and entrepreneurs.

Where did these two kinds of people come from? First, let us consider where the skilled workers came from. In the process of industrialization, skilled workers did not come from the countryside, because there were none of them among the farmers, and the farmers did not adapt to industrialization. When the British built railways, no one was willing to be railway workers. In the end, it was all farmers who built railways because the skills needed were relatively few. At that time, railway workers were looked down upon as mostly the grassroots in the society. Where did skilled workers come from? Artisans in the handicraft industry were the earliest skilled workers. The earliest technicians, who drew, designed, and built machines, were also called engineers at that time. Where did the earliest engineers come from? In Britain and other European countries, they mainly came from watchmakers. Among all the artisans, the ones who were most familiar with and knew how to make mechanical gears were the watchmakers. Besides watchmakers, there were also millers. At that time, the British had not trained technicians from school, so they suffered a loss. In the early days of British industrialization, a large number of watchmakers and carpenters became the earliest artisans who only passed on skills to their apprentices. There was a very strange phenomenon in the process of industrialization in Britain: There were two ways to be an apprentice in a factory: One was called factory apprentice, which was recruited and paid by the factory; The other was called a private apprentice. Each master could train several private apprentices. The private apprentices were not paid in wages, but a little pocket money. In the early nineteenth century, Britain always attached importance to private apprentices.

Germany was the first country to carry out vocational education. In the late nineteenth century, Germany began to set up schools to recruit apprentices and skilled workers, while the US thought that it was not enough to only train middle-class talents. American universities were different from those in Europe. They trained engineers. It was very late for Britain to carry out vocational education. By the end of the nineteenth century, Britain's development fell into a bottleneck because apprenticeship alone could not support development. It had to rely on technical training and vocational education. As a result, the US and Germany later surpassed Britain.

Where did entrepreneurs come from? The emergence of entrepreneurs depended on the social, political, and economic conditions at that time. At first, entrepreneurs were not valued. At that time, those factory owners in Britain were small businessmen who were looked down upon by the upper classes. The status of entrepreneurs was very low. The situation changed gradually. Entrepreneurs who started from small businessmen gradually expanded their factories. After the expansion of the factory, they began to consciously cultivate their children and send them to good schools. The first generation was still looked down upon. By the second generation, they became well educated, and by the third generation, they acquired a completely new outlook. After that, big businessmen and bankers also made investments, so financiers and industrial entrepreneurs came into being. In the early stage of development, there were no entrepreneurs but the government, which acted as entrepreneurs. The government and officials came to run enterprises, which was called "conversion to commerce career." But many people did not adapt to this process.

To be an entrepreneur starts with practice, which is enlightening to us. The greatest shortage in China today is of skilled workers. According to the situation in developed countries, skilled technicians generally account for about 35% of the total workforce, while it only accounts for 5% in China, which is far from enough. Why don't people want to be skilled workers? This is mainly because the society is not aware of the importance of skilled technicians, with the bias that no matter how skilled, one is nothing but a worker. With this concept, people are not willing to enter vocational schools. The treatment of skilled technicians is starting to improve now, but it will take a long time for the whole society to change this view. It is said that we recently exported a set of equipment to Pakistan. After the installation by Chinese workers, Pakistanis always felt dissatisfied. So, after we left, they hired a retired British skilled technician, who knocked a few times and the machine was normal. This is a very serious issue for China. This time we went to Guangzhou to investigate, and found that Guangzhou must pay attention to the cultivation of skilled technicians.

30.3 Industrialization and Technological Innovation

The third problem is technological innovation. There was a fuel crisis during industrialization. The earliest ironmaking in Britain depended on burning wood. The industry needed to burn wood, as did families. As a result, large areas of forests in the northern part of Britain were cut down and the land became barren. Industrialization in Britain encountered great difficulties. Without fuel, industrialization would likely stop. Shipbuilding needed wood too. If all the trees were cut down, how could a ship be built? As a result, they went to northern Europe to import wood. There was a record in economic history: A man bought a leg of lamb, but there was no firewood to cook, so he tried to borrow some from his neighbor. The neighbor said that he could not borrow it, but had to buy it at a much more expensive price. Why not use coal? At the beginning of industrialization, people were already mining coal, but only surface coal was mined. The industrialization needed a lot of coal and fuel. After surface coal was excavated, the most difficult problem of digging the deep coal was that there was no power to drain the water. The steam engine was invented for this purpose and was first used in coal mine drainage. Once the water was drained, it could be dug deeper. How to transport coal out after digging up? By canals and railways. When coal was used as the main fuel, it meant that the age of the steam engine began.

New industries are often bred in crisis. For example, France did not produce sugarcane but needed a lot of sugar. How to get it? Import. At that time, it was mainly the West India that produced sugar. During the Napoleonic Wars, France was blocked, and sugar could not be imported, resulting in a sugar shortage. What if the sugar could not be imported? Then beets were grown all over France. A history book recorded: There was a cartoon in a British newspaper, proposing that when a baby was crying, put beetroot in his mouth. There is a note at the bottom of the cartoon: Napoleon's baby heir had beetroot in his mouth. The nurse said, "Chew it; your father says it is sugar." It can be seen that many new industries were emerging under pressure.

It is said that a new technological revolution often leads to the decline of small and medium-sized enterprises, especially the former. But history has proved that in the process of industrialization, this phenomenon did not exist. Why? In the entire history of industrialization, there were two major rescues for small enterprises, both of which were new technologies. The first rescue was the use of electricity. Originally, it was said that small enterprises would suffer a hard blow after using electricity. As it turned out, the cost would be greatly reduced after using electricity, and very simple machines could work, saving a large number of small enterprises. Therefore, we have gained some new insights and experience on the technical issues in the process of industrialization, one of which is that the process of industrialization is actually the process of industrial upgrade and structural adjustments.

Here are three examples.

The first example is Sweden. In the past, Sweden mainly exported pig iron, a term which coincidentally shares the same name with the animal "pig" in English. Why "pig"? It was mainly because of the ironmaking technology at that time. The iron melted down and turned into iron water flowing into the pit, just like a pig sucking. Both in steel-making technology and steel products, Sweden had always combined the advantages of industries in the process of industrialization. Even now, Sweden is still at the forefront of the world.

The second example is Denmark. Denmark was the first country to produce grain in Europe. However, Denmark's grain export cannot compete with that of Canada and Australia. The grain in these two countries was cheaper than in Denmark, so a large amount of grain was imported from these two countries. Denmark's economic transformation was later than Sweden's, mainly after the Second World War. Denmark had no advantage in exporting grain, so it processed grain into fodder for cattle, sheep, and pigs, or into cheese, condensed milk, sausage, bacon, and other things for export. In this way, the added value of industry had increased, and agriculture had been turned into a food industry. But these were not enough. Denmark thought it needed to have its own industry. At that time, the Danish government contemplated on what industries to be developed. Steel and machinery manufacturing? Machinery manufacturing was certainly not as good as Germany, and steel manufacturing was worse than Sweden. Finally, it was decided to develop shipbuilding and diesel engines. After the target was set, Denmark concentrated resources in this industry, and became a big provider of the marine diesel engine in the world.

The third example is Finland. Finland had been cutting down trees to export timber for a long time, but it was not sustainable. So, Finland began to upgrade materials, making wood pulp for papermaking, and then promoted the high-tech industries, such as Nokia, a famous mobile phone manufacturer.

In technological innovation, every country should realize that it is not enough to identify its own advantages, but also to identify its primary and advanced advantages.

In the process of industrialization, there is a controversial issue regarding the theories of balanced growth and unbalanced growth. These two theories are all reasonable, which have caused debate in the economics field. Balanced growth theory means that in order to improve efficiency, all sectors must grow in balance, otherwise the imbalance would reduce efficiency and cause losses. The theory of unbalanced growth holds that economic development must be based on differentiated growth, i.e., one driving the other. On the surface, walking in unison is coordination, but it in fact hinders speed and leads to a greater loss of efficiency.

A long-term study of economic history shows that both views are incorrect. Because they are all based on the premise that the starting point of the economy is the coordination and balance of the industrial structure, but this premise does not exist. In any place and at any stage, the development of industry starts with people and considers the next step on the basis of the original foundation. Most of the original foundation is that the industrial structure cannot be coordinated. On this basis, to propose balanced growth is actually to continue maintaining the original unreasonable situation. What is the difficult point of unbalanced growth? Choosing appropriate industries can promote the growth of other industries, but it may also lead to the opposite result if a wrong point of unbalanced growth bias is selected. Therefore, economists concluded that distorted unbalanced growth could be worse. In the process of innovation, this problem should be paid attention to.

In the process of technological innovation, a big issue is the protection of intellectual property rights and the environment. Environmental protection mainly depends on technological innovation to turn the waste into the useful. Technological innovation can solve problems, but without the guarantee of legal system innovation, technological innovation may not be effective. Intellectual property is an institutional issue. Without technical protection, developed technology may bring greater disasters to humanity. Without technical protection, there is no technological innovation, for it could be learned and stolen easily.

30.4 Industrialization and Independent Innovation

The first note in self-innovation is the innovation in enterprise organization. The research on economic history is a little different from reality. That is, in developed countries, special handicrafts are still handed down by families. Succession under parochial leadership, family management, and family inheritance should be eliminated because of their backwardness, according to economic theories. But now in some small cities in Western European countries, it is obvious that the best scissors are made by handicraft workshops handed down from generation to generation in small towns. The best knives and forks to accompany the Western food are not made in factories, but in family workshops in Europe. This is also the same case with the pottery and wine industry. Small businesses grow into large ones by the family business, and are then passed from father to son. While large enterprises develop, small enterprises still exist. The big ones do not crowd out the small ones, and they can either cooperate or operate alone. An interesting point that has been widely discussed is that biological inbreeding has genetic problems and should be avoided. But in special handicrafts industry, the best technology was passed on from father to son. This sounds reasonable, and it is true in China as well. For example, traditional Chinese medicine is handed down from father to son, and Chinese opera has been continued for several generations in this way. Technology training is different from biological reproduction. The resemblance to one's father is a biological phenomenon, not a concept typically explored within the humanities.

When it comes to technological innovation, the most important aspect is the evaluation led by the government. In the early stage of industrialization, the government but not entrepreneurs often played a role because the number of entrepreneurs was insufficient. This approach was feasible, but such a government-led approach could not be regarded as the one which is beneficial to the long-term development of the industry. From the perspective of the whole process of industrialization, government dominance has done more harm than good. The investigation of economic history has come to this conclusion, which can be reflected in the following three aspects.

1. For industrialization to continue to make achievements, the domestic market must continue to expand. Government leadership cannot provide a continuous and long-term domestic market. A government-led market depends on government investment. While the government is a force to drive the economy, it cannot ultimately provide consumers. Domestic development depends on final consumption, which is residents' consumption. Only the latter can ensure the continuous progress of industrialization, and the growth of the domestic market can only be sustained on the premise of increasing per capita GDP.
2. Government leadership cannot provide the capital investment needed for industry development, because capital investment depends on the continuous expansion of the domestic market, which should come from the people. From the growth in per capita GDP, part of it would be converted into consumption, part of it into savings, and then savings could be converted into investment.
3. At first, the government protected the emerging industries of a country, but that was temporary. Under government protection, emerging industries may develop, but three disadvantages will also follow:

    (1) Under government leadership and protection, emerging industries are easy to develop without competitors. It is like playing table tennis. If we want to improve our skill, we must compete with the strongest team in the world. Suppose we always compete at home or with teams from weak countries in table tennis, is it fulfilling? It is worthwhile even if we lose when we compete with the strong. Therefore, the development of emerging industries must be based on competition.

    (2) The development of emerging industries needs technological innovation, and technological innovation needs capital. Where does the capital come from? A country must be open. Only when it is open can capital enter.

    (3) Under the government's leadership, efficiency may be limited.

In summary, from the perspective of economic history, the government's leading role needs to be changed into a driving role of the market, that is, an institutional innovator. In the process of industrialization, some management methods emerged in practice. Logistics is a hot topic now. The first link of logistics is goods distribution. How did it come about? The story first took place in England. A peasant woman took a cow to the city, sold milk door to door, and squeezed it in a bucket. Then came the change. Milk sellers began to squeeze and bottle milk at home, then sent it by carriage. Afterwards milk companies were slowly established and became chain stores.

The same case for enterprises. The joint-stock system first appeared in the navigation industry, before or just at the beginning of industrialization. At that time, there was a problem with the safety of ships in the Atlantic trade: The wind and waves at sea were very strong. What if the ships hit rocks or capsize? What if the ships were robbed by pirates and suffered losses? In addition, there was another provision: If the ships were going to capsize due to wind and waves after they left the port, it was necessary to throw the goods into the sea to reduce the ship's weight. Whose goods would they throw? Finally, everyone began to take shares. If one's belongings were thrown into the sea, other shareholders sold their goods to pay him back. If they earned money, they would distribute the profits evenly. In the third volume of *Capital*, Engels wrote about the joint-stock system in the navigation industry. It was too troublesome for every ship to make a contract, and it is better to set up a joint-stock company. Everyone can take shares, including ship owners and sailors.

This is the earliest and relatively primitive joint-stock system, which did not really develop until after industrialization. The railway is regarded as the best case and the most successful example of modern joint-stock operations. First of all, it can be reflected in the raising of capital. Without the joint-stock system, the modern railway cannot be built. In the course of operation, the shareholders would elect the board of directors, which would then appoint a general manager. This set of "railways" was first formed, which is called corporate governance structure today. By doing so, the state and enterprises have also straightened out their positions. The state only formulates and enforces rules, on which enterprises operate. In Germany and Japan, railways were first operated by the state, and was then gradually transferred to private operation, which is institutional innovation. Without institutional innovation, technological innovation cannot succeed.

As for the environmental protection system, there must be three conditions for its formation: the subject of innovation, the scheme of innovation, and the benefits obtained after innovation. The residents who live near the factory could be affected by noise and gas. In this case, the residents become the subject of innovation. How to change the innovation scheme? It would be illegal to disrupt its operation or cut off power. Therefore, the government is required to formulate an environmental protection law. Such a law would ensure innovation, rip benefits, and reduce losses. For example, polluted water must be treated well, and compensation should be paid to those who might be affected and become ill, etc. How to control pollution, how to purify waste water, and how to minimize waste gas? These need technological innovation. The same goes for intellectual property. But in the process of industrialization, what are the differences and similarities between institutional innovation and technological innovation? Obviously, the similarities lie in that they all bring benefits from innovation, but their differences are more important. Technological innovation may be limited by the time horizon of the fixed assets. We just changed a set of equipment, and now we have another chance to get a new machine. Shall we change it again? If we do, the original machine will be redundant. This problem does not exist in institutional innovation, which is a slight difference. Another big difference lies in the costs and benefits.

Technological innovation is mainly about profit and expenditure. If innovation is ineffective, it may result in a loss of capital. However, the case is different with institutional innovation, as its costs could be unlimited. Why? Because it encompasses everything, and those who advocate for institutional innovation may face severe consequences, including detention and even death, with their families potentially being implicated. Therefore, its costs are far greater than that of technological innovation. The same is true of earnings. With the promulgation of the intellectual property rights protection law, the benefits of technological innovation are ensured. If you want to use my invention, you must have a license. If you pirate, you will be sued and punished. However, there is no need to pay patent fees for system innovation. For example, where did the household contract system begin? It was originated in Xiaogang Village, Fengyang County, Anhui Province, where eighteen farmers signed an agreement under an oil lamp to implement a household (contract) responsibility system and had to keep it as a secret. In case anyone was caught, the other households had an obligation to look after one's children. After their success, the whole country would learn, but the villagers were not paid for "the patent." If they get a patent fee, Xiaogang Village must be the richest. But when I visited there a few years ago, it was still very poor because it only grew grain. Now we are able go overseas to visit and learn about technological innovation, but we could learn little about their institutional innovation. The patent fee for system innovation doesn't have to be paid. Why don't you learn it? The scale of institutional innovation varies from large to small, and some may be historical legacy. British cars drive on the left and American cars drive on the right. Why? In Thomson's economic history, it is recorded that in the late feudal era, there were many caravans carrying goods on the road, and there were also many bandits who would rob the goods, so bodyguards were brought in. The bodyguards worn swords and must face to the left. If the people on the opposite side were safe, then they could pass in peace. However, when incidents occurred, the sword could be pulled out smoothly on the left rather than on the right. Why keep right when they get to the US? Because guns were worn at that time, and it was customary to walk with a gun on one's right.

Do you know how banks came into being? The word comes from "bench" in Middle English, which means small bench. Back then, all European countries had their own currencies. In the international trade market, some businessmen would sit on small benches at intersections for currency exchange. The customer would say: I have an upcoming meeting but it's not safe to carry too much cash. Can I leave it with you and I'll pick it up next time? The businessmen would say: OK. This was called "deposit taking." The earliest deposit taking had no interest and the customer had to pay a custody fee. So, the earliest exchange began. Most in the trade were Jews, because they could not buy land or become officials, they could only engage in commerce, so banking industry came into being. New systems have been constantly established in the process of industrialization.

30.5 Industrialization and Agriculture

The decline of agricultural GDP in the industry shows the decline of agriculture and rural areas. This conclusion is wrong. We must look at it from the perspective of economic history. This is an inevitable trend and law in the process of industrialization. Has agriculture declined? There are three main indicators:

Changes in agricultural productivity. Has agricultural productivity increased or decreased?

Changes in farmers' absolute income level.

The growth rate of total per capita investment in public facilities in rural areas, including welfare organizations such as schools, hospitals, and orphanages.

If the per capita investment in public facilities is increasing, it cannot be said that agriculture is on the decline, because it is a matter of regularity.

We should know that the situation in rural areas varies in different national contexts. According to the study of economic history, there is a phenomenon in China in which the growth in urban per capita income is faster than that in rural per capita income. Given this, we can draw a conclusion: In the next stage, the gap between urban and rural per capita income will expand further. Why do we say that? The situation in various countries and China's past have confirmed it, and there are three reasons:

1. The urban fertility rate is low, which is more obvious in China. Generally, there are fewer children in urban areas and more children in rural areas for various reasons. If income growth in rural areas is as much as that in cities, both at 5%, but with more rural children, the per capita income will naturally be lower in rural areas.
2. Education. It is common across countries that urban educational facilities are relatively comprehensive and good. Urbanites also pay more attention to this aspect, so children can receive a better education. Children with a good education can get good employment opportunities, and with good employment opportunities, they would earn more. In rural areas, schools are not as good as those in cities, and they don't pay much attention to education, especially parents of girls. For them, it's better to let their daughters to collect firewood than to go to school. Even collecting firewood would make money. Why go to school? Occupation determines people's income, so the per capita income is different.
3. Health care. Urban medical and health facilities are relatively more comprehensive than those in rural area, and it is not easy for ill children to recover.

That leads to a conclusion. We must increase rural income by a large scale so that rural areas can be comparable with cities. But it is difficult to achieve. How can this be done? It has been a common challenge for all countries to address farmers' issues. In some countries, the approach to industrialization has included the application of agricultural cooperatives, which has been quite successful. For example, New Zealand and Denmark all adopt the form of family farms and pastures. Upon harvest, the farmers would be jointly organized (into cooperatives), including motorcade, warehouse, preliminary processing plant, cheese making, milk bottling, and transportation. Production and circulation are closely integrated. Although its rural population is decreasing, its labor productivity is improving and its per capita income is also increasing. This path is of great reference to China's rural areas.

Another approach is to reduce rural population, which has constantly been migrating to the city. The whole process of industrialization has been an outflow of the rural population. The situation in developed countries is also the result of continuous population flow over the years. Our country should also take note of this issue and encourage population mobility. But mobility also has a problem: Where to find jobs?

The reduction of agricultural population is conducive to raising farmers' income, but there has been a negative example: Italy. The outflow of the population in Italy did not necessarily increase farmers' income, but only the income of the outsiders. In Italy, particularly in the south, the process of industrialization saw an outflux of emigrants when the rural population was high. However, as people began to leave, the fertility rate began to increase, which led to a new wave of emigration as families grew larger... again and again. Later, the Italian government found that immigration alone was not enough. It must popularize education in rural areas and let farmers voluntarily reduce fertility. Why do people voluntarily reduce fertility? If you go to developed countries, many families don't have children at all. First, children are the purpose itself. If raising children is a purpose and giving birth to children is for the sake of sustenance and comfort of the family, it is meaningless; and most parents from developed countries have no plan to rely on children for their senior years. But it is different in China. Many Chinese give birth to children in order to address the issue of aged care. Second, children are burdens. The cost of bringing up a child from birth is very high. Parents would want to start a business when they are young, so they cannot have a baby. When they are slightly older, their careers are just stable. And when they get old enough, it's too late to have a baby. Now China is trying to solve the fertility problem in rural areas. For example, if no boys but only girls in a family, it doesn't matter. After we are sixty, the government will grant us benefits each month, so it is not necessary to have boys just for the sake of it.

30.6 Industrialization and Urbanization

Initially, concentrate the rural population in cities, and subsequently, allow for the dispersion of urban populations into the suburbs to some extent. In the process of industrialization, cities are divided into different categories. Some are cities with special functions, such as religious centers, cultural and educational centers, and political centers. Some are resource-rich cities, which are divided into two types: Mineral resource-based and forest resource-based. Some natural resources in resource-rich cities are coal mines, and there are no conditions for the development of other industries. But what if we run out of resources? I visited the Lesser Khingan Mountains in Heilongjiang a while ago. Now Heilongjiang doesn't allow logging. There are quotas every year. Cutting down trees drives the development of a series of industries. What if logging is not allowed? There is the problem of transformation.

Fuxin is a coal mining city. After all the coal had been dug, people were laid off. What do the people do after being laid off? Some are dismissed, and dismissal is also a problem. Fuxin has a way: Severance pay is not given to individuals, but to build greenhouses. When you go to Fuxin, you will see hundreds of greenhouses. Some people grow vegetables, some raise flowers, and some cultivate mushrooms. The vegetable growers also asked me: Who are we? Are we farmers? I would say: You are not farmers. You have no private lots and homesteads. Are we workers? I would say: You used to be a worker. Who are we? I would say: You are private economic practitioners in emerging agriculture, because you are facing the market. Maybe there will be chicken magnate and vegetable magnate among you in a few years.

Let's turn to big cities, medium-sized cities, and small towns. One school advocated that according to historical experience, cities should be large, and the larger the city, the higher the benefits. China has a population of 1.3 billion. How many cities with a population of more than 10 million? Beijing, Shanghai, and Shenzhen. The advantage of big cities is their high efficiency. In addition, China has a large agricultural population of 800 to 900 million. Since farmers would like to go to cities, we should vigorously develop small towns. Last time we discussed the Eleventh Five-Year Plan, some professors advocated a development of big cities, some others suggested that of small cities, and I advocated that of medium-sized cities. Small cities are too dispersed and hard to manage. It is difficult for the tertiary industry to develop because farmers have just entered the city and there is yet to be any demand for many things. Medium-sized cities are much better. In addition, medium-sized cities are more efficient than small cities. Large cities and small towns can develop appropriately, but the focus should be on medium-sized cities.

Urbanization is mainly about employment. China should learn from foreign experiences in the process of industrialization. Employment is mainly generated by the tertiary industry. There are two reasons for the high proportion of tertiary industry:

1. Under normal circumstances, the share of the primary industry decreases, and the tertiary industry develops rapidly after the secondary industry develops to a certain extent. This is the case in most countries.
2. Under abnormal circumstances, the proportion of the primary industry has not decreased much; the secondary industry is shrinking as workers are laid off, many of which become street vendors; the tertiary industry has developed. This is not normal. It is an abnormal situation of the secondary industry.

The issue of employment lies in the tertiary industry, and the key is to raise per capita income. At the recent meeting of the standing committee of the Chinese People's Political Consultative Conference, I made four basic propositions:

1. Employment is expanded by employment. When a group of people get employed, they would spend their income, and another group of people would get employed. The latter would again spend their income, and others more could get employed.
2. Affluence is driven by affluence. When a group of people get rich, they could help neighbors, relatives, and friends, and also set a role model for the people in the region.
3. Prosperity is supported by prosperity. If private consumption drives the economy, it will prepare for the next prosperity.
4. Harmony is accumulated by harmony. Harmony should start from our small efforts bit by bit.

30.7 Reflections on China's Industrialization

At present, we are in the middle stage of industrialization, and there is still a distance away from its completion. In terms of the total output, we are not there yet. For a population of 1.3 billion, the per capita output is less. The completion of industrialization is marked by the ability to manufacture complete sets of equipment, particularly heavy machinery. Now we are in the stage of renewing large-scale fixed assets. Given that the requirements of environmental protection are becoming stricter, the equipment in the past are no longer proper in this purpose, and the consumption of raw materials should be reduced. Therefore, the renewal is needed. But where did these factories invest first? When we invest abroad, we buy paper from Finland, equipment from Italy, buying what we need in the respective country. We lack the capacity of manufacturing complete sets of machinery and equipment.

In the middle stage of industrialization, the heavy chemical industry is still necessary. Can we bypass this stage? Can't we enter the stage of technology industry directly from the light industry stage? A small country could, but a large country with a population of 1.3 billion like China cannot. Our machine manufacturing industry is based on these foundations. Internationally, it is considered that an aircraft carrier, or the largest airplane Boeing 747, is an embodiment of integrated high and new technologies, and the power, armor, and artillery are the most advanced in the world. But we don't have these technologies. We have to buy it abroad. Our heavy chemical industry has not been complete, and this stage cannot be skipped. The theme of the industrialization in the previous stage is to absorb a large amount of foreign capital to build industries in the coastal area, which is right and inevitable for the early stage. But it should be noted that this has also brought some problems. When I visited the Pearl River Delta recently, I said that if the investment was from abroad, the profits would go to the foreign investors, but the energy it used was provided by China. Our energy supply was already tight. According to the experience of industrialization, we should take our own path today, have more independent innovation ability, and move ahead in the technology of the heavy chemical industry.

—*Peking University Business Review*, issue No. 1, 2006

Chapter 31
2007: Some Views on Current Macro-Regulation

The Seventeenth National Congress of the CPC is an important conference held at a critical stage of China's reform and development. It has great realistic and historical significance for further freeing the minds and maintaining the path of reform and opening-up, promoting scientific development, boosting social harmony, and striving for new victories in building a moderately prosperous society in all respects.

In his report, Comrade Hu Jintao clearly addressed pivotal questions for China's reform and opening-up at this critical juncture, including which banner to uphold, which path to follow, and what kind of development goals to set. Which banner to uphold? It is to hold high the banner of socialism with Chinese characteristics. Which path to follow? It is for the CPC to unite and lead the people of all ethnic groups across the country and follow the path of socialism with Chinese characteristics unswervingly. What kind of development goals to set? It is to continually build a moderately prosperous society in all respects in the new era, accelerate socialist modernization, and accomplish the lofty mission bestowed by the times.

Based on my understanding of the report of the Party's national congress and the current macroeconomic situation, I would like to talk about the issues of macro-regulation. At present, there are three significant challenges in China's macro-economy: inflation, stresses in economic growth, and the social wealth gap. These pressures must be released to develop the economy better and faster. Macro-regulation is one of the measures to tackle the issues.

Macro-regulation is necessary all the time. We are engaged in a socialist market economy, which requires the government to undertake necessary macro-regulation. Only in this way can we better guide the rational distribution and coordination among the industries. Moreover, it can prevent overcooling or overheating in economic practice.

There are three main issues to be addressed through macro regulation.

First, we still suffer from inflationary pressures. A common description in the newspapers is "excessive liquidity," which mainly refers to excessive money supply

Y. Li, *China's Economy Since 1978*, China Academic Library,
https://doi.org/10.1007/978-981-95-5733-2_31

and overcapitalization. The main reason for excessive money supply is the tremendous amount of investment and bank credits, which drives a large amount of money into the market. How to solve this problem? In order to prevent the national economy from overheating, macro-regulation is necessary. The government's measures are to better use fiscal and monetary policies. From the perspective of monetary policy, the government has constantly been increasing the required reserve ratio. As a result, the deposits collected by commercial banks cannot be fully lent out. Deposit reserves must be kept to reduce the amount of money that banks can lend. Moreover, it is vital for reducing the inflation pressure that land sales must be strictly controlled. No projects can be built without land, which is a fundamental resource. After figuring out these issues, we can gradually release the inflation pressure. Then by summing up the experience, we can make macro-regulation more and more comprehensive.

The second issue is the reform of the exchange rate regime. After a long-term study and discussion in academia, there has been a general consensus. A substantial revaluation of the renminbi (RMB) is to the disadvantage of China's economy, which may hurt our exports. Consequently, our enterprises would shrink or even close down with many losing jobs. Agricultural products could hardly be sold, and the livelihoods of the farmers would be affected. Therefore, considering the overall interests of the national economy, a substantial revaluation of RMB is undesirable. However, experts believe that revaluations of RMB by small steps would do some good than harm. Usually, a higher degree of revaluations brings more harm to the exports. As long as the impact of a revaluation is adverse, this disadvantage is always in place.

Small-step revaluations would continuously attract hot money into China, with the expectation of further RMB appreciation. This is also a foreseeable disadvantage.

Economics is the study of the interrelationship between productivity and production relations, and the study of resource allocation. Generally, it is "Choose the lesser of two evils and the better of two good," which means comparing the pros and cons. Therefore, we should make our choice as long as its advantages outweigh the disadvantages. What is the greatest advantage for small-step revaluation of RMB? It is to stimulate and alert Chinese enterprises. From now on, we would see that the currency would appreciate in small steps, so do not count on the exchange rate as the basis for competitiveness as we did. We should waste no time in strengthening management, focusing on innovation, and creating brands. If we miss this opportunity, it will be too late to do it later. Now the signal is out. Companies should seize the time under small-step appreciations of RMB. As long as they seize the opportunity to improve technology and strengthen management, it will be beneficial to improving China's competitiveness in the long run.

To what extent should our exchange rate appreciate in small steps? In the report of the Seventeenth National Congress of the CPC, Comrade Hu Jintao pointed out that "improving the RMB exchange rate formation mechanism and gradually realizing capital account convertibility" is very important. Capital account convertibility is a goal that we should achieve in the future. And now we must follow the direction and achieve it gradually. The market determines the exchange rate of the RMB which should float. For example, the exchange rate of the US dollars to the RMB was around 8.1 some time ago, and now it is below 7.5. This is the exchange rate formed by the market, and it conforms to the rules of a market economy. The free convertibility of the capital account is something we will achieve sooner or later, but we must pay attention to financial risks in this process.

The liberalization of the capital account also has advantages and disadvantages. For example, when the Southeast Asian financial crisis broke out in 1997, Thailand was the first to be under attack, which suffered great losses. This was because Thailand's currency was convertible. Besides, its economic strength was weak, and the banks had many non-performing loans. Therefore, the inflow and outflow of foreign capital had a significant impact on Thailand, so it turned into a tough situation all at once. We must learn from this lesson.

Why didn't the Southeast Asian financial crisis have much impact on China? Because we have a foreign exchange control policy. It is not easy for foreign capital to flow in and out, because it is a gradual process for the liberalization of the capital account.

The third issue is about the financial and capital market.

We should acknowledge that China's shareholding system and securities market were developed under different circumstances. Shareholding systems and securities markets in other countries were established spontaneously in a market economy, while China's were formed in the transition from a planned economy to a market economy when most enterprises are owned by the state. For these firms to go public, on the one hand, they lack experience. On the other hand, we are still unsure about many issues as the shareholding system is gradually being introduced. What should be done, then? At that time, this was implemented in two steps. The first step was the "dual-track system." The increment was demutualized first, and the stock was demutualized later. What does increment mean? One company has 1 billion yuan in assets, which is its stock. Although these assets are converted into shares, they are not traded on the stock market. The company incrementally issued 300 million yuan in stocks, and they are tradable on the stock market. This is the "dual-track system." Because of the implementation of the system, we were able to establish our shareholding system. After more than ten years of operation, the shareholding system has made specific achievements, and securities firms have reached a certain scale, but some problems have become more apparent. What are these problems? The most significant purpose of going public is to transform the corporate operating mechanism. Regardless of the share of non-floating stocks, be it 20% or 80%, the conversion mechanism is still not complete. Incremental demutualization is only to realize the purpose of raising capital. In this way, at the beginning of the twenty-first century, China's shareholding system was facing the problem of a second reform, which is now often referred to as the "split-share reform." The equity had been divided into two categories, and now the dual-track is merging into a single category. In this process, the holders of tradable shares must be compensated to some extent. Some people do not understand why compensation is necessary.

When the SOEs went public, they issued a prospectus, which promised that "state-owned shares won't be traded on the stock market temporarily." If it becomes tradable now, it would violate the promise back then. According to the Contract Law of the People's Republic of China, people who suffered losses should be compensated. If it were written in the prospectus that the state-owned shares would be floated on the stock market, people would not have bought stocks at high prices. Now that they become tradable, which would violate the promise at that time, compensation should be made, for example, in the format of free shares. Only in this way can China's shareholding system step onto the right track. Moreover, the stock market could begin to play the role of a barometer of China's macro-economy.

What about the reform in the next stage? Comrade Hu Jintao emphasized in the report "optimizing the capital market structure, increasing the proportion of direct finance through multiple channels, strengthening and improving financial supervision, and preventing and dissolving financial risks."

These measures are essential. The securities market is already in place, and we need a comprehensive capital market. For example, in addition to the Shanghai and Shenzhen stock exchanges, a "Growth Enterprise Board" would be launched in the future. How can non-tradable shares be traded once a company go public in the future? We must have a complete capital market system and increase the proportion of direct finance. At present, our finance still mainly relies on bank loans, and the proportion of direct finance is relatively low. Particular emphasis is also placed on "strengthening supervision." For now, after many years of ups and downs, China's stock market is on the right track. However, at this time, if financial supervision were not strengthened, there would occur cases such as fraud. Then, market confidence would be hurt, and the gathered morale suddenly disappear.

In addition, risk education must be reinforced along with the development of the securities market. I have said many times that college students should not invest in stocks.

Why are college students not advised to do so? Because the main task at the undergraduate level is to study. Time is too precious. If they would like to trade stocks, there will be ample time in the future. At present, college students must waste no time in study. If they miss the opportunity, they will feel regrettable in the future. Risk education should be strengthened in the financial market to prevent irrational investment. The market is in such a situation now. According to reports, a person mortgaged his real estate to buy stocks. He buys any stocks that others buy, or buys whatever is cheap. This is irrational. Low-priced stocks may be undervalued, or they may be just junk, which nobody wants to hold. Therefore, it is necessary to strengthen risk education for investors so that our macro-regulation can follow a regular track and everyone can follow the market rules.

Strengthening financial supervision is necessary at present, and there was one more point mentioned in the area of macro-regulation. President Hu said, "The financial system reform must be promoted." It has been a consensus that China's financial reform must be further strengthened. Foreign banks have entered the domestic market, and how can we compete with them? How can we directly compete with foreign banks if we do not treat commercial banks as market players in the system and do not have a sound corporate governance structure? In some places of China, the problems of private capital in surplus and the small and medium-sized enterprises in financial difficulty have not been well addressed. Can we absorb much private capital to solve the problem of corporate financing difficulties? This is the issue to be considered in the next stage of financial reform.

For example, the government should allow the establishment of more private small and medium-sized banks. Now our standards have been lowered. We can do pilot projects and set up "township and village banks." Millions of capitals can be used to establish these banks, and more capital can support the development of small and medium-sized enterprises in cities. For another example, we can have various attempts in financial system reform. A pilot project currently being conducted is a kind of financial institutions that engages in lending only. For example, ten of us, each contributing 100 million yuan to establish institution like this, lends out 1 billion yuan. If this loan is recovered, the institution will continue to lend. If not, the loan will become a bad debt. However, the institution cannot absorb public deposits, so not many people will be exposed to the risk. Now we are conducting pilot projects, but the scale is not that large, only tens of millions in capitalization. These are all experiments in financial reform.

There are more and more commercial banks now. What could banks do if there are problems with the deposit? Now there is "deposit insurance," which can guarantee the deposits when a bank fails. Some small companies would like to borrow, but no one guarantees them. The private sector should be allowed to set up financial companies that provide such guarantees.

All kinds of experiments are to be explored in the next stage of the reform. Therefore, in the Seventeenth National Congress Report, Comrade Hu Jintao said, "We must form a modern financial system with multiple ownerships and forms, reasonable functions, complete structures, and high efficiency and security."

—*Zhejiang Today*, issue No. 22, 2007

Chapter 32
2008: The Past and Prospect of China's Joint-Stock System Reform

32.1 Proposing the Joint-Stock System Reform

Although shareholding enterprises and securities markets existed in China before 1949, they successively faded from the historical stage after 1949. When China's economic reform started in 1979, domestic enterprises were mainly state firms, others being collective firms. State firms were directly controlled by the government and lacked clear property rights. The government and enterprises were unclear about their rights, responsibilities, and goals, and the government mandated production and sales. Therefore, enterprises had no investment rights or autonomy at all. To put it simply, enterprises were nothing more than appendants of the government. As for the collective firms, the property rights were also ambiguous. Who owned the property rights? Who were the investors? The concept of "collective" was always vague. The collective enterprises were also controlled by the government, and their production and sales were included in the government's plans, so neither were they autonomous operators. This was the situation at the beginning of the reform.

After the Third Plenary Session of the Eleventh Central Committee of the CPC was held in December 1978, the reform of China's economic system started. The joint-stock reform has been quietly advancing, closely tied to the ongoing experiments and promotion of the rural household responsibility system. The rural household responsibility system greatly mobilized farmers' enthusiasm for production, and as the supply of agricultural products became abundant, the surplus labor force in rural areas transferred to non-agricultural areas, so the TVEs emerged. Many farmers spontaneously raised funds to form shareholding TVEs. Two sentences were popular at that time, "using capital to bring labor force, using labor force to bring capital." After the reform and opening-up, these shareholding TVEs were the rudiments of China's shareholding enterprises. In January 1980, the Fushun Branch of the People's Bank of China, acting as an agent for Fushun red brick factory, issued 2.8 million shares of stock for the enterprise, which was a success. This was the first attempt of the bank to act as an underwriter to issue stocks after the reform and opening-up.

Y. Li, *China's Economy Since 1978*, China Academic Library,
https://doi.org/10.1007/978-981-95-5733-2_32

The earliest involvement of economic theories in the discussion about the shareholding system, as far as I know, was at a symposium on wages and employment held jointly by the Research Office of the Secretariat of the CPC Central Committee and the General Administration of Labor of China in Beijing from April to May in 1980. This symposium had a clear objective, which was to let economists put forward policy recommendations for the severe issue of unemployment. At that time, the employment pressure was very high, because the educated youths who had worked in the countryside and mountainous areas in the past years returned to cities. 17 million of them returned to the cities, plus more than 3 million who always stayed in the cities, totaling more than 20 million people. They were referred to as "to-be-employed youths." They urgently needed to find jobs, but the jobs were far from enough, so in some cities, "to-be-employed youth" surrounded the municipal government to petition. The economists expressed their views during the conference. At the symposium, I suggested that we could call on people to raise funds and establish new enterprises in the form of shares, or let the enterprises increase their capital and scale by issuing shares to solve the unemployment problem. At the meeting, comrade Lin Zili asked me: "So will there be a stock exchange in China?" I answered: "As long as the shareholding system is implemented, the stock circulation will take place, so it will be a matter of time for the establishment of a stock exchange."

Three months later, in August 1980, the CPC Central Committee and the State Council held the National Conference on Labor and Employment. The shareholding system was hotly discussed at the conference. It was seen as an important countermeasure to relieve the pressure of urban employment. At that time, many economists favored the shareholding system. As far as I know, scholars such as Yu Guangyuan, Tong Dalin, Feng Lanrui, Jiang Yiwei, Dong Fureng, Wang Jue, Zhao Lvkuan, Bao Enrong, and Hu Zhiren all agreed on the implementation of the shareholding system. In October 1984, the Third Plenary Session of the Twelfth Central Committee of the CPC was held, and the emphasis on reform shifted from the countryside to cities. From then on, the discussion on joint-stock reform entered a new phase. Where to start with the urban reform and what was the emphasis? The mainstream opinion at that time was the idea of price liberalization. "Shock therapy" was often mentioned, which was the approach of economic reform in the Federal Republic of Germany (FRG) in 1949. The FRG, one of the four occupation zones by the Allied forces, was created by Britain, the US, and France at the end of World War II. And the Democratic Republic of Germany, as one of the four occupation zones, was created by the Soviet Union. The economy of the FRG was in disarray, with severe shortages of goods, inflation, and unemployment, so measures such as price control and coupon-based supply had to be taken. In 1949, the FRG carried out economic reforms, the main measures of which were to liberalize prices and let the market regulate them. In this way, although the economy was in chaos for a while, it gradually stabilized under the conditions of market mechanisms. After a few years, the economy recovered and prospered. This approach was known as "shock therapy." Then some economists thought that, since the economic reform had been effective in the FRG, why shouldn't China implement it? The idea of price liberalization was accepted by the leaders of the State Council at that time.

In 1985, the relevant departments within the State Council proceeded to develop a price liberalization proposal and prepared to implement it in 1986. This led to a dispute between two directions of reform (one was the direction of price reform and the other was the direction of enterprise reform). The dispute was made public in 1986.

In late April 1986, I gave a speech titled "Basic Ideas of the Reform" at Peking University. I pointed out that if China's economic reform failed, it might be due to the failure of price reform, and the success of China's economic reform must depend on the ownership reform, that is, the success of enterprise reform. I also stated: The target model of enterprise reform should be a shareholding system. So far, I no longer merely regarded the shareholding system as a way to raise capital and expand employment, but regard it as a necessary condition for advancing market-oriented reforms in China. I believed that only through the joint-stock reform could the micro-foundations of the market economy be reconstructed and market-oriented reforms be completed. In my mind, although price reform was essential, price liberalization would gradually advance with market-oriented reform, and that marketization of prices should be the final result rather than the starting point of the whole economic reform.

My reform idea attracted the attention of the CPC Central Committee and the State Council at that time. In August 1986, I led some young teachers from Peking University to lecture in Harbin, Heilongjiang Province. Unexpectedly, staff from CPC's Heilongjiang Provincial Committee approached me one night, saying that they had received a long-distance call from Beijing. The comrades in Beijing asked me to return overnight to report my reform idea to the leaders of the State Council. We returned to Beijing at once. When I reported to the State Council leaders, I gave my reasons why it wasn't appropriate to implement price liberalization first. In my opinion, the situation in China and that in the FRG was completely different. The FRG was a country with private ownership. Once the prices were liberalized, private enterprises adjusted themselves according to the market conditions, some survived and some failed. The merger and reorganization, as well as survival of the fittest, led to the recovery of the FRG's economy. On the contrary, China was a country of public ownership, i.e., there were mainly state firms with a small share of collective firms. State firms were not independent commodity producers and operators. Without joint-stock reform, it was impossible for them to adapt to a market economy. Price liberalization could only lead to inflation and economic chaos, and would not facilitate institutional transition. I further analyzed that if the system of state firms didn't change, even if prices were liberalized, once the situation deteriorates, prices would have to be regulated again and the economic system would return to the planned economy overnight. Enterprise joint-stock reform was different because it could be promoted in stages. We could constantly accumulate the experience and promote the reform, so the reform would not be as "radical" as the price reform, and this "gradual" reform would be sound. It could even be said that the price reform seemed to be "gradual," but it was a fundamental reform because it changed the micro-foundation of China's macro-economy.

These views were fully expressed in my book, *The Unbalanced Chinese Economy*.

32.2 The Joint-Stock Reform in Several Twists and Turns

Although the debate between the mainline of price reform and enterprise reform continued, the joint-stock reform didn't stop from 1984 to 1986. In October 1984, the Shanghai municipal government issued Interim Administrative Measures on the Issuance of Shares. In the same year, Beijing launched a pilot joint-stock reform of the Tianqiao Department Store. In 1985, three minor SOEs, the Guangzhou Silk and Sisal Factory, Mingxing Pharmaceutical Factory and Qiaoguang Tannery became experimental units of joint-stock reform. In December 1986, the State Council issued Several Provisions on Deepening Enterprise Reform and Enhancing the Vitality of Enterprises, allowing localities to select a few eligible state firms to carry out the joint-stock reform.

In November 1986, I accompanied Comrade Hu Qili, Director of the General Office of the CPC Central Committee, on a visit to Sichuan Province, preparing to make it as an experimental unit of the joint-stock reform. Back then, the city of Chongqing was still part of Sichuan Province. I gave two speeches on the experimental unit of the joint-stock reform in Chengdu and Chongqing. Comrade Yang Rudai, who was the Secretary of the CPC Sichuan Provincial Committee, was very supportive. Why did we choose Sichuan? Because there were many state firms in Sichuan, some of which were important and influential. Comrade Hu Yaobang supported the joint-stock reform, and approved the proposal of Sichuan being an experimental unit. However, only two months after we came back from Sichuan, Comrade Hu Yaobang resigned as General Secretary of the CPC Central Committee, and the joint-stock reform was vehemently criticized by some. The joint-stock reform suffered a setback under this situation. In May 1987, the enterprise contracting system was formally implemented, which was seen as an alternative to the joint-stock reform. In fact, the joint-stock reform and the enterprise contracting system were not in the same dimension. This could be explained from the following three aspects.

Firstly, the joint-stock reform clarified the property rights of state firms and diversified investment subjects, so that the restructured companies would be active in the market as independent commodity producers. The enterprises would operate independently and the investors would be responsible for their own profits and losses. Thus, the socialist macro-economy had a microeconomic basis that was compatible with the market. However, the enterprise contracting system completely dodged the key issue of property rights.

Secondly, the joint-stock reform made enterprises no longer the appendages of the government, and the government could only regulate the operation of enterprises according to legal provisions, instead of directly manipulating and interfering with enterprises as it did in the period under the planned economy. In this way, the rules of the market economy worked, but this is not the case under the enterprise contracting system, in which enterprises still cannot relinquish their status as government appendages, which made it impossible to establish a market economy.

Thirdly, through the shareholding reform, enterprises would care about the interests of investors, including both the immediate interests and the long-term interests, which would ensure the development of the enterprises. Under the contract system, however, enterprises may only consider the short-term interests because of the uncertainty after the expiration of the current contract. They were likely to have short-term behaviors, such as spending too much on equipment and consuming too much resources. This was not only detrimental to the development of the enterprises, but also to the development of the national economy.

These were my criticisms of the enterprise contract system. At that time, Yang Peixin, also a scholar, insisted on this system. We were good friends with many communications. However, I would never give an inch in the debate between the shareholding system and the contract system.

The enterprise contract system was fully adopted after Comrade Hu Yaobang's resignation, with poor effects, as expected. In October 1987, comrade Li Tieying, director of the State System Reform Commission, proposed that economists who held different views should take the lead in organizing research groups and propose schemes. I was the leader of the research group at Peking University and led a team of young lecturers and students to investigate, study, analyze, and discuss. Finally, we drew up the three-, five-, and eight-year reform plans and submitted them to the State Council. In the schemes, we proposed that although the enterprise contract system had been implemented, it was by no means a permanent solution, and that the transition to the shareholding system should be made as soon as possible, with property rights clarification given the top priority. As the target model of enterprise reform, the shareholding system was the core of our schemes.

By the summer of 1988, the State Council reconsidered the approach to the price reform as mainstay because the enterprise contract system was not very effective. In order to make the price reform work smoothly and prevent inflation, the government planned to adopt the measures of controlling money and liberating prices. However, once the news was spread out, there was a nationwide rush to withdraw deposits and purchase goods. The measure of controlling money failed because it could only contain investment at most, but couldn't stop people from using cash and savings to buy goods. The government had no choice but to announce the suspension of price liberalization and to undertake improvement and rectification. The failure of the price reform proved that under the condition where there was a lack of self-financing and self-operating market entities, the reform idea of taking price liberalization as the mainline was not feasible.

Since the enterprise contract system and the price reform didn't work, the State Council reconsidered the joint-stock reform. At the end of March 1989, some economists in Beijing received invitations from the relevant departments of the State Council. They were asked to make careful preparations for a symposium on joint-stock reform, which would be held in Zhongnanhai on April 27. However, Comrade Hu Yaobang passed away unexpectedly on April 15 and the situation changed abruptly. The symposium, scheduled for April 27, was attended by very few people and no issues could be solved. Then, after the June Fourth Incident, the shareholding system was once again criticized and questioned. The criticism was actually centered on two levels of issues.

Those who had been negative toward the shareholding system believed that its implementation would lead to privatization. They argued that if the shareholding system of state firms was implemented in China, it was tantamount to leading China onto the path of capitalism.

Those who had doubts about the shareholding system were concerned about whether it was suitable for China. They argued that:

Firstly, the Chinese economy was complex and it was not appropriate to adopt the shareholding system. Instead of solving problems, the shareholding system would have a full range of issues, such as encroaching on state assets and causing losses.

Secondly, even if the shareholding system could be adopted, it was only suitable for collective firms and some minor state-owned firms. Large state-owned firms couldn't adopt the shareholding system.

Thirdly, even if the shareholding system could be adopted, it was only suitable for newly formed enterprises that are of less relevance to the national economy and people's livelihood. The existing state-owned firms were not suitable to adopt the shareholding system.

During this period, I still held my view that to establish a market economy, the microeconomic foundation must be reconstructed, and that joint-stock reform must be implemented. Fortunately, during this time, the reform continued to advance in practice. In March 1990, China allowed Shanghai and Shenzhen to experiment with public stock offerings. In November 1990, the Shanghai Municipal Government promulgated the Administrative Measures on Securities Trading in Shanghai. In December 1990, the Shanghai Stock Exchange and the Shenzhen Stock Exchange were established successively and opened for business. In May 1991, the Shenzhen Municipal Government promulgated the Interim Measures for the Administration of Stock Issuance and Trading in Shenzhen. In August 1991, as a self-regulatory organization, the Securities Association of China was established in Beijing. By the end of 1991, eight companies went public on the Shanghai Stock Exchange and six companies went public on the Shenzhen Stock Exchange.

China's joint-stock reform continued to move forward amidst difficulties, reflecting that the shareholding system had to adapt to the trend of the times. At this critical moment, Comrade Deng Xiaoping delivered the Southern Tour Speeches in 1992. When Comrade Deng inspected in Shenzhen, he said, how could we know whether securities and stock markets are suitable for a socialist country? We could observe them, and we should try to adopt them firmly. If our practice was right, we would continue. If the practice was wrong, we would stop and correct them. We could terminate either swiftly or gradually. There was no need to be afraid and if we are to stick to this attitude, we wouldn't make big mistakes (Deng 1993). Comrade Deng Xiaoping's speeches had greatly stimulated the enthusiasm of the people to build a socialist market economy. After several twists and turns, the joint-stock reform finally stepped on a fast lane.

32.3 The Drafting, Discussion, and Adoption of the Securities Law

In 1992, after Comrade Deng Xiaoping gave the Southern Tour Speeches, the Standing Committee of the National People's Congress (NPC), on the recommendation of Chairman Wan Li, appointed me as the head of the drafting group of the Securities Law. The Securities Law was the first legislation drafted by an expert as the head of the group. Some professors in the areas of shareholding system and securities were appointed as advisors or members of the group, including Dong Fureng, Jiang Ping, Cao Fengqi, Gao Xiqing, Wang Lianzhou, and so on. We spent several years writing the first draft article by article, and went to Hong Kong for investigation. We also paid attention to the experiences of foreign securities laws. After a draft of the law was discussed and approved by the Finance and Economics Committee of the NPC, comrade Liu Suinian, the committee chairman, read out the draft in the NPC's Standing Committee. Then the legislative and deliberative procedure of the NPC's Standing Committee was proceeded.

Although there was a close relationship between the enactment of the Securities Law and the promotion of the shareholding reform of state-owned firms, the two shouldn't be considered the same. This was because the adoption and implementation of the Law marked a normative development of China's capital market, which was conducive to the normative development of the shareholding system of enterprises. However, the Securities Law couldn't determine which enterprises would be reformed and listed. If the enterprises which were converted to shareholding firms and listed in the stock exchange were still small or medium-sized (both state and non-state firms), then the reconstructing of the microeconomic foundation of the socialist market economy remained incomplete. Therefore, in the process of deliberating the Law, the shareholding reform of state-owned firms must still be strengthened. Shortly after the publication of *Selected Works of Deng Xiaoping*, Volume Comrade Jiang Zemin invited Wang Jiafu, from the Chinese Academy of Social Sciences, Lu Baifu, deputy director of the Development Research Center of the State Council, and me to his office one afternoon to discuss the issue of the shareholding system. I talked about the necessity and feasibility of the shareholding reform of large state-owned firms in China from the perspective of economics. Wang Jiafu talked about the issues involved in implementing the shareholding system from the perspective of law. Lu Baifu talked about how to implement the shareholding system of enterprises based on his research on reform. Comrade Jiang Zemin said, "I was in favor of implementing the shareholding system when I worked in Shanghai, and now I still agree on it. But now only some small and medium-sized enterprises are subject to the shareholding reform. We should implement the system on a large scale. At present, some leaderships of large state firms still have some doubts about implementing the shareholding system, so we should unify the understanding of the ideological issues."

The issues of expanding the experimental units of the shareholding system and bringing large state-owned firms into the shareholding reform were clearly addressed in the report of the Fifteenth CPC National Congress in 1997. The report pointed out that the shareholding system was a form of capital organization of modern enterprises, which was conducive to the separation of ownership and management. It was also beneficial to improving the operational efficiency of enterprises and capital. Both capitalism and socialism could adopt a shareholding system. It shouldn't be categorized generally whether the shareholding system was public or private, which depended on who had the controlling interest. This was an ideological liberation, as there was a theoretical breakthrough and a major revision of the traditional concept of public ownership that had been firmly dominating people's thoughts during the planned economy. From 1980 to 1997, it had been 18 years. The joint-stock reform of large state-owned enterprises has taken new steps, and the debate over whether these enterprises should be labeled as "socialist" or "capitalist" no longer dominates people's opinions.

And then, the draft of the Securities Law was passed by the Standing Committee of the NPC in December 1998 after several deliberations, and was implemented on July 1, 1999. A few days before the official vote, Li Peng, Chairman of the Standing Committee of the NPC, specifically approached me to ask what issues in the Securities Law needed to be improved. I said that no law could be perfect, and some amendments would undoubtedly be made in the future, but it was an outstanding achievement to submit the Law to the NPC for consideration and adoption. I was very delighted that the Securities Law was passed with a high vote.

Since 1999, the joint-stock reform of large state-owned firms has been greatly accelerated, and the number of listed companies has been increasing. As a result, China's joint-stock reform entered a fast track on full steams.

32.4 Transferring from a Dual-Track System to a Single-Track System: The Reform of Non-Tradable Shares

After the implementation of the Securities Law, an important issue facing China's joint-stock reform and capital market development was how to transfer from a dual-track system to a unified system. It must be solved timely, and it was also a quite tricky problem.

The dual-track system meant that the shares were divided into tradable shares and non-tradable shares. There were historical reasons for the formation of the dual-track system. As mentioned earlier, the joint-stock reform started under the circumstance in which the planned system began to weaken, but still dominated the economy. At that time, the only acceptable solution for the government was demutualizing the increment first, then demutualizing the stock. Specifically, after the state firms were restructured to shareholding enterprises and listed on the stock market, the additional shares issued would be tradable in the stock market. Although the original assets were converted into shares, they were not listed and circulated. The coexistence of tradable and non-tradable shares was the dual-track system of the shareholding system. *China*

Economic System Reform (No. 12, 1986 and No. 1–2, 1987) published my article "Ownership Reform and Management of Shareholding Enterprises" in full. In the article, I wrote, "We should divide the assets of the existing enterprises into two parts: One was the assets already owned by the enterprises, and the other was the new assets of the enterprises. The former would not be demutualized for the time being, while the latter part would be raised by shares. Obviously, this was an interim measure. But in terms of our current state firms, such measure was necessary (Li 1986)." The dual-track system was indeed an interim measure, as the joint-stock reform of state firms faced significant resistance in the mid-to-late 1980s. If we didn't take the measure that temporarily restricted the circulation of existing stocks, the joint-stock reform would be challenging to kick start. In other words, if China had implemented full circulation at that time, except for some collective firms that could go public, it would have been impossible for state-owned firms to break through the resistance and implement joint-stock reform.

The joint-stock reform of state-owned firms was finally launched under the conditions of the dual-track system. Between Deng's Southern Tour Speeches and the beginning of the twenty-first century, it took about ten years to make great progress in the reform of the shareholding system of state-owned firms and the capital market began to take shape. But the problems caused by the dual-track system became more prominent, or rather, the defects left by the dual-track system were exposed more prominently. A few years after the legislation of the Securities Law, the Financial and Economic Committee of the NPC organized reviews on the enforcement of the Law. Comrade Zhou Zhengqing and I led groups to Shanghai and Shenzhen separately for research and inspection. We found that the biggest problem of the dual-track system was that the mechanism of listed companies hadn't really been transformed. State shares accounted for the majority, usually as high as 60 to 70%. Some were even up to 80 to 90%. Shareholder meetings could not be convened because the board of directors was entirely appointed by the state shareholders, resulting in a uniform stance among the members that stifled diverse perspectives. If the mechanism of listed companies hadn't been changed, the goal of joint-stock reform wouldn't have been achieved. After 1999, measures were taken to reduce the proportion of state shares, but they were unsuccessful.

On the one hand, the reduction of state shares didn't change the overall pattern of the dual-track system, nor did it eliminate the institutional defects of the dual-track system. On the other hand, as long as the dual-track system continued to exist, even if the proportion of state shares in some enterprises was reduced, the newly listed companies would continue to increase the total share of non-tradable shares. Therefore, in June 2002, the Ministry of Finance and China Securities Regulatory Commission (CSRC) announced stopping the reduction of state shares in the A-share market. Later as an alternative, the reform of non-tradable shares was announced. This was a major event in early 2004.

The reform of non-tradable shares was actually the second phase of the shareholding system reform, and its main goal was to transform the dual-track system into a single-track system, that is, to change the separation between tradable and non-tradable shares to make them all fully tradable shares. The reform encountered two obstacles. First, some thought that once the state shares were changed from non-tradable to tradable shares, it would open the door for the state assets to be transferred, even reduced, or lost. This went against the principle of state dominance. Second, when the state shares were transformed from non-tradable to tradable shares, should the state shares compensate the holders of tradable shares? Some thought that if the holders of non-tradable shares gave compensation to the holders of tradable shares, it would be a loss of state assets. Why should state assets suffer such a loss?

After a heated debate in the economics community, a consensus finally formed. On the one hand, the transformation of state shares from non-tradable to tradable shares was an important step to improve the shareholding system and the capital market, and it wouldn't represent a loss of state assets. This issue would be properly handled by the regulators of the state shares in accordance with the law. If state shares remained non-tradable and isolated from the capital market, it would be detrimental not only to the state assets, but also to the national economy. On the other hand, in the process of transforming non-tradable shares to tradable shares, it should be a principle that the holders of non-tradable shares should give some compensation to the holders of tradable shares. Because when state firms were restructured to be listed companies, they promised in the prospectus or listing announcement that the shares held by shareholders before the public offering would not be listed for trading, so that the newly issued shares could be sold at a higher price. Now, those non-tradable state shares would be transformed into tradable shares, which was a violation of the initial promise. According to the contract law of the People's Republic of China, this was a breach of contract, and the party who breached the contract shall compensate the other party if it caused losses. Therefore, there was a legal basis for the arrangement of balancing the interests between the holders of non-tradable shares and tradable shares. As for the amount of compensation, it would be decided by the market. The joint-stock reform scheme was finally implemented. By the end of 2006, the second reform of China's shareholding system was basically completed.

32.5 China's Capital Market to Be Improved and the Joint-Stock Reform to Be Promoted

The continued improvement of the capital market and the continued promotion of the joint-stock reform were closely linked, forming a mutual reinforcing relationship.

(I) The Construction of a Multi-Level and Well-Developed Capital Market System

A multi-level and well-developed capital market system should include not only the main board, but also the small and medium-sized enterprise (SME) board, the growth enterprise market (GEM) board, and the over-the-counter (OTC) market for unlisted shareholding enterprises. A well-developed bond market and securities futures market should also be included. At this stage in China, it is necessary to start early on building a multi-tiered and robust capital market system to foster economic growth and stability. This initiative should be complemented by learning from the experiences of mature capital markets abroad, which have closely supported the continued advancement of the shareholding system.

It was necessary first to discuss the joint-stock reform of private enterprises. When private enterprises were first established, they were generally small in scale and were mainly family businesses. The family management system could play a positive role when the scale of the enterprise was not large. Most of the parents were capable and cohesive, so the family businesses grew faster. However, as the size of enterprises increased, the limitations of the family management system became more evident. The parents' personal domination in the enterprise was increasingly unable to adapt to the new situation, and the parents' experience might be assets but more likely to become obstacles in development. Therefore, after reaching a certain scale, it was wise to restructure a family business to a shareholding enterprise. If the structure of the capital market was unitary, it would be negative for the development of these private enterprises. If the capital market was multi-layered, it could be up to the enterprises themselves to choose among the main board market, the SME board, the GEM board, or the OTC market. The construction of a multi-level and well-developed capital market system would greatly promote the development of private enterprises and open up a wide space for private capital to operate.

It should also be mentioned that some graduates of higher education or scientific personnel were likely to develop a career as entrepreneurship and start their own business. They had the enthusiasm to start their own business and may have research findings in science and technology. Besides, they may attract the attention and capital investment from venture capital companies or funds. This also required a multi-level and well-developed capital market as a platform for their activities. Some of them could enter the GEM, and some others could first transfer their shares on the OTC. This would greatly motivate people to start their own business, mobilize enterprises to innovate on their own, and promote self-employment, which was very beneficial to developing the national economy.

Further, with the establishment of a multi-level and well-developed capital market, private capital would be fully mobilized, and they would continuously enter the capital market of all levels to allocate financial resources effectively. As a result, the proportion of direct finance would increase rapidly and change the situation of China's economic development, which traditionally relied heavily or mostly on bank loans. The adjustment of the industrial structure, the transformation of the economic growth mode and the improvement of the quality of economic growth would be accelerated by such a system as well. All shareholding enterprises, whether they were already listed or not yet, would face the pressure of market competition with the capital market in place because it would be more convenient for investors to "vote with their feet." Poorly performing shareholding enterprises in this situation would have to rush to catch up, or they would be abandoned by investors. While shareholding enterprises with good returns to investors would be easier to refinance, and they would be in an even better position. All these were conducive to the sound and rapid development of the national economy and sustainable social economic development.

(II) Improving the Governance Structure of Listed Companies

The rise of the stock market mainly depended on two factors: a favorable macroeconomic situation and the quality of listed companies. Both are important, but the first factor, i.e., whether the macroeconomic situation is good or not, is not determined by the enterprise itself. Instead, it is related to the national economic operation, and is affected by the economic growth, employment, inflation, changes in the balance of payments, etc. The second factor, i.e., the quality of listed companies, is related to the management, core competitiveness and profitability, as well as the perfection of governance structure of listed companies.

The continued exploration of joint-stock reform is not only to convert more enterprises into shareholding enterprises and listed companies, but also to improve their governance structure. The latter refers to the shareholders' meeting, the board of directors, and the board of supervisor that really work instead of being a mere formality. It should be emphasized that the independence of listed companies must be effectively protected and capital are strictly prohibited to be misappropriated. The following situations always occurred in listed companies in the 1990s: irregular use of fund, misappropriation of funds, illegal external guarantee, false financial and accounting information, losses due to the lack of supervision on top management, and losses of shareholders' interests due to disorganized financial management. Such a situation could have been curbed by improving the governance structure and management system of listed companies.

The issue is not limited to this. Improving the governance structure of listed companies is an important guarantee for further expansion as the capital market would help increase the number of people investing in shareholding enterprises. This is because investors' confidence is insufficient under an imperfect corporate governance structure. Investors are worried about the potential losses caused by the misappropriation or the ill-operation of corporate capital, as well as controlling shareholders directly interfering in the corporate affairs without considering the interests of minority shareholders. Moreover, they are concerned about a lack of checks and balances between internal and external directors, board of directors and board of supervisors, and also feel anxious that the senior management of a listed company will be unrestrained in doing whatever they want, resulting in a loss in investors' interests. The decline or loss in investors' confidence would in turn dissipate the popularity of the capital market. As the saying goes, popularity is easy to dissipate but not easy to gather. Once the popularity dissipates, and investors lose confidence, it would be very unfavorable to the development of the capital market, and is also not conducive to improving the quality of listed companies. This shows the urgency of improving the corporate governance structure.

(III) Breaking the Industry Monopoly and Forming a Pattern of Fair Competition

The reform of large SOEs will continue to advance, and in addition to strengthening the adjustment of corporate governance structure, breaking industry monopolies is also one of the critical points. Large SOEs often rely on their special status in certain industries to obtain benefits from monopoly. This is not only undesirable to the market economy (the industry is not freely accessible, which hinders fair competition), but is also harmful to enterprises in monopolistic positions themselves (they are likely to be inactive in independent innovation and improving business management, and enjoy vested interests, preferential policies and other benefits because of their special position). In this sense, breaking the industry monopolies should become an urgent task for the next stage of the reform.

Industry access must be allowed to break the monopoly. This means the field should be open to all qualified entrants unless otherwise stipulated by the law. At the same time, the merger and acquisitions of listed companies should be made more transparent, led by the laws of the market, and determined by market players based on weighing the pros and cons. The administrative authority should only manage according to the law, rather than interfere directly, which is in line with the principle of fair competition.

Once the industry monopoly is broken, the structure of China's securities market will change accordingly. This is because industry monopoly mainly exists in the extractive industry and the transportation and communication industry. In addition, the phenomenon similar to industry monopoly also exists in the financial industry. The listed companies in these industries are basically state-controlled extra-large companies whose shares are over-weighted in the total stock, which is not conducive to the rational allocation of capital. After the formation of fair competition in the industry, these enterprises' shares in the total stock will gradually decrease. At the same time, once private capital is allowed to enter the extractive industry, transportation and communication industry and financial industry, there will be further development of these industries. This will be beneficial to both the development of national economy and the improvement of the capital market.

(IV) Establishing an Effective Supervision and Administration System of the Capital Market

Strengthening the supervision and administration of the capital market does not mean that the government would take administrative measures to interfere with its operation. It means improving the legal system initially so that the capital market can operate in a standardized manner under a legal framework. If the legal system is incomplete, then we would have to rely on the intervention of administrative measures. Therefore, some administrative interventions in the supervision and management of the capital market in the previous stage should be analyzed realistically. They had undoubtedly brought specific maladies and undesirable effects, but they were usually measures taken as a last resort when the legal system was not sound and perfect. As the joint-stock reform has been basically completed, we must improve the supervision and management system of the capital market as soon as possible. To perfect the relevant legal system, we should utilize it cautiously, preferably without simple administrative intervention.

In this regard, there are three tasks that require special attention.

First, there should be a clear criminal liability system and civil compensation system for illegal operation and damage to investors' rights and interests, and the enforcement should be supervised. Only in this way can those who violate the law be punished and the legitimate rights and interests of investors be effectively protected.

Second, we need to strengthen the construction of the supervision and management team for the capital market and attract talents with social responsibility and professional and technical knowledge. At the same time, we should enhance research on the development prospects of the capital market and on new issues that may emerge down the road, and then formulate countermeasures. In this way, the supervision and management of the capital market would be made more effective.

Third, we should strive to prevent financial risks triggered by instabilities in the capital market, and establish and improve early warning mechanisms and rapid response mechanisms against financial risks. Financial risks are not necessarily triggered by turbulence in the capital market, but once they arise, they will undoubtedly affect the stability of the market. Therefore, it is also necessary to strengthen the cooperation and coordination between supervision and management institutions of the capital market and other financial agencies.

(V) Enhancing the International Competitiveness of Listed Companies and the Capital Market in China

To ensure the stable and healthy development of China's capital market, the international competitiveness of listed companies and the capital market itself should be continuously enhanced. This issue needs to be seriously dealt with in the next stage.

If a listed company wants to improve international competitiveness, it must increase the amount of research and development expenses and its share in the total output, possess its own patents and intellectual property rights, and create and maintain its own brand. At the same time, it must also aim at reducing costs and resource consumption, improving management and enhancing marketing capabilities. And to do all these, as already pointed out, improving corporate governance structure is an essential prerequisite.

From the perspective of the capital market, the problem is obviously much more complicated than improving the international competitiveness of listed companies. First of all, it is necessary to define the international competitiveness of the capital market. It should be known that an important aspect of the assessment lies in the capacity of selecting large enterprises with international influence and enterprises with growth potential in emerging industries to list on the market. If a certain capital market is always the preferred magnet, it indicates that this market has strong international competitiveness. Secondly, what makes a capital market internationally competitive? It depends on at least three factors. First is the perfection of the legal system and supervision and management system, as well as the standardization of market operation and market order. Second is the existence of securities companies with adequate capital, sufficient professional talents, as well as credibility and influence. Third is the existence of rational individual investors and standardized institutional investors. Thus, it can be seen that there is still a certain gap between China's capital market and one that is internationally competitive. We should continue our efforts in this direction. Finally, we must also consider the degree of opening-up of China's economy and some relevant issues that need to be dealt with, such as the free convertibility of the RMB's capital account, the establishment of a market mechanism for the RMB's exchange rate, the potential of the RMB's becoming one of the international reserve currencies, etc. These cannot be solved solely by China's capital market. But as long as the Chinese economy has embarked on the market-oriented path, these conditions would be available in China when the time is ripe. Now it is difficult for us to set a timetable for the free convertibility of the capital account. The determination of a market mechanism for the exchange rate is also the general trend of the reform, and there will be a day when everything comes naturally at the right time. Whether and when the RMB can become one of the international reserve currencies will depend on China's comprehensive national power, which is also the direction of our efforts.

32.6 Concluding Remarks

China's reform and opening-up policy has been implemented for thirty years since 1978, so has China's joint-stock reform. Looking back on the past thirty years, all the achievements that China has made are inseparable from the emancipation of our thoughts. These achievements would not have been made without the six-month-long debate on the principle of "practice being the only criterion for testing the truth" that began in May 1978 and the Third Plenary Session of the Eleventh Central Committee of the CPC held in December 1978.

There is no end to the emancipation of our thoughts and theoretical innovation. No one before us has ever engaged in the reform from a planned economy to a market economy. No one can be a prophet and predict how the reform should be carried out, what obstacles the reform would encounter, and how the reform would break through these difficulties. The various debates that have taken place among the economists in the past 30 years should be considered normal. We have achieved growth and improvement in the practice of reform and opening-up. Some ideas may not be accurate and realistic when they are first presented, but they would be added, revised, enriched, and improved in practice. Our understanding is always deepening gradually. In the case of the joint-stock reform, much has happened in the stock market during these years. For example, the gathering, march, and protests occurred during the application for subscription to new shares in Shenzhen on August 10, 1992. Stock trading was launched at Chengdu's Hongmiaozi market in early 1993. Hainan Qiongminyuan Company violated the law by using false information to manipulate stock prices in 1996. Zhongke Venture Company violated the law by manipulating stock prices through self-trading, etc. All these incidents caused considerable social disruptions. But these are by no means the mainstream of China's joint-stock reform and will help accumulate and enrich our experiences. China's joint-stock reform and capital market construction have gone through a difficult path in the process of alternating between bull and bear markets. Investors have gradually rationalized, and the supervision and management institutions have gradually matured and become sophisticated. These offer opportunities to continually promote the shareholding system reform and perfect the capital market in the next stage. We are full of confidence in achieving this goal.

—In Wei Liqun (ed). *Thirty Years of Reform and Opening-Up: Witness and Review*, China Yan Shi Press, 2008

References

Deng XP (1993) *Selected Works of Deng Xiaoping*, Volume 3, People's Publishing House, Beijing, p. 373.

Li Y-N (1986) "Ownership Reform and the Management of Shareholding Enterprises." *China's Economic System Reform*, No.12, p. 28.

Chapter 33
2009: Toward Urban–Rural Integration: Changes of the Urban–Rural System in the Past 60 Years Since 1949

I grew up and studied in the city, so I didn't know much about the countryside. The first time I went to the countryside was in April and May 1955, when I was a senior student in the Economics Department of Peking University. All my classmates went to Xiaojiahe in the Haidian District of Beijing for an internship in agricultural cooperation. We were assigned to different natural villages and lived in the houses of farmers. The main task was to make home visits to the farmers, preaching the Party's policy of agricultural cooperation and explaining its meaning to the farmers. What could be seen in the countryside was that the farmers, after the land reform, lived a stable life and focused on production.

Then, till 1958, some of the faculty members of Peking University were sent down to Mentougou District (known as the Xishan mining region of Beijing) as cadres. The assigned location for the faculty from the departments of economics, law, and biology was Xizaitang Village. It was in the era of the "Great Leap Forward." We went to the construction site early in the morning every day to build a water diversion canal from January to April, and since May, we have turned to work in the crop fields. In August came the climax of the nationwide campaign of establishing People's Communes, and Xizaitang Village was no exception. The village set up a public canteen, and I was called upon to the canteen as an accountant. Later in winter, I was transferred to the newly formed literary propaganda team of the commune as a scriptwriter, creating sketches and allegros to publicize the benefits of the people's commune and touring to various towns. Finally, in January 1959, I went back to Peking University. In retrospect, although I knew something about the rural situation during that year, what I knew was superficial. For example, in 1958, the dual structure for urban and rural areas was institutionalized, as the household registration system was divided into urban and rural sub-systems, and the flow of people between urban and rural areas was strictly restricted. The urban-rural dual structure became institutionalized. What impact this would have on the future development of China's rural residents and agriculture was utterly unknown to me at that time.

Y. Li, *China's Economy Since 1978*, China Academic Library,
https://doi.org/10.1007/978-981-95-5733-2_33

From October 1964 to early June 1966, teachers and students of Peking University went to the countryside in two groups to participate in the socialist education movement, and I participated in both groups. The first group went to Jiangling Tanqiao Commune in Jingzhou, Hubei Province, and the second group went to Gaobeidian Commune in Chaoyang District of Beijing. Immediately afterward, during the Cultural Revolution, I also worked in rural areas such as Liulangzhuang and Yuquanshan in Haidian District, Beijing. Then in 1969, the staff of Peking University was sent to work in the Liyu Zhou Farm in Nanchang County, Jiangxi Province. I was in the first group and lived in a thatched hut by Poyang Lake for two years. During this time, I visited the nearby rural areas and saw that there were often farmers who would flee to the farm of Peking University to beg for food. The fleeing farmers I saw were almost unclothed. By Poyang Lake, it was freezing in winter, but these farmers wore single clothes and straw shoes without socks. Poyang Lake's shore had abundant resources initially, and it had been twenty years since 1949. I was confused as to why the farmers were still so poor. I couldn't help thinking that there was something wrong with our economic system. Otherwise, how could these phenomena be explained? Why couldn't the economic theories I had learned in books at university explain what I saw? That is the time when my economic views started to change.

It was the fall of 1971 when I returned to Beijing from Jiangxi. In the following years, I spent most of my time working in the suburban counties of Beijing and the rural areas of Hebei Province, participating in "open-door schooling." I still saw the poor livelihoods of the farmers, who were deprived of food and clothing. I was perplexed by the situation where the economy was declining and unemployment was soaring, farmers were fleeing, social conflicts were intensifying, and I felt that social unrest might soon occur. In the spring of 1976, I participated in the offered "open-door schooling" with the teachers and students of Peking University in Daxing County, Beijing. When the "Gang of Four" was crushed in October 1976, all Peking University teachers and students who had gone to the countryside to run schools returned to the university. Soon afterward, Comrade Deng Xiaoping was reinstated to his position, and the call for reforms became increasingly prominent. In December 1978, the Third Plenary Session of the Eleventh Central Committee of the CPC was held, and from then on, China entered a new stage of reform and opening-up, and I took the study of China's economic reform as my main research topic.

During the 1980s, I spent most of my time studying the reform of the SOE system. During this period, although I visited some provinces and cities for research, I did not conduct in-depth studies on rural issues because I thought that the reform of the SOE system was the most important issue to be solved. I also thought that since the household responsibility system in rural areas had been promoted and the TVEs had emerged, this basic track was unlikely to change significantly in the short term, so the agricultural and rural issues could be considered later.

In the 1990s, under the rural household responsibility system, a large number of rural migrant workers went to work in cities, which led to a series of new issues. For example, as the middle-aged rural labor had to work in cities, the land was abandoned. When the migrant workers went to the city, their family members went with them, and then there was the issue that children of migrant workers could not study in the city. What's more, the migrant workers would go back to their hometowns to visit their relatives during the Spring Festival, which might overwhelm the railway trains. These issues have prompted me to think about the dual system of urban and rural areas and the urban-rural integration. Besides, the name of "farmer workers" was unreasonable. Workers were workers, and farmers were farmers, which was different. "Farmer workers" were never heard. From the end of the Qing Dynasty to the Republic of China, the first batch of modern factories appeared in Shanghai, Tianjin, Guangzhou, and other places. Where did the earliest industrial workers come from? Didn't they come from the rural areas around the big cities? They were farmers in the countryside and made a living by farming, but they became workers as they worked in the city. Then when they settled down, they could bring their wives and children to the city. Why didn't we have the notion of "farmer workers" at that time? That was a product of the urban-rural dual system. Although their occupation was a worker, their real "identity" was a farmer. Thus the "farmer workers" still could not enjoy the treatment of urban residents. All these issues were exposed in the 1990s.

In 2003, I became the head of the expert advisory group of the central intellectual support coordination group for the Bijie pilot area. In the following years, I took some experts to Bijie every year on a study tour and helped the local communities to eliminate poverty. In the process of poverty alleviation, I found that the most important issue was still institutional reform and a conversion from the previous "blood transfusion mechanism" into a "blood-making mechanism." If we did not focus on institutions and mechanisms and did not regard the reform of the urban-rural dual system as the focus of future reforms, it would always be difficult for farmers to escape from their misery. Moreover, if we did not promote urban-rural integration, farmers would not enjoy the fruits of the reform and development as urban residents. Based on this understanding, the focus of my research shifted to rural issues.

Looking back from 1949 till now, the urban-rural reform can be divided into three stages.

The first stage is from 1949 to 1978. This was the stage when the urban-rural dual system was gradually formed and increasingly consolidated. The institutionalization of the urban-rural dual structure began after the land reform in 1950, in line with the establishment of the socialist planning system. In 1958, the urban-rural dual system finally took shape with the establishment of the people's commune system and the separation of urban and rural areas by the household registration system. The flow of production factors between urban and rural areas was greatly restricted, and urbanization progressed very slowly. In terms of rights, farmers were actually at the position of the "second-class citizens."

The second stage is from 1979 to 2002. This was the stage when the urban-rural dual system was relaxed but still existed. At the beginning of the reform and opening-up, the household responsibility system was implemented in rural areas, which mobilized the farmers' enthusiasm. However, this was only a slight relaxation of the urban-rural dual system. Although the extreme form of the urban-rural division, the people's commune system, has receded from the historical stage, farmers were still affected by social mobility. As a result, farmers still found it difficult to enjoy the fruits of the reform and development.

The third stage is after 2003. This was the stage when we started to reform the urban-rural dual system and gradually promoted urban-rural integration. Under the guidance of the scientific outlook on development, land transfer in rural areas was launched, the large-scale agricultural operation has developed dramatically, and urbanization has accelerated. There were innovations in theory and breakthroughs in practice on the new topic of urban-rural development and reform. As a result, urban-rural integration has become the focus of the new round of reform (Liu and Zhang 2008).

In 2008, on the occasion of the 30th anniversary of China's reform and opening-up, I wrote an article entitled "On the Reform of the Urban-Rural Dual System" (*Journal of Peking University, Philosophy and Social Science Edition*, March 2008) to discuss the issue of realizing urban-rural integration. In this essay, several paragraphs briefly reflect my basic views.

> The dual structure of urban and rural areas has existed for more than one thousand years since the Song Dynasty. However, at that time, despite the urban-rural division, there was no urban-rural dual system until the late 1950s. (p. 5)
>
> From the late 1950s onward, due to the establishment of the planned system, the census register was divided into urban and rural ones, leading to the formation of the urban-rural dual system, and then urban and rural areas were separated from each other. From this point on, both urban and rural areas became closed units, and the flow of production factors was very strictly restricted. (p. 5)
>
> The planned system actually has two important pillars. One is the SOE system, in which government and enterprises are not separated, and property rights are unclear. The other is the urban-rural dual system, in which urban and rural areas are divided, and the flow of production factors between urban and rural areas is restricted. These two pillars support the existence and operation of the entire planned economy. (p. 5)
>
> From the perspective of social coordination, it is necessary to achieve integrated development, including the integration of urban and rural development, regional development, economy and society, domestic development and opening-up, and the harmonious development of human and nature. All of these are related to the reform of the urban rural dual system. (p. 6)
>
> The reform of the urban-rural dual system will lead to an increase in farmers' income and changes in their lifestyle, as well as gradual elimination of the worries of low-income families on the basic establishment of the social minimum life insurance, which will lead to a breakthrough in domestic demand. Where is the world's largest untapped market? It is in rural areas of China. (p. 11)

After this article was published, I continued to conduct more extensive research on this issue by investigating in eight provinces, municipalities, or autonomous regions, including Guangdong, Hunan, Guizhou, Chongqing, Hebei, Jilin, Inner Mongolia, and Tianjin, during the spring of 2008 and 2009. The following is written based on the research in the above places.

33.1 Further Opening the Mind and Gradually Realizing the Urban-Rural Integration

The achievement of thirty years of reform and opening-up has attracted worldwide attention. The traditional planned economic system has been gradually broken down, the traditional system of SOEs has been reformed, and the socialist market economy has been initially established. Thus, the economy and society have developed rapidly, comprehensive national power has been greatly improved, and profound changes have taken place in the vast rural areas. This has been a giant leap. However, in the process of a transition from a planned economy to a socialist market economy, there is still a big issue that has not yet been addressed, i.e., the reform of the urban-rural dual system, which has been in place for decades, has lagged behind, and it can even be said that the urban-rural division has not been touched in the last three decades, because the rural household responsibility system was implemented under the premise of maintaining the urban-rural dual system. As a result, urban-rural development was not coordinated, and the gap between urban and rural areas widened. The slow pace in reform has increased the difficulty of building a moderately prosperous society, achieving common prosperity, and building a harmonious society. It is necessary to increase the efforts of urban-rural integration (Sun 2008a, 2008b). The most crucial task was to reform the urban-rural dual system, which would be the focus of China's next round of reform and development and a significant social change, for which great efforts and hard work were needed.

A view that was once popular among some scholars is as follows. After thirty years of reform and opening-up, the agriculture developed quickly, making China out of the era of running the supply of necessities on coupons. At present, the rural reform has to be put on hold because development was more important. For example, we could give more allowances, collect fewer taxes, relax financial restrictions, and provide more loans for farmers. Let the rural production and living conditions be improved a bit, which will be more conducive to the improvement of farmers' living standards. This view was understandable if it appeared in the late 1980s, and it was justified at that time because the rural land contract had just been promoted and could not be reformed in a hurry. However, it has been twenty years since the late 1980s, and if we do not start to break the urban-rural divide, it will not only hinder the development of agriculture and the increase of farmers' income but also make the income gap between urban and rural areas and the one between workers and farmers continue to widen. Thus, the majority of "farmer workers" had to shuttle between urban and rural areas (The "Migrant Worker Returning Mechanism Research" team of the Chinese Academy of Sciences 2009a, b), which was against the "human-oriented" principle and does not conform to the call for building a harmonious society. In order to make farmers thoroughly enjoy the fruits of the reform and opening-up, it cannot be achieved by increasing government input or relaxing credit policies. Only an imminent reform of the urban-rural dual system should be the focus for the next phase of the reform so that farmers and urban residents could enjoy the same rights and have the same opportunities.

China's reform and opening-up has always been led by opening the mind. Looking back thirty years ago, in May 1978, it was just the six-month-long debate on "practice being the only criterion for testing the truth" that prepared the ideology for the convening of the Third Plenary Session of the Eleventh Central Committee of the CPC. In other words, the successful exploration of the socialist road with Chinese characteristics and the market economy began with an ideological liberation movement. At present, to reform the urban-rural dual system into a new pattern of integrated urban-rural development, we must further emancipate the mind and seek truth from facts. Scholars must carry out forward-looking theoretical research and theoretical innovation, take the lead in theoretical breakthroughs, get rid of all the shackles of thought that fetter the solution of the urban-rural dual system, and create an atmosphere of reforming the dual system in the whole society. At the same time, they must make changes in many aspects such as policies, laws, institutions, and culture that are conducive to promoting urban and rural integration, and reverse the trend of widening the urban-rural gap as soon as possible. In addition, the scholars must be brave enough to explore and practice and coordinate urban and rural areas, opening-up a new road.

Specifically, in reforming the dual system, it is necessary to dispel misunderstandings regarding the following three issues.

First, the urban-rural dual system reform would greatly promote social stability instead of causing social instability.

On this point, one misunderstanding is that farmers have been accustomed to the family-based contracts; therefore, many of them are not willing to leave the local community. Even if they leave the local area to work in the city, they would eventually bring the money back to build new houses or establish new families due to the traditional wisdom that "fallen leaves are bound to return to their roots." They have already been applied to rural life, so why do we have to reform the urban-rural dual system, thus making them feel uncomfortable? What's more, a large number of farmers entering the city may change their lifestyle. In this situation, if urban living facilities cannot be provided in time, this may cause dissatisfaction, and some may want to go back to the countryside, which would then cause societal instability. Most people who have this view do not understand the actual situation. We should know that in the process of reforming the dual system, whether farmers move into the city or not depends on their wishes, and whether rural migrant workers are willing to return to the countryside is also up to themselves. The reform only provides more opportunities for farmers to choose, not to exclude their choices. The city's stability depends on whether the well-being of farmers (whether they go to the city or stay in the countryside) has increased. If farmers' immediate and long-term interests increase through the reform of the urban-rural dual system, then the society should move toward stability instead of unrest.

Second, rather than burdening cities or hindering the deepening of urban economic reforms, the reform of the dual system will facilitate the reform and development of the urban economy.

In this regard, a misunderstanding is that the reform and development of the urban economy are the most important. However, at this stage, proceeding with the reform of the dual system may increase the burden of the cities. Hence, the reform and development of the urban economy will be hampered, and the reform and development of the rural economy will also be affected accordingly. Therefore, it is better to put the reform of the urban-rural dual system on hold and focus on speeding up the reform and development of the urban economy. Once the economic strength of the cities is enhanced, the cities will have more capacity to help the development of rural areas. In Western developed countries, generally in the late stage of industrialization, the government would place rural development in an important position. China is still in the middle stage of industrialization, so why should we be so eager to do what could have been done later? This view is not correct. The problem is that the urban-rural dual structure existed at the beginning of industrialization in the Western developed countries, but there was no urban-rural dual system there, so there was no need to reform the system. The West focused on developing the rural economy in the late stage of industrialization to adapt to the need for social stability. The situation in China is different. Under the urban-rural dual system, China's industrialization has been for a long time at the expense of the farmers. Now the time has come for cities to give back to the countryside. Raising farmers' income and letting them thoroughly enjoy the fruits of the reform and development will significantly promote domestic demand, which is also absolutely beneficial to the further development of the urban economy. Therefore, the reform of the urban-rural dual system will promote, rather than hinder, the reform and development of the urban economy.

Third, the reform of the dual system is not to reduce the scale of rural areas and the number of farmers, nor is it to turn rural areas into towns and cities and change farmers into employees. Instead, it is mainly to reduce the difference between rural and urban areas, so that farmers can fully enjoy the fruits of the reform and opening-up, and enjoy the same treatment in social policies.

A misunderstanding on this is that the city and the countryside are different, and so are workers and farmers. After the urban-rural reform, the countryside would gradually cease to exist, and thus the farmers would gradually disappear. In this way, wouldn't it be forcefully narrowing the urban-rural gap by reducing the scale of rural areas and the number of farmers? It remains to be seen whether this will be a curse or a blessing for the Chinese economy! It should be pointed out that the differences between urban and rural areas, as well as those between workers and farmers in terms of occupation or social division of labor, will not disappear with the breakup of the urban-rural dual system or with the reform. As productivity continues to develop, the disappearance of these differences could take many years. What is needed to reform the dual system is the removal of artificial barriers to the flow of production factors between urban and rural areas and the unequal treatment of workers and farmers under the two types of household registration, which would lead to a reduction in the gap between urban and rural areas. All the above is possible and can only have positive results for national economic development.

33.2 The Reform of Rural Property Rights System Is Imperative, Especially the Management System of the Residential Land

To develop the rural economy and increase farmers' income, one of the problems is a lack of financial services in rural areas, which can be attributed to the existence of the urban-rural dual system and the constraints of the current rural property rights system.

Farmers currently have no relationship with property rights. Therefore, they do not have property rights to the land they contracted, the residential land, and even the houses on the residential land. Even though the houses were built at their own expense, without property rights to the land, farmers do not have property rights to the houses on the land either, not even property certificates. It is unreasonable. Since farmers only have the right to use the land and the houses built on it, rather than actual property rights, neither the land nor the houses can be sold or mortgaged. This restricts the realization of farmers' land rights and interests. This is negative not only to farmers' enrichment and rural economic development but also to the transfer of rural labor, seriously hindering the urbanization process.

At the present stage, the protection of farmers' rights to land (including contracted land and residential land) in China's laws is unclear and inappropriate, and this problem needs to be urgently addressed (Sun 2008a, b). And there have been positive and negative experiences and lessons for urbanization from both sides of the world. For example, in some Western European countries, during industrialization and urbanization, the phenomenon of "slums" did not appear in the cities, mainly because rural land and farmers' houses can be transferred and mortgaged according to farmers' wishes. This helps them work in the cities, start their own businesses, settle down, and become urban residents.

The land and houses built on the land are supposed to be important properties of farmers, and local governments should be encouraged and supported to explore the ways to transfer and mortgage the residential land and houses to protect and realize the due rights and interests of farmers. The practical use of rural residential land and houses would have turned it into a de facto long-term right for farmers. This fact should be legally recognized, and farmers should be given property rights to land and houses, which is of particular importance to protect their land rights and interests and to revitalize the rural economy and finance. Moreover, how to deal with the land issue must fully respect farmers' rights and wishes and must not compromise their interests (Jia and Chen 2009). The direction of future legislation is to give farmers and urban residents the same property rights and protection. In order to realize the integration of urban and rural areas, it is suggested that the laws and related regulations, such as the "Property Law" and the "Land Administration Law" should be revised in due course, and the reform of the property rights system of residential land and houses can activate with full force the rural economy and rural finance. At present, we should actively explore the effective ways of mortgaging the land and the houses built by farmers, summarize the practice of mortgaging land and houses to credit cooperatives or other rural financial institutions for finance in some places, and vigorously carry out pilot projects of this kind in rural areas. Then it is necessary to actively establish the transferability of the residential land and houses, at least gradually promoting the experimental zones of integrated urban and rural development reform.

In the implementation of this reform, some still have concerns in their minds. There are four main concerns.

Firstly, some believe that the house site is like a garden for farmers, and the land around it is carefully cultivated with vegetables or fruits, with high productivity, and a lot of the farmers' cash income mainly comes from this garden economy. If the property rights change hands, not only might it be a greater loss, it would also deprive the retreat for farmers who are migrant workers in cities, because in case they do not do well outside and do not earn much, they would not have somewhere to fall back on. Wouldn't it cause new problems?

In fact, such worries can be dismissed. The vast majority of farmers do not sell their land before going out to work. They would often go out to work first, wait until they have certain arrangements outside and are more financially sound, and then bring their family members to the cities before disposing their land. For them, whether or not to dispose their land rights is a choice made by repeatedly weighting up their immediate and long-term interests. The farmers' behavior in this regard is rational. Of course, one cannot deny the possibilities of contingencies in this process. For example, if the main laborer of the family suffers serious injury while working in the city, what should they do? This tells people to be aware of the importance of insurance because with insurance, the losses could be less, and people will not be in a desperate situation.

Secondly, some people believe that disposing residential land may only be suitable for farmers in suburban areas, not for those in remote areas, and even less suitable for those in mountainous areas. Only those in the suburbs can mortgage the land and houses. But how can those in remote areas, especially mountainous areas, be mortgaged? Who is willing to accept it? Moreover, most farm houses would be dilapidated that no one would want them. Wouldn't the mortgaging be an empty word?

It should be acknowledged that this situation does exist, but the disposal of the residential land still should not be halted. If we halt the process now and resume it when the farmers in the mountains become affluent and their houses are replaced with new buildings, how long would they need to wait? In fact, the implementation of the rural family contract did not spread nationwide and was up to farmers to make their own choices. The contract system was promoted in some places first, some places later, and some approaches other than the household contract was promoted in some other areas. This is also the case with the disposal or mortgaging of the land. Therefore, the approach should be to promote first wherever conditions are suitable, or later at a proper time. Do not make the implementation time as the criteria of "awareness." Sticking to the facts is the most important, or it may lead to mistakes.

Thirdly, it is believed that the disposal of residential land may only be suitable for farmers who work or start a business in the nearby cities, but not for those who go thousands of miles away. For those far away from their hometown, to whom will the land be disposed? For example, many farmers work in the counties and cities in the Pearl River Delta for a long time, but their hometowns are in the rural areas of Western Guizhou. In this case, to whom should the land be disposed?

This concern is reasonable, and the key is to find a solution to the problem. There should be a procedure for land rights disposal, and the problem can be solved by following the procedure. If a farmer settles in a county (city) town, the problem is relatively simple. If a farmer settles in another county (city) in the province, the problem can be solved within the province. If a farmer settles in another province, then the problem can still be solved if the following procedures are implemented. The farmer who would settle down in another province and needs to dispose his land rights would need to apply first. Then, with the consent of the local government, one should apply to the local government in the other province to which one is going to move. Upon obtaining the consent, the farmer would hand over the land to the local government for disposal and will get compensation. Finally, the land will be transferred by the relevant department of the local government to the one in the other province. In this way, this is reasonable for all three parties involved. For the farmer, the transfer could be done, which would enable one to have a place to live in a new location. For the county (city) where the farmer is originally from, it would be reasonable to pay compensation to the farmer. The land surrendered by the farmer could be used for the corresponding urban construction purpose. For the local government in the destination province, it would receive a compensation fee to resettle the farmers who would move in, and there would be no financial losses. Therefore, the problem can be solved as long as it is well coordinated.

Fourthly, it is believed that there are two kinds of risks associated with the mortgage of the rural land, borne by farmers and financial institutions respectively. How to avoid these two kinds of risks is a problem in the reform of the land administration system. If there are no reliable measures to avoid these two risks in place, it should be handled with caution.

It should be acknowledged that these two risks do exist, so there need to be reliable preventive measures. It does not mean that mortgaging the land should be abandoned due to the fear of risks, but to find out the measures that can prevent or defuse the risks in advance. When the Standing Committee of the NPC enacted the "Guarantee Law of the People's Republic of China," the practice of mortgaging contracted land and house was ruled out, considering that land is essential to farmers' livelihood (Chen 2008). However, according to practical experience, the key still lies in the availability of effective risk prevention measures.

How can farmers prevent the risks from mortgaging their land? On the one hand, the financial institutions accepting farmers' land mortgages must be eligible and approved to engage in the business so that farmers will not be subject to fraud. On the other hand, when farmers mortgage their land and housing, they can get a loan for production and operation. What if they lose money? Wouldn't the farmers lose their land and houses from then on? Therefore, a vigorous development of the rural insurance business should be one of the ways to reduce the risk. For example, when a farmer uses the loan to start a farm on his own, open a workshop or go out to work and encounters flood, fire, earthquake, plague, etc., or has a car accident or work injury, compensation can be claimed if one is already insured, thus suffering fewer losses.

How can financial institutions engaged in the mortgage business of rural land avoid risks? The risk here mainly refers to a low repayment rate and the difficulty for financial institutions to deal with the land and houses as collateral, thus getting into financial difficulties. In order to prevent and reduce this risk, the following measures can be taken. Even if farmers use their land and houses as collateral, financial institutions should still investigate their credit status and ability to repay the debt. It would be better to issue mortgages in this regard through cross guarantees among the farmers. In short, risk will always exist, but it can be minimized.

In addition, according to our survey, some farmers have more than one house in rural areas. In this case, why cannot the extra houses be mortgaged? In addition, in some villages, farmers' houses are sometimes three-story or four-story, half of which can be mortgaged. Therefore, even if a loan cannot be repaid later, one would still have half of the house. What is wrong with that?

33.3 Agricultural Scales of Economy Calls for Improving the Rural Land Contract System and Accelerating the Transfer of Farmers' Contracted Land

With the development of the rural areas in the new era, some incompatibilities already occurred in the current rural household contract system. The main problem is that land and other factors of production are highly dispersed among households, which restricts the scale of economy for land operation and land-use efficiency, affects the incentive of increasing investment on land, and influences the improvement of agricultural productivity and the rise of farmers' income. In addition, in the case that many rural middle-aged farmers may go to work in the city, the land under household contracts may be abandoned. Meanwhile, production materials are idled, and only the old and the weak are left to work on land, significantly reducing land-use efficiency. This would cause waste in the vast rural areas where the transfer of arable land is limited. Therefore, a moderate scale of economy is an inherent requirement for developing modern agriculture and improving agricultural productivity. Land resources cannot be used effectively without large-scale operations, which makes it difficult to improve agricultural productivity. The current land contract system urgently needs to be adjusted and improved according to the changing situation. In particular, there is an urgent need to allocate land resources rationally and scientifically and to encourage farmers in different areas to effectively explore ways of transferring land contracting rights (The Law Department of the National Academy of Governance 2008a, b).

Here, let's further analyze the three main forms of land transfer, subcontracting, leasing, and shareholding. These forms are more popular among many, could be applied to certain areas, and have some characteristics.

The transfer of contracted land through subcontracting is applicable in some grain-producing regions. In some regions, farmers who don't work in the countryside anymore would subcontract their contracted land to native or non-native farmers. If a competent grain grower is subcontracted by a dozen farmers, this could result in high yields and profits by hiring only a few employees and adopting machinery. This is beneficial to both the grain growers and the farmers who work in cities. The information obtained from the survey in Hunan demonstrated that a single farmer contracted for a dozen acres of rice fields would have a meager income, just enough to make ends meet. However, by subcontracting over 200 acres of rice fields to a small team of workers equipped with machinery, it is possible to cultivate two harvests per year, yielding approximately 400,000 pounds of rice. Despite the costs of diesel, farm machinery depreciation and maintenance, fertilizers, pesticides, employee wages, and the contractor's income which is equivalent to a wage, a significant surplus can still be achieved. The farmers who subcontract out their land would also earn more than their income from farming when they go to the city to work or do business.

The transfer of contracted land through rentals is also popular in some places. Contracted land is rented out to skilled growers, fruit or vegetable enterprises, or farms to grow fodder, with the amount of rent being negotiated. Some original land contractors go out to work in the city without worries, while others work for the renters after renting out the land and earn a monthly wage. The information from the survey in Xuwen County, Guangdong Province shows that the local pineapple plantations are developed precisely based on the land leased by the majority of farmers.

In the current practice of rural land transfer, three-quarters of the arable land has been transferred in the forms of subcontracting and leasing (Caijing 2009).

The transfer of contracted land through shareholding (i.e., farmers join a professional cooperative as shareholders) may be more valuable to be promoted in some areas where these cooperatives have been formed. Farmers are employed as agricultural workers with monthly wages and dividend income at the end of the year (Liu 2008a, b, c). However, if farmers take equity in their contracted land to form a large company, it may bring three problems:

1. Farmers would have the right as shareholders in the cooperatives, but may lose the shareholders' right in a large company.
2. Since farmers' cooperatives are their economic organizations, at times of distress, farmers can discuss how to overcome the difficulties; while if a large company loses money, it would be difficult to fulfill the farmers' wish to withdraw their shares (return the land they have contracted), which may cause social unrest.
3. If a large company mortgages the contracted land in which the farmers have taken shares and invests the capital in other provinces, the farmers, without their knowledge, are essentially granting the land to the company to use at will, which may contradict with their own interests.

Therefore, farmers should put their contracted land into cooperatives. The "company + farmer" model of land shareholding was once widely adopted. In some districts and counties in Chongqing, this model has been further developed into a "large company + small company + farmer" model. Large companies refer to large leading enterprises, and small companies refer to farmers cooperatives. Farmers put their contracted land into a cooperative. In this way, not only are the farmers assured of their interests, but it is also easy for them to monitor the use of the land. The cooperative (the small company) and the leading enterprise (the large company) then enter into contracts to supply production materials, transportation, and marketing or processing of agricultural products, establishing a market-based relationship of supply and demand.

New forms of land transfer are being experimented in other areas, such as the model of land credit cooperatives. "In terms of business purpose, (land credit) cooperatives do not aim at profit maximization. On the contrary, they serve the 'Sannong (agriculture, countryside, and farmers)' by promoting an orderly transfer of land contracting rights and large-scale operations, which contributes to the transformation of rural production and lifestyle (Cheng 2008a, b)." In terms of economic benefits, "land credit cooperatives have reduced the cost of the transfer of land contract rights. Moreover, through their good demonstration effect, they have not only created local demand for land credit but also attracted the demand from other regions, reflecting the positive effect of successful innovation in the transfer system of land contract rights on agricultural industrialization (Cheng 2008a, b)." In addition, some cities and counties are experimenting with farmers depositing their contracted land with rural credit unions and charging interest. Local farmers refer to such rural credit unions as "small banks." Finally, farmers are relieved to go out to work in the city. Farmers welcome this form of land transfer, which is based on the following considerations:

1. It is less risky. Unlike land renters (individuals or corporates) that could be exposed to greater risks, rural credit cooperatives are considered more reliable.
2. Land rental proceeds are secure and delivered on time without delays, delinquencies, or blank checks.
3. It is flexible and convenient, close to the farmers' residence, and readily accessible.

In some places, if a farmer wants to take back his contracted land, he can notify the rural credit union in advance, and the union would return it on time. It may not necessarily return the original piece of land, but another piece of arable land of comparable size.

According to another survey, the exchange market of rural land established in Chongqing is a new attempt to handle land transfer. Through the "land coupon" (which is a certificate of land-use quota) transaction, the contracted land up for exchange will be organized and reclaimed into arable land, and then listed and sold in the form of "land coupons." Therefore, this market can better communicate with the respective urban and rural construction land-use quotas and protect the farmers' land rights. In this sense, a "land coupon" transaction means a procedure and openness of land quota transfer, which can solve the problem in residential land transfer and increase the urban construction quota without reducing the amount of arable land. Therefore, the red line of 1.8 billion mu of arable land set by the State Council will not be compromised (State Council 2008). In this regard, it is recommended that the rural land exchange market set up in Chongqing be investigated and studied, and experience be summarized promptly. If this kind of market can be standardized, developed, and promoted, it will be conducive to the practical import of urban capital, technology, and other market factors into rural areas. At the same time, we should explore the possibility for farmers' contracted land, other than the residential land, to enter the rural land exchange market, resulting in a new form of land transfer.

Here, an issue needs to be further clarified. The transfer of contracted land and residential land can be separate or combined, but is it better to be "separate" or "combined"? The "separated" here means the transfer of contracted land and residential land can be carried out separately. For example, some farmers would only transfer the contracted land and keep the residential land, while others would transfer the residential land but keep the contracted land and leave the latter to their acquaintances to manage for them. The "combined" here means that the contracted land and the residential land are combined and transferred together. For instance, the contracted land could be sold like a stock, the residential land could be changed in land-use purpose, and the farmers would move out.

It should be said that the transfer of contracted land is more accessible than the transfer of residential land, and if farmers go out to work, they may consider the transfer of contracted land first and then the transfer of the residential land. Because farmers themselves would migrate first and their family members later, and they seldom bring their family members with them initially. Moreover, farmers working in the city may think that the work is temporary, and that once they have enough savings, they would return to their villages to start their own business and build new houses, in which case they would be even less likely to transfer their residential land at the time of going out. This suggests that the transfer of contracted land and residential land should be carried out separately. Of course, this does not exclude that some farmers would be willing to transfer them together. For example, those who have relatives in the city, and those who have arrangements for work and accommodation with the help of their relatives do not necessarily transfer their contracted land first and then their residential land.

33.4 Vigorously Advocate, Encourage, and Support Farmers to Start Their Business and Promote Employment Through Entrepreneurship

In the survey about urban-rural integration, I have compared the situation in Zhejiang and Chongqing. The condition in Zhejiang is better than that in Chongqing. This is due to the different natural conditions and geographical locations, or the different historical situations of the two areas. But more importantly, it is because of the differences in entrepreneurial urge and environment of farmers in these two areas. The main reason why Zhejiang has done a better job in coordinating urban and rural areas is that more farmers leave the countryside to start business there. Just take

Wenzhou as an example, it has about 4 million private business owners, including shop owners as well as investors and operators of large enterprises. While Chongqing has a total of 4 million farmers working in cities. That shows the gap between Zhejiang province and the city of Chongqing.

Working in cities is not the only way for migrating farmers. A more stable, effective, and vital way for farmers would be to start their business and thus entering the non-agricultural sector. Although there is a certain investment risk for farmers to start their business, isn't there a certain risk for working for others? Here are the benefits of farmers' entrepreneurship:

1. When the farmers get rid of poverty and become rich, they can elevate the whole family out of poverty.
2. More farmers could be employed. On the one hand, farmers with their own business could hire other farmers as workers; on the other hand, it could have a demonstrative effect over other farmers.
3. It is conducive to small towns and counties' economic development because the stores and workshops opened by entrepreneurial farmers are mainly located in the counties and towns.
4. It can contribute to the prosperity of the rural economy because in order to expand the scale of business, farmer entrepreneurs would often recruit farmers, buy raw materials from their own townships, use the money earned to build houses and roads in their hometowns, and so on.
5. Farmer workers' returning to their hometowns to start a business is conducive to the expansion of urban civilization, the transformation of farmers' lifestyles, and facilitating the process of urban–rural integration.

In some places, after working in the cities for many years, some excellent young farmers would learn the skills, broaden their horizons, accumulate a certain amount of capital, and then have the desire to start a business in their hometowns. Our investigation suggests that small restaurants, hotels, stores, and workshops could be found along the national highway, from Hunan to Guangxi. Farmers who have returned to their hometowns after working in Guangdong are now successfully operating businesses that are flourishing.

Farmers need government support for entrepreneurship, but there is a lack of a policy support system, resulting in a rather small percentage of farmers returning to their hometowns to start their business.

At present, we should pay full attention to the critical role of entrepreneurship in promoting urban-rural integration. For example, we should introduce policies to further support farmers' entrepreneurship, such as small guaranteed loans with convenient procedures and increased subsidies for entrepreneurs. We should allow farmers to obtain loans with their residential land and the residences built on them as mortgages. We should implement tax reduction policies for farmers' entrepreneurship, particularly for the initial stage. In addition, we should vigorously carry out business training, set role models, and publicize exemplary experiences to encourage farmer workers to return to their hometowns to start their business, etc.

According to theories in modern economics, physical capital, human capital, and social capital are indispensable in starting and operating a business. Physical capital refers to the capital invested in plants, equipment, and raw materials, which can be raised through various channels. Human capital refers to the knowledge, skills, experience, and wisdom embodied in entrepreneurs and operators. Although they vary from person to person, human capital can be gradually accumulated through individual efforts and personal practices. Social capital refers to a great power generated by social networks, interpersonal relationships, and mutual trust, which is embodied in various social relationships. It is intangible but can be transformed into a great power to promote entrepreneurship. What farmers lack most when starting and operating a business is often the social capital. Some farmers are in remote mountainous areas, with few interactions with the outside world, lack of information, and having no relatives and friends working outside. Therefore, it is almost impossible for them to have any social capital to rely on. But this is not set in stone. Social capital can be accumulated, and the key is how to raise it and how to use it. For example, the number of people from one county, township, or village who are working, doing business and starting business in a city is a kind of social capital that can be used for those who are ready to work there. Hometown associations, alumni associations, and fellowship associations, whether tangible or intangible, are likewise social capital. The various professional associations organized by farmers are also social capital. What's more, coastal cities also form institutional connections with the central and Western cities as a helping hand, which is also a kind of social capital that we can tap into. With social capital, farmers could start a business more successfully.

A more far-reaching effect of farmers' entrepreneurship on the reform of the urban-rural dual system is that farmers' entrepreneurial enthusiasm has been stimulated. This is a huge power hidden in the population, which has been suppressed for many years due to the shackles of the urban-rural system. Going out to work is only a tiny part of this force that can be brought into play. Of course, farmers may go out to work to prepare for their own businesses later on, but working is not the same as starting a business after all. At the beginning of self-employment, farmers are investors, operators, and even workers all in one, regardless of the business scale. They must be familiar with the market, care about it, improve management, introduce services, and take risks on their own, which is not the same as the employees. In other words, only after the reform of the urban-rural dual system can the vast number of farmers be truly liberated and become active members of the market economy. When farmers themselves have greater vitality, the market will also be more dynamic. The more the number of farmers who start their own business, the smoother the reform of the urban-rural dual system will be.

There should also be a deeper understanding of farmers' entrepreneurship. Farmer entrepreneurship is manifested not only in towns, i.e., farmers opening stores, workshops, and even enterprises in towns, but also in rural areas. For example, farmers use their contracted land as household farms in the market economy, use their houses and gardens to set up "farm caravanserai" form of rural family hotels and family restaurants, engage in the production and operation of cottage industry products, or even invest personally or collectively in rural enterprises, and so on. It is important to understand that farmers' enthusiasm is greatly restricted under the urban-rural dual system. Even if they grow various crops on contracted land or raise pigs and chickens at home, they do not regard these as a kind of 'entrepreneurship', and they are not motivated to start a business. They just use it to make a living. At the beginning, after the implementation of the household contract system in rural areas, agricultural and livestock production increased significantly. Within a few years, chicken, duck, fish, and meat are all available in the market, thanks to the increase in farmers' enthusiasm. At present, it can be expected that this enthusiasm will be further boosted through the reform of the dual system. In addition, there are always some capable people in rural areas. By being one step ahead, they will make the contracted land and the garden economy achieve greater results. Then, there will be a demonstration effect. In this way, even if they do not go to the city and remain on the contracted land and in their own houses and gardens, they would still do great things. The more and the closer the connection with the market, the higher their enthusiasm for entrepreneurship, and their mental state will be greatly improved. This will profoundly impact the development of the national economy, the improvement in farmers' income, and the renewal of the rural areas.

33.5 Prioritize the Integrated Urban and Rural Comprehensive Reform as a National Strategy, and Vigorously Support the Pilot Areas to Venture and Experiment Boldly

Reform requires great courage and effort, and a relaxed public opinion and policy environment. At this stage, Chongqing and Chengdu are the pilot areas of urban and rural development. Their systems can be in experiment first. It does not matter if it may be wrong, or if the lessons could be learned. Reform is to pay a price to find a new path (Liu 2008a, b, c). Thirty years ago, the path of reform and opening-up was first shaped by the establishment of the special economic zones, which had infinite impact as an example. Chongqing and Chengdu, the two pilot zones for integrated urban and rural development, will also play the role of "pathfinder" in this regard, playing a demonstrative role. The two experimental zones have realized "three concentrations" through reform, i.e., transfer industry to industrial areas, manage land on a large scale, and make farmers live in the neighborhood. The campaign of "three concentrations" has attracted the attention of people who are concerned about a nationwide urban-rural integration (Liu 2009). This shows that promoting urban-rural integration is typical and exemplary in the country. All provinces and cities in the country hope that the two regions will summarize the lessons learned to explore and lead the national urban-rural integration reform.

First, trial in a pilot area has been a valuable experience of China's thirty years of reform and opening-up. When looking back from 1978 to the present, every significant reform went through a path of being piloted, summarized, and then promoted.

Even if the reform experiment might have certain contradictions with the existing law, it could be tolerated. We should consider trying it out in a few places first, wait until the conditions are ripe, then amend the law or formulate a new law. Two examples of rural reforms may be cited. One example is that there was no legal basis from the late 1970s to the early 1980s, when the rural household responsibility system was launched in Xiaogang Village, Fengyang, Anhui Province. If the legal provisions were strictly adhered to, the household responsibility system was obviously illegal. The reform changed the practice of unified land administration under the people's commune system and could be severely labeled as "attempting capitalist restoration." In the early 1960s, during the famine, there were places where the household responsibility system was carried out. But the results were tragic: People were arrested, household contracts were abolished, and the families of some leaders even broke apart. However, the situation changed after 1979 because of the Third Plenary Session of the Eleventh Central Committee of the CPC. The spontaneous experiment of the rural household responsibility system in Xiaogang Village was generally implemented. Another example is that in the early 1980s, the rise of the TVEs has seen many buyers and salesmen dispatched by the TVEs, running across the country to purchase raw materials and sell their products. This led to the formation of an "non-planned market" under the planned economic system. At that time, this was also illegal and could face criminal charge for speculation. However, a large number of TVEs did not stop there. They continued to purchase, market, recruit and hire people, and expand production. In this way, the TVEs gradually developed and expanded. This shows that the reform is improved through experimentation and summary. Therefore, we should fully support and trust the urban-rural integration experiments in Chongqing and Chengdu, and believe that these experiments will explore a new path for the reform of China's urban-rural dual system.

However, China is such a large country, with such a large number of farmers and uneven economic and social development, so it is impossible to expect that the reform of the urban-rural dual system can be completed quickly. It has been thirty years since the implementation of the rural household responsibility system. During that time, the CPC Central Committee and the State Council have studied so many times and issued so many important documents before shifting to the reform of the urban-rural dual system, which is still in the experimental stage. Of course, it may not take another thirty years, but it will take at least twenty years. Therefore, the urban-rural dual system reform will be considered a decisive victory only in 2028, i.e., when China has reached fifty years of reform and opening-up, and it is estimated that by that time, the urban-rural system will have been unified.

The speed of urbanization will accelerate in these two decades. China's situation is different from that of the United States, and it is unrealistic to reduce the proportion of the rural population to 4 to 5% like that in the US. But can it be reduced to 25 to 30%? In other words, can the urban population account for 70 to 75%? This is possible. At that time, the dual household registration will be unified. The occupational division of labor is still necessary. However, people would only have differences in places of residence and occupational divisions. Their rights and opportunities would be equal. This indicates the real meaning of urban-rural integration. The urban-rural dual system will then become an episode in the Chinese history (Li 2008; Zhou 2008).

33.6 The Most Challenging Issues in the Urban-Rural Integration Reform Are Employment and Social Security for the Unemployed and Landless Farmers

What is the most challenging part of the urban-rural integration reform process? It does not lie in the transfer of contracted and residential land, or the change from a dual household registration system to a unified system, but lies in the following big problem. Since so many rural people are moving to the cities, are there enough job opportunities? If not, many of them would become jobless, which will affect the stability and development of the cities. Moreover, if farmers who have already moved to the city cannot find jobs for a long time, they would have to return to the countryside, but is there still land available for them there? For farmers, the land is both a source of income and social security. Once they lose their contracted land in the countryside, how would they make a living after returning home? Here, we will analyze this issue from three aspects.

First, in reforming the dual system, it is necessary to maintain a high economic growth rate.

New jobs always emerge during economic growth as we learn from countries around the world. Although there is an asymmetry between economic growth and employment growth, i.e., employment growth always lags behind economic growth, it is indisputable that economic growth promotes employment growth. However, China's employment problem is complex and will persist for a long time at the current stage. For example, in Western European countries, as long as the annual economic growth rate is maintained at 2 to 3%, the job market is stable and there will not be a big employment problem, but China's economic growth rate should be maintained at more than 9 to 10% in order not to cause severe unemployment. However, if the economic growth rate drops to below 7%, the unemployment problem will be quite prominent. What is the reason?

1. Western European countries have had low economic growth rates for many years, and each year a group of workers would retire, freeing up jobs that could be filled by those who have newly reached the employment age. Therefore, even if the economic growth rate is low, the unemployment problem will not be serious. In those countries, the majority of the unemployed are job seekers among the immigrants from abroad. Furthermore, the industrialization of these countries started earlier, and the release of the rural labor force has been almost finished during this process that ran for one or two hundred years. Now there will not be many farmers who would like to work in the cities, and the employment pressure for those in domestic rural areas will obviously be reduced.

2. More importantly, there is a huge institutional difference between China and the Western European countries, i.e., the urban-rural dual system has long ceased to exist in Western Europe, while the dual system still exists in China. Under this system, urban and rural areas are separated by different institutions, which cause huge differences in social and economic life. If the traditional planning system existed, the human mobility between urban and rural areas would be severely restricted, so no matter how much the rural labor wanted to work in the cities, they could not do so. However, with China's reform and opening-up in the 1980s and beyond, although the urban-rural dual system was not abolished, the labor mobility between urban and rural areas was relaxed, and a wave of rural migrant workers entered the cities. These migrants entered the cities to increase their income, live in the cities, and receive the same benefits as city residents. Moreover, they brought their families into the cities as soon as they found a more stable occupation in the cities. In this way, the supply of rural labor is constant, while the demand for labor in cities is limited, making it difficult to ease the pressure of employment. In addition, since the proportion and number of farmers in China's population are large, some farmers who find jobs in the cities would encourage more of their fellow villagers to go to the cities, so that the employment pressure will definitely exist for an extended period of time. This is not the case in Western European countries, where the urban-rural dual system does not exist.
3. Since China is still in the transition process from a planned system to a market economy, the SOEs still occupy a pivotal position in the national economy while private enterprises have developed gradually only since the 1980s. In terms of scale, the SOEs are mainly mega and large enterprises, with good technical equipment and substantial capital, and even become the monopolies in specific industries. But the SOEs are capital-intensive and technology-intensive enterprises that can only absorb limited part of the labor force. The majority of private enterprises are small and medium-sized ones, many of which are labor-intensive and can absorb more labor. However, private enterprises have not been treated fairly in many aspects (e.g., taxation, finance, government procurement, etc.) and therefore are disadvantaged in the economy. Once the economy is in turmoil, private enterprises are usually the first to be hit, which exacerbates the situation that supply exceeds demand in the labor market. While in Western European countries, although there are SOEs, their number is not large, and private enterprises play a leading role in the economy. As long as the economy grows (even at only 2 to 3%) and the GDP per capita increases, the private enterprises, including a large number of small companies, will develop further and hire more.
4. China is a large country with limited arable land and minimal arable land per capita. According to statistics, 227 million farmers in China have contracted arable land, and the average arable land contracted and operated by each household is only 5.36 mu (Caijing 2009). Farmers do not have enough arable land, and since the 1980s, they have constantly been going out to work and do business. According to other statistics, China has a 950 million registered as rural population. Except for primary and secondary school students and the elderly, there are

about 530 million in their working-age (Caijing 2009), 320 million of them are engaged in agriculture (including forestry, animal husbandry and fishery), and the remaining 210 million are collectively called "farmer workers in the broad sense." The latter includes two groups of people. Eighty million of them are employees working in the TVEs who would never have left their homes, and the remaining 130 million are migrant workers who work in the cities, which is called "farmer workers in a narrow sense (Caijing 2009)." It can be seen that if we do not continue to divert a large number of them off the countryside in the future, the per capita arable land will be even less given a high fertility rate in the countryside. In order to increase the output per unit area of agriculture, it is the trend to increase the scale of economy and agricultural intensification. However, according to the information in 2006, the transfer of arable land in the country (except Xizang) is only 55.51 million *mu*, or only 4.57% of the arable land under the household responsibility system (Caijing 2009). So, it is imperative to accelerate the transfer of arable land. One of the consequences of land transfer is that the number of farmers engaged in agricultural production will decline, which would in turn push farmers to work in cities. This situation does not exist in Western European countries with a small rural population. The farmers there would have their own farms of moderate size and involve the efforts of the entire family to get a decent harvest, and they are not eager to go to the cities and are not willing to lose their land to work for others.

5. In the decades after the end of the Second World War, the social security system in Western European countries has been gradually improved, and both urban residents and farmers can enjoy better benefits. Farmers who entered the cities had the same social security benefits as city residents. Even if the enterprises they work for went bankrupt and farmers lost their jobs, they generally did not return to the countryside because of the social security system. The situation in China is different. For a long time, "the urban-rural dual system is the fundamental reason why farmer workers cannot get the same social security." (The "Migrant Worker Returning Mechanism Research" team of the Chinese Academy of Sciences 2009a, b) China's urban-rural social security reform has just started, and it is still at the initial stage. Therefore, unemployed farmer workers would have to return to rural areas; if the contracted land in rural areas has been transferred without corresponding social security benefits, they would become farmers with no land, job, and social security. This should be most concerning.
6. As for the industrial structure, the high employment pressure in China is related to the small proportion of the tertiary industry. After more than two hundred years of industrialization, Western European countries have finally developed an industrial structure. The primary sector usually accounts for only a few percent of GDP, the secondary sector for more than 20%, and the tertiary sector for more than 70%. The service sector became the biggest industry, absorbing a large number of people, including the owners of small and medium-sized services who started their own businesses. China is still in the middle of industrialization, and the tertiary sector is developing slowly, accounting for only about 40% of GDP. The secondary sector is still the main industry that absorbs the labor force.

Therefore, the slow development of China's service sector is an important reason behind a high employment pressure. The question that needs to be considered is: Why does China's service sector develop more slowly? This can be analyzed in terms of the slow urbanization rate and the low income of most urban and rural residents. Because of the slow urbanization, a large number of farmers, and the low income of farmers, the demand for services is likely to increase slowly. So, why is urbanization slow? Why are farmers' incomes low? This is directly related to the existence of the urban-rural dichotomy. It can be concluded that the problem of industrial structure in China at this stage is linked to the existence of the urban-rural dual system, and the problem of industrial structure cannot be explained without considering the institutional factors.

In conclusion, in the reform of China's urban-rural dual system, the economy must maintain high growth rates, which is determined by the current situation in China. There is a special relationship in China between a high economic growth rate and the urban-rural dual system, i.e., without a high economic growth rate, the pressure of employment will remain high. But the employment problem is difficult to ease, and thus the process of urban-rural integration is bound to be slowed down. The economic growth rate will not necessarily need to be so high once the reform of the dual system has made significant progress, urban-rural integration has been gradually fulfilled, rural and urban residents have become equal in terms of rights, and the pressure on the rural population to work in cities has been reduced.

Second, in reforming the urban-rural dual system, economic transformation must be effectively and efficiently achieved.

As mentioned earlier, China needs high economic growth rates to alleviate the employment pressure in reforming the urban-rural dual system. However, we should also see that a sustained and rapid economic growth could bring great risks. These risks are as follows.

1. Speed would be the only priority, and efficiency could be ignored. As a result, resource consumption would remain high, and the trend of environmental damage would be hard to reverse, which would undoubtedly affect the sustainable development of the economy and the society.
2. Sustained high economic growth rate is often associated with an excessive investment. Therefore, investment demand could expand excessively, and factor prices would continue to rise, leading to inflation.
3. In order to promote economic growth while ignoring industrial upgrading and restructuring, it is likely to lead to overcapacity in specific industries, which would lead to huge fluctuations and downturns in the economy, and thus the need to increase investment again to stimulate the economy.
4. In the above scenario, the proportion of bad loans in bank lending would rise, reflecting an increase in financial risks.

It can be asserted that it is necessary to achieve economic transformation along with economic growth. Without economic transformation, the economy cannot grow well and fast, and achieve the goal of improving the quality of economic growth.

The term economic transformation has two layers of meanings.

Economic transformation is always closely related with structural adjustments and industrial upgrading. Therefore, the key to understanding economic transformation lies in making timely adjustments to industrial and product structures, as well as promoting industry upgrades. It is also crucial to encourage enterprises to innovate independently and prioritize enhancing the quality of economic growth. The second understanding is to grasp the time to realize the adjustment of employment structure or labor force structure, as well as the upgrading of labor force quality, so that the proportion of technicians, R&D personnel, and skilled workers will increase, and to make the most from the vocational and technical training work to embrace the arrival of the new stage.

Only when these two layers of economic transformation are realized can China become a genuine economic and industrial powerhouse and be both a manufacturing and a creative center of the world. At the same time, only when the economic transformation of these two layers is realized can the reform of the urban-rural dual system and the blueprint of urban-rural integration become a reality in the most efficient way. The reason is clear, i.e., the economic growth now is sound and rapid to enable more jobs to be provided and to avoid dramatic fluctuations in the economy, allowing people's income to rise steadily. In other words, when we say that economic growth can deliver more employment, it is not simply referring to the fact that an increase in GDP would result in an increase in the number of jobs, but also means that people's income can rise steadily based on GDP growth, and people's consumption structure can improve. Continuous adjustments have led to changes in the industrial structure, resulting in a continuous increase in the proportion of the tertiary industry in GDP, so that more people can be employed. There are three essential links between GDP growth and employment growth, i.e., per capita income growth, changes in consumption structure, and expansion of the proportion of tertiary industry in GDP, thus forming positive cycles "GDP growth → per capita income growth → consumption structure change → expansion of the proportion of tertiary industry in GDP → employment growth → continuous GDP growth…".

Specifically, we must conscientiously implement the scientific concept of development and pay attention to the quality of economic growth, rather than the one-sided pursuit of economic growth rate, i.e., we cannot blindly compare economic growth rates by talking about "fast." To this end, according to the characteristics of China's current economic growth, we should focus on optimizing the structure, improving efficiency, saving energy, and managing the environment. Development can be faster, but such a high speed should be achieved through economic transformation, and it should lead to effective improvement in people's quality of life. Therefore, the sloppy growth-oriented approach adopted at the beginning of industrialization should be abandoned, which is not in line with sustainable development.

To achieve the second level of economic transformation, it is necessary to develop human capital and implement a new talent strategy. This is also necessary to promote the integration of urban and rural areas. Generally speaking, in terms of talent cultivation, it is necessary to respect knowledge, science, talent, and innovation and raise the innovation consciousness of the whole society. Only by advocating the spirit of innovation and improving the innovation mechanisms can we stimulate the innovative dynamisms of the society and have talents play their roles. At the same time, we should encourage the dare to innovate and compete and accommodate failures. Without accommodation of failures, there can be no real innovation. For this reason, reforms in education, teaching contents, and pedagogical methods are necessary. In the future, attention should be paid to the cultivation of innovative ability, the promotion of quality education, the cultivation of students' independent thinking, and the encouragement of students' participation in social and innovative practice, so that there will be a large number of innovative talents.

There have been many talented people in the rural areas who didn't play their roles for a long period of time, mainly restricted by the urban-rural dual system. Under this system, they lived under the urban-rural division and did not receive good education. But more importantly, there was no environment to utilize their talents, and their enthusiasm was frustrated. At the beginning of the implementation of the rural household responsibility system, although the dual system still existed, it was relaxed a little after all. In this way, some capable people and farmer entrepreneurs emerged from the vast rural areas. Thus, in the future, if the urban-rural dual system is eliminated and the road of urban-rural integration is embarked upon, the general environment will be changed and innovative talents will emerge from the rural areas (Liu 2008a, b, c). After the integration of urban and rural areas, the construction of small towns and new rural areas will require many innovative and entrepreneurial talents, and where will they come from? Shouldn't they be the farmers from rural areas who have transferred to towns and cities?

Third, in the process of reforming the urban-rural dual system, farmers who have lost their land must be allowed to have stable individual social security accounts.

During the reform of the dual system, it is imperative that we prevent farmers from losing their jobs, land, and social security. Those who choose to migrate to cities or remain in rural areas can be categorized as follows.

The first situation is that farmers, whether they stay in the countryside or go to the city to work or do business, have subcontracted, rented out, or taken shares in the land they contracted. In this case, they cannot be considered to have lost their contracted land.

Another situation is if they enter the city to work or live through a transfer of their residential land, and have thus obtained urban household registration, urban housing, and urban subsistence allowances, they cannot be considered to have lost their residential land either (The Law Department of the National Academy of Governance 2008a, b).

The other situation is that, for various reasons, farmers' contracted land or residential land has been expropriated or acquired, such as for building roads, railways, airports, factories, reservoirs, and urban residential areas. In this case, although farmers lose their land, they could receive a compensation. Here, let's not talk about the amount of the compensation, whether the standard of the compensation system is reasonable, or whether the compensation has been embezzled when it is distributed to the farmers. Let's just discuss what to do when the farmers have spent the compensation they received and have no suitable jobs, or have been unemployed after working as migrant workers for a while, or the small shops and workshops they operate have lost money and are closed. What should be done? Wouldn't they become farmers with no job, land, and social security?

In order to prevent this from happening, farmers who lose their land should be allowed to establish a stable personal social security account when their contracted land or residential land is expropriated or acquired, with the social security funds in the personal account consisting of three parts.

1. The government should allocate a portion of the funds from the land transfer to the farmers' social security account.
2. The farmers who have received compensation should allocate part of it into the personal social security account.
3. The developers, enterprises, or construction units who have acquired the land should pay a sum of money to the farmers' social security accounts.

These three parts of the fund are mandatory. With the protection in the individual social security account, farmers can rely on it when they encounter difficulties in life.

The following two situations are special.

The first situation would be that, when the economic situation is good, farmers who work in cities lease the contracted land to large grain growers, and obtain annual rents. When the economic situation worsens, farmers who work in cities and transferred the contracted land return to their hometowns. They would have nothing to live on, thus would ask for land from the large grain growers who lease the land, or become jobless and landless farmers. In this case, the large grain growers should set up farmers' cooperatives and grain processing enterprises to preserve the scale of agricultural operations and allow farmers who rent land to have jobs and stable income. This situation is known as the "transformation of large grain farmers." (Du and He 2009).

The second situation would be that, although farmers can't be considered to have lost their land after putting their contracted land into an enterprise, if the enterprise closes down or goes bankrupt later, farmers will not only lose the dividend income they could have received annually but also lose their original contracted land. In this case, it has already been suggested that, according to the experience of the Chongqing pilot area, farmers should invest their contracted land in professional farmers' cooperatives (small companies) rather than in leading enterprises (large companies). However, since these cooperatives are market players, they will still have investment and business risks. What should be done once the cooperatives are poorly run or invested wrongly and suffer losses, close down or go bankrupt? This is a difficult issue for which effective countermeasures have not yet been found. As the saying goes, "better safe than sorry." When discussing the forms of land transfer in which farmers put their contracted land into shares, we must prevent the possible risk of farmers' losing their land.

One alternative solution could be to try out a land-in-shares insurance system. This is just like the residents' deposits in banks. If the banks fail, the deposits won't be lost because of a deposit insurance system, in which insurance companies insure residents' deposits to reduce the losses of individual depositors. A trial in land insurance system could be set up in some cities in the form of state-controlled insurance companies specializing in farmers' land insurance or subsidiaries under existing state-controlled insurance companies specializing in farmers' land insurance. After converting farmers' contracted land into shares, farmers' cooperatives could be insured by the insurance company and will pay premiums regularly. In case the cooperatives collapse due to market risks, the insurance company would compensate farmers who have participated in the scheme. Usually, the insurance company can supervise and assist the operation of the cooperatives to prevent significant losses and other issues.

In a word, reform requires constant exploration and continuously accumulates experience through experiment. I believe that through endless practice, urban-rural integration will eventually be realized.

—*Journal of Peking University (Philosophy and Social Science Edition)*, issue No. 6, 2009

References

Caijing, No. 2, 2009, p. 62.

Chen X-W (2008) "Land Contract Rights and Homestead land Cannot Be Mortgaged." *People's Daily*, October 23.

Cheng Z-Q (2008a) "Reflections on the Practice of China's land Credit Cooperatives: Taking Pingluo, Ningxia as an Example." *Management World*, No. 11, p. 2.

Cheng Z-Q (2008b) "Reflections on the Practice of China's land Credit Cooperatives: Taking Pingluo, Ningxia as an Example." *Management World*, No. 11, p. 8.

Du A-N, He T (2009) "Farmers Returning Home to Ask for Land, and Major Grain Producers Are Transforming." *Guangzhou Daily*, February 24.

Jia J-H, Chen W-Y (2009) "Execution Hidden Dangers of Homestead land for Housing." *Investor Daily*, March 16.

Li C (2008) "The Chongqing Experiment on the Transfer of Homestead Land." *Beijing Youth Daily*, November 3.

Liu W-T (2008a) "Exploring the Direction of China's New Round of Rural Reform." *People's Daily*, September 3.

Liu W-T (2008b) "Exploring the Direction of China's New Round of Rural Reform." *People's Daily*, September 3.

Liu Y-S (2008c) "Establishing an Urban-rural Coordinated Employment Support System to Promote the Rational Flow of Labor between Urban and Rural Areas." *China Development*, December, pp. 62–65.

Liu Y-G (2009) "Chengdu Urban-rural Integration Consolidates the Foundation for Development." *People's Daily*, March 29.

Liu X-S, Zhang S (2008) "Urban-rural Dual Structure: The Focus of China's Next Round of Reform." *People's Daily*, September 3.

State Council (2008) "Outline of General Plan on National Land Use (2006–2020)." *People's Daily*, October 24.

Sun J (2008a) "Urban-rural Coordination Is an Innovation in Comprehensive Factor Coordination." *China Development*, December, pp. 59–61.

Sun R-F (2008b) "Revision of the Land Administration Law: Promoting the Reform of the Property Rights System of Rural Collective Land or Breaking the Problem." *First Financial Daily*, June 24.

The Law Department of the National Academy of Governance (2008a) "A Case Study and Analysis of the Transfer of Rural Collective Land in Chengdu." In: The Scientific Research Department of the National Academy of Governance (ed), *Government Management Reference*, No. 4, pp. 1–6.

The Law Department of the National Academy of Governance (2008b) "A Case Study and Analysis of the Transfer of Rural Collective Land in Chengdu." In: The Scientific Research Department of the National Academy of Governance (ed), *Government Management Reference*, No. 4. p. 4.

The "Migrant Worker Returning Mechanism Research" Team of the Chinese Academy of Sciences (2009a) "Chinese Migrant Workers Hovering between Urban and Rural Areas." *Guangming Daily*, April 9.

The "Migrant Worker Returning Mechanism Research" Team of the Chinese Academy of Sciences (2009b) "Chinese Migrant Workers Hovering between Urban and Rural Areas." *Guangming Daily*, April 9.

Zhou C-L (2008) "The Chengdu Breakthrough in the Transfer of Homestead Land." *Beijing Youth Daily*, November 2.

Chapter 34
2010: Paying Equal Attention to Aggregate Control and Structural Control: Thoughts on China's Monetary Policy

34.1 Limitations of Aggregate Control in Monetary Policy

At the macroeconomic level, the balance between aggregate demand and aggregate supply has always been the most concerned issue for government regulation. Aggregate demand is composed of investment, consumption, and net export. Therefore, government regulation should be based on aggregate analysis, so is the monetary policy. Monetary regulation relies on the analysis of money flow: When money flow increases, contractionary measures should be adopted, and vice versa. The normal practices in monetary policy include open market operations, adjusting the required reserve ratio, and changing interest rates. Sometimes direct regulation of the scale of credit is also an important tool for changing the total amount of credit. In summary, the flow analysis is reasonable because the fluctuation of monetary flow directly affects aggregate demand and macro-economy. Thus, monetary policy regulation usually includes the above-mentioned aggregate control measures.

The aggregate control of monetary policy is useful, but its limitations cannot be ignored. The drawbacks are mainly reflected in the following four areas.

First, the foundation of the macro-economy is the micro-economy, but the micro-units vary widely in different situations. The aggregate control of monetary policy often falls into the shortcoming of "one-size-fits-all." Therefore, generally speaking, there are pros and cons for the macro-economy. Moreover, the issues caused by "one-size-fits-all" may be severe and could even do more harm than good for the Chinese economy at its current stage of economic transformation.

Second, an aggregate control of monetary policy acts on the expansion or compression of the aggregate demand, but the effect on aggregate supply is uncertain. This is because the regulation of aggregate supply will inevitably involve structural adjustment issues on industry, product, regional economy, technology, labor, and investment. In this way, the limitations of an aggregate control are very clear. Since it cannot affect the adjustment in aggregate supply, how can it effectively balance aggregate demand and aggregate supply? Especially for medium- and long-term equilibrium

Y. Li, *China's Economy Since 1978*, China Academic Library,
https://doi.org/10.1007/978-981-95-5733-2_34

and growth, structural adjustments are extremely significant, which can only be realized by the regulation of both aggregate demand and aggregate supply. So, the two-pronged approach is effective regulation.

Third, China's economy has still been unbalanced so far, including an imperfect market, limited supply of resources, an incomplete pricing mechanism, and an information asymmetry. It limits the control of monetary policy. The effects of aggregate control vary between the coastal and inland regions, between the eastern and Midwestern regions, and between large cities and small towns. The aggregate monetary policy might not narrow the gap between regions and could even widen it.

Fourth, once an economy encounters stagflation, that is, economic stagnation accompanied by rising unemployment and inflation, the aggregate monetary policy would be powerless. For example, the situation that occurred in the United States, an advanced market economy, failed to adjust its aggregate demand through monetary policy in the early 1970s. Therefore, it could also be the case for China. An aggregate control of monetary policy is unlikely to be effective, whether in preventing or in fighting against stagflation.

Therefore, although the aggregate control of monetary policy may be useful, it must be coordinated with the structural control of monetary policy. Both of them are important.

In macroeconomics, there are generally four major policies for government regulation, namely, fiscal policy, monetary policy, price policy, and income policy. Except for monetary policy, the other three all emphasize structural control.

Fiscal policy. Fiscal policy is both an aggregate and structural control but focuses more on the latter. Fiscal policy generally includes fiscal revenue policy and fiscal expenditure policy. In terms of the former, total control refers to control over total fiscal revenue and total taxation. However, in the specific implementation process, it must be coordinated with structural control measures, such as differential adjustments on taxes or differential policies on taxpayers. In terms of the latter, total amount control means controlling the total amount of fiscal expenditure. And the total amount of control must be implemented through specific expenditure items to target and then achieve the goal. Which expenditure should be increased, which should be reduced, and which should remain intact are all related to structural control. Therefore, both total control and structural control in fiscal policy are very important.

Price policy. The regulation of the general price level and the year-on-year growth rate of the price level both fall in the total control in price policies. The target for total control is achieved through the formulation of structural control targets. Specifically, the latter includes the appropriate price levels of the means of production and consumer goods. Firstly, it is necessary to refine the prices of capital goods. The prices of those influential goods, such as oil, natural gas, coal, electricity, construction materials, steel, and non-ferrous metals, should be adjusted according to market supply and demand. Secondly, as for consumer goods, it is also necessary to refine their prices, including those of grain, edible oil, animal products, and cotton, as well as certain services closely related to people's lives (such as transportation, communication, healthcare, education, housing, and rental). Therefore, the price policy also needs to use both total control and structural control, which is also the function of the relevant government departments in charge of policy.

Income policy. The regulation on the income level of residents is an aggregate regulation, but the regulation goal should also be implemented through structural regulation. According to the current economic situation in China, it is necessary to calculate the income levels of urban residents and farmers separately, and formulate measures to increase their income. This is a structural control. Furthermore, the aggregate income is equal to the sum of the income of various production factors, and the income of each production factor and its proportion are issues of an income distribution structure. How to increase the proportion of labor income in aggregate income is the task of structural control of income policy, so aggregate control alone is not enough.

Monetary policy is different from fiscal policy, price policy, and income policy. Monetary policy operations are based on the analysis of money flow and focus more on aggregate control. Moreover, as a method of aggregate analysis, flow-of-money analysis often conceals contradictions and creates illusions, causing people to get incorrect impressions of the economic situation and therefore make wrong judgments.

34.2 Analysis of the Current Credit Volume in China

Since the third quarter of 2009, there has been a discussion in China's economic academia that both the amount of credit and the money flow in the first two quarters of 2009 were too large and that monetary policy should be tightened promptly. This kind of analysis was made from the aggregate perspective, which was not in line with China's reality.

Statistics for the first three quarters of 2009 showed that China's economy bottomed out in the first quarter, and rebounded continually in the second and the third quarters. However, the foundation for China's current economic recovery has not been consolidated yet, which is mainly reflected in the following aspects.

First, the economic recovery was mainly driven by investment. Consumption played a minor role, while exports played a much smaller role. Investment leads to intermediate demand, while consumption and exports bring the final demand.

Second, economic recovery driven by investment is mainly reliant on government investment, which has yet to serve as a lever to prompt private investment. Furthermore, in some regions and industries, there is a crowding out effect, and local governments may even set up barriers to exclude private investment.

Third, the main targets of government investment are infrastructure projects. The government's massive investment in infrastructure construction is of positive significance to ensure the long-term growth of China's economy. The construction of infrastructure, such as high-speed railways, airports, and ports, will help sustain China's economic growth. To stimulate consumer demand, it is essential to create more job opportunities, a goal that cannot be achieved solely by construction projects.

Therefore, at present, to expand employment in China, it is necessary to promote the development of the private economy, foster and help small and medium-sized enterprises and labor-intensive enterprises, and accelerate the development of the service industry. Government investment alone is not enough for such an effect.

Precisely because of the unsolid foundation for China's economic recovery, the moderately loose monetary policy should remain in place. Then, how should we understand the fact that there was too much credit? Currently, the structural analysis might be more useful than an aggregate analysis. Therefore, credit volume should be analyzed from a structural perspective.

First of all, we must figure out how much of the credit released by banks has actually entered into the real economy and how much into the virtual economy. If the credit entering into the virtual economy should have entered into the real economy in a certain proportion of the total credit, then specific measures should be taken to move them to the real economy as soon as possible. Otherwise, it will produce bubbles in the stock market and property market. In this case, simply adopting aggregate monetary policy and tightening money flow will not help solve the problem.

Secondly, how much credit released by banks could really benefit small- and medium-sized enterprises (SMEs), private enterprises, especially small private enterprises, also needs to be clear. Some documents show that banks should assign a certain percentage of their loanable funds to the SMEs. In 2009, this part of the credit market has been realized. But the actual situation is not so simple. At the current stage in China, SMEs account for more than 99 percent of the total enterprises, with the number of employees from a few to 3,000. According to the survey conducted by the Private Economic Research Group of the Economic Committee of the CPPCC in Guangdong Province and Liaoning Province from May to June in 2009, the SMEs that received bank loans were mostly upper- and middle enterprises, while middle- and lower-middle enterprises rarely received loans. As for a large number of small companies, they could not get loans at all. Then they had to rely on mutual aid among themselves to solve the shortage problem of working capital, or even seek loan sharks to overcome their difficulties. Therefore, the current policy of tightening aggregate credit will not help solve the financing problems of the SMEs and private enterprises.

Thirdly, even if a considerable share of the credit enters into the real economy, it is necessary to conduct structural analysis to find out how much credit has entered into the industries with overcapacity, and how much has entered into the short-board or emerging high-tech industries in urgent need of credit support. If these enterprises could not have access to it, while industries with overcapacity could receive excessive loans, then a simple tightening of the monetary policy is bound to be harmful.

It should also be pointed out that the change of monetary policy stance is a major economic event. One of its side effects is that the change in people's expectations could sometimes have an unpredictable impact on economic operations.

As we all know, the forecasts of inflation and market supply and demand are not the same as weather forecast. If tomorrow is a holiday, people may all wish it to be a sunny day. However, nature has its own rules, and the rain might still come. The weather would not change with people's wishes. In contrast, it is not the case for the economy. Inflation expectation will lead to or even accelerate inflation. If there is an expectation of inflation in the society, it will be contagious that everyone would say that inflation is about to come. Accordingly, individuals as consumers and enterprises as suppliers or consumers, will change their consumption and investment behavior. For example, if each household wants to buy an extra bag of grain to prevent the increase of price, then the price of grain would indeed rise. If the company expects an increase in steel and coal prices, then indeed there could be a rise in prices of those materials. On the supply side, the company would be reluctant to sell and temporarily reduce their supply to wait for a better opportunity, which leads to less supply in the market. For the demand side, the company is willing to reserve more production materials, followed by more demand. Therefore, it can be seen that inflation expectations will make inflation come earlier.

Monetary policy, whether it is of aggregate or structural regulation, relies on timely decisions but not ongoing discussions. If it is repeatedly discussed without decision, people may have disordered expectations and change their consumption and investment behavior. Then the direction of the economy may change. In the comparison between aggregate and structural regulation, the former has a greater and more direct impact on expectations, while the latter has a more moderate impact. This is what monetary authorities need to consider.

34.3 Structural Regulations in Response to the Current Excessive Credit in China

According to the above analysis, excessive credit is mainly reflected in an inappropriate structure of credit. Although aggregate regulation has a certain effect, this structure could not be significantly improved. Therefore, under the current circumstances, structural regulation of monetary policy will be more effective, which usually includes the following measures.

First, given the fact that a large amount of credit has entered into the virtual economy but not the real economy, the available regulatory measure is to track the use of credit. Any credit that is not used as the original plan must be returned within a time limit. In some cases, there could even be penalties. In this way, it can not only restrict the flow of credit into the stock market and property market for speculation but also retrieve part or even most of the loans.

Second, with regard to the difficulty of obtaining credit for the SMEs and private enterprises, measures can be taken to target the following four aspects.

1. Establish small and medium-sized banks with private capital as the mainstay, including regional joint-stock commercial banks and village banks. Enterprises can be divided into large, medium, and small ones, and so can banks. Different types of banks mainly serve enterprises of similar size. Thus, there are clear groups of customers for small and medium-sized banks. It means it will be easier for the SMEs to get loans.

2. Establish guarantee companies and funds. Private guarantee companies shall be on equal status with state-owned ones, without differential treatment. In addition, local governments should support the establishment of guarantee funds, which can be raised in many ways to facilitate the SMEs and private enterprises to obtain loans.
3. Expand the scope of collaterals. At present, it is a policy to allow enterprise patents, intellectual property rights and brands to be collaterals, which will help the SMEs and private enterprises in the high-tech industry obtain loans. In addition, according to the survey conducted by the Private Economy Research Group of the CPPCC Economic Committee from May to June in 2009, in some places, large enterprises introduced "zero inventory management," with the SMEs providing raw materials and spare parts exclusively. Then when large enterprises need them, they would call on the SMEs. Those suppliers should deliver within 24 h, otherwise they would have to pay compensation or even void the contracts. As a result, large companies that implement "zero inventory management" could reduce their costs, while their suppliers, the SMEs, would have to increase their inventories and therefore need more funds. Even worse, large companies usually pay three or six months later after receiving the raw materials and spare parts. Therefore, the SMEs are more likely to be in shortage of funds. The solution to this problem is to allow the receipts of account receivables as collateral for loans.
4. Underground finance could operate legally after being guided and standardized, that is, being transformed from informal finance to formal finance. This would be of great help to the small and individual businesses. Then, with the normalization of underground finance, the investors can choose specific forms.

In addition, SMEs' own accounting systems should also be constructed and improved, with complete accounts in accordance with uniform standards. No bank is willing to lend to the SMEs with imperfect accounting systems. Banks or their credit staff should not be the only ones to be blamed.

Third, bank credit should be in strict accordance with national industrial policies in order to prevent industries with overcapacity from expanding blindly. If it is found that a company has transferred the loans to a production line or plans to build a new branch or workshop that has and is about to have overcapacity, the bank should withdraw the loan. This could eliminate the moral hazard and blind expansion of enterprises.

In addition to the above three targeted structural control measures for preventing excessive credit, the aggregate control policies usually adopted by the central bank can also function structurally, such as reserve ratio adjustment and interest rate adjustment.

Let's first talk about the adjustment of the reserve ratio. If the adjustment range of the reserve ratio is uniform across the country, it would fall under aggregate control, but it may have "one-size-fits-all" drawbacks. On the other hand, if the adjustment range varies among the regions, it could reflect the combination and coordination of aggregate and structural control. For example, implementing a differential adjustment of the reserve ratio for the central-western regions and the eastern regions may allow the former to receive more credit. Then the adjustment of the reserve ratio can still be effective in controlling the flow of money.

In terms of interest rate policy, differential interest rate policy is another form of the combination of aggregate and structural control, which can be based on different regions, industries, enterprise scales, and enterprise technology levels. More support for economically underdeveloped areas will promote their growth. Emerging and short-board industries could also be boosted in such way. The enterprises can be divided into extra-large, large, medium, and small (some experts suggest that small enterprises should be separated from micro-enterprises with fewer employees and less capital, which can be considered), so that there can be a certain difference in interest rates. Enterprises have differences in terms of technological level, so government should encourage and support those that adopt new technologies and are committed to independent innovation. For example, companies that have achieved significant results in adopting new technologies, energy saving, and emissions reduction can get preferential interest rates for bank credit, so can those enterprises that have major technological breakthroughs or have made great contributions in the fields of new energy, new materials, biotechnology, environmental protection, etc.

To put it succinctly, the aggregate control of monetary policy encompasses more than just the control measures themselves. The combination and coordination of aggregate and structural controls can achieve better results.

34.4 Three Issues About Liquidity and Its Impact on China's Economy

Recently, liquidity has been one of the concerns in the field of economics in China. How to assess liquidity scale and how much liquidity will affect China's economy are often controversial topics. Here, I want to talk about my views on this. Three issues will be discussed below.

(1) From the impact of the 2008 global financial crisis (GFC) on China's economy, it can be seen that excessive liquidity and insufficient liquidity sometimes coexist, and they will quickly change.

I found the case in the third quarter of 2008 by conducting a survey in some coastal cities. How can this phenomenon occur?

The third quarter of 2008 was a period when the impact of the GFC on China became apparent. By the end of the second quarter, the information we obtained had always been that there had been too much liquidity; by the beginning of the third quarter, however, we had heard that more and more companies had been short of funds; by the end of the third quarter, we heard companies complaining that the monetary condition was too tight and it was almost impossible to obtain funds. The survey results showed that although export companies were the most hit at the time, the decline in exports affected the entire industrial chain, which included the enterprises that supply raw materials, goods in process, spare parts, and services for the export enterprises. Therefore, enterprises in the entire industrial chain were impacted. Once the industrial chain was broken, the normal capital chain had also been broken.

As a result, the concept of "cash is king" quickly spread to many companies. Enterprises feared that a broken capital chain would bring adverse effects, so they held cash and avoided making quick moves. Abnormal corporate cash reserves had become corporate emergency measures. From the central bank's perspective, the amount of cash released was very large and the liquidity was abundant, but in fact the amount of cash actually circulating in the market was not too much, so companies generally exclaimed that there was insufficient liquidity. In this situation, in the second quarter of 2008, the series of measures to reduce liquidity and tighten money supply brought no benefits but more difficulties for the companies.

A lesson that can be summed up from this is: We must consider the reality of China's economy and understand its characteristics. Don't be obsessed with the flow analysis.

(2) The relationship between nominal interest rates, real interest rates, and corporate credit costs is complicated, which reflects another characteristic of China's economic operation.

Here the nominal interest rate refers to the lending rate stipulated by the central bank, that is, the interest rate used when enterprises borrow within the credit quota. Compared with the inflation rate, the nominal lending rate was relatively low, which was cost-effective for companies that can obtain loans at the nominal rate. However, the question is: How many companies can get loans at the nominal rate?

The actual interest rate refers to the lending rate negotiated by the borrower and the lender, that is, the lending rate determined by the market. Loans at this rate agreed by the borrower and lender are not limited by the credit quota. The actual interest rate is usually several percentage points higher than the nominal interest rate. Because companies usually run tight on funds and the credit quota is limited, they have to accept actual interest rates.

The cost of corporate credit refers to all expenses for the enterprises in obtaining bank loans, including the interest (either paid at the nominal rate or at the higher actual rate), the fees charged by the guarantee companies (if the loan is guaranteed), the loss of liquidity of the collateral when the loan is pledged and the resulting losses, as well as the expenditure on lobbying activities, etc. Therefore, the credit cost of enterprises is not only higher than the interests paid at the nominal rate but also higher than that at the actual rate.

The above analysis is based on the actual situation of China's economy in the process of economic transformation. In this regard, the credit quota set by the central bank plays an important role. On the one hand, if the quota is expanded, the gap between the actual rate and the interest rate would decrease, so would the cost of corporate credit. On the other hand, the expansion or reduction of credit quota will affect the inflation rate, which will directly affect the nominal interest rate. As a result, the actual interest rate and the cost of corporate credit will rise or fall accordingly.

From this point of view, the role of credit quota control in China's economy cannot be ignored. It affects the changes in nominal rates, actual rates, and corporate credit costs, and affects inflation expectations, and then the inflation rate. However, as pointed out earlier, China's economy is in a transitional stage, and the market-oriented reform of interest rates is still underway. Credit quota control is still necessary. It is not yet possible to allow credit to expand freely. But we should also be aware of the shortcomings of credit quota control. In particular, in the process of credit quota control, the central bank cannot make decisions based on the size of liquidity alone, because the latter is only one of the reference indicators. Financial authorities must also consider structural issues. A combination of aggregate and structural controls will be more effective and may reduce side effects. In this way, the nominal rate, the actual rate, and the cost of corporate credit could also be adjusted to a more reasonable level. Even if the gap between them exists, it may tend to be narrowed rather than expanded.

(3) Money flow analysis is helpful to clarify the causes of inflation, but it only explains the one caused by an excessive aggregate demand. It is difficult for it to explain the causes of cost-driven or structural inflations.

The cause of cost-driven inflation is mainly not related to aggregate demand, but to rising costs, including labor costs, land costs, and the prices of raw materials and fuel. The rising costs and insufficient supply caused by limited resources will inevitably lead to the rise of prices. The resultant inflation is defined as cost-driven inflation. In this case, the analysis of money flow cannot explain its main reason. Moreover, in fighting against cost-driven inflation, it is necessary to take measures to increase supply, which is often related to an increase in investment. If this type of inflation can be attributed to excessive aggregate demand, then the main measures taken should be to reduce liquidity, credit, and investment. However, these measures cannot contain this type of inflation. If the price policy is adopted at this time (restricting the increase in costs or freezing the price level), it is at best a temporary measure and certainly not sustainable. If the income policy is adopted at this time (restricting the increase in wage, that is, freezing the wage level or limiting an increase in profit rate), it is likely to generate dissatisfaction among wage earners and the investors, which could be more harmful to the economy. It is proved by the fact that the US government failed in curbing the cost-driven inflation by measures such as price control and income freezing in the early 1970s. The main cause of structural inflation lies in the imbalance of the industrial and product structures, which brings an excessive demand for some key products but an insufficient supply of some other key products. In this sense, structural inflation has the nature of both excessive demand and insufficient supply. Because structural inflation is driven by the rise in the prices of key products, it is difficult to solve the problem with the measures of reducing the aggregate demand. Furthermore, the aggregate analysis of whether liquidity is large or small cannot guide the effective countermeasures. Structural inflation should mainly be dealt with by measures that coordinate aggregate and structural controls. Meanwhile, industrial policies must be adjusted to curb excessive demand and increase the supply of some key products. The issue of economic system reform is bound to be relevant here. This is because the excessive demand for some products may be related to the government-led investment decisions, while the insufficient supply of some products may be related to the inappropriate resource pricing system and the industry monopoly system.

This once again confirms the limitations of money flow analysis and the aggregate control of monetary policy.

—Speech at the Economic Situation Seminar at the Guanghua School of Management, Peking University on January 15, 2010

Chapter 35
2011: Ten Questions About China's Economic Development

35.1 What if Capital Floods into the Asset Markets?

After the GFC, China's economy was the first to recover. However, there has been a large flow of capital into the asset markets rather than the real economy. To be sure, such phenomenon should be expected in the aftermath of each financial crisis when, despite indications of an economic rebound, the profitability of the real economy is not clear. Hence, investors remain hesitant, adopting a wait-and-see attitude. Therefore, a large amount of capital would flow into real estate, stock market, and other asset markets for speculation. This phenomenon has not entirely disappeared so far, leading to the formation of a bubble. If managed poorly, the bubble could burst and cause a double-dip recession. Therefore, many economists have been calling for vigilance against a double-dip recession over the past year.

The solution to this problem is to build up enough confidence for private enterprises and private capital to enter the real economy. The promulgation of the so-called 36 articles for the new non-public economy (Opinions on Encouraging and Guiding the Healthy Development of Private Investment [State Council, 2010 No. 13]) has created a suitable environment. For a long time, private enterprises have been worrying about unfair treatment and uncertain investment prospects. Therefore, it is practical and feasible to earnestly implement the Opinions and facilitate private capital flow to the real economy through institutionalized protections, thus reducing speculation in the asset markets.

35.2 How to Expand Domestic Demand?

Expanding domestic demand is crucial as we can no longer rely solely on investment or foreign trade to stimulate the economy. Although foreign trade is important, economic growth would not be sustainable if we relied too much on it. Investment

Y. Li, *China's Economy Since 1978*, China Academic Library,
https://doi.org/10.1007/978-981-95-5733-2_35

demand is only intermediate. The ultimate demand should be the consumption of the residents. There are many ways to expand domestic demand, among which the most important measure is to increase farmers' income. Some policy measures in this regard are more or less helpful but cannot address the fundamental issues, such as encouraging the purchase of home appliances by rural residents and providing subsidies for agricultural machinery and tools. Increasing the procurement prices of agricultural products can also be helpful, but the scale of the price hike has not been big enough. There are other policy measures in increasing rural income, but the most fundamental solution should be to grant property rights to farmers. Farmers have almost no properties. Even the houses built by themselves cannot be given any property certificates, which is an issue worthy of great attention. The Seventeenth Party Congress has stressed again that farmers should have asset income. In order to solve this problem, the first step is to issue property rights certificates to farmers. With the certificates in hand, the whole problem of expanding domestic demand will be solved.

On June 5, 2010, the experience of Jiading District of Shanghai appeared on the first page of *The Shanghai Mercury*. A new village was built after the demolition of the farmers' houses. Each household can get three moderate-sized apartments in 60, 80, and 110 square meters. They can choose to live in two of the three units, with the third as a rental property. All three units can be freely traded on the market after three years. This is the Shanghai experience. Now let us look at a rural community not far from the downtown area in the city of Weihai, Shandong Province. The "Story of a Small Town" community was formed by integrating several administrative villages. When the new village was built, each family got two apartments of 100 square meters in size. One is owner-occupied and the other is for rent. With property ownership certificates, farmers can rent their houses and thus significantly increase their income and expand domestic demand. Another experience comes from the countryside in the city of Laiyang, Shandong Province. Rural land is collectively owned, but farmers are given ownership certificates for their properties, which means they could use them as collateral to get loans for their production, thus expanding domestic demand.

35.3 How to Mitigate the Employment Pressure?

The main unemployment groups include laid-off workers, rural migrants, university graduates, the disabled, and emigrants from the reservoir areas. Therefore, it is necessary to reduce the employment pressure by vigorously promoting the SMEs, especially micro-enterprises. A micro-enterprise is an enterprise with no more than 20 employees, including the owners themselves, and with less than 100,000 yuan in initial capital. Micro-enterprises should be granted more preferential treatment, such as fiscal subsidies, tax exemptions, staff training, government guarantees for bank loans, simplification of registration procedures, fast-track opening of bank accounts, etc., which is conducive to encouraging entrepreneurship and creating jobs. Therefore, to address the employment issue, China must rely on the development of the private economy and micro-enterprises. Assuming there are many micro-enterprises, each of which employs 20 people, the employment pressure in China could be greatly lessened.

35.4 What Are the Critical Issues in the Transition of Economic Development Models?

Industrial upgrading and self-innovation play the central role in the transition of economic development model. The key is to cultivate a group of high-quality private enterprises that can lead innovation. The experience of Shenzhen suggests that the private economy has great potential for innovation. Thus, we need to exploit their potential and cultivate more high-quality private enterprises. At the same time, it is necessary to improve the existing capital market and develop new capital markets to establish a comprehensive capital system, including the main board, the SME board, the growth enterprise market (GEM) and the third board (trading ownership rights of unlisted companies), which is conducive to accelerating the transition of the Chinese economy.

35.5 How to Deal with the Current Increase in the Prices of Agricultural Products?

The current increase in agricultural product prices is a concern for everyone, especially the urban working class.

How can the price of agricultural products be stabilized? Increasing supply is the primary way. When the supply of agricultural products is insufficient, prices are bound to rise. To solve this problem, administrative price restriction is not a fundamental solution. Therefore, on the one hand, a differentiated credit policy should be implemented to develop agriculture and expand supply; on the other hand, private capital should be encouraged to enter into the vast rural areas. After that, the situation could be greatly improved.

35.6 How to Deal with the Fluctuations in the RMB Exchange Rate?

A sharp appreciation of the RMB is not feasible because its impact could be too severe for our economy to bear. However, a modest appreciation could be acceptable. Modest appreciation involves relaxing the upper and lower trading band, thereby allowing the market to play a more significant role and enabling a genuine two-way mechanism in which the RMB exchange rate could rise or fall.

China's international trade should be adjusted according to two aspects. First, the companies should adjust the export products and markets and make them more diversified according to changes in situations in international trade. Second, the government should facilitate domestic innovation, further broaden market entry, increase the involvement of private capital in high-end export industries, and earnestly implement the new 36 articles in the State Council Opinions. With the new upsurge of independent innovation, the industry will be further optimized and upgraded.

35.7 How Can Local Governments Address Urbanization and the Associated Livelihood Issues?

Currently, we are in the process of urbanization. We need to gradually solve the problems of people's livelihood in education, healthcare, public welfare, social security, and the improvement in broader living conditions. The key to solving these problems lies in the participation of private capital. Some pilot projects should be carried out in order, including issuing public construction investment funds and attracting private capital into the tertiary industry and public utilities. Private enterprises need to have expected returns from these investments. If the market is monopolized by the government and the SOEs, the urbanization process may be delayed forever.

35.8 How to Meet the Primary Demand for Housing of Residents Below the Middle-Income Level?

The central government has implemented a series of administrative measures to curb the excessive increase in housing prices and "limit speculative purchases." These measures are necessary but not enough. Housing supply should also be increased, especially low-rental housing and affordable housing. This alternative of public housing initiatives should be credited as being positive and effective for government regulation. However, the winning bidder in development should not be the one who offers the highest bid, for this will only drive up the land price, resulting in ever-rising property prices.

In my view, we should adopt the method of government procurement. The government should decide the price and areas of land as well as the specifications and quality of the houses according to citizens' purchasing power. The winning bidder should be the developer who offers the best quality at the lowest price.

35.9 What Is the Driver for China's Long-Term Economic Growth?

The main driving force for China's economic growth lies in fully mobilizing the enthusiasm of the people, which has been proven effective in China. For example, the rural household responsibility system in 1979, the rise of the TVEs, and the reform of joint-stock enterprises have all successfully motivated farmers' enthusiasm, the vast rural areas, and the people, respectively. Therefore, the driving force for China's economic growth still lies in the general public's enthusiasm. It is necessary to learn from previous experiences and lessons and avoid dampening the enthusiasm. We should promote mass entrepreneurship, encourage people to improve their quality of life and promote China's economic growth. Once the people's enthusiasm is fully mobilized, China's massive potential for economic growth can be realized.

35.10 How to Accelerate Ecological Development Amidst Economic Growth?

At present, the most critical task is to speed up ecological development. We should continue to implement the collective rights system for forests and to accelerate reforms to the property right system of state-owned forest farms.

After reforming the collective rights system for forests, farmers could start building plantations spontaneously. Many provinces, such as Hunan, Jiangxi, Fujian, and Yunnan, stipulated that the 70-year contract period remains unchanged, enabling the benefits to be passed on for generations. Hence, it is conducive to increasing individual income, meeting market demand, improving the environment, and stimulating the local forest rights system. Therefore, it is necessary to further advance the reform through pilot projects by the state-owned forest farms, which will form an ideal system in which economic and ecological development are equally important.

—*Globalization*, issue No. 1, 2011

Chapter 36
2012: Ten Comments on Expanding Domestic Demand

Recently at several Central Conferences on Economic Work, it has been emphasized that stimulating domestic demand is a much targeted decision. How to boost domestic demand? Here are my views.

36.1 Expanding Domestic Demand Mainly Refers to Boosting Private Consumption

Expanding domestic demand mainly refers to boosting private consumption, which means increasing the latter's contributions to the economic growth. Both expanding investment and government consumption can boost demand. However, compared with expanding private consumption, these approaches might incur certain restrictions and significant side effects, even long-term ones. There has been enough evidence from history.

36.2 Expanding Private Consumption Is a Gradual Process Which Can't be Done Overnight

Expanding private consumption is a gradual and continuous process. It is impossible and even detrimental to enhance private consumption capacity through quick fixes, such as relying on the government to distribute money or even plundering other countries, both of which would have very negative consequences. There are two lessons in history. The first example dates back to the end of the fourth century BC, when King Alexander of Macedonia took control of Greece and crossed the sea to attack the Persian Empire. The Persian Empire was destroyed, and the treasures in its palace were pillaged by King Alexander. How did he spend them? He distributed a

Y. Li, *China's Economy Since 1978*, China Academic Library,
https://doi.org/10.1007/978-981-95-5733-2_36

portion of them to each city in Greece (except Sparta, for it didn't support Alexander) and gave a lot of money to veterans for retirement. Officials were also dispensed a part of the treasures. As money flew into the society, consumer prices inevitably rose, leading to a century of continuous inflation in recorded history. Obviously, spending money in this way could cause only inflation, for the supply didn't increase at the same time. The second one happened in the sixteenth to the seventeenth centuries when Spain occupied Latin America (except Brazil). Some gold and silver ores had been exploited, which were shipped back to Spain and became the private properties of the royals, officials, and military officers. However, the domestic supply in Spain was insufficient, so the Spanish had to buy goods from France, the Netherlands and Britain, causing prices to rise in the whole of Western Europe for 200 years. It is the so-called "price revolution." These two examples tell us that we must gradually improve the private consumption capacity with economic growth and let the supply meet the demand. Only in this way can we achieve stable and balanced development.

36.3 There Must Be a Transition from Investment-Led to Private Consumption-Led Economic Growth

If we ignore the necessity of a transition and change abruptly, China's economic growth rate could decline sharply to 5 percent due to insufficient consumption capacity, which is unacceptable. Therefore, we must go through a transition stage first: From the stage of equal emphasis on investment and consumption to one that is led by private consumption. Are there any such examples in history? Yes. The most typical example occurred immediately after World War II. The growth in Western Europe and the United States had been depending equally on investment and consumption, which worked together to drive the economy for more than 20 years. This was because the war-ravaged economies of Western Europe urgently needed reconstruction. Why could they give equal values to consumption and investment? After being suppressed during the Great Depression of the 1930s, personal consumption rebounded in the post-World War II era. Families needed to rebuild their houses and buy cars. Under such circumstances, it was possible to give equal values to both consumption and investment. Therefore, if we want to expand domestic demand that is mainly supported by private demand, we should transit from the investment-led model to one that features equal importance of investment and consumption and ultimately to one led by private consumption.

36.4 To Increase the Earnings of the Low-Income People Is Currently the Main Task of Expanding Domestic Demand

Low-income families typically have a higher marginal propensity to consume, so we should help more of them become middle-income families. Moreover, the latter tend to have more diversified consumption patterns, whereas the former mainly focus on basic necessities such as food, clothing, and housing. Only in this way can we achieve stable long-term growth.

36.5 To Expand Domestic Demand, We Must First Eliminate the Worries of Low- and Middle-Income Families. This Requires Integrating the Urban and Rural Social Security Systems

During the great recession of the 1930s, a debate occurred in Western economics. At that time, the mainstream economics was the Neoclassical School. There were two economists, Lionel Robbins and Edwin Cannan. They argued that there was a way to solve the unemployment problem. If one's work was to be done by two, one's salary would be divided into two, and one's meal would be for two, then the problem would be solved. However, a young Swedish economist, Karl Gunnar Myrdal, together with his colleagues, submitted a report to the Swedish government, arguing that the solution to the social problems in Sweden must first be to eliminate the worries of the everyday people. The specific policy proposed was to construct large-scale affordable houses and low-rental houses, which could be sold or rented out for the people in need. This policy, together with unemployment relief, free education, public healthcare, and pension, started the age of Sweden as a welfare state.

After the end of World War II, Western economists once again met to discuss whose judgments were right in the early 1930s, when Keynesianism was yet to emerge. Everyone agreed that the Neoclassical School was wrong while the Swedish School was right. What was wrong with the Neoclassical School? Sharing one's work, food, and money between two people does not increase the society's purchasing power. It was merely an internal corporate approach to address employment issues and was ineffective in addressing broader social unemployment. The Swedish School was right in this regard. To increase consumption, it's necessary to address consumers' concerns. The increase in consumption would then generate demand for more jobs and then income for new employees. The increased income would in turn lead to more consumption, and this process will continue in positive cycles. This is the employment multiplier theory.

36.6 Let Farmers Have Property Incomes

It is important to raise farmers' income and expand private consumption. Households' property rights must be protected by law. In recent years, the reform to the collective rights on forests has been carried out. The forest rights have been granted to the households, and the forest right certificates have been issued to the farmers. In this way, the enthusiasm of the farmers can be mobilized. For example, if the protection of property rights is limited only to the village level in the rural areas, it would not have had the impact as today.

36.7 To Establish Small and Micro Enterprises Is an Important Way to Expand Domestic Demand

Small and micro enterprises are fundamental to various types of private entrepreneurship. To mobilize their enthusiasm, government support, including financial assistance, is necessary. Farmers' family orchards, vegetable sheds, workshops, farms, and forestry centers are all small and micro enterprises directly connected to the market. Farmers' income can be increased through the operations on their own forestry centers, vegetable sheds, orchards, and farms. In this way, the rural economy will gain vitality, so will small towns' economy.

36.8 To Keep Vertical Mobility in Unblocked Channels Is an Important Measure to Increase Residents' Income

After the 1970s, a dual labor market theory emerged in the Western economics community. What is the dual labor market? It refers to a market divided into an upper labor market and a lower labor market. The occupations in the upper labor market are good, while those in the lower labor market are bad. What is the difference between "good" occupations and "bad" occupations? Good occupations are well paid while bad ones are poorly paid. Compared with the bad occupations, the good ones have more welfare, career prospects and opportunities for promotion. What's more, good occupations could enable one to continue to learn knowledge and enhance personal capabilities, while bad occupations are simply repetitive work. There may exist a situation in China today where social mobility channels are blocked. Parents are engaged in a job, their children and grandchildren would do the same job, which means parents and children are hereditary. Farmers could work outside of their villages, but they are still rural migrant workers from generation to generation. What can we do if these mobility channels are blocked? How can we avoid the solidification of social classes? First, we must create an environment of fair competition where everyone competes for employment and is recruited based on qualifications. In addition, we should continually increase the number of good occupations and gradually upgrade the bad ones. For example, it is possible to increase wages, raise service standards, improve the working environment, provide learning opportunities, etc. These are all beneficial to increasing the income of farmers and low-income earners.

36.9 To Increase Education Investment and Improve on an Even Distribution of Education Resources

Without sufficient investment, especially in education, private consumption cannot be effectively promoted. The unbalanced distribution of educational resources is a significant issue, which in turn leads to unbalanced employment opportunities. Unbalanced employment can further lead to income inequality, resulting in a more stratified society. In such a society, the next generation would start from an unequal position.

36.10 To Change the Identification of Luxury Goods

The perception of luxury goods should gradually evolve with the times. Thirty years ago, wearing gold chains or pearl necklaces and using cosmetics were considered signs of a luxurious lifestyle. But nowadays, when people travel abroad, especially to Europe, they tend to buy many items, including luxury goods, also known as "high-end consumer goods." This trend is hard to resist. Instead of encouraging overseas consumption, it would be better to create favorable conditions for domestic purchases. Therefore, the import taxes on these products should be reduced. The premise is that the definition of luxury goods must be adjusted to keep pace with the times.

—*Xinhua Wenzhai*, issue No. 7, 2012

Chapter 37
2013: Discussions on China's Dual Transformation

37.1 China Has Been Gradually Achieving Dual Transformation

According to traditional development economics, economic transformation refers to the shift from an agricultural society to an industrial society. The implementation of the planned economy is considered to be another way to an industrial society, which the Soviet Union has practiced after the October Revolution.

China's experience from the 1950s to the 1970s proved that the attempt to transition to an industrial society through a planned economy was unsuccessful because in a developing country like China, setting up several large industrial enterprises was possible, but it was too inefficient and costly. In addition, the issues associated with the traditional agricultural society have not been solved but rather solidified in new forms. Agricultural development was a failure, leaving the countryside still in a backward state, farmers' life still hard, and their freedom remained restricted.

Since 1979, China has entered into a dual transformation process, which refers to the combination and overlap of institutional and development transformations.

What is institutional transformation? It refers to the transformation from a planned economy to a market economy.

What is development transformation? It means transformation from the traditional agricultural society to the industrial society.

The combination or overlap of the two kinds of transformations was unprecedented and has not been discussed in traditional development economics. After World War II, in some newly independent developing countries, where the planned economy had not been practiced in the past, there was only development transformation, i.e., the gradual transformation from traditional agricultural societies to the industrial ones. However, this was not the case in China after 1979. On the one hand, China had to break the shackles of the planned economy and replace it with a market economy, which was the institutional transformation. However, on the other hand, China needed

Y. Li, *China's Economy Since 1978*, China Academic Library,
https://doi.org/10.1007/978-981-95-5733-2_37

to transform from a traditional agricultural society to an industrial society, growing into a modern country, which is called the development transformation.

In the past 30 years of reform and development since 1979, China has accumulated some experiences in the process of carrying out the dual transformation, which can be summarized into the following eight aspects.

First, the priority in dual transformation should be given to institutional transformation, that is, transitioning from a planned economy to a market economy, and driving development transformation through institutional transformation. This is because there are a lot of shackles and restrictions imposed by the planned economy on China's development, such as those between urban and rural areas, industry and agriculture, and among city dwellers and farmers. Without breaking those shackles and restrictions, China will not be able to transform from a traditional agricultural society to an industrial society and will not achieve the goal of making China a modern country.

Second, we must liberate our minds and eliminate the influence of planned economy theories; otherwise, the reform and development would be difficult. In 1978, the great debate in China that "practice is the sole criterion for testing truth" liberated people's minds and launched the reform and opening-up. In early 1992, Comrade Deng Xiaoping's speech on his visit to the south further liberated people's minds and led China to the rapid reform and development. Therefore, it can be said that the reason why China's dual transformation has had such outstanding achievements in a short period of more than 30 years is inseparable from "liberating thoughts first."

Third, clarifying property rights must be the priority of the reform. Under the planned economy, vague property rights, uncertain investment subjects, and unclear rights and responsibilities of investors pose severe obstacles to reform and development. Therefore, property rights reform is the breakthrough and the mainline in the institutional transformation, while the definition and clarity of property rights are the driving force. For the vast majority of farmers, land and housing rights also need to be confirmed for each household, which will help protect the legitimate rights and interests of farmers and enable them to obtain property incomes that can be used to expand reproduction and start business.

Fourth, improving people's livelihoods should go hand in hand with economic growth. Improving people's livelihood is critical to narrow the income gap between urban and rural residents and local governments. Among macroeconomic policy objectives, employment is the top priority and cannot be overlooked at any time because the transfer of rural labor force to cities is an urgent problem that needs to be seriously solved in the dual transformation. At the same time, new jobs are created as the economy develops, so the economy needs to maintain a specific growth rate. Too high an economic growth rate certainly is not feasible, but too low rate would result in higher employment pressure.

Fifth, in the dual transformation, the competitiveness of enterprises should be continuously enhanced, with self-innovation at its core. The inadequacy of self-innovation ability will lead to the inadequacy of corporate competitiveness. With the international competition becoming increasingly fierce, China will undoubtedly lose its market share, or return to the previous situation of relying on the export of resources and primary products to obtain foreign exchange, making it difficult for China to achieve the goal of modernization. Moreover, the effectiveness of self-innovation depends not only on the protection of intellectual property rights but also on the training and motivation of professional and technical personnel. Therefore, human resource policies should be paid more attention to and implemented more effectively.

Sixth, China faces more prominent environmental pressures than countries that achieved modernization and industrialization earlier. Therefore, China must attach importance to the sustainable development of the economy and the society in the dual transformation. Experiences since 1979 have taught us that, although a country's economic growth is essential, improving the quality of this growth is even more critical. One indicator of the quality of economic growth is the improvement in economic structure, and others are environmental protection, energy conservation and emission reduction, rational use of resources, and a cleaner production. We and our future generations share the environment and resources. Only by pursuing sustainable development can we enjoy brighter prospects for development.

Seventh, the increase in urbanization has been both a result of the dual transformation and a driver for its continued progress. Under the planned economy, the urbanization process was prolonged. In some years, there was even an "anti-urbanization" trend, of which farmers were not allowed to go to the cities and some urban residents were forced to move to the countryside. It was not until the dual transformation began that things turned better. Therefore, it is inevitable to increase the degree of urbanization, which will be the most promising investment opportunity over the next few years, and ensure that China's economic growth will continue advancing at a high speed.

Eighth, vigorously promoting the private economy in the dual transformation can ease employment pressure while mobilizing the initiatives of the private sector and unleashing the potential of the private capital. Whether "the state advances" or "the private advances," the relationship between private enterprises and SOEs should not be dictated by state's policy. The state's policy is the joint development of the SOEs and the private enterprises. There should be cooperation and competition, thus forming a win-win situation in the country's best interests.

The above eight experiences illustrate how China's dual transformation has progressed step by step. However, in general, the above aspects show one thing: China has its national conditions, and there would be no experience if the transformation has not been implemented according to the national conditions.

37.2 To Continuously Promote Development Transformation through Institutional Transformation

China has not finished dual transformation yet. The reform and development need to be deepened and to reach new levels.

Then, has the relationship between reform and development changed? The answer is no. We should continue driving development through institutional transformation, as we have done for more than 30 years; we will continue promoting development through reform that paves the way for development. Three aspects will be discussed below.

1. Endogenous and Exogenous Forces

What is an endogenous force? It refers to the forces originating within a system and its mechanisms. Reform aims to remove obstacles to establishing new systems or mechanisms.

What is an exogenous force? It refers to external forces that affect economic operations by intervening in economic activities or by stimulating or restraining them. The purpose of reform is to reduce the intervention of exogenous force to an average level, preventing it from weakening the system's self-regulation and its mechanisms.

Take one's health as an example. One who can live and work healthily must have a perfect endogenous mechanism. If one gets sick, the endogenous regulatory mechanism can overcome the obstacle and restore health. Exogenous forces are like drugs or surgery if necessary and are of less importance compared with endogenous forces.

Although we have carried out reform and opening-up for more than 30 years, our endogenous forces are still not sound, and we mainly rely on exogenous forces to regulate the economy. For example, there is a phenomenon of "investment impulse cycle" in China. In recent years local governments and institutions have clear incentives in speeding up development through more investment, projects, and credit. With the increase of investment and projects, credit has been expanded and the economy has grown, resulting in inflation. The central government has relied on the exogenous forces to curb inflation, which has made it difficult for local governments. As fiscal revenue and output fell, enterprises were depressed, and employment also decreased. The central government has had no choice but to initiate regulation of exogenous force again to stimulate the economy and restore rapid economic growth. This cycle has gone over and over again. The economy would go up for a while, and then be depressed, indicating that the endogenous force has not played a positive role, and the exogenous force has to some extent replaced it.

Continuously advancing the reform is to improve the institutional system so that its endogenous mechanisms can play their due role and the regulation of the exogenous force becomes supplementary.

2. Phased Achievements and the Target Goal

Over the past 30 years since 1979, we have achieved remarkable progress in reform and opening-up. However, these achievements are just phased results, and we have not achieved the target goal. Our target goals are clear. From the perspective of institutional transformation, our target goal is to establish a complete socialist market economic system. From the perspective of development transformation, our target goal is to realize industrialization, establish a modern society, and make a society of common prosperity and harmony. Reform must be deepened, and development must be redoubled. We cannot slacken our efforts or give up halfway. If we do, we may lose everything.

It is essential to know that many economic problems cannot be solved only by macroeconomic regulation but by the continuation and deepening of reform. For example, the "social class solidification" phenomenon is now worse than it was in the early years of the reform and opening-up. At the initial stage of reform and opening-up, the social mobility channels for college graduates from 1977 to 1979 were unobstructed. Vertical and horizontal social mobility is the primary way to incentivize people. However, "social class solidification" has now caused the blockage of horizontal, but mainly vertical mobility channels, which has led to another phenomenon, namely "career inheritance." For example, if the father is a rural migrant worker, the son would still be a migrant worker, and the grandson would also be a migrant worker in the future, which is a manifestation of "social class solidification" and "career inheritance." This situation cannot be solved by macro-regulation but only by structural transformation.

Moreover, the urban-rural dual system still exists. The planned economy has two pillars: the SOEs and the urban-rural dual system. In the past 30 years, the reform has mainly focused on the SOE system, which has made significant progress so far. Of course, there are still some issues to be solved. Although the issues of urban-rural dual system have been dealt with in the past, they are mainly unresolved.

The urban-rural dual system is different from the urban-rural dual structure. The dual structure has existed since ancient times and will exist for a long time in the future. But the dual system is the product of the planned economy. In 1958, the household registration was split into rural and urban regimes. Rural and urban household registration were segregated, and neither rural nor urban registration could be changed freely. This division isolated farmers from the cities and greatly hindered economic development. However, breaking the dual system cannot only rely on macroeconomic regulation. Reform must be deepened in order to change the status quo.

In short, a phased result is not our target goal.

3. Consider all Things and Make Overall Arrangements

As has already been pointed out, China's transformation from a planned economy to a socialist market economy is unprecedented in the world and must be explored and moved forward by ourselves. There was a vivid saying of "crossing the river by touching the stones." This was accurate at the time, but it may not be applicable anymore. Why? Because once the water is too deep to reach the stone, how can we move forward? If the stones on the riverbed are not evenly distributed, what if we touch the stones but go in a wrong destination?

Therefore, it is essential to consider the entire situation when planning comprehensive strategies. A reformist leader must stand atop, see ahead, think deeply, and have the vision, courage, and decision. This is now referred to as top-level design, which is also the target goal of the reform.

Take the reform of the collective forest rights as an example. In the initial stage of the reform and opening-up, some rural areas have undergone the contract reform without allocating the collective forests. However, forests were allocated to individuals in some rural areas, resulting in severe deforestation because it was at the beginning of the reform and opening-up when many farmers lacked confidence in CPC's policies and were afraid of change. Many of them cut the trees down after the allocation. As a result, the central government had to stop granting rights to collective forests. The reform of the collective forest rights has been overdue, which should have been implemented more than twenty years ago. In 2003, the reform of the collective forest rights was carried out first in Fujian and Jiangxi Provinces, and the central government released related documents on June 8, 2008, a decision to promote the reform to the entire country.

This reform has three innovations. First, to allocate property rights of the forests to each family, rather than to each village, or countryside, or forestry cooperatives and associations organized by authorities, as some in the academia had suggested. The reality proved that farmers' incentives could only be induced by the allocation of property rights to individuals. Second, the rights can be mortgaged. If farmers have the rights to manage their allocated forests, they could become richer by raising chickens in the forest, growing medicinal herbs, and producing mushrooms and fungus, making every family forest farm into small enterprises. If the asset could be revitalized, everything could be revitalized. Third, the contract period for the allocated forestland is 70 years. Moreover, the texts of the farmland contract were permanently fixed, but for how long exactly? The farmers were still not at ease. At the same time, collective woodland is set as 70 years in contract period, when the third generation could grow up. Therefore, the incentives for planting trees have increased because the later generations can enjoy the benefits. In conclusion, the reform of the collective forest rights is an overall arrangement. If there is decision by the central government, how do the local governments dare to have this on trial?

Many issues need to be considered and done when it comes to overall planning, including how to reform the financial system and the fiscal decentralization system, and determine the management system of the SOEs. Of course, pilot reforms will still be applied in the future, but it is important to consider from the above with a strategic vision.

37.3 Structural Adjustments in Dual Transformation

There is no end for structural adjustment. With the progress of science and technology, the changes in consumption habits and concepts, the changes in domestic and foreign situations, as well as the rich experience in management and the improvement in the quality of management personnel, today's structural optimization only represents the current stage of structural optimization, not the understanding of economic optimization in the future. From this point of view, structural optimization is always relative, and the adjustment will continue.

Although different stages have different standards for structural optimization, the concept of emerging industries persists in any period of development. Therefore, structural optimization should conform to the reality of each stage and take the development of emerging industries as one of the measurements for the degree of structural optimization. In any period of development, there have been the overcapacity industries and under-capacity industries. Therefore, structural optimization should be measured by the increase or decrease in the proportion of the output value of these industries in the GDP, and only a decrease in the proportion of these industries represents structural optimization. On the contrary, an increase in the proportion of these industries represents structural deterioration. Therefore, to discuss China's structural adjustment at this stage, we must first focus on the development of the emerging industries, the decrease in the proportion of the industries of overcapacity and under capacity, and the rise in the proportion of the industries with basically balanced capacity.

Another issue in the process of dual transformation that deserves our attention is that structural adjustments must move toward cleaner production, a circular economy, and a low-carbon economy. High-polluting, energy-consuming, and resource-consuming industries need to undergo a technological transformation, and some of them need to be eliminated to prevent further damage to the environment and an excessive consumption of resources. Therefore, China must be determined in environmental governance. Otherwise, it will not be easy to maintain sustainable social and economic development.

In the process of dual transformation, the rationalization of regional economic structure is also an essential issue in structural adjustment. According to China's situation, the imbalance in regional development has been caused by natural conditions as well as historical and cultural factors. As a result, the gaps in terms of development and residents' income are widening between the Eastern and Western regions. Therefore, policies leaning to the Western region must be carried out to alleviate and gradually reverse the trend of widening regional disparities, helping the Western region promote development through preferential policies. The two most important measures for adjusting regional economic structure are to promote the transfer of industries to the West and to change the situation in which the Western region only depends on exporting resources.

As for the industrial transfer, it is mainly related to the efforts of reducing costs in manufacturing enterprises, especially the labor-intensive ones. For example, the cost of labor, land, construction, logistics, etc. has been rising gradually with industrialization. The less developed regions become the hosts of inter-regional industrial transfer because they have relatively affluent labor, land, and mineral resources and can use these advantages to attract industrial transfer to accelerate the development of the region and increase local revenue and employment. In the industrial transfer, institutional reform remains the most important because the system decides the policies. Only in this way can responsible, efficient, honest, and law-abiding officials be promoted to their posts. Only in this way can the economy of the less developed areas prosper. At the same time, due to the transfer of industries to less developed areas, the economic structure of developed areas can better take their advantages, make more significant achievements in self-innovation and industrial upgrading, and continue enhancing the competitiveness of local enterprises.

How to transform the Western regions and some less developed regions in the eastern developed provinces also need to be discussed. In the past, the development of the West was only about exporting resources. A new arrangement based on the nature of the systems and the policies for these regions needs to be made. For example, revenue could be improved by developing local processing industries to increase output. Besides, the cultivation of local private enterprises must be accelerated in the process of industrial transfer and the development of resource processing industries in the Western and less developed regions because key workers and managerial personnel with management experience would come from the developed areas along the industrial transfer. However, enterprises supplying raw materials and marketing the outputs do not necessarily move in. Therefore, in the West and other less developed areas, local enterprises that can support and serve the transferred enterprises are in need, which will depend on the efforts of local private entrepreneurs. Moreover, industrial transfer and development resources provide several business opportunities for processing enterprises, which are often instantaneous. If local private enterprises do not seize these opportunities, the private enterprises from other areas will soon get these opportunities.

Moreover, relocating industries to the West and other less developed areas is only one stage in the regional economic restructuring. With the less developed regions hosting the transferred enterprises from developed regions, it is bound to promote the industrial upgrading of local enterprises and the transferred enterprises, which is an unstoppable trend. That is to say, developed regions are ready to transfer enterprises to the less developed regions to take advantage of these regions' resources and their market prospects. Once the industrial transfer happens, these industries will sooner or later be upgraded to improve their competitiveness, develop a larger market volume and gain more market shares, which also means that the structural adjustment in this case cannot be limited to industrial transfer but may include future industrial upgrading.

The structural adjustment may involve stock adjustment or increment adjustment, each with its own advantages and disadvantages. Generally speaking, stock adjustment is often quicker, with noticeable effects. However, its impact could be very significant, making this kind of adjustment difficult. A typical example is that if enterprises are forced to shut down, stopping some business or products would hurt local fiscal revenue and local employment. Therefore, the local government has to adopt "nominal shutdown instead of real shutdown." The increment adjustment refers to structural adjustment as the economy grows and government revenue continues to rise. The disadvantages lie in the slow effect and long delay, but it also has advantages.

First, the economy still maintains a specific growth rate, thus providing better conditions for structural adjustment, which prevents more enterprises from going bankrupt or closing down and causing more unemployment. Second, under the condition of economic and revenue growth, more investment expenditure can be used to improve technology, to realize structural adjustment in the process of industrial upgrading, and to realize economic transformation in a relatively stable environment.

A practical approach could be that the economy still maintains a specific growth rate, so does the fiscal revenue then the implementation of increment adjustment could be carried out. At the same time, some enterprises with heavy pollution and energy consumption should be selectively forced to close or stop making certain products. In conclusion, incremental adjustment is more feasible compared with stock adjustment.

37.4 Macro-regulation Should Be Moderate and Preventive in the Dual Transformation

As pointed out in the relationship between the endogenous and the exogenous economic forces, the former should play a significant role. In contrast, the exogenous force should play a supplementary role in deepening the reform, which can be done step by step in a dual transformation. This is in accord with the requirement of establishing a perfect market economy.

The first problem lies in the correct orientation of government functions. The government cannot be omnipotent, and its role in regulating the economy is limited in any case. There are too many variables in the economy, whose influences over economic operations are often uncertain and unpredictable. Moreover, the information the government could access is always limited. The government cannot acquire all the information in a short period of time. Even if more information can be obtained in an extended period, the actual situation may have changed during this period, and part of the information the government has would definitely be out of date. Therefore, governments generally make decisions on the basis of incomplete information, which is one of the inevitable limitations of its macro-regulation.

Another inherent challenge in macroeconomic regulation is the need for the government to balance the interests of the public. The government is usually in a passive position because there is one government but there are thousands of people. Millions of eyes are upon the government, but the government cannot keep its eyes upon millions of people. Therefore, every policy made by the government would trigger a public response, or in other words, as soon as the policies are released, the countermeasures of the public follow immediately. Many people, whether investors, consumers, or depositors, deal with the effect of government policy by choosing their responses based on their expectations. This suggests that the expectations and countermeasures from all walks of life can make the government passive.

Another inevitable limitation in the government's macro-regulation is how to control the scale of the measures. Public decision-making is always under the condition of incomplete information, and public policy is always in a passive position, so macro-regulation tends to be excessive. If the policy is tightened, the market would become rigid. If the policy is relaxed, the market would become chaotic because the government always believes in its capacity. Once the government cuts back the regulation, the economy would suffer and business would lose their vitality. Then if the government switches from tightening to easing in afraid of hurting the economy, the investment would be overheated, credit would be swelled, and inflation would surge. So again, the government feels the need to tighten.

In the dual transformation, this kind of fluctuation between tightness and looseness, and between stagnation and chaos, occurs repeatedly due to both the imperfection of the market mechanism and the incorrect positioning of government functions.

The conclusion can only be drawn that, based on the achievements in the dual transformation so far, the government's role should be more accurately defined. We cannot consider the government omnipotent like in the past. The government should follow market rules and avoid disrupting the normal expectations of investors, consumers, and depositors. There should be no significant tightening or loosening, or drastic fluctuations in conducting macro-regulation. Otherwise, either it would lead to bubbles in the economy, or the bubbles in the economy would burst suddenly. All these would hurt the economy and undermine public confidence in macroeconomic regulation.

In economic operation, there will be an omen of abnormal operation. Even if the government's information is always patchy, it can still pick up signs that the economy may not be doing well. Therefore, the government's macro-regulation should be moderate in nature, taking as few aggregate control measures as possible and focusing on structural regulation measures instead. The latter would cause less shock than full-scaled measures with more significant impact.

In the future, macro-regulation should be not only moderate but also be preventive. Therefore, it is essential to choose a starting point of macro-regulation. In the past, the timing to launch macro-regulation was often lagging, and the timing to conclude was even more likely to lag. These two kinds of delays will cause losses to the national economy and increase the difficulties of managing the economy in the future.

In macroeconomic operations, the government's regulation was originally aimed at adjusting aggregate demand, which mainly applies to the short-term adjustment of unemployment and inflation. However, since the 1970s, due to stagflation in the United States, only adjusting demand or focusing on short-term adjustment could not solve the problem. As a result, the United States, followed by other countries, shifted the macro-regulation from a simple adjustment in aggregate demand to an equal emphasis on demand and supply, from short-term adjustment to an equal emphasis on short-term and medium-term, and from aggregate regulation to an equal emphasis on aggregate and structure. As a result, this has become the common approach for developed market economies to regulate the economy, which could be used as a reference in China's dual transformation.

In China, the main reason for the lag in macro-regulation is that the government does not have complete information, and more importantly, the government often fails to sift through the information it has. Therefore, the government is easy to be disillusioned by the good news, rather than the bad news, reported by various regions and departments, while many real situations in economic operation may not be understood by the government so the macro-control is often lagging. Therefore, for future macro-regulation, the government should learn from past experiences, grasp the actual economic situation as much as possible, and emphasize the importance of preventive measure, making the latter equally important with policy fine-tunings.

Finally, the price-fixing policy in macro-regulation also needs to be reconsidered. If we continue our institutional transformation, we must understand the limits of the price-fixing policies, as they can undermine the functions of market mechanisms. In addition, commodity prices always affect each other and are also the cost of each other. In macro-regulation, price caps are sometimes imposed to prevent commodity prices from surging. However, experiences show that a price cap policy is only effective in the short term and may bring uncertain damages to the economy, inevitably making the structural imbalance more prominent and more serious. The reason is that prices cannot be regulated for all commodities, but only for those of a few. In this case, the costs of commodities are interrelated, so that some commodities whose prices cannot float, could only be reduced in supply under a price cap, together with those of other commodities whose prices can float. This would cause disruptions in the supply chain and economic structure and bring a series of difficult problems to the economy.

Controlling resource prices has similar consequences. The resource supply is absolutely not unlimited, be it land, water, minerals, or labor. Although China's labor resources are relatively sufficient, there is still a limited supply if it is classified by age, type of skills involved, professional expertise, and living area. Therefore, in terms of land, water, and mineral resources, the rules of use and allocation cannot be entirely formulated according to market demand. If necessary, the government can implement quota regimes. However, quota management has its advantages and disadvantages and cannot be used randomly. Otherwise, it may be harmful to the economy. As for the price adjustment of resource products, the reality of their limited supply should be considered. Price adjustment may also lead to the breakdown of the industrial chain, distortion in the current structure, and even more severe structural imbalances. Therefore, the most effective countermeasure to address the unreasonable prices of resource products is to promote the reform of the resource pricing system. Only through this reform can we make the prices of resources reasonable and avoid adverse consequences.

This once again confirms the primary role of institutional transformation in the dual transformation.

—*China Market*, issue No. 1, 2013

Chapter 38
2014: Discussing Several Issues on Property Rights Reform

In recent years, I have been concerned with the issues related to property rights reform. Here, in line with the spirit of *the Decision of the CPC Central Committee on Some Major Issues Concerning Comprehensively Deepening the Reform (hereinafter referred to as the Decision)* adopted at the Third Plenary Session of the 18th CPC Central Committee, I would like to discuss some issues in the property rights reform.

38.1 Property Rights: No Property Rights, no Market Economy

One of the most critical practical issues in implementing the Decision is defining property rights. Without this definition, no real market players can exist, not to mention a market economy.

The issues of property rights and market players in an unbalanced economy were elaborated in my book *Chinese Economy in Disequilibrium*, written in the late 1980s and published in the early 1990s. Generally, disequilibrium is a common phenomenon and is composed of two categories: One is the disequilibrium in capitalist countries, which is mainly caused by market imperfection (such as monopoly); the other is like China's disequilibrium (besides market imperfection, there is also a lack of genuine market players). Why is there a lack of market players? Because property rights are not clarified and not defined. Without defining property rights, there could not be genuine market players. Therefore, the main point I put forward then was the reform of the shareholding system. In my view, this is the most effective way to clarify property rights. Only with clear property rights can market players exist, so that China can embark on the path to a market economy.

The reform of property rights in China has not been completed yet. Why? Although the property rights reform of the SOEs has made considerable progress, it is yet to be completed, and further efforts are needed. In addition, from a national perspective, the

Y. Li, *China's Economy Since 1978*, China Academic Library,
https://doi.org/10.1007/978-981-95-5733-2_38

property rights of farmers have still yet to be clearly defined. Lots of farmers, growing and selling agricultural products, are supposed to be market players. However, they haven't become real market players so far because there are both no defined property rights and consequently no property income.

To accelerate the development of the socialist market economy, we still need to promote the reform of property rights. If we do not properly solve the problem of farmers' property rights and do not continue to address other issues in the SOE reform, it would be difficult for our market economy to become effective. Therefore, *the Decision* points out that "We should improve the modern property rights system with clear ownership, definite rights and responsibilities, strict protection and smooth circulation." These are necessary requirements for promoting the socialist market system.

38.2 The Confirmation of Land Rights: The Most Important Part of Rural Reform

"Rural collective profit-oriented construction land is allowed to be sold, leased, or bought as shares, and has the same prices and rights as those of the state-owned land." "Improve the secondary market for land lease, transfer, and mortgage." These provisions in *the Decision* are of great significance to promoting rural reform and further solving the "Sannong" issues (agriculture, countryside, and farmers). At present, where should rural reform start? What is the most important part of the reform? I think it's the confirmation of land rights. Shortly after the 18th CPC National Congress last year, I led an investigation group from the Economic Committee of the CPPCC National Committee to do a survey on land rights confirmation in three counties of Hangzhou, Jiaxing, and Huzhou in Zhejiang Province. After the investigation and discussion, we listened to the report of the municipal governments and thought that the confirmation of land rights was indeed a major reform that was welcomed by the farmers.

1. Farmers feel much more relieved. As for the confirmation of land rights, the farmers said, "We are no longer afraid that other people will occupy the land at will. The management rights to the contracted land, the operational rights to the residential land, and the property rights to the houses on the residential land have all been clarified. Can one occupy my land at will? Can one tear down the house without our consent? One dares not!" The transfer of land also makes the farmers feel relieved. We should know that the transfer of rural land has been rare up to now. Because in the past, if farmers pooled land into shares, they would be afraid that the land would be owned by others. Now it is different. After the confirmation of land rights, the shares of the farmers are guaranteed. After the land is leased, the property rights remain unchanged, so the farmers are relieved.

2. The gap between the per capita income of urban and rural residents has significantly narrowed. For example, the report from Jiaxing made it clear that before land rights were confirmed, the ratio of urban to rural per capita income was 3.1:1, and it was 1.9:1 after the confirmation of land rights according to the survey. Why did it narrow so much? When we held a symposium in the countryside, we heard some farmers say: "After the land rights were confirmed, I feel reassured. On the one hand, I expanded the planting and the breeding. On the other hand, the old houses on my residential land were pulled down to build new houses with several floors." In the village we visited during our research, many farmers built four-story houses. I asked a farmer, "Isn't it too large for you to live in?" The farmer replied, "My family has few members and two floors would be enough to live in. The first floor is rented out to others to open shops or workshops, and one of the other three floors can also be rented out, with different prices for different floors. The tenant can choose any floor. In this way, I can get rental income. In addition, I am not afraid of the rental because the land rights have been confirmed. After the land transfer, I can go out to work." All these suggest that the urban-rural income gap is narrowing.
3. Another unexpected benefit is the increase in the area of cultivated land. This is because the land has to be remeasured before the confirmation of land rights, and then we find that the area of cultivated land has increased by 20 percent. How can this happen? The main reasons are as follows: First, at the beginning of the contract system, there was a big difference in land quality, so one unit of fertile land was regarded as one unit, and two units of infertile land were regarded as one unit. After 30 years of contracting and intensive farming, there is little difference in land quality. Therefore, at the time of remeasurement before the confirmation of land rights, one unit of land is regarded as one unit, leading to more cultivated land area. Second, in the past, the land was divided into small plots with ridges and people farmed with cattle. When the land was originally measured, the ridges were not counted as cultivated land, and the area where there was no sunshine on both sides of the ridges was not considered as cultivated land, either. Now, the ridges have been removed, and the farmers use tractors to plow, so there is more cultivated land. Third, farmers had to pay agricultural taxes previously, so the villagers basically understated the area of cultivated land. For example, if a family had 1.3 units of land, they would report 1 unit of land, and so would other families. Now it's different. Farmers don't have to pay agricultural taxes. Everyone reports according to the actual area when the land was remeasured. No one lies or underreports because underreporting would lead to self-losses. The less land area is reported, the fewer shares it will be, and the less land area can be leased. In this way, the cultivated land has increased by 20 percent when it was remeasured. All farmers were happy.

The confirmation of land rights will bring great hope to agriculture. This year's "No. 1 Central Document" calls for an introduction of the family farms system. The Decision also makes it clear to "encourage the transfer of contracted management rights in the open market to large specialized entities, family farms, farmers' cooperatives, and agricultural enterprises, and develop large-scale operations in various forms." This will also bring some big changes to the countryside. At present, only Western Europe, the United States, and Canada have real family farm systems, while China does not. China should promote the family farms and improve the technical level and labor productivity of the farmers. Farmers also need to know how to operate and adopt measures for the economy of scale.

38.3 For the SOEs: Too Much Administrative Interference

The Decision will have an important impact on the reform of China's state-owned capital system in the future. Generally speaking, the reform of the state-owned capital system is composed of two levels: State-owned capital allocation system reform at the higher level and the SOE management system reform at the lower level. *The Decision* suggests that we should "improve state-owned assets management system, focusing on managing capital and strengthening the supervision of state-owned assets." Therefore, it is advisable to reform as follows: A number of professional or comprehensive state investment fund companies shall be established by the guidance of the State-owned Assets Supervision and Administration Commission (SASAC) to be responsible for the state-owned shares. We should increase investment in sectors in shortages and emerging industries, and withdraw state capital in sectors with overcapacity and poor efficiency. In this way, the efficiency of resource allocation can be improved.

The Decision proposes that the market should play a decisive role in the allocation of resources, which highlights the position and function of the market. Why do we emphasize resource allocation? The efficiency originally considered in economics is production efficiency. Production efficiency has been a traditional concept for many years, focusing on the relationship between the input and output of production units. A given amount of input results in an increase in the amount of output indicates an improvement in efficiency; A given amount of output based on a decrease in the input also indicates an improvement in efficiency. This is called production efficiency. Since the 1930s, the concept of resource allocation efficiency began to appear in economics, and it is different from the meaning of production efficiency. With fixed input, by combining production factors and changing the allocation method, we could get different levels of efficiency. For example, in mode A, N number of products can be made; and in mode B, N + 1 number of products can be made, which suggests an improvement in the resource allocation efficiency. Therefore, we must attach importance to the allocation of resources.

The concept of resource allocation efficiency is different from that of production efficiency, which can be more meaningful to the macro-economy. The efficiency of resource allocation will bring about two conceptual changes. The first one is to recognize the importance of non-productive personnel in the improvement of efficiency. They usually include the staff in charge of financing, personnel organization, publicity, and administration, who are not on the front line of production and were previously considered irrelevant to production efficiency. After resource allocation efficiency was introduced, the situation changed. People in charge of financing ensure the better allocation of resources. Those people tasked with the personnel organization work to allocate human resources to their best positions. Those undertaking propaganda work motivate every worker. And those who are in administrative management combine better material resources with human resources, which can improve efficiency. The second is that the views on capital market and property rights market have changed. They are considered to be the best means to improve resource allocation efficiency. Therefore, developing the capital market and property rights market is conducive to a rational allocation of resources.

At present, the property rights reform of SOEs is not yet complete, and these enterprises still face excessive administrative interference. *The Decision* suggests that we should improve the corporate governance structure with coordinated operation and effective balance. In the future, SOEs should all be managed under a corporate governance structure, as they are already joint-stock enterprises and independent market players, with some being publicly listed companies.

38.4 For Private Enterprises, Property Rights Must be Clearly Defined

Regarding the reform of private enterprises, I propose avoiding the term "structural reform" as it may cause misunderstandings: Private enterprises could mistakenly think that they are going to be nationalized! I propose to use the term "structural transition," which means that the property rights of the private enterprises must be clearly defined.

According to the survey, the property rights of some private enterprises remain ambiguous. For example, why are some private enterprises in trouble now? One important reason is that property rights were not well defined when they were established. Conventions in the past led to the situation that property rights were not clarified at the beginning. A private enterprise may have a paternalistic structure because a parent is often a capable actor with cohesion, experience, etc. Later, the scale of the private enterprise would expand. When it comes to the second generation, is it necessary to continue with the paternalistic management? According to our investigation in Guangdong and Zhejiang provinces, some founders of the second generations of private enterprises came back from overseas. They studied abroad and may not necessarily be management talents but experts in a particular industry. The question is who will take over the enterprises. There are almost two choices for the family business in private enterprises: One is to choose the best, indicating that it is not necessary to recruit family members but can select people with strong capabilities in the society; the other would be to choose within the family, such as the eldest son or the most trusted son. But the second choice does not tend to adapt to the trend of development. In the future, private enterprises should also improve their corporate governance. After the expansion in scale, they must follow the path, i.e., adopt a professional management system in which managers could be hired from the market or within the family. The key point of recruitment lies in a strong competence for the job so that the enterprise can continue to develop.

The Decision states that "both the public and non-public economies are important components of the socialist market economy and important foundation for China's economic and social development." This involves an understanding of the relationship between the SOEs and private enterprises. In my view, this relationship is not mutually exclusive so that one is strengthened and the other has to be weakened. It could be a win-win result, which, of course, has not been achieved yet. Since many of these enterprises are not fully independent market players, we need to continue the structural reform of the SOEs and the structural transition of private enterprises in the future. If private enterprises do not carry out structural transition, they will not be able to develop in the future. This is the current situation in China.

38.5 For Income Distribution, the Primary Distribution Is more Important

As for the reform of the income distribution system, my basic idea is that the primary distribution should be the key focus. This is different from the view of some who think that the secondary distribution is more important, and that it is easier to contain the rich and assist the poor. Some others consider that the primary distribution and the secondary distribution are equally important. My view is very clear, that is, the primary distribution is more important. Here, I will elaborate on a few examples.

The first example is about farmers. Farmers must have property rights, the absence of which will result in the inadequacy of their primary distribution. This has been mentioned before.

The second example is about the labor market. There are both the supply and the demand sides in the labor market. Most of the suppliers are rural migrant workers or those of the middle and lower classes in cities. These people enter the market individually, and they are the weak side. The demand side is large enterprises and public institutions, which are the strong side. The balance of power between supply and demand is thus asymmetric and unequal. On the demand side, large enterprises have strong power to decide wage level, and the supply side has no choice about that. Is it acceptable that this situation remains unchanged? How do developed countries solve this problem? They rely on the power of labor unions. The labor unions protect the rights and interests of low-income workers. If the wages are too low or not paid, the unions will speak for the workers. The labor union is a powerful group. When they intervene in supply and demand, the balance of power between the two sides may change. Rural migrant workers have been working in cities for so many years. They are also workers, but labor unions cannot assist them because they are registered as rural residents. Therefore, this situation needs to be changed.

The third example is about the market for agricultural products. The main sellers of agricultural products are individual farmers and herdsmen, who are disadvantageous in the market. Even if the buyers go to their doorstep to purchase their products, they are still the weaker bargainers. The buyers, usually composed of big supermarkets, food processing enterprises, and other buyers, are powerful groups. If they say they don't want your products, where else could you sell them? If you go out to sell, it will cost you more. Therefore, this situation needs to be changed. In developed countries, farmers form agricultural cooperatives, which facilitate further organization. I have visited the Netherlands, Denmark, and New Zealand. Their agricultural cooperatives are very powerful, having motorcades, fleets, warehouses, cold storages, wharves, etc. Their agricultural products are sold to foreign countries directly. However, this system does not work in China because our agricultural cooperatives have just been set up, all of which are small-scale operations based on villages and towns. The associations are yet to be formed.

The fourth example is about the education system. The education system is relevant for the wages of first-time job seekers. In China, due to the existence of the urban-rural dual structure or the urban-rural dual system, per capita education expenditure in the urban area is often more than that in the rural area. As a result of poorer conditions in rural schools, such as inadequate facilities, teachers, and equipment, the learning quality of students in rural compulsory education suffers accordingly. Rural children do not want to go to senior high school after finishing junior high school. They say that it is no use going to senior high school. If they cannot get into college, they would prefer to find a job now; therefore, many of them end up finding jobs after graduating from junior high school. However, what good jobs can rural children get when they graduate from junior high school? They can only be simple, repetitive manual works. This situation is like the dual labor markets in Western developed countries. Some can only engage in labor jobs with low-level income, which will gradually form a social class solidification, or an occupational hereditary system in China's society: Rural migrant workers' children are at risk of inheriting their parents' status, and this pattern may continue into the next generation. They don't have other skills or better access to education. What else can they do if they don't work as rural migrant workers? This affects the primary distribution of income. Therefore, the allocation of educational resources must be made more equitable.

On the issue of income distribution, I would emphasize the importance of primary distribution, in which the issue of property rights matters a lot. The power of both sides in the labor market should be equal, so should the power of supply and demand in the agricultural products market. The allocation of education resources should be equal and fair. These are the issues that can witness the importance of primary distribution in China. Of course, secondary distribution is also important. In China's current secondary distribution, the most important is the integration of urban and rural social security, which shows that we can have the same welfare system as Western developed market economies. The situation there is that, if the primary distribution is insufficient in some areas, the secondary distribution could be supplementary. Then the income gap would be narrowed through secondary distribution. The current situation in China is that, there are gaps within the primary distribution, and the secondary distribution further widens these gaps. For example, within different social security systems of urban and rural areas, urban workers have free healthcare or medical insurance, while rural migrant workers who have access to cooperative healthcare still have to pay quite a lot to see a doctor, let alone those who do not even have cooperative healthcare. This situation needs to be changed.

—*Xinhua Wenzhai*, issue No. 3, 2014

Chapter 39
2015: Current Issues to Note in China's Economic Development

39.1 Two Essential Conditions for Realizing a Medium-High Economic Growth

For the development of China's economy in the next stage, we should start with the new normal.

We should have a correct understanding of the new normal. It means acting according to economic laws; otherwise, it could violate market principles. For example, China's economy has been growing at a high speed in the past few years, but the continuous high growth rate does not conform to the laws of economic development and may not be sustainable. Therefore, deceleration is necessary. A medium-high growth rate may be more consistent with China's current situation.

The prolonged high-speed growth could bring five adverse effects: Excessive consumption of resources, ecological degradation, and overcapacity in some industries, general inefficiency, and missed opportunities for technological innovation and structural adjustments. After the outbreak of the global financial crisis (GFC) in 2008, Western developed countries, including the United States, Germany, and Japan, have been trying their best to find a way to develop the economy through technological innovation, while we have been busy with a high growth and might have let slip some good opportunities. This is an important issue that we should take seriously.

Therefore, one of the essential features of the new normal is that our economy should shift to medium-high growth. Generally speaking, economists believe that an economic growth rate of 6–7% is a medium-high growth rate. However, this is indeed not easy to achieve. Entering into the new stage doesn't mean the realization of a medium-high growth. There are two more important conditions: economic structural adjustment and innovation. Without them, even a medium-high growth rate could not be achieved.

Y. Li, *China's Economy Since 1978*, China Academic Library,
https://doi.org/10.1007/978-981-95-5733-2_39

39.2 Finding the Real Reasons for the Economic Slowdown

At present, we are facing downward pressure on the economy. We must analyze how the downward pressure was formed and what we should do if it increases? We should clarify the problem first and then try to find a countermeasure.

First, the issue is not the growth rate itself, but the slowdown of the growth rate. At the same time, we should also realize that maintaining rapid growth for a long term is too costly. For example, the recent problems, such as overcapacity and low efficiency, are the consequences of various issues, including a large number of low level, repetitive construction projects and overcapacity in many places under a rapid growth over the past few years. The most significant impacts of overcapacity include overexploitation and waste of resources. In the past few years, the superfast growth has involved wasting resources and inefficiency to some extent.

Second, from an economics perspective, steady growth is characterized by a consistent growth rate over time, which is not necessarily dependent on the size of the comparison base. Our economy at present is much bigger than ten years ago (let alone twenty years ago). Therefore, every further increase of 1% makes it more difficult to sustain at the same growth rate. The growth will sooner or later undergo a diminishing process. Thus, the rapid growth in previous years has made current growth more challenging.

Third, the instability of the international market causes a number of problems. It has some adverse impacts on China's imports and exports. The current difficulties imposed by the international economic situation on our economy are mainly manifested in two aspects. On the one hand, Japan is our main competitor in high-tech products. On the other hand, Southeast Asian countries are our main competitors in low-end products. Although the productivity of these countries is dwarfed by that of China, the labor is cheaper because of their lower wages.

Fourth, downward pressure on the economy has increased, and it is not easy to turn it around. The current situation could be improved through structural adjustment, but it is not easy. Too much over-investment has been made, and it is hard to reverse. Structural adjustment requires great determination and could also bring losses, so our endurance and persistence are essential. Therefore, we must fully recognize the arduous nature of structural adjustment. If we do not persist, all our previous efforts would be in vain.

Fifth, technological innovation should not be rushed. The technological innovation that can genuinely be applied to the market requires years of accumulation. For example, the Huawei company in Shenzhen did not succeed overnight but has developed step by step and day by day. It may have entered a conservative phase now, but it should keep innovating and never stop.

In addition, the rapid development of the Internet is highly significant. Internet development in China is still in the initial exploratory stage. It is difficult for economists to predict where the Internet will push us in the future, but this is undoubtedly a trend of future development. The role of the Internet is significant, nurturing many new technologies that could make structural adjustment smoother, but whether it can stimulate economic development remains to be seen.

Above all, we should adhere to two points when dealing with the downward pressure on the economy: structural adjustment, which is indispensable; and technological innovation. People should be encouraged to innovate and start business. We must have a determined mind and clear thoughts for these tasks without any illusions. Worrying about economic ups and downs is of no benefit. Furthermore, macroeconomic regulation must be carried out simultaneously, emphasizing targeted regulation. We must pay attention to fine-tuning and pre-adjustment to cope with the current downward pressure on the economy.

39.3 High Investment May Not Bring High Employment

This is a new issue we encounter. We need to change our mindset. In our minds, new jobs are usually generated from economic growth, i.e., high economic growth creates more new jobs. It was indeed the reality in the past because China's economy was still at a relatively low level. However, the situation has changed. Economic growth could only be achieved through industrial upgrading with high technology. Therefore, the employment issue cannot be solved solely by significant investments.

When I was investigating a company recently, the head of the company said that they had made significant investments. Then I asked him how many new jobs had been created, and his answer was simple: "None, and worse still, some staff might have to be laid off." I tried to find out the reasons. The current investment differs from that of the past. The investment in technological innovation makes the production process more modernized. For example, using robots to replace labor increases efficiency but not employment. Some older workers would be reassigned, and others might even directly retire. Younger ones would have to be retrained. Moreover, newly hired employees must be skilled, which is quite different from the past.

I also asked other heads of enterprises how to solve the current employment issue. They thought that we couldn't solely rely on high investment as well. On the one hand, the entrepreneurial incentives of the private sector should be mobilized. Encourage them to start a business, and then it would increase employment. On the other hand, the enterprise system needs to be decentralized. Each sector should be an innovative unit. Nowadays, many people's concepts have changed. Even rural residents do not just go out to work like before. Instead, they learn skills first, and then they could adapt to more positions in more places or start a business (including business startups in their hometown). There is incredible entrepreneurial enthusiasm among people, which is one of the main approaches to address China's employment issue in the future. It is predicted that in 20 years, ordinary enterprises will not need office buildings at all because employees can work from home. Therefore, we need to change our perceptions of employment, which means addressing the employment issue may not rely on high investment. Although technology is improving, sensible investment in infrastructure construction and human resource training should still be in need.

39.4 High Interest Rates May Not Curb Inflation

This is also a new point of view.

Classical theories suggest that inflation is caused by excessive demand from too much investment and consumption. Thus, austerity measures can be taken to tackle it. However, in the early 1970s, stagflation occurred in the United States with inflation and high unemployment in coexistence. The mainstream economists at that time felt overwhelmed. According to the Keynesian theory, inflation would occur when aggregate demand is swelling, and unemployment would occur when aggregate demand is depressed. Therefore, inflation and unemployment would not coexist. At the time, US President Nixon asked mainstream economists why stagflation occurred. In fact, the main reason lay in the presence of two types of monopolistic power in the economy. One was the labor union, believing that it could control the actions of workers and insisting on rigid wages that should only increase, not decrease. If the wages fell, workers would strike, making it challenging to increase the employment rate through decreased wages. The other was the multinational corporation, believing that it could control prices and make the prices rigid. Likewise, the prices should only increase but not decrease. A multinational corporation would rather destroy the products than reduce the prices. In this way, two kinds of rigidity existed simultaneously, leading to a high unemployment rate and inflation. The phenomenon similar to a "seesaw" effect would not appear in reality. Mainstream economists advocated "holding down the baby." If two hands held both "babies," neither wages nor prices would rise. This view was entirely against the laws of a market economy, but Nixon accepted it and implemented the New Economic Policy, which was the famous wage freeze and price control measures in the United States in the 1970s. Later, the measures could not work anymore, and Nixon's New Economic Policy failed. By the 1980s, President Reagan accepted the argument of the Supply School, which advocated reducing taxes, promoting market competition, and creating new products through technological innovation to drive economic growth. As a result, the US economy jumped out of the stagnation trap, and the inflation was tamed.

This tells us that we cannot be short-sighted. Current inflation is caused by excessive investment and demand. However, necessary investment should still be maintained, and lower interest rates might still be needed at the proper time. Only in this way can we adapt to the new situation. What has caused the "money shortage"? To get the answer, I have explored several cities in Zhejiang Province and found that it was not a shortage in money supply because the M1 and M2 money stocks are pretty significant. The main reason for the "money shortage" was the difficulty in obtaining loans. Banks believed that private enterprises are unreliable, and if the loan cannot be repaid, it would become a big problem. Therefore, they prefer to lend to large and creditworthy SOEs. Nevertheless, the SOEs favored by banks may not need so much money, and the lending rate is relatively low, so the SOEs re-lend the borrowed funds. Private enterprises cannot get credit, and have to borrow from the SOEs at high interest rates. There are also many owners of private enterprises who cannot get credit and have to resort to their relatives and friends for help. A famous saying in Zhejiang Province is "cash is king," i.e., the most important thing for a company is to hold cash in its account. With cash, everything is available. The capital chain would not be broken, and the industrial chain would operate smoothly. Once there is an investment opportunity, actions can be taken promptly. As a result, each company would have a cash reserve beyond the average level. However, many M1 and M2 money in circulation would still be in short supply. Therefore, if there is an inflation, we should consider these aspects because tightening the credit may not work under the new situation.

39.5 Markets Can Be Created

This is a new proposition, which is understandable for each industry. During my investigation in Cangzhou, Hebei Province, I went to Suning County that mainly engaged in the fur business. Some people said, "It has been difficult to do business recently. In the past, fur was mainly sold to Russia, but now even if Suning's fur is much cheaper than that from Europe, Russians are still not willing to buy." Then I gave them several suggestions. First, "produce more personalized products," because current consumption is different from that of decades ago. In the early or even late 1990s, it was herd-styled consumption with people following the fashion while nowadays it is personalized consumption. Second, "provide more human-oriented services," and make the shopping experience more enjoyable. Third, "establish Chinese brand and sail abroad." Building a brand depends on creating high-quality products that last long, but at present, the brands of Chinese products have not been fully recognized by the market. Fourth, "retain domestic customers." If good-quality toilet seats are available in China, why would people rush to buy them in Japan? It is entirely possible to keep customers from home. Moreover, establishing Free Trade Areas would also be beneficial.

At Guanghua School of Management, Peking University, I often told graduate students the following case. A company that produced wooden combs recruited four salespeople and let them take a batch of samples to the designated temples to sell them to the monks. The results were quite different. The first salesman did not sell any because the monks said a bald head would not need a comb. The second salesman told the monks that combs had other functions besides combing hair, such as scratching the scalp, reducing fatigue, activating blood circulation, improving eyesight, clearing up the head, beautifying the skin, etc. Then dozens of combs were sold. The third salesman observed endless streams of pilgrims in the temple. Their hair was somewhat messy after praying to the Buddha, and sometimes the incense ash fell on their hair. Then he went to the abbot and said that, since there were so many enthusiastic pilgrims, the temple should care more about them. Putting a few combs in front of each hall would make them feel looked after so that they would return more and more frequently. The abbot agreed, and hundreds of combs were sold. The fourth salesman told the abbot directly that gifts were needed for public relations when the monks worked outside the temple. Wooden combs could be the best gifts. The most famous couplet of the temple could be carved on one side of it while the words like "Buddha in Mind" and "Accumulate Goodness" could be carved on the other side, making the comb a symbol of the temple. Then thousands of combs were sold at once.

This story tells us that market can be created and product functions may undergo various changes. If companies want to sell their products abroad, they must add new functions to the products, making them meet the new demands of consumers. Only in this way can new markets be created, followed by more overseas sales.

39.6 Pay More Attention to the "Social Man" Perspective in the "Internet +" Era

In the past, almost all works in economics mentioned the "economic agency hypothesis," i.e., people consider minimum costs and maximum benefits, the two principles that must be conformed with. Therefore, economics was built on this hypothesis. However, with the continuous change of the world, the "economic man hypothesis" alone is obviously incomplete and insufficient, so the "social agency hypothesis" is gradually emerging. Under this assumption, people consider issues from both the "economic agency" and "social agency" perspectives.

For example, there are two places, A and B, where investment can be made. The investment returns in A are higher than those in B, and the cost is lower than B. If we consider the "economic agency hypothesis," people would always choose to invest in A. However, some people prefer to invest in B. There may be various reasons. One reason may be that: "B is my hometown. Since I have prospered while my hometown is still poor, I am willing to invest and set up factories there to solve the employment issue in my hometown." This is from the perspective of the native place. Some may consider: "When I studied and worked there previously, many people looked down on me and thought I was good for nothing. After leaving there to start a business, I have made some achievements, so I would go back to establish a big company to prove myself. I want to change the previous prejudices and views on me." In addition, some people might have made some mistakes or even done some malicious things to the local people when they lived there, and later they felt guilty and regretful. Thus, with successful entrepreneurship, they would like to set up factories there to make up for the mistakes.

People have various ideas. Nowadays, in the "Internet +" era, people are more likely to consider issues from the "social man" perspective. Thus, the economic perspective alone is increasingly limited.

39.7 Pay Attention to the "Tertiary Regulation"—Cultural Regulation

The "Tertiary regulation" is to regulate through moral forces, that is, cultural regulation. The primary regulation featured in the past was market regulation. The market is like an invisible hand, regulating through market laws. Later, there is the secondary regulation, namely, government regulation. Government regulation is to regulate by the tangible hand of the government with laws, rules, and policies. Is there a third type of regulation? Thousands of years ago, commodity exchanges occurred, and the market was created. Government regulation appeared later after the formation of the state and government. Before the emergence of market and government regulations, people mainly regarded moral forces as a discipline. Later, moral regulation still plays its role. The saying goes that "Cities are better during mild turbulence, and the countryside is better in a big chaos." When a minor turmoil occurs, villagers will go to the city to seek refuge from relatives and friends there. They would stay in a city that is safer in their mind. In contrast, during the big chaos, the market is malfunctioning, and the government is paralyzed, but there is a higher possibility for the human society to survive and move forward in the countryside. It does not matter if there is no market or government because moral force plays the role of regulation.

Therefore, we must pay attention to the tertiary regulation, that is, regulating through moral forces, or namely cultural regulation. Cultural regulation means that everyone is self-disciplined, and everyone abides by general rules. Community, corporate, and campus culture constructions, etc., are all promoting people to enhance self-discipline, which is helpful for future social and economic development.

39.8 Improve the Efficiency of Resource Allocation and Increase the Value of the State-Owned Assets

For many years, production efficiency, studied in economics, is the ratio of input to output. The output increases with a given input, indicating improved efficiency; with a certain output, the input decreases, and the efficiency is also improved. Thus, production efficiency is essential. After the 1930s, the second type of efficiency emerged in economics, which is called resource allocation efficiency. With fixed input, by combining production factors and changing the allocation methods, we could get different levels of efficiency. For example, N products can be made in mode A and $N + 1$ products can be made in mode B. Thus, the two efficiencies coexist. Production efficiency focuses on enterprise and production management in the micro-field. The focus of resource allocation efficiency, on the other hand, is at the macro level, that is, how to improve the efficiency of resource allocation. Therefore, we must pay more attention to improving resource allocation efficiency in the future, mainly to improving the allocation of state-owned assets, leading to higher efficiency with more added value.

39.9 Conclusion

We can draw two conclusions about the future development of China's economy. One is that the changes could far exceed expectations, and the other is that the changes would be drastic and accelerating. Under this circumstance, it is difficult for us to predict what the economy will look like in 30 or 50 years. For example, will there still be any differences between blue-collar and white-collar workers? When everyone works with the computer, can they be distinguished? What is more, how useful is cash? Since people all use credit cards, who will still carry cash? Will the scale of enterprises become small? Will people still buy cars? Will people still need to rush to work in the morning and hurry home in the evening? Many are beyond our imagination today. However, we should still keep our minds open and imaginative. Ideas that often cause significant changes in economic life may be whimsical at first, and with great efforts, we can eventually turn these ideas into reality. So, everyone needs to keep studying and exploring.

—Speech at the "2015 China Internet+ Innovation Conference ·Hebei Summit" on June 13, 2015

Chapter 40
2016: How to Enable the Supply Side to Contribute More Effectively

Xi Jinping, General Secretary of the CPC Central Committee, proposed at a meeting of the Central Financial and Economic Leading Group on October 10, 2015, that "China should deepen the supply-side structural reforms and improve the quality and efficiency of the supply system, while moderately expanding aggregate demand." Subsequently, at the G20 meeting on October 15, General Secretary Xi Jinping reiterated that we should pay much attention to the synergy on the supply side and the demand side. So far, supply-side reform has entered the stage for public discussion on the decision-making.

40.1 What Does It Mean to Reform on the Supply Side?

Supply-demand equilibrium is a crucial issue in economics. Economists believe that this equilibrium could be reached by adjusting either supply or demand. Then what is the difference between the two sides? Adjustments on the demand side would be made soon. We can either increase fiscal revenue and credit to stimulate demand or reduce fiscal revenue and credit to restrain demand.

Supply-side adjustment, on the other hand, is usually considered as medium-term reform that involves mainly the structural adjustments in industrial policies, technological policies, and resource allocation. It takes time for these adjustments to be effective.

Supply-side reforms may occasionally restrain supply. For example, it seems easy to close enterprises with excessive capacity and extra consumption of energy and resources, but many obstacles could occur in practice, such as relocating unemployed workers and disposing idle equipment and factories. Therefore, efforts on both supply side and demand side can be effective to certain extent. However, the former is generally more complex and riskier than the latter.

Y. Li, *China's Economy Since 1978*, China Academic Library,
https://doi.org/10.1007/978-981-95-5733-2_40

What is the biggest risk? It is an increase in unemployment. If a high unemployment rate lasts for long, social stability would be at risk. When we consider the reform on the supply side, it is usually about increasing supply, not about shutting down the enterprises.

40.2 What Are the Difficulties in the Supply-Side Reform?

In the case of insufficient capacity in supply, it would be problematic to blindly expand production. These expansions could allow the suspended enterprises to resume operation on re-acquired loans. However, this would cause inflation in the macro-economy and result in a more distorted economic structure, which makes the structural adjustment more difficult. In addition, the increase in supply could also bring about "three deficiencies": insufficient capital due to increased investment; the shortage of professionals and technicians; the lack of land and freshwater supply as well as marketing capability. All these "three deficiencies" need to be planned and resolved in a coordinated manner, which is the reason why supply-side reforms are regarded as medium-term reforms.

Hence, how to overcome these difficulties and obstacles in the current supply-side reform? The first is to adopt targeted regulation, that is, structural regulation, which enhances existing production capacity and increases supply through targeted tax cuts and tax exemptions. The second is to encourage the development of high-tech enterprises and support the industries in difficulties, which can make up for the lack of production capacity. The third is to vigorously develop new products so that increased goods and services could satisfy residents' expanded demand. The fourth is to strengthen vocational and technical training, which could improve the quality of the labor force and alleviate the shortage of human resources as well. The fifth is to streamline administration, delegate power to the lower levels of the government and clarify the "three lists": negative list, power list, and responsibility list. This will motivate private capital into the supply side to have more supplying entities in the market. The sixth is to mobilize the enthusiasm of enterprises for innovation and accelerate the reform of mixed ownership of the SOEs. At the same time, it is also essential to boost the transformation of private enterprises. When they reach a certain scale, the family management system would have to be transformed to a modern one with the implementation of the professional manager system and refinement and rewards of property rights.

40.3 What Is the Relationship Between Increasing Supply and Increasing Demand?

Investment entities on both the supply side and the demand side are not passive. They have their own profit goals and ways to achieve them, and their actions influence each other. In short, to increase supply, we must increase input, including capital input, various productive input, and human capital input. While to increase demand, private consumption is even more significant, besides the government procurements. Private consumption depends on the purchasing power of residents, which requires a narrowing in the urban-rural income gap and motivate residents' desire to consume. More importantly, we should strengthen the willingness to buy. The consumption patterns of the younger generation are different from those of the older generation. Younger people are willing to invest but are less inclined to spend, no matter how much funds they start with.

However, as an investor, whether the investment goes into the supply side or the demand side, one must firstly consider the cost of recycling and the level of interest rates. How about demand if all investment goes to the supply side? Demand-side investors could turn to the supply side because they may be attracted to do so. If the power of the supply side is not as high as that of the demand side, investors would tend to withdraw funds from the supply side and invest in the public facilities of the demand side. Therefore, there is an interactive process between the two sides. Do not assume that if there is an increase of investment in supply, more private capital would be flowing in. It is not necessarily the case here. Private investors would have to observe before making decisions. So, this process is often slow.

In addition, an increase in supply also means adjusting the human resource structure. We must pay attention to both capital investment and human capital investment on the supply side. If human capital is insufficient, there would not be enough skilled workers and professionals. Then the effect of supply-side reform would be limited. Therefore, an important issue is that we must guarantee the increased supply through the upgraded human resources. We often say that the original demographic dividend has gone, but the new one could continue to emerge.

Mass entrepreneurship and innovation have created conditions for the upgrade of human resources. For example, farmers are keen to start family farms, or small and micro-enterprises. These are all innovations in human resources. Therefore, in the future, China's human resources should gradually be improved with the increase of supply. Otherwise, the supply cannot keep up with the demand.

How to keep up the supply? One is to rely on the innovation and entrepreneurship I mentioned earlier. The second is to reform the education system. For example, the Bijie College, located in Guizhou Province (southwest of China), was upgraded into Guizhou Institute of Engineering. The Institute began to focus on training technicians, with more than 90% of graduates assigned to enterprises. In Yunnan (another southwest province), we have also seen that vocational schools began to train mechanics for coastal areas. These changes are taking place in the supply of human resources.

40.4 What Are the Insurmountable Obstacles to the Increase of Supply?

Increasing supply is not a panacea, and it must also comply with economic laws. We should pay attention to the long-term benefits of increasing supply, even though there could be issues emerging in the near future.

First, an increase in supply could encounter some insurmountable obstacles, mainly including the limited resources of land, freshwater, transportation, etc. The land supply on the southeast coast of China is already in shortage, while it is also difficult to invest in the west. There are adequate lands in the west, although other resources are insufficient and transportation costs are high. These problems could not be solved easily within a short period of time.

Second, the supply-side reform interacts with demand, but there are still many issues on the demand side. For example, not long ago, I mentioned four points during an investigation in Hebei Province. First, we should make more individualized products. Second, we should make the services more user-friendly. Third, we should make our brands well-known abroad. According to a survey by the China Brand Association, foreign investors were sent a questionnaire asking them for a list of Chinese brands they knew. As it turned out, there was only one entry in the list of known brands—Maotai, a brand for liquor. They know nothing but "Maotai" for China's manufacturing industry. Fourth, we should encourage people to consume in China. Many people now travel abroad and spend a lot of money buying daily necessities. Why are they willing to buy abroad? One reason is that they can buy genuine goods, the other is that they can buy the same product at a lower price. Why are they sold more expensively in China? Because tariffs are high. Of course, they are allowed to buy goods abroad, but it will increase foreign tax revenues and promote foreign employment. However, if the tariffs could be reduced on the imported goods, we can stimulate local consumption, contributing to domestic tax revenue and employment.

How to solve these problems? The supply-side reforms require medium-term adjustments, which then involve government planning. The central government is currently formulating the "Thirteenth Five-Year Plan." In this Plan, we should consider some measures to deal with the above issues so that the supply side can work better.

—*Money China*, issue No. 2, 2016

Chapter 41
2017: Realizing the Glorious and Arduous Historical Mission of Making China Strong and Prosperous

41.1 The Connotation and Practical Significance of "Prosperity and Strength"

Since the Opium War, China had been in a state of poverty and weakness with the invasion of the European powers. People with lofty ideals had longed for the country's prosperity and the people's wealth, but this state of poverty and weakness had lasted for a long time, and China hadn't realized such goal. In 1949, the People's Republic of China was established. The Chinese nation stood up from then, but it has been far from getting rich. Compared with industrialized countries in the world, China was still in poverty. This became a big worry for the old generation of revolutionaries. They devoted themselves to finding the path to prosperity but have yet to fulfill this wish.

The amount of a country's gross domestic product (GDP) is often used to measure its prosperity and strength. GDP is seen by economists as the best indicator that reflects whether or not a country is prosperous and strong, or to what extent it is. But economists are coming to realize that GDP cannot indeed tell whether a country is prosperous or strong. The structure of GDP, that is, the structure of the economy, is more illustrative than the total amount of GDP. Let's look at the example of China and Britain during the period of the Opium War, which broke out in 1840. At that time, China's total GDP was much larger than that of Britain, but there was a huge gap in the structure of GDP. China's GDP was made up of agricultural and handicraft products, and the exports were mainly tea, silk, porcelain, tung oil, and pig bristles. China also exported cotton textiles, but they were hand-loomed products. Things were very different in Britain. The industrial revolution began around 1770, and by the time the Opium War broke out in 1840, Britain had been industrialized for 70 years. Britain's GDP included all kinds of machinery and equipment, steam engines, steel, etc. Its cotton textiles were machine-made. The main means of transportation in Britain were trains and ships, while in China, they were horse-drawn carriages and sailing ships. At that time, the continental European countries were promoting industrialization,

Y. Li, *China's Economy Since 1978*, China Academic Library,
https://doi.org/10.1007/978-981-95-5733-2_41

and the machines and equipment, steam engines, locomotives, and railroad tracks made in Britain were continuously exported to these countries. The GDP structure of Britain was in line with the global trend of scientific and technological progress, while that of China lagged far behind. This fully demonstrates that the structure of GDP is even more important than GDP itself. Today, although China's total amount of GDP has ranked second in the world, there is still a certain gap in GDP structure between China and the developed countries, such as an inadequate proportion of high-tech industries in GDP. Furthermore, China is a developing country with a large population and is still at the middle-income level in terms of GDP per capita. These are also what we need to catch up.

Then we can analyze the issue of the aggregate and the structure of human resources that are closely related to prosperity and strength. When the Opium War erupted in 1840, China's total population had well exceeded that of Britain, but the human resource structure was seriously flawed and far inferior to Britain's. By that time, it had been 70 years since the beginning of the Industrial Revolution in Britain. Primary education was already popular, with many secondary schools established in urban and rural areas. Moreover, some universities were founded there as well. In Britain, a number of scientific researchers, engineers, skilled workers, economic managers, and finance professionals were cultivated year after year. The proficient skills of British workers were known worldwide. At that time, countries such as France, Germany, the Netherlands, and Belgium were actively promoting industrialization, and they absorbed British skilled workers together with the imports of capital, machines, and equipment from Britain. According to historical records, British railroads had been built for some time, so British workers were invited by France to build the railroad from Paris to Rouen, and French workers were impressed that their British counterparts were much more proficient than themselves. The British were well-off, and workers were supplied with meat in every meal. Therefore, British workers tended to be stronger, resulting from their improved nutritional intakes.

How about China? In many years after 1840, China had a large population but an inferior human resource structure. The majority of farmers and women were illiterate, and only a few people could read the Confucian canons and classic writings in order to take the imperial examinations. How many people in China knew modern science and technology at that time? How many of them knew modern economic and business management? And how many of them knew modern finance? The comparison of human resource structure between China and Britain showed how backward China was. Nowadays, China ranks second in terms of total GDP and has the largest population in the world. But the gap in human resource structure between China and Western developed countries is still quite large. For example, the proportion of graduates in the total population in China is smaller than that of Western developed countries. The proportion of skilled workers in the labor force in China is also smaller. This suggests that the adjustment of human resource structure, the same as that of GDP structure, is an important issue that influences China's goal of prosperity and strength. Therefore, in terms of human resource structure, we should clearly understand that there is still a wide gap to catch up, and we cannot be complacent, just like we cannot merely emphasize on the total GDP but not GDP structure in China.

As a goal, "prosperity and strength" is directly related to institutional reform to a greater extent. Looking back on the Sino-Japanese War of 1894–1895, around 120 years ago, we can see a disastrous defeat of China, with ceded land and suffering of humiliation. Why did China lose? The reason lied in the corruption of China's system, which was the most important lesson we have learnt. Before the war, the difference in national power between China and Japan was not so large. That is to say, the naval fleets of the two countries were almost equal in combat power. The reason why the Chinese navy was defeated did not lie in the naval failure in the battle of the Yellow Sea but in the performance of the Chinese army when the Japanese landed in Liaodong. At that time, the Chinese army was afraid of war and the enemy and would collapse at the slightest provocation. Hence the Japanese were able to encircle the back of the Weihai base on land, resulting in the destruction of the entire Beiyang fleet of China. The Chinese army in Korea and Liaoning was virtually defenseless, collapsing upon encountering the enemy, which further illustrated the corruption within the Chinese military. Immediately, the Japanese army crossed the Yalu River and then marched rapidly, eventually defeating the Chinese army. The crushing defeat of the Chinese army in the War obviously demonstrated that institutional corruption was the biggest cause. No wonder this national shame of the War led people of vision to ponder deeply at that time, realizing that it was not enough to revitalize the country in peril without the political and institutional reform. Thereby, for the China that was poor and weak, it would have been important to adjust the structure of its GDP, to promote education, and to cultivate talents. However, without reforming the institutions and eliminating corruption, China cannot truly achieve the transformation to prosperity and strength.

The Revolution of 1911 put an end to the feudal dictatorship of the Qing Dynasty, but China remained poor and weak. The May Fourth Movement awakened the Chinese nation, followed by the founding of the CPC in 1921. After a long period of exploration and struggle led by CPC, the Chinese people finally defeated the invasion of the Japanese militarists and overthrew the autocratic rule of the Kuomintang. With the joint efforts of the first generation of the CPC leadership with Mao Zedong as the core, the People's Republic of China was established in 1949. The Chinese nation finally "stood up" after more than 100 years of hard struggle. However, a correct path had not been found on our quest for prosperity and strength. The first generation of leaders chose a planned economy after the founding of New China, which also reflected the characteristics of the times. In the early days of the new regime, the Western imperialist powers were not friendly to China. They began imposing an embargo against China so that we had to copy the experience from the Soviet Union. China had to imitate the planned economic system implemented by the Soviet Union and a highly centralized government to manage the economy. It was completely understandable why the Chinese leadership did so. If they did not learn from the Soviet Union at that time, who would they learn from? Machines were bought from the Soviet Union, and experts were hired from the Soviet Union, resulting in the inevitability of China to embark on the planned economy. This was due to a certain circumstance at that time.

Although the implementation of the planned economy conformed to the international and domestic political situation at that time, it had left China in a state of "neither prosperous nor strong" for a long time. Together with the "ten years of turmoil" of the Cultural Revolution, by the middle of the twentieth century, China had been mired in a difficult situation where the national economy was on the verge of collapse.

The second generation of the CPC leadership, with Comrade Deng Xiaoping as the core, deeply explored China's reality and put forward the theory on socialism with Chinese characteristics, with reference to the experience from Western developed countries in the promotion of industrialization and modernization since the end of the Second World War. In terms of the ideological line, they reviewed the principle of "seeking truth from facts," and launched a nationwide debate on "practice is the only criterion for testing truth." They objectively evaluated our experience in the 30 years before reform and opening-up, and proposed a general direction of the path to follow. Therefore, China had embarked on a new historical process with the goal of "prosperity and strength." This is what Comrade Xi Jinping says recently: "We should look back on the past and sum up the experiences of the past." There are specific characteristics in the past, and it's not possible to forget how China managed to "stand up" in the early 30 years before reform and opening-up. We need to understand not only how to "stand up," but also how to become "prosperous and strong." This is the valuable experience we should draw from the past.

Comrade Deng Xiaoping pointed out in the 1980s that the world was overall in a period of peace and development, and that China must seize this opportunity to make further economic development. To this end, China should accelerate reform and opening-up. Reform means to transform the planned economy which has been an ill fit to the development in productivity. Opening-up means to learn the new achievements and successful experience in science and technology from Western developed countries so that China's economic development can keep pace with the world and enter the ranks of prosperous and strong nations. It has been under the guidance of the theory of socialism with Chinese characteristics that China's economy has gone through a rapid development since the early 1990s. The living standard of the Chinese people has also experienced a leap forward from subsistence to well-off in the process of economic reform and development. China has been gradually approaching the goal of prosperity and strength during this period. Learning from practice, Chinese people generally recognize that without reform and opening-up, China would not have made such tremendous and respectful achievements.

The 18th National Congress of the CPC and the Third Plenary Session of the 18th CPC Central Committee summarized the 35 years' experiences of reform and opening-up since the Third Plenary Session of the Eleventh CPC Central Committee (held in 1978). The review pointed out that the basic task at that time was to deepen reform in all aspects, to hold high the great banner of socialism with Chinese characteristics, to further emancipate the mind, to liberate and develop the social productive forces, to liberate and enhance social vitality, to resolutely break down all the drawbacks of the system and to exploit a brighter prospect for socialism with Chinese characteristics. In the speeches since the 18th National Congress of CPC, Comrade Xi Jinping has put forward the strategic idea of national rejuvenation, discussing such major issues as how the New China successfully rise on the world stage and how the Chinese nation rejuvenated itself under new historical conditions. This is a new elaboration of China's goal of achieving "prosperity and strength."

According to Comrade Xi Jinping, the reason for emphasizing the concept of "successful rise" instead of "peaceful rise" is that the latter depends on the international situation. It is not possible for China alone to achieve it by following a peaceful development path. If other countries in the world interfere with China's peaceful development, China could not realize its desire. If the core interests were trampled on, China would never give in and would fight resolutely to defend its national interests. In such circumstances, "successful rise" depends on the country itself, and "peaceful rise" depends on the international situation.

Therefore, we should have a deeper understanding of the goal of "prosperity and strength" for our country. It has always been combined with the great task of national rejuvenation, and is included in the strategy to achieve it. "Prosperity and strength" are our dream, so is peaceful development. Meanwhile, these must be in line with the core interests of China. It is difficult to achieve "prosperity and strength" without the great task of national rejuvenation.

41.2 The Two Major Historical Missions and the Unremitting Pursuit of the Chinese People

When we focus on achieving the goal of "prosperity and strength," we must not forget the two major goals entrusted to the Chinese people by history. One is to strive for national independence and people's liberation, and the other is to achieve national prosperity and people's wealth. The first and second generations of the CPC leadership were dedicated to leading the people of all ethnic groups in their unremitting struggle to achieve these two historical missions. This is the main theme and principal line of the historical development of the Party.

Among the two major historical missions mentioned, the foremost priority is to achieve national independence and people's liberation; without this, the other would remain a daydream. It was the first generation of the leadership, with Mao Zedong as the core that led people to realize national independence and people's liberation, which would always be remembered by people of all ethnic groups in China.

We shall not also forget the great achievements of the second generation of leadership with Comrade Deng Xiaoping as the core. When the national economy was on the verge of collapse after the "ten years of turmoil," it was the second generation of the leadership that set things straight, adhering to the principle of seeking truth from facts. Then China could embark on the path of reform and opening-up. They clarified that the road of socialism with Chinese characteristics should be the direction. They also led people of all ethnic groups in China to keep pace with the times, laying the foundation for building a moderately prosperous society and then a modern socialist country.

In fact, since 1979, under the guidance of the reform and opening-up policy, China has begun to enter the stage of dual-track transformation. It refers to the combination or integration of institutional transformation and development transformation. The former is a shift from a planned economy to a socialist market economy, and the latter is a shift from a traditional agricultural society to an industrial and modern society. Development economics actually examines development transformation, although the latter includes many aspects. Western development economics emerged near the end of the Second World War (around 1944), when some economists realized that a group of colonies might become independent after the war and take the path of developing countries. The developing countries would need to realize the transformation from an agricultural society to an industrial society, therefore development economics mainly approached the issues from this aspect. For example, it was necessary to address the issue of capital shortage because developing countries had insufficient capital. It was necessary to address the issue of land distribution because land was managed by capitalist countries previously. It was necessary to address the issue of human resources and foreign trade because some local plantation products and land products were exported previously. Development economists did not think about the issue of dual-track transformation before.

Thus, there were no precedent studies on the combination or integration of institutional transformation and development transformation. From 1979 to the first decade of the twenty-first century, China had accumulated some experience in the process of reform and opening-up, i.e., in the process of dual-track transformation. These experiences can be summarized as follows.

First, in the dual-track transformation, the focus was on institutional transformation, which led to development transformation. This is because the shackles and restrictions imposed on China's economy by the planned system had been omnipresent. If they were not broken, it would be impossible for China to achieve the transformation from a traditional agricultural society to an industrial society, nor is the goal of transforming into a modernized country attainable.

It is impossible for all developing countries to backtrack in the process of transformation from an agricultural to an industrial society since they have to abolish the pre-capitalist mode of production, build capitalist cities, and take the capitalist road under the guidance of economics. Nobody, except the landlords, wanted to go back to the pre-capitalist society and live a life of servants. So it is acceptable to transform slowly, but impossible to go backwards. However, retrogression could occur in China's institutional transformation, and that's why it is essential to emancipate the mind. The reason why such a heated debate took place in the 1980s in China and had not been settled until Comrade Deng Xiaoping's Southern Tour speeches in the spring of 1992 was that the benefits of a planned economy were discussed before the collapse of the Soviet Union. Deng's speeches were followed by the Fourteenth National Congress, which set a socialist market economy as the goal. But in reality, the planned economy had an obstacle to further industrialization, and the 1980s were not an easy time for reform and opening-up. It was a time of trial and error when all kinds of ideas were exchanged. By the 1990s, the Fourteenth National Congress formally set a socialist market economy as the goal, which was a significant change.

Second, people's livelihood should be improved along with economic growth. It is imperative to narrow the income gap between urban and rural residents and improve regional income distribution. According to China's actual situation, it is essential to care about employment. This is because the massive transfer of rural labor to coastal and urban areas is an inevitable phenomenon during the transformation period. Among the macroeconomic policy targets, employment should be the top priority.

Third, it is necessary to continuously innovate independently and promote industrial upgrading. In the dual-track transformation, the competitiveness of enterprises should be constantly enhanced, which is centered on promoting independent innovation. At the same time, industrial upgrading is also inseparable from the independent innovation of enterprises.

Fourth, property rights reform is the most important reform. In the dual-track transformation, clarity and certainty of property rights must be put at the forefront of the overall reform. Whether for existing enterprises, new enterprises, or urban and rural residents, ambiguous property rights in investments are obstacles to economic growth. For the majority of farmers, both land rights and housing property rights need to be defined, and the confirmation of rights should be implemented to households in rural areas. This will not only help to protect the legitimate rights and interests of the farmers, but also enable them to obtain property income for the improvement of their livelihood and to mobilize their enthusiasm for more reproduction and entrepreneurship.

Fifth, the private economy is an important part of the socialist market economy. In the process of dual-track transformation, it is necessary to vigorously develop the private economy and encourage the establishment of more small and micro enterprises. These not only help to relieve the pressure of employment but mainly help to mobilize the enthusiasm of the private sector, realize the potential of private capital, and allow private capital to play a greater role.

Sixth, urbanization could bring the most investment opportunities over the next several years. In China's dual-track transformation, the institutional transformation came first. Urbanization aims to break down the urban-rural dual system, including the unification of the dual household registration systems. It will enable farmers to fully enjoy the fruits of reform and opening-up and equalize the rights for urban and rural residents. Urbanization offers great opportunities to continuously promote growth in investment and consumption, and it will play a driving and leading role in the long-term prosperity for China. Through urbanization, "farmer" would no longer be an identity, but a mere profession. China will see the emergence of a large number of family farmers with advanced agricultural technologies and good management skills, as well as many forms of professional cooperatives. This would help realize agricultural modernization and agricultural industrialization.

The above characteristics of China's dual-track transformation model suggest an essential path for China to shift from a planned economy to a socialist market economy, and from a traditional agricultural society to an industrial and modern society.

In 2013, the Third Plenary Session of the 18th CPC Central Committee adopted the Decision on Some Major Issues Concerning Comprehensively Deepening the Reform, which stated that "there is no end to the development of practice and no end to the emancipation of the mind." Now, we are facing a new situation and tasks, so we must deepen reform comprehensively at a new starting point in history. My thoughts upon studying the decision are that there are two crucial points that would directly affect the overall situation of future reforms. One is the proposition that the market plays a decisive role in resource allocation, and the other is the statement on actively promoting mixed ownership. My take is elaborated below.

The first is about the decisive role of the market in the allocation of resources.

Generally, economists have three strands of views on whether the government or the market should play a decisive role in the allocation of resources. The first one is the government. The second one is a combination of the government and the market, and the third one is the market. There has been ongoing debate on these for years.

The first view, that the government should play a decisive role, has been proved to be inefficient by history, leading to distorted resource allocation, low product quality, waste of resources, and suppression of public initiatives and incentives. The second view, that the government and the market jointly play a leading role, has also proved inefficient. This is because once the government intervenes directly in the resource allocation, the market cannot play an equal role as the government and usually has to retreat, or even lose its original role. Another flaw in this view is that this may look ideal to theorists, but it is difficult to achieve in practice. Since the government often has a stronger influence than the market, it tends to exploit its power and crowd out the market in many instances.

The third view, which considers the market as a decisive role in the allocation of resources, is consistent with the law of a market economy. The key lies in how to clearly define the boundary between the government and the market. The government intervenes only under market failure. What are the things that the market does not excel at? They include supplying public goods (national defense, justice, law and order, compulsory education, social security, etc.), balancing regional development, coordinating individual income distribution, regulating macroeconomy, allocating scarce materials, planning for social and economic development, and so on. What are the things that the market is unwilling to do? Things that have large social benefits but small or even no economic benefits. For example, the market is generally reluctant to engage in basic research.

With a distinct boundary between the government and the market, we can clearly distinguish the functions between the two. When the market plays its decisive role, the government still functions in leading, planning, and supervising. This would guarantee a better environment, ensuring ongoing improvement of market efficiency.

Thus, the proposal that the market plays a decisive role in resource allocation is a major innovation in socialist economic theory.

Now let's turn to my second view, which is about the argument on actively promoting mixed ownership. I consider it another great innovation in socialist economic theory because we had adopted a simplistic dichotomy for the economy for a long time, which seems to be either public or private, without understanding the objective existence of the "intermediate territory." In fact, there are mixed-ownership entities with both public and private ownership. Furthermore, there are also different forms in the public or private economies.

Why is it urgent to develop a mixed-ownership economy? Let's start with the concept of production efficiency, which has always been the focus in economics. It refers to the relationship between input and output. Either decreased input with the same amount of output or increased output with the same amount of input indicates an increase in production efficiency. Since the 1930s, especially after the end of World War II, there has been another concept of efficiency, i.e., resource allocation efficiency. It means that changing the way of an allocation of the same amount of input can lead to different levels of efficiency. Thus, resource allocation efficiency is actually more important than production efficiency. While production efficiency is mainly examined from a microeconomic perspective, resource allocation efficiency is not only applicable to the analysis of microeconomic units (e.g., how to improve resource allocation efficiency in an enterprise) but more suitable for analyzing efficiency issues from a macroeconomic perspective. In other words, only by making resource allocation more rational and effective on the macro level would deliver the continued improvement in resource allocation efficiency.

The capacity of capital does not lie in the amount of capital stock but in the power of capital management. Assuming that the capital stock of a wholly state-owned company is 100 billion yuan, then the management capacity of state-owned capital in this case would only be 100 billion yuan. Under the condition of decentralized equities, if 25% of shares would enable a control of a company, the management capacity of capital would increase to 400 billion yuan, which represents a big expansion. Therefore, the establishment of mixed-ownership enterprises and the reduction of state-owned shares don't necessarily lead to losses in state-owned assets but rather precisely be a method to optimize the allocation of state-owned capital and be a step forward to improve the capital allocation efficiency.

Some worry that the establishment and development of a mixed-ownership economy is a phenomenon of "a retreat of the state and an advance of the private sector." This assertion is incorrect, especially for the former part. We should not focus on specific SOEs in a competitive industry but on revitalizing and activating the stock of state-owned capital and improving its allocation efficiency. Currently, there are more than trillions of yuan in the stock. There would be a huge loss if these resources were used inefficiently or even left idle. Therefore, it is all the more important to improve the allocation efficiency of the state-owned capital. We should adopt a mixed-ownership regime and revitalize the state-owned capital. So, it should be "an advance of the state with an advance of the private sector" instead of "a retreat of the state."

It should be emphasized that the key to developing a mixed-ownership economy lies in establishing a sound corporate governance structure, not just a diversification of investment entities or the demutualization of the enterprises. An SOE could be transformed through restructuring into a shareholding enterprise with diversified investment entities or even going public. This should only be considered as the first step on the road to a mixed-ownership economy in that the enterprise hasn't become an independent and autonomous market entity yet. If the corporate governance structure of the enterprise has not been established, or is only superficially in place, i.e., it is neither complete nor operating properly, it is still not a modern enterprise. Therefore, the enterprise reform must be continually deepened so that the shareholders' meeting, the board of directors, and the board of supervisors can play their respective roles. Besides, the general manager appointment system, the tenure system, and the responsibility system should also be established.

In the current progress of the mixed-ownership economy, there is also a practical obstacle that the SOEs, private enterprises, and private investors all have their respective concerns. Thus, they would not participate easily in the transition into mixed-ownership enterprises. Private enterprises and private investors are worried about the annexation of their enterprises or investments by powerful SOEs. And the heads of the SOEs are not willing to take the initiative to discuss with those of private enterprises on the establishment of new enterprises. They fear that they could be scrutinized later and that some may say that they have sold state-owned assets at a low price, leading to the loss of state-owned assets, or they could be suspected for taking bribery. Private enterprises and investors would also like to avoid potential trouble and suspicion. In fact, there may be three reasons behind this concern. First, the laws and regulations are not sound enough, resulting in suspicions of the negotiation between the state-owned and private enterprises. Second, the guidelines and policies of the central government are not understood deeply, so the heads of enterprises are afraid of making mistakes. Third, there are not many successful cases in practice, so the heads of the SOEs often do not know where to start and tend to retreat when encountering difficulties. Therefore, we must recognize that it is essential to speed up the formulation and publication of relevant laws and regulations, to study carefully the guidelines and policies of the central government, and to understand the spirit of *the Decision* of the Third Plenary Session of the 18th Central Committee. In addition, there is a need to find out some successful cases of developing mixed ownership in the relevant departments of the central government jointly with the business community and use these to facilitate the reform.

41.3 Poverty Is Not Socialism

Comrade Deng Xiaoping once proposed that "the essence of socialism is to liberate and develop productive forces, eliminate exploitation and polarization and eventually realize common prosperity." Regarding the characteristics of socialism, he argued that "socialism is not characterized for poverty, but for wealth," "poverty is not socialism, and slow development is not socialism either," and "to uphold socialism, we must get rid of poverty." When he listened to the report of the Standing Committee of the Jilin Provincial Party Committee on September 16, 1978, he remarked that "according to historical materialism, correct political leadership must ultimately be manifested in the development of social productive forces and the improvement of people's material and cultural life. If within a long historical period, the pace of development of productive forces in a socialist country is slower than that in a capitalist country, then what is the superiority of socialism?" These remarks on the essence and the characteristics of socialism clearly tell us that since poverty is not socialism, eliminating poverty and realizing the country's prosperity and the people's will should definitely become the main tasks of socialist construction. Otherwise, how to reflect the superiority of the socialist system?

Since the reform and opening-up, we have been conducting in-depth discussions on two major issues. First, what is the fundamental reason behind persistent poverty? Second, how to eliminate poverty and elevate the vast number of low-income families out of poverty and embark on the road to gradual affluence? Now, we can illustrate our explorations of these two major issues during the past 30 years' opening-up.

First, why has the phenomenon of poverty existed for so many years after the founding of the New China?

Since the reform and opening-up, the faculty and students at Peking University had investigated the central and Western regions, especially the Wumeng Mountains, the Wuling Mountains, the Qinba Mountains, and the Qilian Mountains. They found that the poorest were the farmers in these mountainous regions. Not only did they have meager income and tough life, but the income gap between them and urban residents had widened over a long period of time. In order to explain their poverty, it is necessary to start from three concepts of capital in economics: physical capital, human capital, and social capital.

The first is physical capital. It is supported by money. Monetary input is converted into means of production and housing. With housing, one can settle down and live a stable life. However, it is difficult to narrow the gap between urban residents and farmers in physical capital, and it even tends to widen.

In terms of land and property, urban land is state-owned, but the inherited houses have property rights so that they can be used as collateral. When urban residents want to start a business with small capital, they can mortgage their houses and then invest in workshops and stores. Things would be different for farmers because the land is collectively owned. In fact, farmers do not have property rights except for those in the pilot reform areas. Their houses and contracted land cannot be mortgaged. Without physical capital, they had to live in poverty for a long time.

The second is human capital. In economics, it is defined to include the skills, knowledge, wisdom, and experience embodied in human beings. There are a variety of ways to form human capital, the most important of which is education. People enter all levels of schools and learn knowledge and skills to increase their human capital. One could continue to study, accumulate experience, and enhance his/her own quality after entering an enterprise, which also leads to an increase in human capital. But the problem lies in the unequal allocation of educational resources. Urban schools have more investments and sufficient funds, with excellent faculty and a full range of equipment. However, children in rural areas can only enter schools with a bad environment, poor equipment, and a shortage in teachers, therefore they obviously tend to be less educated than their urban counterparts. This inevitably affects the employment and income prospect of young people in rural areas.

The third is social capital. Here it refers to intangible capital, which is a social relationship. It is important for a person to have social capital. Farmers have less social capital than urban residents. If an urban resident wants to start a business, one could usually have support and help from some relatives or friends. There are even more opportunities for a kind, hardworking, and reliable person. However, things would be different for farmers. They often have few acquaintances and their relatives also live in the countryside, so it's difficult to get a connection with the market. Particularly, some may live in a house on the mountain, knowing few people and unfamiliar with the market economy. Once they set foot in the market, what social capital can be used? In this way, the income gap between the urban and rural residents would inevitably widen.

Precisely because of the wide gap between urban and rural residents in terms of physical capital, human capital, and social capital, it is not surprising that the income gap had become even larger after the reform and opening-up.

After investigating in some poor mountainous areas, the faculty and students at Peking University found that it was a quite common phenomenon that "the capable would move out and the weak would remain." In the countryside, competent people who had relations with the outside had gone to the city. Some did manual work, some opened workshops, and some started business. In contrast, those who were old, weak, ill, or disabled were left in the countryside. If young people of ability were still engaged in farming, it would be difficult to make a living with insufficient output and low income. Thus, there would be a series of social problems such as "no one to support the elderly," "no one to take care of the sick," and "no one to raise the children."

Second, how to eliminate poverty so that these low-income farmers can gradually embark on the road to prosperity? It is undoubtedly important for the government to strengthen poverty alleviation and relief programs in poor areas, mountainous areas, and areas with formidable natural conditions in the southwestern and northwestern regions. The central government and local governments at all levels have been doing so in recent years, followed by many achievements. But it would be more important to deepen the rural reform through the confirmation of land rights.

41.3.1 The Confirmation of Land Rights

A new round of rural reform in China started with the confirmation of land rights. Since the 1950s, due to the establishment of the planned economy, the household registration system was divided into separate urban and rural regimes. Thus, the urban-rural dual system was formed, and the urban and rural areas were separated as a result. In the early 1980s, when the household responsibility system was actively promoted in rural areas, the dual system and household registration system were kept largely intact. At that time, the focus of reform shifted from rural to urban areas, and the reform of the SOEs (into contract or shareholding enterprises) became an issue of wide concern. This was obviously the main realm of the reform. Consequently, further rural reform was neglected and delayed at that time.

Until the twenty-first century, the reform of the collective forest right system was launched, which played an important demonstrative role. This reform was implemented for households, and forest rights certificates were issued to foresters, which could be seen as the confirmation of the land rights. Forest rights can be mortgaged, and foresters can set up their own family forestry farms, or form forestry cooperatives voluntarily. The forest economy was enlivened, followed by the mobilization of foresters' enthusiasm. Therefore, the achievements of the reform inspired and motivated a new round of rural reform, leading to a wider implementation of land rights confirmation.

A research group of the National Economy Committee of the CPPCC Economic Committee investigated in a city of Zhejiang Province and found that local farmers enthusiastically supported the implementation of land rights confirmation, believing that it would surely protect their property rights and interests. It is important to know that under the system of collective land ownership, farmers' contracted land, residential land, and houses (whether left by their ancestors or built by themselves in recent years) were not recognized as their own belongings, not to mention the contracted farmland that had become increasingly fertile after years of labor. If the government and large enterprises would decide to demolish houses and seize the land, the farmer contractors had to obey the arrangement and watch helplessly on the demolishment of the old and new houses on their residential land. Moreover, the compensation that farmers could receive was much lower than the market price. This had led to the occurrence of resistances to land occupation, land enclosure, and anti-demolition of residential houses almost everywhere.

Therefore, land rights confirmation as an experiment could enable farmers in rural areas to secure their property rights, which is the most important thing. If land rights could be confirmed, farmers would have certain rights recognized in certificates. The rights would include: (1) the right to operate the contracted land; (2) the right to use the residential land; (3) the property right to the buildings on the residential land. All three kinds of rights would be accompanied by respective certificates and protected by law. If a farmer's land is to be expropriated or the house is to be demolished, legal procedures would have to be strictly followed. There should be a negotiation between farmers and the government or enterprises and institutions authorized by the government, and the transaction would only be done at a mutually agreed price based on the contract. Therefore, farmers could feel at ease because their rights and interests are protected.

41.3.2 Land Transfer

Land transfer is a manifestation of farmers' rights to operate and use the land. In recent years, land transfers have been gradually promoted in China's rural areas, in the forms of subcontracting, leasing, entrusting, and so on. One rule that needs to be strictly obeyed to is that the purpose of land use cannot be changed, which restricts the conversion of limited arable land or rural residential land to other types of uses. Some rural residents who go out to work, set up stores and workshops or start businesses believe that it's better to carry out land transfer so as to generate more income, instead of leaving their contracted land idle or be operated by the left-behind elderlies who market their products in an inefficient way.

According to the research conducted by the faculty and students at Peking University in some provinces and cities, a common concern of farmers who engaged in the land transfer was that they were not sure whether the contracted land still belonged to them after the transfer. They wondered whether the land that had been subcontracted, leased, entrusted, or even lands that had been exchanged shares into a union could generate subcontracting fees and rents in the future as usual. And whether they could recover the right of management. After land rights confirmation, farmers could possess "three rights and three certificates," and that's why they attached special importance to this rural reform. Farmers could "have a bottom line" and were no longer concerned about their property rights. In this way, land rights confirmation was combined with the land transfer. Farmers had great confidence, and the land transfer area would be enlarged year by year.

41.3.3 Increasing Farmers' Income and Narrowing the Income Gap Between Rural and Urban Areas

We did a survey in Jiaxing, Zhejiang Province. After land rights confirmation, farmers' income had increased rapidly, and the income gap between urban and rural areas had narrowed significantly. According to a preliminary estimation of the Jiaxing City, the ratio of urban to rural per capita income was 3.1:1 before and reduced to 1.9:1. Such a change was not due to a decline in urban per capita income but an increase in rural per capita income. We once conducted an in-depth investigation on this issue in Pinghu City, which belongs to Jiaxing, and found that the reasons for the increase in rural per capita income were generally as follows.

First, farmers' property rights could be clarified after land rights confirmation. Their confidence in production and management has increased, motivation has been fully mobilized, and potential has been exerted.

Second, through land transfer, farmers could not only receive subcontracting fees and rents but also go out to work or start small business, resulting in an increase in their income.

Third, farmers have demolished old houses and built new ones on their residential land. Generally, there are four floors, with two floors for their own and others rented out as stores (including the shopfront on the first floor). In this way, the income grew rapidly.

Fourth, some farmers with expertise in agriculture could increase their income through land transfer, followed by the establishment of family forestry, family breeding farms with scale of economy.

Fifth, some farmers have participated in specialized farmers' cooperatives, getting both wage income (undertaking certain works in the cooperative, such as management, farming, and breeding) and dividends on shares.

Thus, it seems that land rights confirmation is indeed an effective way to help farmers get rich and narrow the income gap between urban and rural residents.

41.3.4 Agricultural Industrialization

Who would farm in the future? There are two main concerns when the question is put forward. One is that the young and able in the countryside have gone out to work or start business, and only the elderly, the sick and the disabled would continue to farm. Would the future of Chinese agriculture depend on the latter? Second, who would be willing to farm with less income?

In fact, we need to think from the perspective of development and reform. A new phenomenon is emerging in China's rural areas that there are people who would like to farm and keep the fields up. There are at least three kinds of people who are actively preparing to engage in agriculture and lead Chinese agriculture on the road to industrialization. Who are they? They are farming families, members of farmers' cooperatives, and agricultural entrepreneurs.

Let's start with farming families, who are competent farmers in plantation and breeding in rural areas, some of whom have embarked on establishing scale of economy through land transfers. Farming families are new emerging forces in China's rural areas, and they are a new type of farmers. After the reform of the household registration system, the dual system has been unified. The productivity of these farming families is raised through mechanized farming and harvesting. Farming families are the main forces in the realization of agricultural production, and their own income would increase with the further development of family farms.

Let's turn to the farmers' cooperatives, which are organized in a formal way, with farmers organized under the leadership of the competent in the village. Farmers join the cooperatives with shares of their land and grow appropriate crops according to the local soil quality, climate conditions, water irrigation, and transport accessibility. We had visited professional cooperatives of citrus, watermelon, tea, and vegetables in Liangping County, Changshou District, and Jiangjin District of Chongqing City and found that farmers who joined the cooperatives were highly motivated and their income grew rapidly. However, these cooperatives were newly created with less capital, therefore in an urgent need for support from rural financial institutions.

Moreover, unions should be organized to expand the scale of production and sales of products.

Finally, let's talk about agricultural enterprises. The agricultural enterprises mentioned here mainly refer to private enterprises which take agriculture as their main business. The entrepreneurs bring capital and technology to the countryside, rent land from farmers by leasing and other means, and engage in agricultural production and operation. The scope of business varies from place to place, but they all provide agricultural products for domestic and foreign markets. They have their own technical teams and marketing channels. After local farmers rent their lands to these agricultural enterprises, some are willing to go out to work and the rental from the land becomes part of their income. And those who are not willing to go out to work sign contracts with these agricultural enterprises, become contract workers and receive wages from the enterprises, which has greatly improved their lives. The main problem is that the purpose of the land leased by farmers must remain unchanged, and land cannot be used for real estate or industry.

Thus, a new type of agricultural production team is gradually emerging in China's vast rural areas, bringing the hope in Chinese agriculture. The phenomena that have plagued us for years, such as low productivity in agriculture, low income of farmers, widening income gap, and "the capable moves out and the weak remains," will gradually change with the promotion of reform measures such as land rights confirmation, agricultural industrialization and modernization, and unification of the dual household registration system. It is conceivable that as long as farmers' income grows, the prospect of the countryside and the farmers will both take on a new look. As for the next generation, would they be undoubtedly engaged in agriculture? It is hard to say. Would the children of the farmers stay in the countryside and engage in agriculture? Not necessarily. With the equalization of educational resources, schools in rural areas will be greatly improved, and children in rural areas can decide which industry to work in on their own. If one is willing to follow the footsteps and establish a new farmer family, he/she must pass a qualification test first. The land can be transferred, but would the owner subcontract the land to a person who is not good at farming and agricultural technology? It should be a relief for the owner if the transferred land is operated by a skilled agriculturalist. Only talented people would be chosen as subcontractors in land transfer. At present, there are subcontract and lease of the rights to operate land in Jiangsu, Zhejiang, and Shanghai.

Only when the majority of farmers embark on the road to prosperity can we appreciate the true meaning of Deng's famous saying "poverty is not socialism."

41.4 "Goals for the Two Centenaries" and the Realization of the "Chinese Dream"

The successful rise of China would be a long process. It had been 174 years since the Opium War in 1840 until 2014. China had achieved a transformation from a poor and weak country that was bullied and humiliated by the great powers to a country that has both "stood up" and "grown prosperous," for which so many people had spared no pains and even sacrificed their precious lives. However, we still have a long way to go in the process of rejuvenating the nation and enriching the people. The "goals for the two centenaries" were proposed by the 18th National Congress of the CPC, which is complementary to the "Chinese Dream." The "goals for the two centenaries" can be illustrated as follows.

The goal for the first centenary refers to that, by 2021, which is the 100th anniversary of the founding of the CPC, the goal of building a moderately prosperous society in all aspects would be achieved.

The goal for the second centenary refers to that, by 2049, which is the 100th anniversary of the founding of New China, the dream of the great rejuvenation of the Chinese nation would be realized.

Shortly after the 18th National Congress of the CPC, Comrade Xi Jinping proposed and explained the "Chinese Dream" during his visit to the exhibition "The Road to Rejuvenation." He pointed out that "Everyone has ideals, pursuits, and his/her own dreams. Now, everyone is discussing the Chinese Dream, and I believe that achieving the great rejuvenation of the Chinese nation is our greatest dream in modern history." He elaborated the connotation of the "Chinese Dream": "This dream, which unites the aspirations of several generations of Chinese people, embodies the overall interests of the Chinese nation and Chinese people, and shows the common expectation of descendants of the Chinese nation. The core connotation of this dream is the great rejuvenation of the Chinese nation, that is to say, in the new historical period, the Chinese Dream means we must achieve national prosperity and rejuvenation as well as people's happiness."

In order to achieve the "goals for the two centenaries" and our "Chinese dream," what are the essential tasks at this stage? According to my recent investigation and analysis in some provinces and cities, I proposed four points. The first is to transform the mode of economic development. The second is to establish the concept of "the new normal." The third is to promote urbanization based on the principle of equal emphasis on fairness and efficiency. The fourth is to strive for the greatest dividends of social harmony. These will be discussed respectively as follows.

41.4.1 Transforming the Mode of Economic Development

Western developed countries have summed up lessons from the global financial crises since 2008. In the coming period of time, they have strived for improving the vitality of independent innovation, driving economic development with innovation, and realizing the integration of industrialization, modernization, and informatization. These could be great inspirations for us.

Reviewing China's economic development since the 1950s, it was clear that China had not actually got rid of the unsophisticated mode of economic growth, and as a result, China lagged behind Western developed countries in terms of independent innovation. Our consumption of raw materials and energy has been a lot higher than that of Western developed countries. There are two obvious examples in manufacturing. One is that by the end of the twentieth century, we had been in a leading position in conventional television manufacturing in the world, but we did not pay enough attention to new type televisions. As a result, after entering the twenty-first century, new type televisions internationally replaced conventional ones in general, and we suffered a great loss in the market. Therefore, we were provoked to follow closely and catch up fast, and it took ten years to make the situation better. For another example, by the end of the twentieth century, we had been in a leading position in camera manufacturing in the world. However, after entering the twenty-first century, digital cameras replaced traditional cameras, indicating that we fell behind again and had to catch up. These two examples both show that economic development must focus on independent innovation and that we must unswervingly follow the path of innovation-driven development. Otherwise, we can hardly realize the dream of becoming a powerful industrialized country and occupy the height in the international manufacturing market.

At the same time, we should implement the green and low-carbon production mode as an important direction for economic development. In the process of industrialization and modernization, we must promote a coordinated development of industrial civilization, modern civilization, and ecological civilization. Moreover, we should strive to achieve a clean production process and efficient use of resources, reduce the emission of waste water, gas, and residue as much as possible, and build a green production system that is economical, clean, safe, and low-carbon. In this way, a sustainable economy and social development could be achieved.

41.4.2 Establish the Concept of "the New Normal"

China's high GDP growth rate over a long period of time came from an unsophisticated and quantitative mode of economic development built on the exploitation of massive use of cheap labor and non-renewable resources. As a result, we have paid a huge price for rapid economic growth. What are the costs? Briefly speaking, the first is the irrational structure of the economy. The second is the excessive consumption of resources. The third is the low productivity of labor. The fourth is the great damage to the ecological environment. And the fifth is the serious overcapacity in certain industries and products. In addition, there has been a significant drawback that the best time to adjust the structure and reform the irrational system was missed in order to achieve the predetermined high growth rate.

According to the trajectory of economic growth in the industrialized countries, one could achieve a high economic growth in the short term, but once the growth peak was over, the growth rate would inevitably decrease and turn into moderate. As for China, the moderate reduction of economic growth rate in recent years is in line with the economic law. The growth rate of about 7%, or even 6.6–7% still indicates high-speed development and is at the forefront in the world. In other words, as long as China maintains a high-quality growth rate that is adapted to structural adjustment and conducive to coordinated regional development, it should be suitable for China's national condition. To this end, macroeconomic regulation and control should be adjusted accordingly, in a steady and orderly manner. This is the new normal. There shouldn't be sharp fluctuations in economic growth. Macroeconomic regulation and control should focus on fine-tuning and pre-adjustment, which is necessary to maintain the new normal.

Here, it is necessary to explain why some domestic economists suggest the GDP growth target should be set as a forecast (expected) value. Because rigid GDP growth target set by the governments (including central government and local governments at all levels) would lead to the following four drawbacks.

First, setting a rigid GDP growth target often becomes a mandate for governments at all levels. They will make every effort to achieve this target regardless of the changing economic situation. Finally, it would result in decreased quality of economic growth, more wasted resources, higher costs, and make the economic structure more irrational.

Second, setting a rigid GDP growth target would lead to overcapacity and increased government debt, making it more difficult to adjust the economic structure in the next step.

Third, setting a rigid GDP growth target would force macroeconomic regulation and control to go back to the old pattern that centered on drastic measures, making it difficult to fulfill the policy of macroeconomic regulation mainly through fine-tuning and pre-adjustment.

Fourth, setting a rigid GDP growth target is inconsistent with the principle of the Third Plenary Session of the 18th Central Committee of the CPC on the decisive role of the market in resource allocation, which would easily lead to strong administrative intervention and the destruction of market discipline.

In conclusion, among major economies in the world, China is the only one that specifies rigid GDP growth targets. Other major economies have successively changed to forecast short-term GDP growth rates and frequently modify their forecast value based on the economic situation. Therefore, China should also timely transform its rigid GDP growth targets to a flexible target (adjust the forecast value annually or quarterly), which is conducive to a more stable economic growth. And the focus of economic work should be shifted to adjusting the structure and improving the quality of economic growth.

41.4.3 Promoting Urbanization on the Principle of Equal Emphasis on Equity and Efficiency

So far, China's urbanization rate is still less than 40%. Although the number of permanent residents in urban areas has accounted for more than 50% of the total population, some of them, such as migrant workers, their spouses, children, and dependent elderlies are still registered in rural areas, and cannot enjoy the social security and rights granted to urban residents. Migrant workers cannot enjoy preferential treatment such as low-cost housing in cities, and their children still cannot attend schools for compulsory education. These manifest the problem of "dual household registration" that must be solved in the urbanization process as early as possible.

According to the suggestions of the government, there are two ways to address the issue in the dual urban-rural household registration system. One is the points-based system adopted by big cities (especially mega cities), i.e., each migrant worker can be formally transferred to be urban residents after accruing a certain number of points based on education, experience, years of working in the city, and various awards. This is a good way to retain migrant workers who have certain technical expertise. After calculating the points, even if they have not yet reached the threshold of transfer, they would at least have something to look forward to. The other is the elimination of the discrimination against migrant workers in employment, children's schooling, healthcare, and housing that exists in the city. Citizenship is equal, and the phenomena that those who live in urban areas can be taken care of but those who live in rural areas have fewer rights should no longer exist.

In the process of urbanization, it must be repeatedly explained to the cadres in cities and rural areas that the goal should be "the urbanization of population." While in the past, the appearance of the streets was considered the priority, such as wider roads and taller buildings. Cities were compared blindly with others, but government debt was not taken into serious considerations. How could it be! This is against the original intention of urbanization, and we must stop this kind of so-called "urbanization."

How to raise funds needed in the process of urbanization? This is another serious issue. With a certain amount of debt, the funds should be spent economically and sparingly. Do not rely on the government to underwrite the debt in the promotion of urbanization. It is basically impossible to sustain the local governments by land sales. Therefore, in the process of urbanization, it is necessary to plan early for the funding of public facilities. One way is to draw on the experience of some Western countries and set up urban public utility investment funds, combining the power of the central government, local governments, and financial institutions to attract private capital to participate in urban construction by issuing long-term investment bonds. This should be a feasible approach.

41.4.4 Striving for the Greatest Institutional Dividend—Social Harmony

When referring to institutional dividends, we usually think of the benefits in terms of institutional adjustment that could be generated within the market system rather than the traditional planned system, such as the increase in resource allocation efficiency, the rise in the incentives of production units and workers, and the fruits of the opening-up policy, etc. These are all included in institutional dividends. In addition, when referring to institutional development mode, we also think of the benefits brought by the transformation from extensive growth to intensive growth, from an expansion mode that only values quantity to one that values economic growth, etc. These also belong to institutional dividends. However, it should not be forgotten that the biggest institutional dividend is social harmony.

Why did some Latin American countries suffer economic stagnation, social unrest, widening gap between the rich and the poor, and finally fall into the so-called "middle-income trap" after entering the ranks of middle-income countries? The specific circumstances of each country are different, and the reason cannot be generalized. But one thing is in common, i.e., these societies were extremely disharmonious, and the disharmony went over a certain threshold, which is the main reason why these countries fall into the "middle-income trap."

For China, the realization of social harmony should be closely related to our socialist system with Chinese characteristics. Social harmony is a manifestation of the superiority of our system. In fact, a series of reforms we are carrying out now are the prerequisites that enable us to achieve social harmony systematically. For example, the reform of the dual urban-rural household registration system would bring equal rights and opportunities to both urban and rural residents. The reform of the social security system would lead to comparable social security benefits for urban and rural residents. The poverty alleviation program in mountainous rural areas sponsored and implemented by the government would enable the poor in these areas to receive assistance, learn the skills to become rich, and get introduced to work outside. Furthermore, the vigorous development of vocational and technical education would make it easier for young rural population to seek employment opportunities or start their own businesses. All of these contribute to social harmony.

It should also be noted that the third distribution in modern Chinese society is attracting more social attention. It is relative to the primary and secondary distribution. The market-based distribution, i.e., the primary distribution, refers to that under the regulatory role of the market, people who participate in work or investment can receive their share of income according to the law of the market. However, there would exist an income gap, and excessive income disparity is not conducive to social harmony, thus there will be the secondary distribution. The secondary distribution is the government-led income redistribution, which means that the government regulates income according to laws, regulations, policies, etc. In general, individual income tax and corporate tax are imposed on those who earn more. Property tax is imposed on those who have more properties. Allowances and subsidies are given to poor households. The government narrows the income gap in society through income adjustment. After the secondary distribution, everyone's income becomes after-tax income. People with lower income do not have to pay income tax or property tax and could receive allowances or subsidies from the government.

The secondary distribution should be followed by the third distribution in society. It usually refers to the redistribution of income based on moral authority, including social institutions that organize voluntary donations to help low-income families out of poverty, help widows, orphans, the sick, the disabled, and children, as well as voluntary provision of scholarships to schools at all levels, etc. In addition, in disaster relief programs where floods, earthquakes, mudslides, and prolonged droughts occur, there are also many who either donate to charitable organizations or donate to the afflicted people on their own, which all belong to the third distribution. According to the experience of Western developed countries, the amount of donations for the third distribution is gradually expanding. China also has the same trend, so the relevant laws and regulations should be gradually improved.

The role of the secondary and the third distributions in promoting social harmony obviously cannot be underestimated. However, it is also necessary to pay attention to the primary distribution, which is dominated by market regulation. Two examples are cited here to illustrate this.

The first is about the labor market. At present, the power of buyers (employers) and sellers (employees) in China's labor market is extremely asymmetrical, because employers are usually enterprises and institutions, while employees (including migrant workers) are usually individual job seekers. With unequal power, it is often the employees that suffer losses. If the supply exceeds the demand in the labor market, the employed have to bear the burden. It is also common for employers to default on wages. Labor unions at all levels in China have paid attention to these issues in recent years and are actively participating in labor negotiations and resolutions of labor disputes. This is a welcome phenomenon, and I hope that labor unions could expand their influence.

The second is about the situation of farmers and herdsmen selling their own agricultural and livestock products. If a single farmer or herdsman is facing a big buyer of agricultural products, the power distribution of the two sides is obvious. The single farmer or herdsman is the weaker party, and the buyer of agricultural products is the stronger party. With farmers and herdsmen being the supply side and agricultural products buyers being the demand side, it is impossible to deal at the market equilibrium price. Generally, the price would be depressed, resulting in less income that farmers and herdsmen could receive in the primary distribution. How to change this situation? Referring to the experience of some developed countries in Western Europe, a feasible way to protect the interests of farmers and herdsmen would be to form a farmer and herdsman cooperative first and then a union, which can either be in a closed form (i.e., expands into a large agricultural cooperative) or in a loose form (i.e., productions are still carried out by individual cooperatives, while sales are unified). These unions are tremendous in power and large in scale. They have their own fleets, docks, and warehouses. With their marketing channels, they can directly sign supply and sales contracts with large supermarkets at home and abroad, thus generating more income. It seems that China could gradually realize the formation of unions based on specialized farmers' cooperatives.

In conclusion, social harmony will be achieved under the guidance of the 18th National Congress of the CPC and the decisions of the Third Plenary Session of the 18th CPC Central Committee. The superiority of our system is the decisive factor, and comprehensively deepening the reform provides the conditions for us to achieve social harmony and reap its dividends. Moreover, there is no end to social harmony and its dividends. Let's work together to achieve the "goals for the two centenaries" and the "Chinese dream"!

—*Casting the Soul: Twelve Lectures on Socialist Core Values* (the Propaganda Department of the Party Committee of Peking University), Peking University Press, 2017

Name Index

Y. Li, *China's Economy Since 1978*, China Academic Library,
https://doi.org/10.1007/978-981-95-5733-2

Subject Index

Y. Li, *China's Economy Since 1978*, China Academic Library,
https://doi.org/10.1007/978-981-95-5733-2

MIX
Papier aus verantwortungsvollen Quellen
Paper from responsible sources
FSC® C105338

If you have any concerns about our products,
you can contact us on
ProductSafety@springernature.com

In case Publisher is established outside the EU,
the EU authorized representative is:
Springer Nature Customer Service Center GmbH
Europaplatz 3, 69115 Heidelberg, Germany

Printed by Libri Plureos GmbH
in Hamburg, Germany